John Dewey's Ethical Theory

This book provides a wide-ranging, systematic, and comprehensive approach to the moral philosophy of John Dewey, one of the most important philosophers of the 20th century. It does so by focusing on his greatest achievement in this field: the *Ethics* he jointly published with James Hayden Tufts in 1908 and then republished in a heavily revised version in 1932.

The chapters in this volume are divided into two distinct parts. The first features chapters that provide a running commentary on the chapters of the 1932 *Ethics* written by Dewey. Each chapter is introduced, situated within a historical perspective, and then its main achievements are highlighted and discussed. The second part of the book interprets the *Ethics* and demonstrates its contemporary relevance and vitality. The chapters in this part situate the *Ethics* in the broader interpretive frameworks of Dewey's philosophy, American Pragmatism, and 20th-century moral theory at large. Taken together, these chapters show that, far from being a mere survey of moral theories, the 1932 *Ethics* is a theoretical highpoint in Dewey's thinking about moral philosophy.

This book features contributions by some of the most influential Dewey scholars from North America and Europe. It will be of keen interest to scholars and students of American pragmatism, ethics and moral philosophy, and the history of 20th-century philosophy.

Roberto Frega holds a PhD from Paris 8. He is Permanent Researcher at the CNRS (French National Center for Scientific Research) in Paris. He has published several books and articles on pragmatism and American philosophy. He is Founder and Co-executive Editor of the *European Journal of Pragmatism and American Philosophy.*

Steven Levine is Professor in the Department of Philosophy at the University of Massachusetts Boston. He has recently published a book entitled *Pragmatism, Objectivity, and Experience*, and he has published a wide variety of article on classical and contemporary pragmatism.

Routledge Studies in American Philosophy

Edited by Willem deVries, University of New Hampshire, USA and Henry Jackman, York University, Canada

The Ethics of Wilfrid Sellars
Jeremy Randel Koons

Wilfrid Sellars and Buddhist Philosophy
Freedom from Foundations
Edited by Jay L. Garfield

The Network Self
Relation, Process, and Personal Identity
Kathleen Wallace

Deweyan Experimentalism and the Problem of Method in Political Philosophy
Joshua Forstenzer

Pragmatic Perspectives
Constructivism beyond Truth and Realism
Robert Schwartz

Wilfrid Sellars and Twentieth-Century Philosophy
Edited by Stefan Brandt and Anke Breunig

Challenging the New Atheism
Pragmatic Confrontations in the Philosophy of Religion
Aaron Pratt Shepherd

John Dewey's Ethical Theory
The 1932 *Ethics*
Edited by Roberto Frega and Steven Levine

For more information about this series, please visit: https://www.routledge.com/Routledge-Studies-in-American-Philosophy/book-series/RSAP

John Dewey's Ethical Theory

The 1932 *Ethics*

Edited by
Roberto Frega and Steven Levine

NEW YORK AND LONDON

First published 2021
by Routledge
52 Vanderbilt Avenue, New York, NY 10017

and by Routledge
2 Park Square, Milton Park, Abingdon, Oxon, OX14 4RN

Routledge is an imprint of the Taylor & Francis Group, an informa business

Library of Congress Cataloging-in-Publication Data
Names: Frega, Roberto, editor. | Levine, Steven (Steven Matthew), editor.
Title: John Dewey's ethical theory : the 1932 ethics / edited by Roberto Frega and Steven Levine.
Description: New York : Routledge, 2020. |
Series: Routledge studies in American philosophy | Includes bibliographical references and index.
Identifiers: LCCN 2020015629 (print) |
LCCN 2020015630 (ebook) | ISBN 9780367201593 (hbk) |
ISBN 9780429259869 (ebk)
Subjects: LCSH: Dewey, John, 1859–1952. | Ethics. |
Dewey, John, 1859–1952. Ethics.
Classification: LCC B945.D44 J635 2020 (print) |
LCC B945.D44 (ebook) | DDC 170—dc23
LC record available at https://lccn.loc.gov/2020015629
LC ebook record available at https://lccn.loc.gov/2020015630

ISBN: 978-0-367-20159-3 (hbk)
ISBN: 978-0-429-25986-9 (ebk)

Typeset in Sabon
by codeMantra

Contents

Dewey Citations

Citations of John Dewey's works are to the thirty-seven-volume critical edition published by Southern Illinois University Press under the editorship of Jo Ann Boydston. In-text citations give the series abbreviation (EW, MW, and LW) followed by volume number and page number.

Dewey, John. 1985. *The Early Works of John Dewey, 1882–1898*, edited by Jo Ann Boydston. Carbondale: Southern Illinois University Press.

Dewey, John. 1985. *The Middle Works of John Dewey, 1899–1924*, edited by Jo Ann Boydston. Carbondale: Southern Illinois University Press.

Dewey, John. 1985. *The Later Works of John Dewey, 1925–1953*, edited by Jo Ann Boydston. Carbondale: Southern Illinois University Press.

Preface

John Dewey (1859–1952) was one of the greatest philosophers of the 20th century. Though Dewey worked in nearly all areas of philosophy, his contribution to ethical theory stands out. The *Ethics* is undoubtedly his greatest achievement in the field. The book, co-authored with James Hyden Tufts, was published for the first time in 1908 and was intended as a textbook. The book was far more than a textbook, however, as its organization, perspective, and topics were clearly shaped by the authors' respective philosophical views. Indeed, it should be said of the *Ethics* what Dewey said about his first book on ethics, the 1891 *Outlines of a Critical Theory of Ethics*: "although the following pages have taken shape in connection with class-room work, they are intended as an independent contribution to ethical science" (EW 3, 239). The *Ethics* was almost completely rewritten for a second edition, published in 1932. The chapters included in this volume are devoted to this edition of the *Ethics*. The second edition is divided into three major parts. The first part concerns the history of ethics; the second, ethical theory; and the third applies ethical theory to concrete social and political issues. Dewey wrote all of the chapters of the second part and the first two chapters of the third part, which examine the social and political implications of Dewey's ethical theory. All in all, Dewey wrote eight chapters of the *Ethics* (10–17).

The present publication is the result of a four years research project involving both European and American scholars. All of the papers in the book were discussed during a series of workshops that took place between 2016 and 2018 in Bologna, Boston, and Berlin. We thank CNRS for generously funding the project, and the University of Bologna and the University of Massachusetts Boston for their support.

The project stems from a belief that Dewey's work requires a more rigorous and analytical form of exegesis than is currently on offer. Despite their often-undeserved reputation for clumsiness and awkwardness, Dewey's texts demand the kind of scrutiny that can only be given by a close chapter-by-chapter reading. This is what we have attempted to provide, first through collective discussion, and then through close commentary.

This book's structure follows from this methodological starting point. Part I is comprised of two introductory chapters, written by Gregory Pappas and Steven Fesmire. Pappas and Fesmire contextualize the 1932 *Ethics* within the context of Dewey's ethical theory and philosophy as a whole. Pappas' chapter puts the 1932 *Ethics* in the larger framework of Dewey's ethical thought, focusing on the relationship between the 1932 *Ethics* and the 1908 *Ethics*, as well as other of his texts in moral philosophy. Fesmire takes a different tack, investigating the relationships between the 1932 *Ethics* and the 1930 article "Three Independent Factors in Morals," whose central insight provides the baseline for Dewey's reconfiguration of ethical theory.

Part II is composed of seven chapters, each of which is devoted to a chapter of the 1932 *Ethics* written by Dewey.[1] Stéphane Madelrieux interprets Chapter 10 in light of Dewey's critique of dualisms, contending that the major innovation of the chapter consists in Dewey's criticism of moral atomism. As Madelrieux shows, Dewey reconstructs character and conduct, motives and consequences, in terms of habits, considered as general ways of behavior. Federico Lijoi's contribution focuses on Chapter 11, discussing Dewey's account of ends. It examines the relationship between thought and desire, and the differences between inhibition and transformation of desire, and between the quality of an enduring satisfaction of the whole self and that of a transient satisfaction of some isolated element of the self. Conor Morris examines Chapter 12 of the *Ethics,* focusing on Dewey's critique of Kant. Morris discusses the Kantian distinction between the right and the good, and lays out Dewey's critique of Kant with respect to the problem of moral change. Roberto Frega devotes his essay to Chapter 13, where Dewey takes up the place of virtue in moral life. Frega reconstructs Dewey's views about the virtues from a historical perspective. He identifies three major conceptions of the virtues spanning Dewey's career, and concludes by contending that the 1932 *Ethics* provides a final synthesis of Dewey's views on virtue. Céline Henne's chapter tackles Dewey's treatment of sympathy as a basis of moral knowledge, emphasizing the originality of Dewey's position with reference to David Hume, Adam Smith, and John Stuart Mill. Focusing on the closing chapter of the middle section of the *Ethics*, Steven Levine takes up Dewey's conception of the self. Levine shows that although Dewey overcomes his earlier ethics of self-realization, Hegelian strands remain in Dewey's mature ethical theory. Finally, Justo Serrano Zamora's chapter discusses the implications of Chapters 16 and 17 for democratic theory. He demonstrates, in particular, how Dewey's ideas of democracy and democratic method complete his moral vision, assigning to democracy an emancipatory potential that is inseparable from the vision of the good that Dewey lays out in the previous chapters of the *Ethics*.

Part III contains five interpretive chapters, all of which situate Dewey's ethics within the larger framework of contemporary ethical theory. In her chapter, Roberta Dreon highlights the bodily and aesthetic dimension of Dewey's ethics, arguing that an anthropological treatment of ethics must be rooted not only in Dewey's theory of habits but also in the qualitative, aesthetic, and affective meaning of experience. Matteo Santarelli devotes his chapter to a reconstruction of Dewey's theory of interest, showing how the 1932 *Ethics* systematizes and analytically develops insights about interest introduced in Dewey's previous psychological, pedagogical, and political essays. In his contribution Mathias Girel explores Dewey's treatment of the ethical notion of obligation, highlighting its relation to William James's account of this concept. Girel emphasizes Dewey's idea that the sense of duty is related to a certain state of society, which implies that certain social settings can imperil the justification of moral claims. In his chapter, Sarin Marchetti discusses Dewey's ethical thought from the perspective of recent meta-ethical debates, particularly with reference to the question "What is moral philosophy (good) for?" Marchetti finds at the heart of Dewey's ethical thought the problematic yet productive coexistence of a conception of moral philosophy as piecemeal criticism of conduct from within moral practice and as prescriptive device for moral education and growth governing practice from without. Finally, Jörg Volbers devotes his chapter to another meta-ethical question, asking how Dewey's moral theory can answer the challenge posed by moral anti-theorists like Bernard Williams. Like Marchetti, Volbers investigates Dewey's practice-based account of ethics as the key to finding the limits of ethical reasoning, showing that instead of opposing moral sensitivity and rational inquiry, Dewey seeks to establish a common ground from which we can understand both modern moral philosophy and its critics.

Note

1 With an exception, since Justo Serrano Zamora's contribution covers two chapters.

Part I

Introduction

1 Contextualizing Dewey's 1932 *Ethics*

Gregory Fernando Pappas

In this chapter I argue for the importance of contextualizing Dewey's 1932 *Ethics* in order to appreciate its claims, importance, and limitations. There are a variety of different contexts that may be relevant in understanding the text of a philosopher, for instance, his or her personal life, historical events, intellectual trends, and commonly shared assumptions of that period. While I consider some of these contexts, I mainly focus on appreciating the place of Dewey's 1932 *Ethics* in the context of the larger framework of his moral philosophy and the rest of his philosophy. Dewey's philosophy was holistic in the sense that a part is dependent on other parts and the whole. Moreover, each part was the result of a continuous process of inquiry so that each text is the result of the development and reconstruction of prior ideas.

In this essay three related general issues are considered. First, are there important changes between the earlier texts in *Ethics* (e.g., the 1908 *Ethics*) and that of 1932? Are there changes in Dewey's own larger inquiries in philosophy (metaphilosophy, metaphysics, epistemology, aesthetics, education) that may be important for understanding the changes in his ethical thought? How do his inquiries into other areas of philosophy bear on the changes he made to his 1932 *Ethics*?

Second, what is the significance, place, or importance of the 1932 *Ethics* in Dewey's overall ethics? How does the 1932 text compare with and relate to Dewey's other texts on morals? Are there other works that must be consulted to complement and enhance one's reading of the 1932 *Ethics*, and also to appreciate how radical his mature ethical thought was compared to mainstream ethical theory?

Third, what characterizes Dewey's mature and overall ethics by 1932?

Important Changes between Earlier Texts in *Ethics* (e.g., the 1908 *Ethics*) and the 1932 Edition

To appreciate the importance of the 1932 text and why it represents Dewey at his most mature, sophisticated, and radical (in comparison with traditional ethics), it is worth comparing it with his earlier version of the same text (1908). In their introduction to the 1932 edition Edel and Flower highlight the most important changes. There is no point in duplicating their work here. However, there is a need to revisit these changes today in light of Dewey's overall philosophy. One must keep in mind that by 1932 Dewey had the benefit of working out and significantly improving his theory of inquiry and experience.

Let me address, even if briefly, some of the most important changes in each of the following topics.

The Historical-Natural Aspects of Morality and the Relation between Customary and Reflective Morality

A commonly shared assumption of many thinkers at the beginning of the 20th century was the notion of a linear theory of the evolution of morality. Some of the terminology (e.g., "primitive") is present in early Dewey, especially because it coincided with the distinction between customary group morality and the reflective individual morality of the more modern human. This distinction gradually disappears in Dewey as he questions some of its background assumptions about history and culture.

By 1932, and already in "Anthropology and *Ethics*" (LW 3, 11–24) and *Public and its Problems* (LW 2, 1927), there is no determinate linear evolutionary pattern or historical substructure. Dewey's approach or understanding of history is different. Dewey became worried about grand abstractions and totalizing metanarratives about history in the hands of philosophers. Instead, undertaking specific historical inquiries and examining specific groups and conflicts are the proper context-sensitive approaches. As Edel and Flower observe,

> What replaced the linear view was simply a more genuinely socio-historical analysis of the social phenomena in their specific sociohistorical contexts. ... Emerging moral forms are now seen not as general stages of moral evolution but as specific responses to challenges in the specific historical problems and conflicts.
>
> (LW 7, xv)

In the 1932 *Ethics* the earlier distinction between customary and reflective morality remains, but it is a functional distinction at any time and not two separated historical epochs or domains. Custom is redefined as valued social habit, and there is an acknowledgment that the customary can embody previous reflection. Edel and Flower speculate that Dewey's stay in China may have had some influence on this issue. Perhaps seeing the extent to which China relied on custom and not being able to assert that they were at an early developmental stage, Dewey comes to appreciate "the conservatism of the Chinese as more intellectual and deliberative rather than as merely clinging to custom" (LW 7, xxiii).

Relevant to this last change is the development in Dewey's view of "habit" between 1919 and his 1922 *Human Nature and Conduct*

(MW 14), an important text that should be consulted to fully understand the richer view of the moral self presupposed in the 1932 *Ethics*. The continuity between custom and intelligence can be shown in terms of habits and impulses (his social psychology). Habits, learned via one's social environment, give social shape to impulses (biological). They constitute the self and character as an interpenetration of habits. Conflicts of habits, new needs and conditions, prompt reconstruction via reflection. Reflection becomes "intelligence" as a special set of habits.

The Nature and Function of "Moral Intelligence"

Reason and rationality have been the favorite categories of ethical theory in Western ethics. Dewey's pragmatism questioned the modern conceptions of reason and even the entire traditional way of doing epistemology. This made a difference in his resulting ethics. Drawing the implications from his epistemology (or theory of inquiry) to ethical thinking and theory accounts for many of the changes in Dewey's ethical writings. Between 1908 and 1932 Dewey worked and reworked some of his more-advanced views on the nature of thinking and intelligence. Reason as a faculty is rejected, and instead, intelligence as a complex set of habits is embraced. More significant is the extent to which by 1932 Dewey had significantly moved away from even the most liberal understanding of reason, rationality, and knowledge in Western philosophy. Dewey's reconstruction of epistemology in such works as his 1910 *How we Think* (MW 6), the 1916 *Essays in Experimental Logic* (MW 10), the 1929 *Quest for Certainty* (LW 4), and especially his 1931 "Qualitative Thought" (LW 5, 243–261) must be consulted to understand how radical the mature view of moral deliberation and reflection presupposed in the 1932 *Ethics* is. Moral thinking beyond analytic and conceptual reasoning includes creative elements, imagination, and feelings. Flower and Edel admit this much, but Dewey's brief and general descriptions of the role of feelings, the imagination, and the non-cognitive context of the situation in the 1932 *Ethics* fall short of what he could have written, given the state of his epistemology at that time. This is understandable since the book was intended to be an introduction to ethics, but there is the risk that readers that do not consult, for example, Dewey's "Qualitative Thought" (1931) may not appreciate how rich and radical Dewey's view of moral deliberation is. Reasoning and reasons are only a fraction of what goes on in moral inquiry as a process.

Individual/Social

Dewey never ceased finding new dualisms to question in philosophy. By 1932 it became clear to Dewey that using the dualistic categories of individual/social in general tended to adversely affect sociopolitical and ethical inquiry. This is too abstract a starting point. In addition, the distinctions between the psychological and the social in the study of moral experience (life) were merely functional. Individuality was important but is self-nurtured by its relations. By 1932 "the idea of the common good is now enriched by specific ideas of sharing and participating. And it becomes intelligible why morality is neither wholly social nor wholly individual" (LW 7, xxi). There is no conflict between the social and the individual, but it contains aspects of any moral thought and action. The backdrop and full arguments to be consulted in understanding why Dewey insisted on this point in his 1932 *Ethics* are works from the same time period in which he became critical of how sociopolitical inquiry tended to start with abstract categories and large historical narratives of conflicts. Instead, he felt the starting point should be conflicts of particular groups and people at particular times and places, that is, "specific inquiries into a multitude of specific structures and interactions" (MW 12, 193).

From the Self to Situations as the Context and Locus of Moral Life

By 1932, as a result of his parallel inquiries into other areas of philosophy such as metaphilosophy, metaphysics, epistemology, and aesthetics, Dewey's notion of moral experience became more centered on particular morally problematic situations. The starting point of the 1932 *Ethics* is not some moral development of mankind nor is it the self, as is obvious in his 1908 *Ethics*, but situations, which are the ultimate context and locus of moral life. The importance of the self remains, but it is a more-transactional conception bounded by situations. In Dewey's ethics the moral self becomes an integral part of the process of reconstructing morally problematic situations. The self therefore affects and is affected by what goes on while transactions take place in a particular situation. This establishes a very important, organic relation between the quality of what we do and the quality of the character we bring to a situation. A growing educative moral life requires improvement of both the habits that determine the quality of present experience, and of the present experiences that determine the quality of our habits.

Edel and Flower account for the difference between Dewey's earlier and mature ethics in the following way:

> As long as he was doing chiefly psychological ethics, supported by the individualism of the theory of moral evolution, the ethical concepts were interpreted wholly in terms of inner-individual process. Now, however, the view is no longer simply of an individual ... it is rather a direct focus on the full complexity of natural and social relations that occur in the field itself.
>
> (LW 7, xxvi)

However, more should be said about what this "field" or context of moral experience comes to. While Dewey does provide some descriptions of this concrete context in his 1932 *Ethics*, consulting other texts of Dewey on how lived experience is a matter of living in "situations" during this same period is desirable. A situation is the field or context of all inquiries. Dewey makes clear in his discussion with Bertrand Russell how important this notion is for understanding his philosophy: "Mr. Russell has not been able to follow the distinction I make between the immediately had material of non-cognitively experienced situations and the material of cognition—a distinction without which my view cannot be understood" (LW 14, 33). Indeed, Dewey's *Ethics* cannot be fully understood unless one understands what he means by a morally problematic situation. This was the subject of his essay "Three Independent Factors in Morals" (LW 5, 279–288). Dewey's empirical approach to philosophy demands that ethical theory begins with the primitive situations of life in which moral experiences are had. In this sense, moral subject-matter is always experienced as a part of the field that constitutes a situation, in particular those situations that pose a moral problem.

In Dewey's view, the tendency to absolutize or universalize in ethics by providing theories of "the good" constitutes a failure to see that any meaningful quest for the good is always tied to a particular inquiry within the unique context of a morally problematic situation. The dualisms or splits that have plagued most moral theories (self versus act, character versus conduct, and fact versus value, to name but a few) are also a result of the failure to begin with situated experience rather than with theory. Instead of starting empirically then with the "integrated unity" and "unanalyzed totality" found in a lived situation, modern moral philosophy begins antiempirically, with ontological gaps. These dichotomies have in turn generated all kinds of false dilemmas and debates, such as on egoism versus altruism, subjectivism versus objectivism, and an "ethics of character" versus an "ethics of the act."

By 1932 the amelioration of specific morally problematic situations became the alternative to traditional views of moral life as the search from some telos (some ultimate good), or of ethics as the application of rules or the avoidance of transgressing moral laws. The moral life is not a quest for the acquisition of some good (happiness or even virtue). This is important to keep in mind since the temptation in the history of the secondary literature on Dewey has been to try to find evidence somewhere in the text that Dewey assumes some ultimate good or telos, or assumed a form of consequentialism, or is another virtue ethics. By 1932 Dewey had totally abandoned the language of self-realization as the aim of moral life (found in his earlier ethical writings). His ethics became much more pluralistic, complex, and context sensitive, as we will explore in the next sections.

Pluralism of Moral Experience

In the 1908 *Ethics* the "good" as a category is central—everything is filtered through it, and the self is the central focus. However, by 1932 "the three major ethical concepts of good, right or obligation, and virtue; originally analyzed in terms of the good, were now declared independent, each resting on a different force in human life" (LW 7, xv). This shift represents a fresh way of looking at what goes on in moral life. The new view was set forth in a 1930 lecture in France "Three Independent Factors in Morals" (LW 5, 279–288). Edel and Flower explain the significance of this shift in Dewey's ethics:

> The changes in conceptual structure that are carried through in the 1932 *Ethics* consolidate the central Deweyean outlook on ethics: that it is the concrete task of bringing the broadest lessons of experience and the resources of inventiveness to the solution of particular problems, not the application of fixed and pre-set code of moral universals.
>
> (LW 7, xxviii)

However, I think more can be said about the important relation between the "Three Independent Factors in Morals" and the 1932 *Ethics*.

In "Three Independent Factors of Morals"[1] Dewey argues that the history of moral philosophy is characterized by one-sidedness because philosophers have abstracted one factor or feature of situations that are experienced as morally problematic, and then made that factor supreme or exclusive. Hence, moral theories have been classified according to whether they take good (teleological-consequentionalist), virtue (virtue ethics), or duty (deontological theories) as their central category or source of moral justification. As Dewey points out, however, good, virtue, and duty are all irreducible features that are intertwined in moral situations.

While "Three Independent Factors of Morals" is a short essay, reading the 1932 *Ethics* without reading the essay amounts to not having the benefit of reading the full argument for why an empirical ethics must be radically pluralistic. In the essay Dewey concludes that we must find an alternative to the narrow, reductionistic views that have dominated the history of moral philosophy. The 1932 *Ethics* is his attempt to develop further and with more detail some of the implications and insights of that short essay. Hence, reading both texts is necessary to appreciate and evaluate whether Dewey succeeded in laying out the pluralistic ethics he believes is needed. It is important to note that the three middle, and arguably most important, chapters of the 1932 book correspond to each of the three independent factors in morals distinguished and argued for in the essay.

The chapter in the 1932 *Ethics* on the good (Chapter 11) extends the very-brief analysis in the essay. In the 1908 *Ethics* the good is analyzed in relation to the self-realization of the whole self, but in 1932 the good is more pluralistic and equated with the cultivation of interest, and understood in terms of its functional role in deliberation as a process. The chapter on duty (Chapter 12) moves away from any introspective-subjective or rationalistic account of the sense of duty; instead, Dewey explains how duties emerge from the relationships themselves. The relational self in a situation becomes central. Similarly, the chapter on virtue (Chapter 13) explains how virtues emerge naturally and socially from the affective and immediate aspect of praise and blame in social relations. Both the 1908 and the 1932 *Ethics* include a chapter on virtues as traits or habits in a character, but in the 1932 edition their instrumental function in the context of ameliorating morally problematic situations is emphasized.

The Nature and Function of Ethical Theory

By 1932 Dewey had developed his more mature views on metaphilosophy, i.e., on what should be the starting point of theory and philosophy in general (see Chapter 1 of *Experience and Nature* LW 1). He applied this view to the reconstruction of philosophy in its different areas. In the chapter "Reconstruction in Moral Conceptions" in *Reconstruction in Philosophy* (MW 12), Dewey develops some of these implications for ethics. The 1932 *Ethics* builds on this text and makes explicit both the limitations and potential of ethical theory. It was important to be critical of the traditional ambitions of mainstream ethical theory but without undermining the possible ameliorative role of ethical theory, even if the role was a humbler one in regard to moral practice.

His argument became clear. For Dewey, moral theory is developed in a bottom-up way, starting from the particular facts and the deliberation that are the features of a particular moral situation. Moral philosophy is thus a function of the moral life, and not the reverse. Moral theory thus involves refined and secondary products of moral deliberation, but these products are not absolute. They are instrumentalities that assist or illuminate daily effort and give intelligent direction to the affairs of primary moral experience. When theory is conceived as something within practice (i.e., situations) and not just imposed on it from the outside, it takes on the responsibility of being a part of the available means for the intelligent amelioration of practice. If moral theory is in and for our moral life, then one cannot determine what an adequate ethical theory will be without considering what kind of moral theory works better within our actual moral lives. For Dewey the problem with most ethical theories is simply that they do not really assist our moral practice.

The Significance, Place, and Importance of the 1932 *Ethics* in Dewey's Overall Ethics

The 1932 *Ethics* is necessary and central to Dewey's ethics, even if it is not sufficient to fully grasp the depth and unorthodox character of his ethics. This should not be surprising since Dewey did not intend it to be his definitive book on ethics. It was a book clearly written for a particular audience: teachers and students interested in ethics. In the preface to 1932 edition he states that his aim is to "induce a habit of thoughtful consideration ... and aid the students with tools and method." The text is an "effort to awaken a vital conviction of the genuine reality of moral problems and the value of reflective thought in dealing with them" (LW 7, 5).

This pedagogical purpose and audience also explain the overall structure of the book. He explains the pedagogical value for classes in having the historical material in Part I, prior to the examinations of ethical theories in Part II. To describe moral-social life via different historical epochs enables students to realize that morals are about habitual practice. He reasons that had he placed the more theoretical ideas (i.e., what became Part II) at the start of the book, there is the danger that instead of "serving as tools for understanding the moral facts, the ideas are likely to become substitute for the facts" (LW 7, 6). The historical material of Part I permits students to be present at the "social situation in which intellectual instruments were forged," appreciating moral ideas as tools to deal with moral problems and conditions.

The aim of Part II is not to inculcate theories as some ready-made system, but to present them as arising out of problems and used for their analysis. "Theories are not treated as incompatible rival systems ... but as more or less adequate methods of surveying the problems of conduct." Therefore, "the student is put in a position to judge the problems of conduct for himself" (LW 7, 6). The aim of Part III is to introduce students to the examination of some particular social and economic issues, and encourage them to abandon a priori ways of dealing with them, and instead utilize the "methods of more deliberate analysis and experiment." The fact that Dewey aimed the 1932 *Ethics* at teachers and students does not devalue its philosophical merits. There are texts that Dewey clearly wrote for teachers that are better explanations of his philosophical ideas than those written exclusively for philosophers. For instance, the explanations of the operations of inquiry found in his 1910 *How We Think* (MW 6) may be better than those found in his 1938 *Logic: The Theory of Inquiry* (LW 12), in which his language gets a bit more technical and obscure.

My point is not to try to undermine the significance of the 1932 *Ethics* but to give it its proper place in the context of Dewey's overall ethics. It is a key text of his mature ethics, deserving of more attention and worth new and fresh reconsideration today. However, it needs to be complemented with other texts in order to do full justice to how rich and unique is his ethical thought. In any case, the expectation to find a single, comprehensive, and self-sufficient text of Dewey's ethics goes against how he conceived and practiced philosophical inquiry as a process that requires continuous reconstruction. Dewey's books on any area of philosophy are stages that are both the culmination of and a step in a lifelong process. Dewey's ideas about ethics, just as with his ideas on other subjects, underwent gradual but continual reconstruction during his 71-year public career. In his first writings on morality (1887) Dewey was an absolute idealist, but by his 1908 *Ethics* there is almost no residuum of this early idealism. Dewey's early concerns on reconciling ethics with experimental science led him to investigate the ways in which scientific inquiry and moral inquiry can share a way of forming and justifying judgments (i.e., a general method). By 1932 he had even worked out a general but more-sophisticated and pluralistic view of inquiry and experience.

In general, what distinguishes Dewey's later ethical writings from his early writings is a more-acute awareness of the complexity of the particular, of the indeterminacies and elements of novelty in situations, and of the social and instrumental nature of our character. Although these modifications are important they are not substantial or drastic enough to support a sharp distinction between an "early" and a "later" Dewey. It is probably more accurate to say that Dewey developed his views about moral experience early in his career, and that he then tended to revise his thinking as the implications of his views became apparent, and as he felt the need to present his case in fuller detail or wider scope. The works that best represent Dewey's mature treatment of ethics are *Democracy and Education* (1916), *Reconstruction in Philosophy* (1920), *Human Nature and Conduct* (1922), "Three Independent Factors in Morals" (1930), and *Ethics* (1932).

The expectation of finding a single text that summarizes Dewey's ethics also underestimates the holistic character of Dewey's ethics and philosophy in general. Unlike many contemporary approaches to ethics, the one that Dewey constructed does not rest on a set of postulates and arguments that are recognizable as an ethical "system." When reading Dewey it is therefore important to resist the philosophical habit of trying to find a system: Dewey's ethics, like the rest of his work, has an organic structure. What this means is that his treatment of a particular moral issue cannot be understood in isolation from his larger moral project. Each thread of that larger moral project is in turn interwoven within the still-larger fabric of his whole philosophy. This means that he is the kind of philosopher whose ethics are better understood and evaluated when we have further knowledge of the rest of his philosophy. In this he is no different from other great ethical theorists such as Aristotle, Kant, or Mill. One implication and challenge is that Dewey's ethics therefore cannot be judged or appreciated from the standpoint of assumptions that are foreign to his wider philosophy. Dewey entertains one of the most unorthodox and complex views of moral life in the 20th century. To appreciate this it is necessary to complement his view of moral experience presented in his 1932 *Ethics* with texts that demonstrate how at that time he was engaged in an overall reconstruction of philosophy. There one can find further supporting reasons for his deviating so strongly from traditional approaches to ethics.

I hope the above is useful in determining how to approach and complement the reading of Dewey's 1932 *Ethics*. However, my effort to contextualize the text in light of the rest of his ethical thought assumes a view of what his overall ethical thought comes to. Therefore, full disclosure requires me to lay out what Dewey's ethics comes to, so that as they read the 1932 *Ethics* others can examine whether my account is on target, misleading, or incorrect.

Dewey's Mature and Overall Ethics by 1932

Dewey's contributions in ethical theory are in three general areas:

1 A critical stand on the limits, nature, problems, and function of the type of inquiry that takes our moral experience as its subject-matter (his metatheory);
2 A treatment of the generic traits and components of moral experience (his descriptive ethics);
3 A constructive, though not explicitly articulated, proposal regarding how we should live, and how we can improve our appreciation of morally problematic situations (his normative ethics).

The metatheoretical, the descriptive, and the normative facets of Dewey's ethics are found intertwined throughout his writings, and the 1932 *Ethics* is no exception. These facets are supportive of one another and of what Dewey regarded as his larger inquiry, namely an investigation of the conditions and instrumentalities required to ameliorate concrete, existential, lived experience. Dewey's concern with ethics arose out of his perception that individuals and institutions had not been able to find a viable alternative to the moral absolutism offered by custom and authority. He believed that such ethical theories, as well as the economic and political institutions that depend on and perpetuate them, have tended to encourage habits and attitudes that impoverish moral life.

The main problem with rigid ethical theories and the institutions that support them, Dewey argues, is that they are built on distrusting the capacity of human intelligence to find innovative ways of coming to terms with experienced problems. Such theories and institutions thus assume a profound dualism—a split between what they take to be a dignified, autonomous moral theory, on the one side, and what they take to be common, contingent, everyday experience, on the other. Dewey charges that the major theories advanced to date by moral philosophers, including subjectivism, rationalism, and transcendentalism, and those outlined throughout the middle chapters of the 1932 *Ethics*, have been constructed squarely on top of this dangerous fault line. He believes that in their efforts to achieve incontrovertible theories and indubitable foundations they had abandoned any effort to come to terms with experience as it is actually lived.

In order to recover morality from "otherworldly" views, on the one hand, and arbitrary subjectivist views, on the other, Dewey had to engage in a critical redescription of moral experience. He believes that traditional ethics had become bankrupt because it begins with an isolated subject or self that has a purely cognitive apprehension of moral truths. However, this abstraction ignores the social (transactional) and affective (qualitative) character of moral experience. Dewey's ethics thus point to dimensions of moral life that tend to be overlooked and undervalued in much of modern ethical thought. He rejects their intellectualist, passive, and possessive views of our moral life in favor of a conception of morality as a social, creative, imaginative-emotional, hypothetical, and experimental effort to ameliorate situations and to bring new goods into existence.

Dewey argues that there is no area of our experience that has suffered more from distortion and misleading conceptions than our moral experience. Among the most troublesome misconceptions has been the reification of morality into something that is separate from ordinary experience. Morality has thus been isolated and honored as something "spiritual." It has been cut off from lived experience and placed in an extra-experiential or subjective realm of its own. This understanding of morality, which has dominated Western culture, has been fostered in large part by the dualisms (such as the fracture that opposes "fact" to "values") that have been assumed and nurtured by traditional philosophy. As a part of his goal of reconstructing traditional philosophy, Dewey attempts to heal these conceptual fissures. Dewey warns against separating morality from relationships in the workplace, from the technical-scientific use of intelligence, and from the "material" orientation of the business world.

This persistent separation of morals from experience is one of the ways in which men and women seek to escape responsibility for their actions. If morality is perceived as something external to the material-natural realm of industrial and economic relations or something that is just sometimes added to them, then the instrumentalities of technology, science, and business are not properly perceived as tools that can be taken up and used to improve unsatisfactory moral conditions. This is a costly mistake; it diverts intelligence from the concrete situations where moral demands are encountered. If the continuity between morals and the rest of experience were acknowledged, however, then a fuller range of resources would become available for moral action.

Moral philosophers have consistently sought to prove that, independently of the "phenomenal" changes that occur in the world, special moral precepts exist that are universal, fixed, certain, and unchanging. However, in Dewey's view, change, conflict, contingency, uncertainty, and struggle are at the very heart of moral experience. This is not to say that he was a pessimist, but simply that he presented a more-honest assessment of our potential to ameliorate existing conditions. He thought that amelioration requires the recognition that even our most stable moral principles will have to be revised over time.

Dewey characterizes the generic elements and phases of our moral life as a process. There are three predominant stages in Dewey's model of moral inquiry. First, the agent finds herself in a morally problematic situation. Second, the agent engages in a process of moral deliberation. Finally, she arrives at a judgment that results in a choice. It is in light of this process that Dewey provides novel and provocative reconstructions of the traditional notions of character, moral deliberation, value judgments, principles, and moral problems. In contrast to the usual rationalistic-sterile account of moral deliberation, for example, Dewey describes moral deliberation as an experimental, emotional, and imaginative process. Moral deliberation results in a moral judgment—a decision to act in one way or another. But judgments are not static; they continue throughout the entire deliberative process, and they are transformed as deliberation proceeds. Within this process Dewey distinguishes between the direct judgments of value ("valuing") and reflective judgments ("valuations").

In Dewey's ethics the self is not a substance but an organization of habits that is relatively stable and enduring. The self therefore changes as habits are modified. Because we are selves in a process of continuous formation, what we do at any point in time is not a creation ex nihilo. Instead, what we do depends on the history of the self. In deciding what to do we rely on the habitual tendencies, projections, and desires that constitute our character as it was formed, at least in part, from previous experience. Although having a good character does not guarantee that we will always do the right act, it does increase our chances of doing so. The good habits we bring to a situation are among the means by which we are enabled to discover and do what is right. It is only by doing what we ought to do, however, that we can improve our habits. This is how being good and doing good are mutually dependent within any moral life that is both growing and educative. The most important moral learning that a person can acquire in a situation is not information (or rules), but the indirect cultivation of the habits that tend to affect the quality of future situations. This is to say that although the moral decisions we make depend on our characters, they also affect the habits that are carried forward by a growing self. The reconstruction of situations and the reconstruction of the self are not things that can be separated.

To take situations as the starting point of ethical theory does not entail a narrow or scaled-down view of moral experience. On the contrary, Dewey thought that much of the reductionism and oversimplification of the subject-matter of contemporary moral theory had been caused by the failure to consider the complexity and richness of our moral experiences as they are had in unique situations. Dewey mounts a devastating and systematic critique of contemporary moral theory as a part of his proposal for a new starting point. Ethical theory does not have answers to the problems that a particular situation poses. Theories are tools open to revision as applied to problems and open to new knowledge from the sciences. The constancies that we can rely on from the past (funded experience) are general and thin in content. Life has stabilities but not the degree or kind that many wish for or presuppose in their ethics. What ethics is possible or needed in light of the fact that life in general, especially moral life, has change, novelty, complexity, pluralism, and some indeterminacy?

The ethics that Dewey ends up proposing is one that abandons common traditional pretensions (e.g., universal standards, solutions, and rules). Instead, it concerns itself with reconstructing what is worth saving from the usual traditional theories but as tools. Instead of seeking new rules, it prescribes more attentiveness, and sensitivity to generic traits found in our concrete and particular moral problems. Instead of "what to do" it can prescribe a "how to" approach to morally problematic situations in terms of certain habits (as ways of interacting) in a community and in a situation. To find the guidance for rectifying a particular situation, it is necessary to give up looking for a universal theoretical formula and go on to the difficult task of studying the needs and alternative possibilities lying within a unique and localized situation. Dewey thus advocates an approach to moral decision-making that may be termed "situational." However, the flexibility and anti-theoretical character of his view does not entail less work, intelligence, or responsibility than fixed-theory approaches. Dewey argues that his view does not destroy responsibility, it only locates it. This implies that the work of intelligence cannot be accomplished once and for all. We cannot rely solely on the theoretical use of intelligence to construct rules that will relieve us of the need to make hard decisions. A situation ethics of the sort that Dewey advances demands that we try a fresh and wholehearted use of intelligence each time there is a new situation that requires amelioration.

For Dewey ethical theory can aid moral practice only indirectly, not in the direct way that has been assumed by most of contemporary philosophy. He favors an ethics that treats theory neither as cookbook nor remote calculus, but as a tool of criticism. His ethics is open to and encourages a method for generating and testing hypotheses about the conditions for living a richer moral life. In his ethics there is also an important role left for principles and ideals, but he knew these tools needed to be conceptually reconstructed so that they are no longer associated with old conceptions that tend to function as blinders in dealing with moral problems.

One of the most important of these conditions is what has been called "character." From Dewey's standpoint, moral philosophy has had the tendency to either overestimate or underestimate the importance of character. Underestimation is usually the result of denying the participatory role in moral experience. Overestimation is usually the result either of assuming that the direction of moral experience is totally within our control, or of making character an end in itself. Character and habits occupy a central place in Dewey's ethics, but they do not thereby occupy a place of ontological or epistemological primacy, as some other approaches argue. Character and habits are central to moral reflection and to ethical theory simply because they are among the most controllable factors of moral experience. To a great measure, habits determine how we interact with particular situations. This is how Dewey was able to propose an ethics with a strong character orientation and a commitment to amelioration of present morally problematic situations.

Even though what is right or wrong in a particular situation is determined in and by its particular context, not all characters are equally prepared for moral tasks. Dewey's contextualism thus advances a view about how moral agents as participants should confront moral situations. It demands the participation of the whole character of a moral agent in a moral situation. Moral anarchy and chaos are not avoided by fixing moral rules, but by the proper cultivation of character. For Dewey the kind of character we should develop is thus a more-important consideration than what decision procedure we should adopt.

In the final analysis, that part of Dewey's ethics that could be treated as a virtue ethics is complementary to his situation ethics. He holds that the most important instrumentalities for morality, the cardinal virtues if you like, are the traits of character that make it possible to determine what morality requires here and now. Dewey's situation ethics exhibits a positive-normative position in the sense that it undertakes judgments about what kinds of habits will serve as virtues, that is, as instruments for the development of better moral lives. Such virtues include sensitivity, conscientiousness, sympathy, and open-mindedness. These are the habits he identified as contributing to moral intelligence.

Note

1 Dewey's article "Three Independent Factors in Morals" is a centerpiece of his moral thought. The tripartite description of our moral experience of this essay explains why Dewey discusses good, duty, and virtue in separate

chapters of his 1932 *Ethics*. Without this essay one misses important support for the situational and pluralistic thrust of his moral philosophy that is not evident in his discussions about value in general. Dewey's faith in the instrumentalities of experience was tempered by the honest realization that the most intense moments of our moral life are tragic in the sense that there is an irreducible and sometimes-irresolvable conflict between positive moral demands or values. This is a different view and has different consequences than the general view of our moral life as merely a struggle between good and evil.

2 Dewey's Independent Factors in Moral Action

Steven Fesmire

Three Independent Factors in Morals

On November 7, 1930, Dewey addressed the French Philosophical Society in Paris, giving what his French colleagues recognized as "a première of his new ideas" (quoted in LW 5, 503). He hypothesized that each of the primary Western ethical systems (represented for him by ancient Greek teleologists, Roman and German deontologists, and British moralists) represents an irreducible experiential factor or root of moral life: aspiration, obligation, and approbation. Each basic experiential factor is expressed in that system's leading fundamental concept: good, duty, and virtue, respectively. Each system seeks to bring divergent experiential forces wholly within the logical scope of its own monistic category while treating other factors as derivative. For example, rationalistic deontologists conceive a character trait to be virtuous because it maps to what is antecedently determined by reason to be right. Dewey, however, contended that aspirations, obligations, and approbations are distinctive experiential/existential phenomena that often conflict with each other and cannot be fully blanketed by a single covering concept.

Sorbonne professor Charles Cestre immediately translated Dewey's 1930 English presentation, along with highlights from the ensuing discussion, and published it in *Bulletin de la SFP* as "Trois facteurs indépendants en matière de morale."[1] Decades later, in 1966, Jo Ann Boydston translated the French article back into English for *Educational Theory* as "Three Independent Factors in Morals," which she eventually included in the critical edition of Dewey's works (LW 5, 279–288).

Soon after Boydston published her back translation, an unpublished and undated typescript (mss102_53_3) was discovered in the Dewey archives at Southern Illinois University, titled in Dewey's hand "Conflict and Independent Variables in Morals."[2] A copy of this typescript was available to Abraham Edel and Elizabeth Flowers, who introduced the 1985 critical edition of Dewey's 1932 *Ethics* (LW 7; cf. Edel 2001). Pages 1–5 and 13 of the typescript remain unpublished, though these pages clarify several substantive points about Dewey's ethical outlook and offer unique angles and metaphors. The first five pages were likely presented in 1926 to Columbia University's philosophy club (Dewey to Horace S. Fries [1933.12.26 (07682)]). Pages 6–12 closely track "Trois facteurs indépendants en matière de morale," though Boydston decided not to include Dewey's substantive handwritten revisions for those pages in the critical edition.

Assuming that Dewey was reworking the typescript for an English publication, why did he never follow through? A plausible reply can be inferred from the fact that Dewey incorporated its basic insights into his chapters of the 1932 Dewey-Tufts *Ethics* textbook (LW 7, chs. 10–17). The "three roots" hypothesis in the 1930 presentation serves as an organizational chart for those chapters, especially Chapters 11–13. But he incorporated the three roots in a less theoretical form that he judged to be better suited to the practical and pedagogical needs of undergraduate students (Dewey to Horace S. Fries [1933.12.26 (07682)]. He set aside the theoretic key once it had served his pedagogical goal for the *Ethics*, which was to reforge historical theoretical tools in light of contemporary moral needs so that students can use them to become more comprehensively conscientious in their deliberations and character development. Specifically, Dewey's goal in the 1932 *Ethics* was to help students become more perceptive of moral complexity, study and assess their own circumstances in light of prior systems, and competently use diverse theories as deliberative tools (reforged to see connections that had escaped our notice) in predicaments that require practical coordination among disparate elements.[3]

The theoretic key he left behind is among the most practically significant things Dewey ever wrote on ethics, and its significance has arguably increased as rampant moral fundamentalism and homogeneous narrowness continue to build walls of exclusionary oppression (see Collins 1998) and block the way to discovering shared toeholds to debate and achieve social goals like security, health, sustainability, and justice. Moral fundamentalism encourages antagonism toward excluded standpoints, closure to being surprised by the complexity of many problems, neglect of the context in which decisions are made, obtuseness about one's own truncated framework, and a related general indifference to public processes and adaptive policies. It may be progressive in one dimension of a problem, but typically at the cost of being regressive with respect to concerns that are off the radar of our idealizations. These concerns are habitually overlooked or relegated as externalities.

Meanwhile, reactionary nihilism is merely moral fundamentalism's mirror image, setting up a false dilemma between nihilism and fundamentalism. Dewey rejected both of the principal alternatives on offer: moral monism (the quest for a single ethical ruler to govern deliberation) and moral skepticism (which takes the absence of such a ruler to spell the end of ethics). Instead of joining monists in an outdated quest for a theoretical hierarchy that subdues variety among fundamental moral concepts, or merely venturing "an eclectic combination of the different theories" (LW 7, 180), Dewey approached philosophical research into ethics as a way to help create a shared cultural context in which we cultivate conditions for communicative inquiry that refreshingly steers clear of any tendency to autocratically predefine what is relevant and to prejudge alternative formulations without dialogue.

In a letter to Horace S. Fries [1933.12.26 (07682)], Dewey identified the key conceptual shift he made between the 1908 *Ethics* (MW 5) and the 1932 revision. He had, he wrote, been committed in 1908 to a "socialized utilitarianism" that foreshortened moral action from the teleological perspective of the good. This monistic consequentialism is also apparent in *Outlines of a Critical Theory of Ethics* (1891, EW 2, 238–388) and *The Study of Ethics: A Syllabus* (1894, EW 4, 219–362). Note, importantly, that Dewey nowhere *reduced* moral life to a triumvirate of root factors; he did not have a universal, cover-all ethical theory. But by 1932 he had transitioned to a strong axiological pluralism that maintained the intellectual distinctness of variables in moral action, variables that are selectively—often helpfully—emphasized in key abstract ethical concepts.

Dewey's typology of "at least three" relatively independent factors in moral action developed in the 1920s as the organizing principle of his spring 1926 course in "Ethical Theory" at Columbia University. Thanks to Donald Koch's editorial work on *The Class Lectures of John Dewey* (2010), researchers have access to material unknown to Edel or Flowers, including Sidney Hook's class lecture notes on that 1926 course. Hook's notes take readers into the classroom as Dewey surveys the history of ethical theory to lay bare "certain categories found to be involved in judgments which men actually pass in the course of moral conduct and which concepts have become the foundation stones of theories about ethics" (in Koch 2010, 2.2230). The 1926 course—akin in its topic to a course in meta-ethics today in that it was "not concerned with what is specifically right, but with the category of right" (2.2230)—was organized around a hypothetical explanation for the variety of ethical theories.

In the 1926 course, Dewey struggled with whether right and duty are fundamentally different concepts. For example, he explored Sidgwick's notion in *The Methods of Ethics* that the right is the "Rational Good," which Sidgwick contrasted with a merely *natural* good (cf. Lazari-Radek and Singer 2014). Dewey said in the class's opening days:

> These remarks [identifying good, right, duty, and virtue as fundamental concepts that enter into moral conduct] presuppose the possibility of a hierarchy of these different ideas, i.e., all deduced from a supreme one. But an alternative is possible, i.e., that none are derivative or subordinate. They may be independent variables, i.e.,

> ideas representing facts which while they overlap, are still intellectually distinct so far as the meaning of the four terms is concerned. The originality in the [Spring 1926] course will largely be concerned with the inability to find a single central notion from which the others can be derived or around which they can be organized. Two or three may be connected, but there are at least three independent variables.
>
> (in Koch 2010, 2.2231)

Urging that moral uncertainties arise from conflicts inhering in situations, and that moral problems do not come prepackaged with a correct formulation or a single justified course of action, Dewey in 1926–1932 broadened his scope beyond his prior focus on moral psychology in *Human Nature and Conduct* (1922)—e.g., his theory of dramatic rehearsal in deliberation (see Fesmire 2003, ch. 5)—to encompass the wider scene of moral action. "Three Independent Factors in Morals" is Dewey's resulting conceptual map of the existential terrain of moral action. The essay foreshortens his mature ethical theory.

In what follows, I draw on the aforementioned unpublished and published sources from 1926 to 1932 to clarify Dewey's analysis in "Three Independent Factors in Morals" of good, duty, and virtue as distinct concepts that in many cases express different experiential origins.

Is There a Conceptual Home Range of Moral Action?

Is there a single empirical source of moral action, or are there plural sources? This was Dewey's central question as an ethical theorist from 1926 to 1932—again, aside from any normative prescriptions or constraints regarding what specifically is good or bad, right or wrong, virtuous or vicious. His hypothesis was that moral problems require us to reconcile and coordinate "heterogeneous elements" (in Koch 2010, 2.2270) that include "at least three independent variables in moral action" (LW 5, 280) which "pull different ways" (Dewey, undated ms, 4). These variables are independent in the sense that one is neither logically derivable from another nor translatable without remainder into the terms of another. If Dewey is right that there are several empirical roots of moral action, then one radical implication is that any ethical theory that strives like logical or mathematical theories to solve any moral problem with the single "right" method or procedure will be inadequate to the heterogeneity of moral experience.

In the 1930 presentation, Dewey began his analysis with a simplified binary of independent factors in morals before expanding to "at least" a trifecta. He operationalized the two most familiar "opposing systems of moral theory" by rejecting the false dilemma that binds them: either what's morally Right derives from what's Good (so we get a teleological morality of ends, where right action is defined as the means to the supreme good of *eudaimonia*, pleasure, self-realization, liberty, equality, sustainability, or the like), or what's morally Good derives from what's Right (so we get a deontological morality of laws, where right action is prescribed by "juridical imperative"). Dewey argued that "neither of the two can derive from the other," there is no "constant principle" tilting the balance "on the side of good or of law," and that both good and law are conceptions that "flow from independent springs" (LW 5, 281). Consequently, in moral education, learning to desire the good and learning to do one's duty are equally legitimate expectations, yet each frequently gets in each other's way and tugs in different directions. Reflective morality consists, then, in the capacity to determine a "practical middle footing" *between* practically incommensurable claims, "a middle footing which leans as much to one side as to the other without following any rule which may be posed in advance" (281).

Moral situations, in Dewey's view, are not just *occasions* for uncertainty about what to do; problematic moral situations more typically *justify* our uncertainty. "Moral experience is a genuine experience" of real, systemic conflicts (in Koch 2010, 2.2270), so we generally *ought* to be reflective. And yet, Dewey argued, traditional theories have treated conflict as specious rather than as part and parcel of moral experience. Moral philosophers have not failed to acknowledge angst, but they have for the most part postulated "one single principle as an explanation of moral life" (LW 5, 280), a correct standpoint from which we will at least in principle see that our initial hesitancy had been based on momentary ignorance.

If there is a unitary conceptual home range of moral action, moral conflict boils down to hesitancy on our part about what to choose. On that view, what is good or virtuous or right is already licit, ready to be laid bare by intellectual analysis. But in fact morally uncertain situations require us to reconcile conflicting factors with multiple conceptual ranges. Consequently, Dewey urged: "It is not without significance that uncertainty is felt most keenly by those who are called conscientious" (Dewey, undated ms, 13). Should an expectant mother of triplets selectively reduce to twins? Should we globally follow a principle of per capita equity for carbon emissions? Should John have had the affair with Anzia? To see these questions through the lens of only one factor—as at bottom a matter of rights not downstream consequences, of what is right not what is good, of duty not virtue, of what I should do and not what kind of person I should become—risks lop-sided, partial, and exclusionary deliberation that pretends as a matter of course to have precisely captured all that is morally or politically relevant to the choice. In actual experience, it would be an atypically easy case in which tensions among values could be resolved by appealing to a supreme value, principle, standard, law, concept, or ideal that exhausts whatever is of moral worth in the rest of our concerns.

Under the narrow monistic assumption legitimized by traditional ethical theorizing, conflict and diversity are merely apparent (LW 5, 279–288). A situation may at first *seem* to be a quagmire, the supposition runs, but rigorous examination, or more data to feed into our utility calculations, or comparison to an egalitarian island of rational albeit hapless contractors (see Dworkin 2000), will reveal that (a) there had been a good, right, or fair path through it all along, and (b) the path's goodness, rightness, or fairness overrides other considerations when it comes to justifying the choice.

From that angle, uncertainty is seen mostly as a "hesitation about choice" between the moral and the immoral: we assume we must choose the good (vs. evil), will the obligatory (vs. giving way to appetite, inclination, and desire), or do the virtuous (vs. the vicious). "That is the necessary logical conclusion if moral action has only one source, if it ranges only within a single category" (LW 5, 280). "*We* may be in doubt as to what the good or the right or the virtuous is in a complicated situation," but under the traditional one-way assumption "it is there and determination of it is at most a purely intellectual question, not a moral one. There is no conflict inhering in the situation" (Dewey, undated ms, 3).

Yet contemporary moral and political conflicts are rarely so superficial that a theoretically correct rational analysis could, even in principle, sweep the path clear toward what is "truly" good, right, just, or virtuous. Entanglements of often-incompatible forces inhere in typical moral predicaments (cf. Latour 1993). It is typical to find ourselves tugged in multiple ways, none of which has overriding moral force. This relative incommensurability of forces presents, for Dewey, a *practical* problem that requires moral imagination and artistry (cf. Alexander 2013). For example, anyone who has worked on administrative policies for allocating faculty workloads at a university is at least implicitly aware that an institution or department can purchase greater aggregate happiness at the price of some unfairness. One can also demand an exactingly rational fairness in workload at the cost of some unhappiness. Is the job of the theorist to discern which of these ways of organizing reflection is the most justified? That is, is the theorist's job to show a priori which antecedently defended and relatively static principles should govern choice? A Deweyan alternative is not to override one of these conceptual frameworks on behalf of a purportedly more rational monistic framework, but to democratically elicit the generative possibilities of a situation that may be shackled by an overly legalistic approach that is insensitive to intractable tensions.

In the Q&A that followed the 1930 presentation, Dewey admitted that

> he exaggerated, for purposes of discussion, the differences among the three factors, that indeed moral theories do touch on these three factors more or less, but what he wanted to emphasize was the fact that each particular moral theory takes one of them as central and that is what becomes the important point, while the other factors are only secondary.
>
> (LW 5, 503)

The central dogma of ethical theory is that any adequate account of metaethics and normative morality must be given in terms of one supreme root (Fesmire 2003, 2015). Yet proponents of each primary ethical system miss, at least in their explicit theorizing, the tensions that constantly underlie moral action as irreducible forces, as when binding social demands conflict with aspirations. Dewey insisted that it is not possible to theoretically settle moral problems in advance of their occurrence because each variable in moral action "has a different origin and mode of operation," so "they can be at cross purposes and exercise divergent forces in the formation of judgment." "The essence of the moral situation is an internal and intrinsic conflict; the necessity for judgment and for choice comes from the fact that one has to manage forces with no common denominator" (LW 5, 280). Dewey's alternative for future ethical and political theorizing would be to lay bare and classify these practical entanglements within a wider "framework of moral conceptions" that puts basic roots in communication (LW 7, 309), so that we might "attend more fully to the concrete elements entering into the situations" in which we must act (LW 5, 288).

From Three Factors to Three Foundations

To recap Dewey's hypothesis, problematic moral situations are heterogeneous in their origins and operations. They tangle and diverge in ways that elude full predictability and are typically not controllable by the impositions of any abstract monistic principle. Moral life has *at least* three distinct experiential roots that cannot be encompassed in one ideal way to think about morals. Hence, most importantly for reconstructing traditional ethical theories, there is no universal foundation of ethics—whether procedurally constructed or "foundational" in the now old-fashioned sense—that would allow us to single out, in Thompson's phrasing, "the most fully justified course of action, even in situations where beneficial outcomes are offset by costs, or where rights and duties conflict" (Thompson 2016, 70). Dewey's unpublished typescript clarifies the hypothesis:

> The three things I regard as variables are first the facts that give rise to the concept of the good and bad; secondly, those that give rise to

> the concept of right and wrong; thirdly, those that give rise to the conception of the virtuous and vicious. ...What I am concerned to point out [is] that the concrete conflict is not just among these concepts, but in the elements of the actual moral situation that, when they are abstracted and generalized, give rise to these conceptions.[4]
>
> (Dewey, undated ms, 2)

In this section, I clarify Dewey's hypothesis by interspersing the three experiential factors and concomitant abstract concepts, as emphasized in the 1930 presentation, with the parallel chapters in the 1932 *Ethics* (Chapters 11–13).

Ends, the Good, and Wisdom

The Good as a leading concept in reflective ethics springs from desires and aspirations. People have purposes they aim to realize; pervasive wants, drives, appetites, and needs that demand to be satisfied. Yet what *seems* good at short range may not in fact *be* durably good. If only miracles would intervene to keep our choices from having their usual side effects! But in the universe we are obliged to inhabit, the *satisfaction* we crave may not be judged *satisfactory* when we take a wider view. So we need practice and wisdom to thoughtfully discriminate between the real good and the mirage. Consequently, the teleological conception of goods that approvably speak to human cravings and aspirations is "neither arbitrary nor artificial" (LW 7, 309). When we make hasty choices without intelligent foresight, we just follow the strongest impulse and fulfill an inclination without taking its measure. "But when one foresees the consequences which may result from the fulfillment of desire, the situation changes" (LW 5, 282). Intelligent foresight involves judgment and comparison as we envision consequences *ex ante* and track them *ex post*.

Dewey analyzes the imaginative capacity to crystallize possibilities and transform them into directive hypotheses in his theory of "dramatic rehearsal" in deliberation (e.g., MW 14, ch. 16; cf. Fesmire 2003, Alexander 2013, and Johnson 2019). We imaginatively rehearse alternative avenues for acting in a dynamic social context, and judgments can be "examined, corrected, made more exact by judgments carried over from other situations; the results of previous estimates and actions are available as working materials" (LW 5, 282). In this way, we learn to organize and prioritize desires with an eye to their bearings, and this led historically to candidates for the "chief good," the *summum bonum* (Aristotle 1999, Book I) such as hedonistic pleasure, success, wisdom, egoistic satisfaction, asceticism, and self-realization.[5] Wherever this factor is the dominant emphasis in philosophical theorizing, *reason* is conceived as "intelligent insight into complete and remote consequences of desire" (LW 7, 217). The envisioned action is right and virtuous because it is truly, far-sightedly good; it is wrong and vicious because it is short-sightedly bad.

As a contemporary example, take Singer's hedonistic utilitarian approach to "effective altruism." For Singer, reason objectively calculates the best quantifiable way to "maximize the amount of good you do over your lifetime" (Singer 2015, 65). Reason counters our emotive tendency to discount the lives of those who are physically or temporally distant. Singer argues that reason also checks our tendency to mistake "warm glow giving," as with the Make-a-Wish Foundation, with cost-effective philanthropies like GiveWell. One need not be morally "on the clock" 24/7, as this would reach a point of diminishing returns (what Singer calls the point of marginal utility). But weighing your options—say, alternatives for charitable giving—to objectively determine the most good that you can do, is what it *means* to be moral. If you can work for Goldman Sachs and donate your considerable discretionary cash to effective charities, you may do more life-saving and quality-of-life-improving good than if you strictly adhere to a deontological "do no harm" principle and refuse to participate in the capitalistic financial system due to its putative unfairness. The good that you do *justifies* your participation in the system, unless you could have aggregated more good in some other way. If struggling against structural inequalities by minimizing involvement in financial markets adds up to the most good you can do, then it is justified. But for Singer, fighting for justice is *not* good "in itself" independent of its utility.

For Singer, answering a moral problem is analogous to answering a math problem. It requires us to calculate payoffs and pitfalls and thereby determine the objective good (145). For instance, what priority should we give to expenditures on decreasing existential risk (from asteroids, climate change, etc.)? Singer quotes Bostrom, an Oxford utilitarian specializing in existential risk, who calculates that it should be our highest global priority: "If benefiting humanity by increasing existential safety achieves expected good on a scale many orders of magnitude greater than that of alternative contributions, we would do well to focus on this most efficient philanthropy" (174).

In the unpublished typescript, Dewey included such mathematizing, neo-Benthamite approaches in a sweeping criticism of traditional moral philosophies: : appeals to "the dictates of conscience," intuition, a moral calculus, moral law, or divine command acknowledge moral hesitancy and puzzlement, but they mask existential uncertainty when they presuppose "that the answer to a moral problem is already licit, like the answer to a problem in a text on arithmetic that it only remains to figure correctly." Dewey held that moral problems typically bear little analogy to elementary arithmetic tasks, or to being stumped by a hard puzzle. When calculating the square root of 25, there is a clear-cut way to formulate the problem and a right solution, so the only real problem is momentary ignorance of the answer. In moral life, however, the answers are not already licit.

In the undated manuscript Dewey wrote, "Genuine uncertainty is an essential trait of every moral situation" (Dewey, undated ms, 1). He is not merely remarking here on the uncertainty that arises from the *difficulty* of a puzzle, or to lack of *access* to relevant data to plug into our diagnostic machinery. Dewey contended that a typical moral choice among viable alternatives cannot *even in principle* be definitively formulated and finally answered by assembling information and then calculating profits and losses on a moral accounting spreadsheet. Utilitarianism's economic-mathematical balancing model can function well as a heuristic for some purposes. Dewey does not deny this. But he did challenge the aggregationist's obsession with predetermined metrics whereby we judiciously weigh matters so that the balance tips toward the good or "optimal" outcome supported by some welfarist principle. Insofar as such metrics economize deliberation without occluding morally relevant factors, then they are pragmatically valuable to that extent, but insofar as any approach fails to prioritize sensitivity to context, creative social inquiry, and experimental understanding of complex underlying structures, their actual results are too often reminiscent of an offhanded criticism that Dewey once made about "popcorn" solutions: put the right amount in the right mechanism and you get some "unnutritious ready-made stuff" that will not sustain anyone for long (1951.02.14 [14090]: Dewey to Max C. Otto).

Right, Duty, and Loyalty

The way we express our concerns and make sense of problems is acquired through interaction with a sociocultural medium. Dewey argued that the intimacy of the Greek polis supported teleological intelligence and the idea that laws reflect our rational ability to patiently set and achieve goals together. Accordingly, theories of the good made sense to classic Greek theorists. However, the far-flung hodgepodge of peoples in the Roman Empire favored the historical development of centralized order and the imposition of demands. Consequently, in the transition from Greek teleology to Roman law, as exemplified by Stoic philosophers, compliance with authorized duty was placed at "the centre of moral theory" (LW 5, 284).

The resulting deontological or jural theories speak to fact in everyday human behavior: we inescapably make claims on each other through living together. This includes the control of desire and appetite, companionship and competition, cooperation and subordination. Our desires are impeded and regulated, sorted into the forbidden and the permitted. These demands appear arbitrary unless they square with each other's purposes. So, Dewey proposed, "there finally develops a certain set or system of demands, more or less reciprocal according to social conditions, which are ... responded to without overt revolt." In this way, authorized rights and duties evolve through demands and prohibitions on others' behavior. "From the standpoint of those whose claims are recognized, these demands are rights; from the standpoint of those undergoing them they are duties." This "constitutes the principle of authority, Jus, Recht, Droit, which is current" (284).

Dewey hypothesizes, then, that duty as a leading concept in morals arises from authoritative control of individual satisfactions and temptations. As such, the concept of duty (along with the related concept of loyalty to what is *right*) is independent of the concept of good. The concepts of duty and good are independent both in their existential origins and in their logical operations. These concepts pivot on different elements: the good pivots on aspiration; the right pivots on exaction.

As Kant recognized, because imperatives often inhibit the fulfillment of desires, the concept of duty is not "reducible to the conception of the good as satisfaction, even reasonable satisfaction, of desire" (LW 7, 214). Kant additionally recognized that there is no moral quality in binding our choices to an authority we deem ultimately arbitrary. Several years ago, my young son was happily picking flowers in a public garden, and we told him "don't pick the flowers." To him, our curtailment of this good seemed to be an arbitrary imposition. Asked about this a few years later, he said it was reasonable for his liberty to be restrained in this way. What had begun as compliance had been converted into something with moral standing, something *right*. He now acknowledged it as a *moral* demand that he should meet.

Taking these insights a step further, Dewey distinguished the *origins* of root factors from their eventual *operations*. For example, that which operates as a good that one sincerely aspires to may have originated as a duty with which one had to comply. Today my son wants to help that garden flourish. What began as an alien injunction that thwarted his desires developed into something right to which he personally realized the wisdom of submitting, and then it became a good that he pursued absent any requirement. The same might eventually be said of his enforced duty to do school work, which can also originate in obedience to communal regulations. When cultivating a garden or going to school enter one's personal aspirations "it loses its quality of being right and authoritative and becomes simply a good" (LW 5, 285).[6]

To summarize, "the Good is that which attracts; the Right is that which asserts that we *ought* to be drawn by some object whether we are naturally attracted to it or not" (LW 7, 217). When the latter factor is foremost, *reason* (or alternatively a presumed innate faculty of conscience) is conceived as "a power which is opposed to desire and which imposes restrictions on its exercise through issuing commands" (217). An act is good and virtuous *because* it is right; it is bad and vicious because it is wrong. To the degree that a deontologist is a monist, it follows there are no morally relevant aspects of virtue or good that cannot be blanketed under the concepts of duty, right, law, and obligation. To will and be loyal to what is right purely *because it is right*, and not because it is prudent, is consequently a common way of framing moral judgments, and the conception of lawful duty and compliance with constraints of the right is thus taken by many to be the universal foundation of ethics.[7]

Dewey applied these insights to Kantian deontology in the 1932 *Ethics*. According to Kantians, what is morally Good "is that which is Right, that which accords with law and the commands of duty" (214–216). Contemporary representatives include Rawls (1971), Donagan (1977), Gewirth (1978), Darwall (1983), and Korsgaard (1996). For example, central to his conception of justice as fairness, Rawls distinctively holds with Kant that a principle of right must take priority over consequentialist concepts of good (1971, 31; cf. Freeman 2007, 72). Rawls references *The Critique of Practical Reason*: "the concept of good and evil must not be determined before the moral law..., but only after it and by means of it" (Kant 2002, 37). One should struggle against inequality or strive to change an unjust system *independent* of any welfarist purpose such as anticipated net utility. For Kantians, the good is a path to the right, and the right gets its legitimate governing authority by reasonably obliging. In Korsgaard's idiom on the "source of normativity," on the Kantian view moral obligations are assigned by autonomous consciousness (1996; cf. Schaubroeck 2010). Complying with your duty and thereby at least attitudinally intending to uphold the rights of others is what it *means* to be moral.

Rawls or Korsgaard would reasonably wonder how social expectations take on justifiable moral authority on Dewey's naturalistic and pragmatic view. In other words, how does Dewey reinterpret the locus and ground of rightfulness without falling back on any of the traditional sources of normativity: God, the state, an inner law of pure practical reason, autonomous consciousness, a law of nature, or idealized rational actors? Dewey's general reply was that relationships naturally bind us to each other—as parents and children, spouses or partners, friends, and citizens. These relationships expose us to "the expectations of others and to the demands in which these expectations are made manifest." This is equally true of social expectations within institutions and political alliances. Explicit and implicit claims upon us are "as natural as anything else in a world in which persons are not isolated from one another but live in constant association and interaction" (LW 7, 218). Although a child, friend, spouse, or citizen might be coerced into conformity, they experience this as a brute imposition of power without moral standing. Social expectations become *moral* claims because, even when inconvenient or exasperating, conscientious parents, friends, spouses, or citizens respond to relations of parenting, friendship, marriage, and citizenship as "expressions of the whole" to which they belong rather than as extrinsic impositions (218).

> If we generalize such instances, we reach the conclusion that right, law, duty, arise from the relations which human beings intimately sustain to one another, and that their authoritative force springs from the very nature of the relation that binds people together. (219)

In moral life we must meet the demands of the *situation*, and this requires us to perceive and comprehensively respond to more than our own private hankerings. The word duty is apt for the many occasions in which our own preferences run at cross-purposes from relational demands that should not be shirked merely because they may be irksome, inconvenient, *or* dangerous. In Dewey's pragmatic-operational reconstruction of duty and the right, not only are Kantians right that we cannot rationally will a world of liars or thieves; they are also right to call for an inner sentinel alert to the exceptions we make of ourselves even as we make demands on others. Who is better than Rawls, for example, for shining a light on the way we benefit from a practice while shirking to do our share in sustaining that practice for others? (cf. Appiah 2017, 203). Though for Dewey, the general social demand to do our fair share is justified in practice, not by compliance with the first principles of idealized contractors.

Kantians typically reject Dewey's style of aspectual pragmatizing and operationalizing as an abdication of morality. Nevertheless, Dewey agreed with Kant that "to be truthful from duty is ...quite different from being truthful from fear of disadvantageous consequences" (Kant 1993, 15). Duty, right, and obligation are concepts that serve an experiential function as *one* among several constant and distinctive streams of morals. Kant's mistake was to hypostatize this factor and sharply separate moral conduct from our natural aspirations and practical purposes, inferring that "All so-called moral interest consists solely in respect for the law" (14n14).

Approbation, the Standard, and Virtue

A third independent primitive factor in morals is centered on praise and blame, approval and disapproval, reward and punishment (LW 5, 285). "Acts and dispositions generally approved form the original virtues; those condemned the original vices" (286). This factor differs fundamentally, at least in principle, from both the deliberative pursuit of ends and the demand for compliance.

Deontologists use praise and blame as sanctions for right and wrong , while teleological thinkers acknowledge the instrumental importance of social approval and disapproval (Dewey, undated ms., 10).

> But as categories, as principles, the virtuous differs radically from the good and the right. Goods, I repeat, have to do with deliberation upon desires and purposes; the right and obligatory with demands that are socially authorized and backed; virtues with widespread approbation.
>
> (LW 5, 286)

Virtue ethicists search for consistency and coherence about which character traits *ought* to be approved or censured. This requires a non-arbitrary standard of approbation to critique the "original," socially preestablished virtues so that more appropriate and defensible ones can be discovered. Typically virtue theorists turn, like Anscombe (1958), to some eudaemonistic conception of living well.

In his 1933 letter to Fries, Dewey credited his mature meta-ethical typology—which complicates any simple categorization of Aristotle (1999) as a virtue ethicist, or Mill as an aggregator of good consequences—to his careful re-reading of 18th- and 19th-century British moral philosophers such as Hume, Smith, Bentham, Mill, and Sidgwick. Hook's 1926 course notes (in Koch 2010) allow us to witness this re-reading as it unfolds. Dewey settled on a Jeckyll-and-Hyde reframing of utilitarianism: it's far better to be an inconsistent Millian than a consistent Benthamite. Whereas the Benthamite strain persists in its "untenable hedonism," at the cost of some consistency Mill received and renewed the torch of moral sentiment theory by shifting the primary focus of ethics away from what we should *do* in pursuit of pleasures and toward cultivation of character. "Although Mill never quite acknowledges it in words, a surrender of the hedonistic element in utilitarianism" enabled him to develop, or mostly develop, a welfarist standard implicit in our approbations that favors "worthy dispositions from which issue noble enjoyments" (LW 7, 245).

Commentaries on Dewey's ethics, including some of my own, have tended to treat utilitarianism under the category of the good. But this is a half-truth, as Dewey revealed in his close readings of Smith and other 18th century sources of the utilitarian tradition. For British moral sentiment theorists like Hume and Smith, morality is founded on sympathetic sentiments. Hume wrote in the *Treatise*, "Sympathy is the chief source of moral distinctions" (1978, 618).[8] Sympathy always brings approval, while antipathy always brings disapproval. We approve because we sympathize, and whatever elicits our sympathy we call good; we disapprove because we feel antipathy, and whatever calls out this sentiment we call bad. Nevertheless, in their theories of moral judgment Hume and Smith do not merely equate being praised with being praiseworthy. Dewey was especially interested in the way in which, for Hume and Smith, our moral sentiments can be corrected and regulated by rational considerations. Dewey observed of moral sentiment theory: "In individuals, the exercise of sympathy in accordance with reason—i.e., from the standpoint of an impartial spectator, in Smith's conception—is the norm of virtuous action" (LW 11, 11). The job of reason in moral judgment, for Smith in *The Theory of Moral Sentiments*, is to inform and secure the correctives of an impartial standard of approbation so that it plays a formative role in critically reflective ends. *Reason* seeks "a *standard* upon the basis of which approbation and disapprobation, esteem and disesteem, *should* be awarded" (LW 7, 255).[9]

Dewey spotlighted Smith's approach to this problem of non-arbitrary standards that do not merely bow to customary esteem and ridicule. Dewey argues that this problem is uppermost in moral sentiment theory "even when the writer seems to be discussing some other question" (LW 5, 286). Again, within sentiment theory what is good or dutiful is derived from what our sentiments approve as virtuous and disapprove as vicious. And according to Hume and Smith, what we spontaneously sympathize with and favor are benevolent actions that serve others. Meanwhile, ill will arouses antipathy. Ethical theory extrapolates from this and gives its seal of rational approval to the implicit standard in such judgments: "the Good must be defined in terms of impulses that further general welfare since they are the ones naturally approved" (Dewey, undated ms, 10). This is the natural and non-arbitrary standard we arrive at when, in Smith's idiom, we take up the standpoint of a fully informed impartial spectator. In this way, moral sentiment theorists accounted for aspiration (for the good) and compliance (with duty) in terms of what they took to be *the more fundamental fact* of approval and disapproval (the virtuous and vicious). Mid-nineteenth-century British utilitarianism inherited this legacy, as is especially evident in Mill's focus on social sympathy. But in Dewey's view Mill illogically tried to combine "Dr. Jekyll" with "Mr. Hyde": (a) the pursuit of general welfare as the legitimate natural standard implicit in social approval (or reproach) of dispositions and practices with (b) the hedonistic idea that individual pleasure is the *summum bonum*.

To summarize, for monistic theories rooted in the third factor, a practice or disposition such as generosity, courage, honesty, industriousness, or compassion is deemed good and dutiful because our moral sentiments naturally approve it (and ought legitimately to approve it when considered from an impartial perspective) as virtuous; a predisposition such as miserliness or retaliatory payback is bad and wrong because it is vicious (and rationally merits disapproval). To the degree that virtue theorists are monists—and Hume was a pluralist of sorts, at least with respect to fundamental conflicts among moral ends (see Gill 2011)—they infer that concepts such as goodness, welfare, duty, and right can be systematically organized without remainder under a conception of virtuous character traits, taking these traits to be those we should approve because they are contributory to a rationally defensible conception of living and being well. Monistic virtue theorists hold that cultivating stable behavioral traits that are as virtuous as possible is what it ultimately *means* to be moral. Or, to update Dewey's analysis, the virtue theorist must at least fictionalize (see Alfano 2013) stable character traits. Situational psychologists and ethical theorists are currently debating whether we are capable of exhibiting these traits in the trans-contextual way that is required by strong monistic virtue theories (Appiah 2008, ch. 2).

Conclusion

In the spirit of Hume's *A Treatise of Human Nature: Being an Attempt to Introduce the Experimental Method into Moral Subjects*, Dewey sought to bring experimental method to bear on value inquiry. "The growth of the experimental as distinct from the dogmatic habit of mind," he asserted, "is due to increased ability to utilize variations for constructive ends instead of suppressing them" (LW 1, 7). Accordingly, he saw variability in valuing and valuations as a useful entry point for further inquiry, rather than as a troublesome deviation to be flattened.

Dewey recommended abandoning the old quest for a completely enlightened ideal standpoint secured prior to struggling with difficulties in particular contexts, a standpoint from which our general way of thinking about morals will be fully adequate to meeting every situation with what is best in us. Our actual experiments in living assuredly involve ideals and idealizations—often one-sided–through which we appraise alternative avenues for acting, as Appiah has argued (2017). But they have always proceeded without access to a non-contingent ideal standpoint. What ethical theory can do, despite (and at times likely because of) its one-sided idealizations, is to help lay bare "the factors causing [problems] and thus make the choice more intelligent" (in Koch 2010, 2.2241–2.2245).

Dewey understood that ad hoc rationalizations can masquerade as intelligent deliberation. In Haidt's recent phrasing, so-called "moral reasoning" often amounts to little more than a self-justifying, ineffectual "rider" atop the headstrong "elephant" of habituated intuitions (Haidt 2012). This is from Dewey's angle an everyday deliberative vice. But at the other extreme, we may be like Hamlet in his indecision, "sicklied o'er with the pale cast of thought" (Shakespeare, Hamlet, Act III, scene ii) so that we shirk responsibility for choosing. Excessive deliberation amounts to dawdling, or signifies a manically imbalanced character (LW 7, 170). Dewey observed a related tendency to slough off responsibility among intellectuals who retreat to remote abstractions even when immediate conditions require more than begrudging notice. Those who "devote themselves to thinking are likely to be unusually unthinking in some respects, as for example in immediate personal relationships" (MW 14, 137). Mike Parker humorously wrote in *Map Addict*: "I'm the one in the car with the map in his lap, ...often at the expense of seeing the actual landscape it depicts rolling past on the other side of the window" (2010, 2). Like Parker, moral and political philosophers tend to be more map-oriented than terrain-oriented. There are consolations of retreating from the ambient buzz, but at our *philosophic* best we do not escape from existential peril into symbolic formulations and indulgently remain there.

But how do we work out which choices are progressive or regressive? Dewey offers no pat answer to this question. Instead of offering yet another iteration of the old escape through faith or reason to an antecedently established "aperspectival position" (Johnson 2014, 120), Dewey embraced the fact that when we ask different questions, we see different connections and possibilities. As is often observed, to ask the Kantian question (What is my duty?) or the utilitarian question (Which actions help us do the most good we can do?) is not to ask the Aristotelian question (Which character traits contribute to the *eudaemon* life?). To appropriate Heisenberg, what we observe is not the moral situation in itself, but the situation exposed to our method of questioning (see 1958, 32).

As Dewey framed his pluralistic ethical theory, his central questions were as follows: when we are morally conflicted, is this a superficial hesitancy that would dissipate if only we could conduct our reasoning rightly, marshal enough data, consult our inborn moral sense, or pray harder? Or, is the experience of moral conflict often rooted in something intractable, a conflict *intrinsic* to the situation itself? Should we strive for a one-size-fits-all approach that organizes moral cognition under a single covering concept? Do the traditional blanket concepts of good, right, and virtue arise from the same empirical source in our moral experience, or do they express distinctive roots? If leading moral categories express independent forces with different empirical roots, are these roots ultimately fully compatible? Or do they pull us in different directions, leaving us in a muddle about what to choose? If there are practical incommensurabilities between primitive springs of moral action, then how can we practically manage and evaluate the normative claims made on us by these disparate forces?

Dewey's typically-for-him-programmatic stab at answering these questions pivoted on the thesis that there are "independent variables in moral action" (LW 5, 280), these diverse experiential factors are in tension with each other, and they are reducible neither to an ideal starting point for moral inquiry nor to a changeless universal foundation. The three primitive strands that Dewey analyzed are conceptually distinct and have independent sources, but in actual moral experiences they intertwine and "cut across one another." For moral deliberation to be at all comprehensive, it must search for a way to reconcile conflicting variables to each other by weaving them into a tapestry of action that more-or-less satisfactorily expresses the tensions that originally set the problem at hand (Fesmire 2003, ch. 7).

Dewey developed a hypothesis to clarify how often-conflicting basic values relate to one another and how they might be put into communication with each other without being hypostatized. He thereby showed how functionally isolated theories can be critically appraised within a wider normative context even as these theories retain distinctive emphases as idealized partial mappings of the terrain of moral action. Maps are tools, so when these partial mappings of normative ideals are clung to as though they are true "independent of what they lead to when used as directive principles" (LW 4, 221), dogmatism is fueled and deliberation remains incomplete. But when normative models are reframed as revisable experiments in living (cf. Mill 1986), as what Dewey in *The Quest for Certainty* called instrumentalities of direction, then they can be progressively reformed through our interactions.

Dewey concluded "Three Independent Factors in Morals" with a call for our moral imaginations to become more perceptive and responsive to concrete situations. His insights from the early 1930s can be supplemented with contemporary research on DuBoisian "double consciousness," or better, Jose Medina's "kaleidoscopic consciousness" standing democratically in the intersections of race, class, gender, ethnicity, sexuality, religion, nationality, and culture. Insofar as moral problems are entanglements, then "zeal for a unitary view" oversimplifies moral life (LW 5, 288). Striving for systematic coherence can be a philosophic virtue, and abstracting some factor of moral action as central and uppermost has great instrumental value. But when we hypostatize it, then treat this factor as the self-sufficient starting point for moral inquiry and the bedrock for all moral justification, we perpetuate the same problems as when we indulge in the popular habit of singling out one trump value or concern among a wide range of relevant values.[10]

In summary, Dewey hypothesized that good, duty, and virtue are distinct moral categories that express different experiential origins, and none fully includes all that is morally relevant in the rest. Hence, moral life does not have a single central and basic source of justification. Instead of beginning moral reflection with a single abstracted factor, Dewey proposes that we should begin our reflective excursions with a practical predicament in lieu of a theoretical starting point (Pappas 2008, 2019). In this way, we discover that diverse factors are already in tension with each other. Our foremost practical need is for fine-tuned habits that enable us to comprehensively coordinate and integrate these tensions.

Theories and practices that open communication between conflicting factors can better inform our moral deliberations. Dewey consequently sought in his work in ethical theory from 1926 to 1932 to analyze the main categories through which ethical theories have concentrated attention on these factors, in order to put them in communication for the sake of more responsible choices.

Dewey doubtless hoped to inspire theoretical projects reconciling these diverse factors. Such projects could change the terms of debate within and across ethical traditions. Dewey approached historical ethical and sociopolitical theories as resources for social inquiry, not as finalities to be accepted *or* rejected wholesale (LW 7, 179; cf. Koch 2010). He thought that rejecting such zero-sum theorizing could open a door for research into classic moral philosophies as compensatory emphases, in dynamic tension with other selective emphases.[11] These monistic philosophies were forged in part as idealized tools to make sense of and navigate social situations. In "Three Independent Factors in Morals," Dewey reveals how their durable practical value can be liberated through philosophical research that at last gets over both the quest for, and the tone of, finality and instead rededicates itself to experimentally developing robust communicative projects with distinctive emphases, angles, and inferences.[12]

Notes

1 Originally published as "Trois facteurs indépendants en matière de morale," trans. Charles Cestre, in *Bulletin de la SFP* 30 (October-December 1930): 118–127.

2 This typescript was subsequently misplaced and retrieved in 2016 in a careful search by staff at Morris Library, Special Collections, Southern Illinois University at Carbondale.

3 In his theory of moral judgment and knowledge (LW 7, ch. 14), Dewey argued that the "comprehensive object" of moral choice is the option one foresees *ex ante* as most reliably expressing the situation's conflicting factors and recovering its dynamic equilibrium. In Dewey's experimental view we must act and also review *ex post.*

4 Dewey's typos silently corrected throughout.

5 Some commentators misrepresent Dewey's *mature* ethics as an ethics of self-realization. However, he argues in the 1932 *Ethics* in a Kantian vein that self-realization as an ideal may deaden people to the experiences of others so that we value them like pleasantries.

6 Along these lines, Edel (2001) argues that Dewey respects the independence of each factor while making the content of each "responsible to the idea of the good" (11).

7 Of course there are many hybrid ethical theories that defy tidy categorization. Rule utilitarianism, for example, operates in the main via compliance with universal rules, albeit rules theoretically justified on welfarist grounds: if you aspire to maximize the good, then conform to the rule.

8 In *The Theory of Moral Sentiments*, Smith (1790) followed Hume in tracing the source of morals to the principle of sympathy: "By the imagination we place ourselves in his situation" (I.I.2).

9 As deontologists rightly emphasize, one's own cravings may run counter to the "comprehensive object" of moral choice. Taking a cue from Hume and Smith, Dewey was skeptical of the Kantian contention that our moral mettle is truly revealed only when we are motivated to pursue the comprehensive object by the force of reason independent of desire (cf. Trianosky 1990).

10 For example, in environmental policymaking economic criteria are typically presumed to have supremacy over other key values (aesthetic, spiritual, recreational, ecological, etc.; see Norton 2005, 2015).

11 For example, with notable exceptions such as McKenna and Light's *Animal Pragmatism* (2004), McKenna (2018), and the work of Paul Thompson (e.g., 2010, 2015), scholars contributing a pragmatic pluralist perspective have taken a back seat to the zero-sum theorizing of many utilitarians and deontologists in responding to the far-reaching impact of human practices on other species and rising concern about animal use and treatment.

12 I am grateful to Oxford University Press for permission to draw, in revised form, from research that appeared in my article "Beyond Moral Fundamentalism: Dewey's Pragmatic Pluralism in Ethics and Politics" in *The Oxford Handbook of Dewey* (2019).

References

Citations of Dewey's correspondence are to *The Correspondence of John Dewey*, 1871–2007, published by the InteLex Corporation under the editorship of Larry Hickman. Citations give the date, reference number for the letter, and author followed by recipient. For example: 1973.02.13 (22053): Herbert W. Schneider to H. S. Thayer.

Alexander, Thomas. 2013. *The Human Eros*. New York: Fordham University Press.

Alfano, Mark. 2013. *Character as Moral Fiction*. New York: Cambridge University Press.

Anscombe, Gertrude Elizabeth Margaret. 1958. "Modern Moral Philosophy." *Philosophy* 33, no. 124 (January): 10.

Appiah, Kwame Anthony. 2008. *Experiments in Ethics*. Cambridge, MA: Harvard University Press.

Appiah, Kwame Anthony. 2017. *As If: Idealization and Ideals*. Cambridge, MA: Harvard University Press.

Aristotle. 1999. *Nicomachean Ethics*. Translated by Terence Irwin. Indianapolis, IN: Hackett.

Collins, Patricia Hill. 1998. "It's All in the Family: Intersections of Gender, Race, and Nation." *Hypatia* 13, no. 3: 62–82.

Darwall, Stephen L. 1983. *Impartial Reason*. Ithaca, NY: Cornell University Press.

Dewey, John. Undated manuscript (mss102_53_3). "Conflict and Independent Variables in Morals." Morris Library, Special Collections, Southern Illinois University at Carbondale.

Donagan, Alan. 1977. *The Theory of Morality*. Chicago, IL: University of Chicago Press.

Dworkin, Ronald. 2000. *Sovereign Virtue: The Theory and Practice of Equality*. Cambridge, MA: Harvard University Press.

Edel, Abraham. 2001. *Ethical Theory and Social Change: The Evolution of John Dewey's Ethics, 1908–1932*. Piscataway, NJ: Transaction Publishers.

Fesmire, Steven. 2003. *John Dewey and Moral Imagination: Pragmatism in Ethics*. Bloomington: Indiana University Press.

Fesmire, Steven. 2015. *Dewey*. London and New York: Routledge.

Freeman, Samuel. 2007. *Justice and the Social Contract: Essays in Rawlsian Political Philosophy*. Oxford: Oxford University Press.

Gewirth, Alan. 1978. *Reason and Morality*. Chicago, IL: University of Chicago Press.

Gill, Michael B. 2011. "Humean Moral Pluralism." *History of Philosophy Quarterly* 28, no. 1: 45–64.

Haidt, Jonathan. 2012. *The Righteous Mind: Why Good People Are Divided by Politics and Religion*. New York: Pantheon.

Heisenberg, Werner. 1958. *Physics and Philosophy: The Revolution in Modern Science*. New York: HarperCollins.

Hume, David. 1978. *A Treatise of Human Nature*. Edited by Lewis Amherst Selby-Bigge. Oxford: Clarendon Press.

Johnson, Mark. 2014. *Morality for Humans: Ethical Understanding from the Perspective of Cognitive Science*. Chicago, IL: University of Chicago Press.

Johnson, Mark. 2019. "Dewey's Radical Conception of Moral Cognition." In *The Oxford Handbook of Dewey*, edited by Steven Fesmire. Oxford and New York: Oxford University Press, 175–194.

Kant, Immanuel. 1993. *Grounding for the Metaphysics of Morals*. Translated by James W. Ellington. Indianapolis, IN: Hackett Publishing Company.

Kant, Immanuel. 2002. *Critique of Practical Reason*. Translated by Werner Pluhar. Indianapolis, IN: Hackett Publishing Company.

Kitcher, Philip. 2014. *The Ethical Project*. Cambridge, MA: Harvard University Press.

Koch, Donald, ed. 2010. *The Class Lectures of John Dewey*. Volume 2. Ethical Theory (1926) Class Lecture Notes by Sidney Hook. Charlottesville, VA: InteLex Corp, 2.2230–2.2284.

Korsgaard, Christine M. 1996. *The Sources of Normativity*. Cambridge: Cambridge University Press.

Latour, Bruno. 1993. *We Have Never Been Modern*. Translated by Catherine Porter. Cambridge, MA: Harvard University Press.

Lazari-Radek, Katarzyna de and Peter Singer. 2014. *The Point of View of the Universe: Sidgwick and Contemporary Ethics*. Oxford: Oxford University Press.

McKenna, Erin. 2018. *Livestock: Food, Fiber, and Friends*. Athens: University of Georgia Press.

McKenna, Erin and Andrew Light, eds. 2004. *Animal Pragmatism*. Bloomington: Indiana University Press.

Mill, John Stuart. 1986. *On Liberty*. Amherst, NY: Prometheus Books.

Norton, Bryan. 2005. *Sustainability: A Philosophy of Adaptive Ecosystem Management*. Chicago, IL: University of Chicago Press.

Norton, Bryan. 2015. *Sustainable Values, Sustainable Change: A Guide to Environmental Decision Making*. Chicago, IL: University of Chicago Press.

Pappas, Gregory. 2008. *John Dewey's Ethics: Democracy as Experience*. Bloomington: Indiana University Press.

Pappas, Gregory. 2019. "The Starting Point of Dewey's Ethics and Sociopolitical Philosophy." In *The Oxford Handbook of Dewey*, edited by Steven Fesmire. Oxford and New York: Oxford University Press, 235–253.

Parker, Mike. 2010. *Map Addict*. London: Collins.

Rawls, John. 1971. *A Theory of Justice*. Cambridge, MA: Harvard University Press.

Schaubroeck, Katrien. 2010. Interview with Christine Korsgaard. *The Leuven Philosophy Newsletter* 17: 51–56. www.people.fas.harvard.edu/~korsgaar/Schaubroeck.Korsgaard.pdf; accessed June 4, 2020.

Singer, Peter. 2015. *The Most Good You Can Do*. New Haven, CT: Yale University Press.

Thompson, Paul B. 2010. *The Agrarian Vision: Sustainability and Environmental Ethics*. Lexington: University Press of Kentucky.

Thompson, Paul B. 2015. *From Field to Fork: Food Ethics for Everyone*. Oxford: Oxford University Press.

Thompson, Paul B. 2016. "The Emergence of Food Ethics." *Food Ethics* 1: 61–74.

Trianosky, Gregory. 1990. "What is Virtue Ethics All About?" *American Philosophical Quarterly* 27, no. 4: 335–344.

Part II

Commentary on the Chapters of the 1932 *Ethics*

3 Moral Holism and the Pragmatist Character

Stéphane Madelrieux

Overview of Chapter 10

Chapter 10 can be read as a general introduction to "Theory of the Moral Life," the second part of the 1932 *Ethics*. It presents the general topics that concern the nature of moral theory, while the subsequent chapters examine and reconstruct Dewey's three key moral theories—the theories of the Good (Chapter 11), the Right (Chapter 12), and Virtue (Chapter 13). At first sight, this chapter seems to have a very linear, straightforward structure that reflects the function of an introduction. Indeed, its seven sections could be divided into three main parts. Part 1 corresponds to the first section on "Reflective Morality and Ethical Theory" (LW 7, 162–166), which gives an account of the *origin and function* of moral theory. Moral reflection stems from the perplexities and doubts that arise within our customary ways of acting and systematic moral theory is but an extension of such a common-sense reflection. The purpose of philosophizing about our customary ways of acting is not to substitute a rational system of rules for traditional moral codes, since such a rational catechism is the kind of extension that would tend to discourage reflection by giving ready-made answers to our perplexities. Instead, moral theory should provide us with some methodological principles that help common-sense reflection cope with moral perplexities. In short, moral theory should take the form of a methodology of moral judgment for testing and use in particular situations rather than take the form of another moral doctrine which should be learned and applied in any situation whatsoever.

Part 2 includes Section 2 on "The Nature of a Moral Act," Section 3 on "Conduct and Character," and Section 4 on "Motive and Consequences" (LW 7, 166–176). Its apparent purpose is to define the *object* of any moral theory. Dewey claims that only voluntary acts are subject to moral evaluation. However, he adds that acts are voluntary if they are the expression of a "formed and stable character" (LW 7, 167), so he assumes that ultimately character is the proper subject-matter of moral theory. This shift from the act to the character seems to correspond to the shift from customary to reflective morality. Social codes manifest themselves by saying "do this", but a more reflective morality, in keeping with the progress of individualism in modern times, seems to express itself in a more perfectionist form by saying "be this." This new focus could explain why the second part of the book culminates with a chapter on "The Moral Self" (Chapter 15).

Part 3 includes Section 5 on "The Present Need of Theory," Section 6 on "Sources of Moral Theory," and Section 7 on "Classification of Problems." It presents the starting point, the materials, and the instruments for guiding anybody willing to elaborate a systematic moral theory which corresponds to their times. Social, political, and scientific changes have brought new moral problems to the fore which neither old customs nor past moral theories can cope. Dewey believes, however, that we are not without resources in this situation. First, human sciences, including history, give us a considerable amount of *data* on human conduct from which moral theory can draw its material. Second, past moral philosophies give us several "working hypotheses" (LW 7, 178) that shed some light on the moral situation, even if these philosophies, by their plurality and antagonism, produce new perplexities, of a theoretical character this time, to be resolved. In other words, after the origin and function of moral theory and its subject matter, Dewey introduces the student to the kind of *resources* that should be used in any moral inquiry, both in terms of already accessible scientific facts and philosophical ideas.

From Moral Dualism to Moral Atomism

As straightforward as it may appear on the surface, Chapter 10 is disrupted by an imbalance operating in Part 2. The general discussion on the relation between act and character as appropriate subject-matter of any moral theory develops into a lengthy discussion on the relation between motive and consequences (Section 4). This seems to overly anticipate the discussion of specific moral theories that will only begin in Chapter 11. Indeed, the antagonism between Kantian philosophy and "the school of Bentham" (LW 7, 173) is explained at this point and even quickly resolved. This discussion is all the more strange as mention of the various types of moral theory will not be made until the end of Chapter 10, where the trichotomy between the Good, the Right, and the Virtue will be introduced (Section 7). Dewey himself acknowledges this abrupt leap forward in the first sentence of Section 4: "In reaching the conclusion that conduct and character are morally one and the same thing (…), we have virtually disposed of one outstanding point of controversy in moral theory" (LW 7, 173). After this initial tantalizing incursion into the discussion of particular moral theories, the return to the "present need of theory" in Section 5 seems indeed somewhat anticlimactic.

How can we explain this apparent breach in the linear construction of the chapter? One way would be to show how Dewey has condensed the substance of no fewer than four chapters from the first edition of *Ethics* (1908) into a single chapter. Chapter 10 in the 1908 edition is about "The Moral Situation," and points to the origin and function of moral reflection; Chapters 11 ("Problems of Moral Theory") and 12 ("Types of Moral Theories") identify the main problems of moral theory by referring to the dominant dualisms in moral philosophy. In these two chapters we already find a copious presentation on the opposition between "teleological" and "jural" theories (those that take right, duty, and law as the dominant factor). Then, and only then, does Chapter 13 disclose the relation between "Conduct and Character" in the form of an "independent analysis" of the moral situation (MW 5, 221). This is supposed to help us resolve the opposition between teleological and jural theories.

Ethics 1908	*Ethics 1932*
Chapter 10. The Moral Situation **Chapter 11. Problems of Moral Theory** **Chapter 12. Types of Moral Theories**	**Chapter 10. The Nature of Moral Theory**
§ 1 Typical Divisions of Theories (Teleological [Good]/Jural [Right]; Individual/Institutional; Empirical/ Intuitional) [A]	§ 1 Reflective Morality and Ethical Theory
§ 2 Division of Voluntary Activity into Inner and Outer (Separation into Attitude and Consequences) **[B]**	§ 2 The Nature of a Moral Act, § 3 Conduct and Character **[C]** § 4 Motive and Consequences **[B]** § 5 The Present Need of Theory § 6 Sources of Moral Theory § 7 Classification of Problems [A]
§ 3 General Interpretation of These Theories	1 Theories of Good 2 Theories of Right and Duty
Chapter 13 Conduct and Character [C]	3 Theories of Virtue

However, the difference that accounts for the breach of construction in the second edition is not only due to size—a whole chapter on "Character and Conduct" being reduced to a mere section—but to place and function. Along with the reduction there is also an inversion in the order of the topics in the 1932 edition, as indicated by the three markers [A], [B], and [C] in the comparative chart. In the first edition, the discussion on conduct and character takes place after the presentation of the different theories, while in the second edition it takes place before. This creates the imbalance we have noted. My hypothesis is that between the two editions, the emphasis in the meaning of the discussion has been shifted. In the first edition, it is quite clear that the discussion on character and conduct works as a *criticism of moral dualism*. This so-called moral dualism consists in dividing human action into two separate parts: the inner and the outer, motives and consequences, and character and overt conduct. Such a dualistic way of thinking is a presupposition shared by Kant's deontological theory and Bentham's teleological theory, each highlighting only one of the parts as being essential from a moral perspective. Dewey's main claim about this issue is that a better psychology of voluntary action could allow us to overcome the opposition between the two dominant theories by helping to reconstruct moral theory in a non-dualistic way.[1]

In the second edition, the criticism of the dualistic character of the dominant theories is still there, but the fact that the discussion on conduct and character now occurs before the presentation of these theories indicates that it has acquired a new function. This function is of course also present in the first edition, but less explicitly. In the central sections of the chapter, the criticism is not so much aimed at moral dualism than at what I would call "*moral atomism*." Moral atomism refers to the idea that we can judge the moral value of a given act by only considering this particular act, whether it be from the point of view of its particular motives or the point of view of its particular consequences, without placing it within the whole line of conduct and the agent's general ways of thinking and doing. Moral atomism thinks that "good" and "bad," "right" and "wrong," and "virtuous" and "vicious" are fixed, absolute terms that can be predicated with certitude to a single particular act. In contrast, Dewey holds that when applied to a particular act, these terms are only relative and probable, and serve as landmarks in the direction of the general tendencies of the agent's moral development. More precisely, "good" and "bad", "right" and "wrong", etc., should not be applied to particular acts taken independently of one another, but to the general tendencies and ways of acting. A particular act is good insofar as it displays a way of acting that is good "in the long run" (MW 14, 37), that is, in the formation of a better moral self. The second edition of *Ethics* specifically foregrounds what I would accordingly call a kind of *moral holism* in its discussion of character and conduct: the idea of conduct "expresses continuity of action" (LW 7, 168); a "continuity of sequence in which one act leads on to others and to a cumulative result" (LW 7, 169); a "chain" or "series" of acts, a "serial whole," and not "a mere succession of disconnected acts" (LW 7, 169); "a course of action," a "line of behavior" (LW 7, 171).[2]

The shift between the two editions helps us better distinguish between two kinds of criticism that could be made from a pragmatist standpoint toward traditional moral theories. On the one hand, the psychological examination of the relation between conduct and character provides the means to highlight the moral continuity between the inner motives and the outer consequences of a given particular act on the grounds that an act is not composed of the union of two separate parts, that is, a mental part and a physical part. This criticism is akin to the more general criticism of the mind-body dualism in Dewey's theories of experience and knowledge (subject/object, mind/world). The reason why moral philosophy is divided into opposing schools, such as Kantianism and utilitarianism, is that human action has first been divided into two irreconcilable parts: the inner and the outer, motives and consequences, and character and overt conduct. According to Dewey, each philosophical school concentrates on one part to the exclusion of the other as the true subject-matter of morality. Despite championing their chosen part and rejecting the other, both schools in fact agree on the dualistic way of thinking about these irreconcilable parts. A non-dualistic analysis of human action is thus the way to resolve philosophical antagonisms in favor of a theory that takes into account the whole of a moral act without artificially dissociating the inner and the outer. This hence explains Dewey's order of topics in his first edition: the presentation of the antagonisms between moral theories [A] is shown to be dependent on a psychological view that separates the inner motives and the outer consequences [B], and then is resolved by a proper non-dualistic conception based on the identification of character and conduct [C]. Moral holism, in this first sense, is opposed to moral dualism and denotes the method of judging the morality of an act by taking into account the whole of it, or rather, by considering it as an indivisible whole.

On the other hand, the same analysis of the relation between conduct and character examined from a temporal perspective rather than a synchronic perspective, which is based on the examination of a single act, leads to the idea of a continuity between *several particular acts*. When a particular act allows for the consequences of a previous act and prepares the motivation for some future act, the whole of these acts forms a series which exhibits a type of generality. This continuous series is a *conduct*, which means that it is not only an action or even a collection of disconnected acts. It displays a *character*, that is, a complex mix of active interests and permanent dispositions which makes the individual open to certain aims and indifferent to others. As such, a character is not reducible to a particular motive or even a disconnected collection of aims and intentions: it exhibits a type of generality observable in the continuity of enduring interests and dispositions. Character and conduct refer to general *ways* of thinking and acting. Now Dewey's focus is not only upon the inseparability of motives and overt action (in any single act), but on the inclusiveness of particular motives in a general character as well as the inclusiveness of particular overt acts in a general line of conduct. In this second sense, moral holism is opposed to moral atomism and denotes the method of judging the morality of an act, its motives and its consequences by placing them inside the whole of the agent's conduct and character, that is, the temporal whole of their moral development.

In the 1932 edition, this second point of view is even given as the reason for the first, which leads me to think that it is Dewey's definitive point of view. We see that Section 3 on "Conduct and Character" precedes Section 4 on "Motive and Consequences," while in the 1908 edition it is the reverse. The purpose of this inversion is to make clear that the motives and consequences of a particular act are inseparable *because* what really matters from a moral standpoint is not any particular motive or consequence, but rather, character and conduct considered as wholes. The unity of the inner and the outer, as claimed by Dewey, is indeed not the unity of every particular motive and every particular consequence because such a unity cannot be achieved for every particular act. In every particular act, some motives do not make us act and are thus disconnected from any practical consequences; conversely, some of the consequences that happen following a particular act are not intentional and may be due to external and contingent circumstances. Dewey acknowledges that for a given particular act, taken in isolation, there are some motives that are disconnected from the consequences and some consequences that are not internally connected with the motives. Nonetheless, the unity takes place and is constituted at the general level of the character and the conduct, each of which is considered as a serial whole. This is because there is no character without continuity across a series of particular overt *acts*, and no conduct without the continuity of *interests* and *dispositions* that constitutes the unity of somebody's character. We might accept a good person, that is, a person of good character, doing a bad thing in a particular situation from time to time: it happens to everybody, but we could not accept such a person *usually*, *regularly*, *generally* not doing the right thing. We would not call this person good in that case, as there is no such thing as a good character in the abstract (MW 5, 225).

We are now in a strong position to understand what Dewey means when he asserts that since "conduct and character are morally one and the same thing (…) we have virtually disposed of one outstanding point of controversy in moral theory" (LW 7, 173)—the controversy that opposes the theories of Kant and Bentham. According to Dewey, moral holism, as understood in the second sense, that is, a criticism of moral atomism, is also and by the same token a means to "dispose of" moral dualism. Moral dualism is based on a flawed dualistic psychology, but the continuity between our particular acts that constitutes a line of conduct and expresses a persistent character explains the *moral*—as distinguished from the *psychological*—continuity between particular motives and particular consequences within a single act. From a psychological point of view, inner motives are generally inseparable from outer results, whereas from a moral point of view, what matters are the motives and results that exhibit general tendencies in the ways an agent thinks and acts, because according to Dewey, only these should be the subject-matter of moral judgment.

A New Philosophy of Habit

As I have already mentioned, both kinds of holism are present in both editions of Dewey's *Ethics*, and the shift from one to the other is a question of degree and emphasis: the more Dewey focuses on the criticism of the dualism between motive and consequence, the more he emphasizes the generality of character and conduct as a way to unify the inner and the outer. How can we account for this progressive shift in Dewey's work?

The first reason is that Dewey embraces the idea of there being three kinds of moral theory rather than two. In the 1908 edition, the unity of character and conduct helps him resolve the opposition between the two dominant theories: the motives-theory, as in Kant's philosophy, and the consequences-theory, as in Bentham's philosophy, each selecting and abstracting one side of a whole act. In his 1930 address on "Trois facteurs indépendants en matière de morale" (cf. LW 5, 279–288), which would serve as a blueprint for the rewriting of the second part of the new edition of *Ethics*, Dewey adds a third theory to the two previous theories by acknowledging virtue and approbation as independent factors in each moral act. This new trichotomy does not sit neatly with the criticism of dualism and may have compelled Dewey to reorganize his general presentation.

The second reason is more positive and more important. Between 1908 and 1932 Dewey wrote *Human Nature and Conduct* (1922) in which the criticism of moral atomism comes to the fore in light of a new psychology and philosophy of habit. In the first part of the book, which deals with habit, one finds another chapter entitled "Character and Conduct" (Chapter 3), which may be considered as the missing link between the two editions of *Ethics*. The main difference that was introduced to the second edition on this topic is indeed the reference to habit as the best way to analyze the notion of conduct, the notion of character, and their unity. Dewey makes his point forcibly:

> if an act were connected with other acts merely in the way in which the flame of a match is connected with an explosion of gunpowder, there would be action, but not conduct. But our actions not only lead up to other actions which follow as their effects but they also leave an enduring impress on the one who performs them, strengthening and weakening permanent tendencies to act. This fact is familiar to us in the existence of *habit*.
>
> (LW 7, 170)

What Dewey implies is that "conduct" only refers to the fact of the continuity of action or the binding together of several acts so as to constitute a temporal whole; "habit," on the other hand, denotes the psychobiological factor *explaining* this continuity. Without habit, there would not be any conduct, but only a mere succession of acts exterior to one another, for example, in the case of "physical events" (LW 7, 170), like an explosion caused by a flame, which does not keep the memory of this explosion the next time it is in contact with gunpowder.

From a biopsychological standpoint, habit is the natural basis of moral conduct (even if habits are social in content and depend on cultural environments). Dewey acknowledges that as a characteristic of living organisms, any act brings about changes, not only to its environment but also to the organism that performs this act. Habit is the name for the cumulative result of acts on the agent themselves due to such an organic retention, so that future acts are determined not only by particular present stimuli occurring in the environment, but also by past and general dispositions and tendencies on the part of the agent. If a child does not merely react to the present sensorial excitement of a bright and dancing flame that they impulsively tend to grasp, but to the idea that if they were to grasp it, they would be burnt, then their act follows a general rule they believe to be true for every particular occasion, past, present, and future. They have become accustomed to react to the flame in this way rather than in any other way. As such, habits bring continuity to our acts by making any particular act the outcome of past acts and the preparation for future acts. If our acts did not leave a trace in our organic (nervous) substance, there would be no continuity between our past, our present, and our future. Moreover, there would be no possibility of moral education and moral progress.[3]

This biopsychological standpoint is the key to resolving the moral opposition between consequences and motives. Indeed, to judge the morality of a given act it is necessary, according to Dewey, to take into account not just one, but *two* sets of consequences. There are of course the "overt consequences" that are brought about by the act, in terms, for example, of pleasure and pain, as in orthodox utilitarianism. However, the consequences that are of greater importance from a moral perspective are those which affect the agent's character in terms of habits and permanent dispositions to act in certain general ways. To take an example from *Human Nature and Conduct,* the overt immediate consequences of an act of gambling may be "consumption of time, energy, disturbance of ordinary monetary considerations" (MW 14, 35), which are particular and momentary, but contrastingly, the most significant consequences are the setting up of permanent dispositions that will form or change the agent's character: "the enduring love of excitement", the "persistent temper of speculation," the "persistent disregard of sober, steady work" (*ibid*), etc. As these long-term consequences of a particular act are incorporated in the forms of permanent dispositions to act, they are not dissociated, but are at one with what constitutes the agent's character, which is the real motivational force behind the whole conduct.

Conversely, this character tends to make the agent "aware of and favorable to certain sorts of consequences, and ignorant and hostile to other consequences" (MW 5, 234), so that such complex mixes of interests and intentions cannot be dissociated from what constitutes their conduct. The long-term consequences are the condition for future motives, that is, future acts, while the habitual motivations are the condition for the interest in future consequences caused by future acts.

A third reason for this growing emphasis on generality should also be mentioned, namely, the re-reading of Peirce's work after his death. In his 1916 essay entitled "The Pragmatism of Peirce," Dewey stresses the difference between Peirce's pragmatism and James's more famous pragmatism by stating:

> Peirce puts more emphasis upon practice (or conduct) and less upon the particular; in fact, he transfers the emphasis to the general (...) pragmatism identifies meaning with formation of a habit, or way of acting having the greatest generality possible, or the widest range of application to particulars (...) he emphasizes much less the *particular* sensible consequence, and much more the habit, the generic attitude of response, set up in consequence of experience with things.
>
> (MW 10, 73, 76)

The first volume of the *Collected Papers of Charles Sanders Peirce* was released in 1931, and the following year Dewey published both his revised edition of *Ethics* and a review of Peirce's volume where he once again highlights Peirce's originality in his defense of the reality of "generals": "Peirce understands by the reality of a 'general' the reality of a way, habit, disposition, of behavior" (LW 6, 276). This is not to say that Dewey adopts Peirce's metaphysics, but that he agrees on the fact that, as a form of "general," a conduct is irreducible to any particular act and that the most important consequences from a moral, as well as from an epistemological point of view, are those that are good or bad in the long run after the idiosyncratic elements of the particular circumstances have been sifted.

Moral Holism as a Method for Making Our Acts Morally Clear

What are the material changes when one adopts such a holistic point of view in moral theory? According to Dewey, as moral theory is first and foremost the logic rather than the doctrine of moral deliberation, such distinctions and shifts of emphasis between action and conduct, motive and character, and particular and general consequences could be reinterpreted as entailing several methodological reorientations. These reorientations are part of a more complex and general picture in which moral holism within Dewey's whole philosophy agrees with his continuism, his pragmatism, his meliorism, his fallibilism, and his anti-exceptionalism. They could be expressed in terms of *rules* of moral inquiry, such as the following (without claiming exhaustiveness):

First Rule. From a practical point of view, keep track of your acts so that you can reconstitute the continuity of your conduct—as the "competent physician" holds the "complete clinical record" (MW 14, 35) of their patients to better diagnose their health over time. It is a diary of your moral life which allows you to know yourself and your character.

Second Rule. Take into account the immediate and overt consequences of any act, not for itself as if it were final and self-enclosed, but as part of the temporal development of your whole moral experience. In other words, place your acts in "a wider context of continuing consequences" (MW 14, 32)—which, from a methodological perspective, is what moral holism is all about. The point is not to deny the importance of the immediate and overt consequences or to neglect them, but to discriminate between those consequences which are only accidental through external circumstances and not connected with the agent's true motives and character, and those which can be said to be the expression of a past or future habit. Only the latter consequences, which are the indications of a general trend, have a true moral meaning and value, and therefore must be the object of moral judgment.

Third rule. Evaluate not only the consequences of an act in the present or the consequences of a one-off past act (like gambling), but evaluate past and present acts in light of the *future* acts and the *future* consequences they might engender for your moral life in the long run. This rule clearly connects moral holism with a pragmatist point of view on moral theory. The point is not only to determine what kind of practical difference such and such act has made or would make here and now, but to be able to predict the future course of the agent's moral experience in order to prevent it, encourage it, or change it:

> while the material of the judgment comes to us from the past, what really concerns us is what we shall do the next time; the function of reflection is prospective. We wish to decide whether to continue in the course of action entered upon or to shift to another.
>
> (LW 7, 172)

Moral holism (the general-consequences perspective) and moral pragmatism (the future-or-conditional-consequences perspective) should themselves be understood from the perspective of moral *meliorism* (the ascertainment of better consequences). The goal of moral reflection is not only to know whether we should do this or that, but to know whether we should do this or that in order to change or to persevere with our present dispositions and habits. The purpose of moral inquiry is thus practical as well as theoretical: it endeavors to evaluate both our action and our conduct, which means the kind of person, character, and moral self we are and are going to be—as our character is more or less the organic interaction of our habits:

> No individual or group will be judged by whether they come up to or fall short of some fixed result, but by the direction in which they are moving. The bad man is the man who no matter how good he *has* been is beginning to deteriorate, to grow less good. The good man is the man who no matter how morally unworthy he *has* been is moving to become better.
>
> (MW 12, 180–181)

In Chapter 15, Dewey claims accordingly that "the fact that each act tends to *form*, through habit, a self which will perform a certain kind of act, is the foundation, theoretically and practically, of responsibility. We cannot undo the past; we can affect the future" (LW 7, 304). It is useless to blame or praise someone for a course of action that cannot be changed, and Dewey denies that stones, plants, and "animals lower in the scale" (LW 7, 303) have any moral self as they will not change their behavior as a result of our approval or blame. Moral judgments of approbation and blame are thus prospective and not retrospective. They are what Dewey refers to elsewhere as "judgments of practice" (MW 8, 14–82, LW 12, 161–181), which endeavor to have an effect on the self and transform it by changing or comforting its general tendencies to act rather than by describing and classifying the particular act that has just been completed. Understanding moral judgments as being only the application of terms of value such as "good" and "bad" to a particular act abstracted from the temporal development of conduct is to reduce them to judgments of fact. Moral judgments are moral, not because they are judgments about some already given moral facts, but because they are normative judgments made to introduce a change in future facts or to produce better facts in the future, either by modifying bad tendencies or encouraging good tendencies.[4]

Fourth rule. Do not look for moral certainty by focusing on the moral value of one isolated act as if moral values were intrinsic proprieties attributed to this particular act, but content yourself with probabilities (MW 14, 37). Moral judgments are hence always judgments of tendencies and not of fixed realities. A genuinely modest theory

> will never assume that a moral judgment which reaches certainty is possible. We have just to do the best we can with habits, the forces most under our control; and we shall have our hands more than full in spelling out their general tendencies without attempting an exact judgment upon each deed.
>
> (MW 14, 36–37)

Probabilism is as important in the logic of moral inquiry as it is in the logic of scientific method. The surest way to block the path of moral progress is to imagine that we already know without any possible doubt what we should morally do in any given situation because "good" and "bad" would be absolute proprieties that could be predicated with certainty of any moral situation.

Fifth rule. Do not overlook the evaluation of ordinary acts that do not seem moral at first sight because you may on these occasions take a new disposition that will have consequences for your conduct in specifically moral situations. There is thus no sharp demarcation between moral situations and ordinary practical situations, such as eating and walking, which initially seems morally indifferent. The very idea of only locating morality in typical situations, such as tragic dilemmas, could be detrimental to the conduct of inquiry. As Dewey pleads in his philosophy of art against "the museum conception of art" (LW 10, 12), which places aesthetic experience in a separate realm of experience, we should be wary of all theories that focus exclusively on experiences so unique and exceptional that they tend to identify moral acts with heroic feats instead of analyzing them in terms of habitual tendencies. By stressing the continuity between practical and moral situations (as well as between natural and moral goods and values), moral holism can be seen as a criticism of the kind of *exceptionalism* exhibited by the heroic conception of morality that makes morality alien to our ordinary life.

Reflective Morality and the Pragmatist Character

While Dewey begins Chapter 10 by recalling the distinction between customary and reflective morality as the clue to "the nature of moral theory," there is a final issue to be raised concerning the implication of such a philosophy of habit on ethics. On the face of it, the distinction is based on the fact that customary morality provides a set of moral rules. An agent has to incorporate these rules into habitual ways of doing in order to be recognized as a moral agent by their community, while reflective morality begins when a stage of critical reflection on the rules is reached. For this reason, reflective morality does not seek to substitute other rules for those criticized, since any "attempt to set up" ready-made rules to be applied in any situation would "contradict the very nature of reflective morality" (LW 7, 166) by preventing personal reflection. Reflective morality, and more generally, moral theory, is moral in as much as it can help us break with old customs and habits without trying to replace them with new habits. This distinction between the two kinds of morality seems inconsistent with the role and importance of habit in its relations with character and conduct.

The solution to this apparent paradox lies in the distinction, made in *Human Nature and Conduct*, between two kinds of habit: "we are confronted with two kinds of habit, intelligent and routine" (MW 14, 51). Some habits are mechanized into routines, and some are flexible dispositions that have a reflective character. Thinking and intelligence are themselves only habits: habits of reflection, doubt, inquiry, and experiment. Reflective morality is thus opposed to customary morality, not that reflection is opposed to habits as such, but that one kind of habit is set against another. Embodied in habits (sufficiently flexible as to take into account the particularity of each situation), the rules of inquiry we listed above would provide us with the intelligence we would need to ascertain our problematic moral situations. There is even a sense that, insofar as habits are never purely individual, being formed "under conditions set by prior customs" (MW 14, 43), reflective morality could be another kind of customary morality in a society where habits of inquiry have become the ruling customs. This is why the moral growth of individuals cannot take place in a social vacuum and why Dewey relies on the reorganization of education to bring about "the production of good habits of thinking" (MW 9, 170), "effective ways of dealing with subject matter" (MW 9, 180), and "intellectual attitude[s]" (MW 9, 185) in children. Dewey's ultimate aim is to produce the kind of democratic society where the disposition to experimental reflection in matters of morals and values in general becomes institutionalized.

The notion of habit is central, not only to Dewey's conception of moral theory but also to his ideas about philosophy. Dewey does not see philosophy as a discipline or a body of truths. First and foremost he sees it as a "general attitude" (MW 9, 180) which he relates to the experimentalist type of thinking that developed along with the emergence of modern sciences and their new methods of inquiry. While the scientific revolution of the 16th and 17th centuries has deeply transformed our conception of nature and humanity, and has had a lasting impact on our technological progress, Dewey claims that the major practical outcome is a moral outcome. This has produced a revolution in our general ways of thinking, which has introduced a new type of character—the anti-dogmatic, experimentalist temper, and a new type of conduct—the logical conduct of inquiry. Before applying the logic of scientific inquiry to questions of value, Dewey seeks to ascertain the moral significance of scientific inquiry, because the dispositions that are learned and developed within the conduct of experimental inquiry—such as persistency of interest, honesty, willingness to give up past beliefs if proven inadequate and open-mindedness—are the true virtues. These dispositions are "second-order habits" (Pappas 2008, 189), indispensable for criticizing and reconstructing all our habitual/customary ways of believing and living. Extending the application of the logic of scientific method beyond the traditional subject-matter of natural sciences does not mean reducing morality to a kind of positivistic science or introducing the specific methods and procedures of natural sciences into moral reflection, but adopting the experimentalist type of mind and character to solve the problems of associated living.

Such a definition of philosophy explains why Dewey starts Chapter 10 of *Ethics* with the idea that the function of moral theory is not to elaborate a new kind of catechism, and that the aim of moral philosophy is not to develop a moral doctrine which would present a body of moral truths. The principles formulated by moral philosophy are not substantive rules of action, but methodological rules of inquiry into moral situations. The final aim of moral philosophy is thus to enable everybody to adopt a moral character, which is not defined in any substantive way, but only in terms of second-order habits and dispositions of reflection. From this point of view, incorporating the logic of moral deliberation into the various forms of permanent dispositions of thought would not guarantee the morality of future action, but it would at least be a minimal condition for moral growth not to be blocked. In as much as any doctrine that claims to have already reached moral certainty, and hence professes some definitive moral truths and principles, would be not only intellectually but morally wrong because it would instill bad habits of thinking in moral reflection—the sorts of habits that may be said to define the dogmatic character as opposed to the pragmatist attitude.

A Theory of Being Moral

This dispositionalist account of morality constitutes a common thread throughout the second part of the book. We may divide the latter into two sets of chapters. The first set, consisting of Chapter 10 on moral theory, Chapter 14 on moral knowledge and Chapter 15 on the moral self, gives a general account of Dewey's own outlook on ethics. In Chapter 14, the change from customary to reflective morality, construed in terms of the difference between a direct and spontaneous kind of *valuation* and a deliberate kind of estimation or *evaluation*, leads to the conclusion that "all growth in maturity is attended with this change from a spontaneous to a reflective and critical *attitude*" [italics mine] (LW 7, 265). There is no special, ready-made moral knowledge inherent to the various forms of principles or theories that should be acquired once and for all, but only a "*will* to know" that should be maintained: "the active desire to examine conduct in its bearing upon the general good" (LW 7, 281).[5]

Accordingly, in Chapter 15, where the "circular arrangement" and "essential unity" (LW 7, 287, 288) between conduct and character, and the acts and the self, are overtaken, the moral self is presented in terms of its capacity to change its habitual tendencies and modes of conduct. However, to be able to change our past habits and "being interested (...) in acquiring new attitudes and dispositions" (LW 7, 305), we first have to acquire the will to learn and to incorporate the second-order attitudes and dispositions that make us open to the perpetual reconstruction of ourselves instead of being satisfied with the way we customarily behave.

The second set of chapters deals with specific moral theories—Chapter 11 on the Good, Chapter 12 on the Right, and Chapter 13 on Virtues—and Dewey engages in conversation with specific moral philosophers and schools of philosophy. We would expect these theories to be less personal and more constrained due to the necessity of writing a handbook on ethics for students, but Dewey actually presents them in a way that would seem to support his own outlook. With reference to the good, the change from customary to reflective morality corresponds to the "development of inclusive and enduring aims" (LW 7, 11)—they are goods in the long run—rather than the satisfaction of immediate desires, so that the very "cultivation of interests" (LW 7, 208), that is, the holistic attachment to ever more inclusive ends, is in itself the end to be sought and the good to be attained. The examination of the ideas of Right and Law leads to an apology for toleration as "not just an attitude of good-humored indifference," but as a "positive willingness to permit reflection and inquiry to go on in the faith that the truly right will be rendered more secure through questioning and discussion" (LW 7, 231). The chapter on virtue finishes with a complex mix of virtues (whole-heartedness, persistency, impartiality), which represents the moral character and overlaps with the list of "attitudes," "personal qualities, traits of characters," and "habits" that "are favorable to the use of the best methods of inquiry and testing" (LW 8, 136, 139). This would be included a year later in the second edition of *How We Think*.

The building of such a moral character is not an end in itself, even if Dewey finishes the second part of the book with a chapter on the moral self. Abstracting the moral self from the situation we are experiencing would be a case of moral dualism. The purpose of moral reflection is to solve specific moral problems and not only to perfect ourselves—in as much as the acquisition of the scientific attitude is only a means to solve scientific problems. The focus on the personal side of moral life in this part is in accordance with the distinction, which is not a division, between the psychological and the social aspects of conduct—the attitude and the content, the *how* and the *what*, the means and the ends. Such a distinction appears in the introduction of the book: "Part II will analyze conduct or the moral life on its inner, personal side (...) Part III will study conduct as action in society" (LW 7, 15). However, as the beginning of Part III reminds us: even if in Part II, "the emphasis fell upon the attitudes and responses of individual persons,"

> we repeatedly noted, however, that the social environment has great influence in calling out and repressing the thought of individuals, and in sharpening or dulling their moral sensitiveness. From the social human environments proceed ultimately the problems which reflection has to deal with.
>
> (LW 7, 314)

Habit and the psychology of action refer to ways of acting, and from this first point of view, the discussion on the nature of moral theory leads to the experimental attitude of inquiry as *the* moral disposition. Nevertheless, the ends for conduct are given by the societies we live in and we should not abstract the question of the moral growth of the self from the question of the kind of society where our conduct will take place. Although the question of the unity of conduct and character will thus have to be reconsidered from this second social point of view, there is no implication that the first point of view will be overlooked. The problem of social growth will be related to the way our social environment simultaneously tolerates and encourages reflective morality. The notion of character will hence be preserved in this new interrogation and will even provide us with the criteria for evaluating social environments and political institutions. The value of social environments and political institutions will indeed be judged according to the kind of character and self they tend to produce—reflective and growing selves or routine-driven and closed selves (cf. MW 12, 186). Consequently, the internal relation between the personal and social points of view in ethics is another way to state Dewey's major thesis about the identity between science as an attitude and democracy as a way of associated living.

Notes

1 Such a take on ethics is still very apparent in the final chapter of *Democracy and Education* (1916), which is devoted to "Theories of Morals," and where Dewey claims:

> The first obstruction which meets us is the currency of moral ideas which split the course of activity into two opposed factors, often named respectively the inner and the outer, or the spiritual and the physical. This division is a culmination of the dualism of mind and the world, soul and body, end and means, which we have so frequently noted. In morals it takes the form of a sharp demarcation of the motive of action from its consequences, and of character from conduct (...) Different schools identify morality with either the inner state of mind or the outer act and results, each in separation from the other.
>
> (MW 9, 356)

2 The difference on this issue between the two editions is only a matter of degree and emphasis, cf. "the appropriate subject matter of moral judgment is the *disposition* of the person as manifested in the *tendencies* which cause certain consequences, rather than others, to be considered and esteemed – foreseen and desired *[italics mine]*" (LW 3, 241).

3 There is no way to minimize Dewey's biological naturalism on this point, as can be seen in his essay "The Need for a Recovery of Philosophy" (1917): "Organic instincts and organic retention, or habit-forming, are undeniable factors in actual experience. They are factors which effect organization and secure continuity" (MW 10, 14). Instincts account for the continuity between a perceptual stimulation S and a motor reaction R in a reflex action which is "native, unlearned, original" due to the "established connections of neurons" (MW 10, 14). The continuity mentioned here is the S-R continuity grounded on the pre-established neural paths between the sensory and the motor apparatus. Habits, on the other hand, account for the continuity between several acquired actions in similar circumstances: continuity in the S-S'-S" series and in the R-R'-R" series. On this biological naturalism that Dewey inherits from James's scientific psychology (cf. Madelrieux 2016, 57–75).

4 In a way, Dewey is Aristotelian insofar as he bases moral life on habitual dispositions. However, he completely reverses the relation between the permanence of habit and the value of change, as good habits are flexible and they do not block the possibility of continuous moral growth. It is interesting to note what Dewey writes about Peirce's own conception of habit: "he dwells upon the fact that the habits of things are acquired and modifiable. Indeed, he virtually reverses Aristotle's thinking in holding that the universal always has an admixture of potentiality in it" (LW 6, 276). This shift from eternity to the future is a hallmark of pragmatism.

5 Peirce talks about the first rule of logic and science as only being "the will to learn" (Peirce 1998, 47).

References

Madelrieux, Stéphane. 2016. *La philosophie de John Dewey*. Paris: Vrin.

Pappas, Gregory Fernando. 2008. *John Dewey's Ethics: Democracy as Experience*. Bloomington: Indiana University Press.

Peirce, Charles Sanders. 1998. *The Essential Peirce, Volume 2*, The Peirce Edition Project. Bloomington: Indiana University Press.

4 Forming New Ends Creatively

Federico Lijoi

Overview of Chapter 11

Chapter 11 of Dewey's *Ethics* is dedicated to the analysis of "Ends, the Good and Wisdom." The chapter is divided into seven sections. In the first section, entitled "Reflection and Ends," Dewey's intention is to demonstrate how customary morality does not allow us to tackle those moments when customs, or habits provided by elders and old institutions, fail to give the necessary guidance. Therefore, when old institutions break down and when habit fails, "the sole alternative to caprice and random action is reflection" (LW 7, 185). Nevertheless, according to Dewey, reflection alone is not sufficient to ensure morally good conduct, because without the propulsive force provided by habit, the continuity of conduct would be absent.

In the second section, entitled "Ends and the Good: The Union of Desire and Thought," Dewey's critique of the traditional dualism between custom and reflection leads to the idea that desire should not be simply contained or repressed by thought because it is intrinsically bad, but should instead be *transformed* by means of thinking, in order to obtain a thoughtful—more inclusive and enduring—desire.

Following the distinction between inhibition and transformation of desire, Dewey, in the third section, entitled "Pleasure as the Good and the End" discusses Mill's utilitarian theory, focusing on the difference between the enduring satisfaction of the *whole self* and the transient satisfaction of some isolated element within the self. The pleasures that satisfy the whole self are more lasting and therefore less incidental than those that satisfy isolated desires: the "happiness" caused by the former, unlike the "pleasantness" produced by the latter, "is a stable condition, because it is dependent not upon what transiently happens to us but upon the standing disposition of the self" (LW 7, 198).

In Sections 4–6, entitled, respectively, "The Epicurean Theory of Good and Wisdom," "Success as the End," and "Asceticism as the End," Dewey continues to examine the distinction between the harmonious expansion produced by transformed desires and the disruptive disaggregation brought about by isolated desires. He reaches the conclusion that, by separating moral goodness from interest in all those objects which make life fuller, and by confining it to a narrow set of aims, these doctrines state "the negative for the sake of the negative," thereby creating an obsession with guilt and its avoidance, and fostering "a sour and morose disposition" (LW 7, 207).

In the last section, Dewey sums up his most fundamental insight, i.e., the connection between reflection and ends. This operates in two different ways: on the one hand, the role played by reflection as a factor that operates creatively to form new ends, and on the other hand,

> the need to remake social conditions so that they will almost automatically support fuller and more enduring values and will reduce those social habits which favor the free play of impulse unordered by thought, or which make men satisfied to fall into mere routine and convention.
>
> (LW 7, 211)

The Original Plasticity of Moral Life

The distinction between customary morality and reflective morality, with which Dewey opens Chapter 10 of the 1932 edition of *Ethics* and which he discusses in Chapter 11, can be considered as belonging to the same conceptual framework expounded in *Human Nature and Conduct*:[1]

> The intellectual distinction between customary and reflective morality is clearly marked. The former places the standard and rules of conduct in ancestral habit; the latter appeals to conscience, reason, or to some principle which includes thought.
>
> (LW 7, 162)

The attention that Dewey dedicates, in Chapter 11 of *Ethics*, to Greek philosophy and its various different currents (Hedonism, Epicureanism, Cynicism, and Asceticism) is very significant in this context, due to the fact that:

> [o]ne great source of the abiding interest which Greek thought has for the western world is that it records so clearly the struggle to make the transition from customary to reflective conduct.
>
> (LW 7, 162–163)

According to Dewey, this "transition" represents a genuine "revolution," not only because "it displaced custom from the supreme position, but even more because it entailed the necessity of criticizing existing customs and institutions from a new point of view" (LW 7, 162). The figure of

Socrates played a decisive role, for by posing the question whether virtue was teachable, thereby addressing the crucial problem of the education of the young,[2] he inaugurated a reflective conception of morality:

> the essence of morals, it is implied, is to know the reason for these customary instructions; to ascertain the criterion which insures their being just.
>
> (LW 7, 163)

In Chapter 4 of *Human Nature and Conduct*, Dewey observes that the same "plasticity" that allows adults to impose the barriers of custom upon young people "also means power to change prevailing custom" (MW 14, 47). For him "plasticity of impulse" (MW 14, 69) therefore means at one and the same time reception *and* activity, habit *and* reflection. This is a fundamental point for Dewey, because it underlies his critique of a radically fallacious dualism, that which opposes "body and mind, practice and theory, actualities and ideals," and which here is expressed by the "separation of habit and thought" (MW 14, 49). After all, although "all habit involves mechanization," Dewey points out that "mechanization is not of necessity *all* there is to habit" (MW 14, 50). It is therefore not possible to set up an opposition between "life and mechanism" (MW 14, 51). Rather than a "leap" from habit to reflection, from automatism to intelligence, we are, according to Dewey "confronted with two kinds of habit, intelligent and routine."[3]

Dewey therefore sees moral life as a dynamic and dialectical balance between the tendency of custom toward *inertia* and the explosive potential of the impulse. It is important to note that a few years earlier, in *The Quest for Certainty* (1929), Dewey had shrewdly understood that the opposite extremes of habit and spontaneity, considered separately, offered the same answer, albeit with opposite polarities, to the difficulty of accepting the fact that reality is not "something fixed and therefore capable of literally exact mathematical description and prediction" (LW 4, 163). Dewey thought that the emergence of a separation between theory and practice as a "compensatory perversion" (LW 4, 182) was due to the fact that the human being "lives in a world of hazards" and is therefore "compelled to seek for security" (LW 4, 3). This is the case when the ideal world, devised by theory to escape from the problematic contingency of the real, reveals the secret ambition of human beings to attain a mechanized world, in which the illusion of freedom without friction ends up coinciding with the desire for a necessity that is free of risks.[4]

In his text of 1929, moreover, Dewey's task was not only to stigmatize the perverse and compensatory character of dualism, but to show that it is the experimental method that puts an end to the deleterious isolation of knowledge from action. According to Dewey, in the experimental method—the premise of which is precisely the abolition of tendencies directed toward ultimate and fixed ends[5]—resides the capacity of humans to make both the natural and the social environment "a plastic material of human desires and purposes" (LW 4, 82). In short, it consists in a creative application of *reflection* to reality: "Intelligence in operation, another name for method, becomes the thing most worth winning" (LW 4, 163).

Dewey therefore replaces the unpredictable and contingent course of events, underlying the "perverse" dualism between theory and practice, with the concept of the *problematic situation*. To this he attributes, in a controversial opposition to the foundational proposal that modernity has devised in order to repair the crisis of the cosmic order established by the classical world, the positive role of *experiment* for the creation of new ends. For Dewey the *problematic situation* represents the *doubt* which the scientific attitude "is capable of enjoying," and which urges it to revise its own premises and to propose new ones: "quest for certainty, that is universal, applying to everything, is a compensatory perversion. One question is disposed of; another offers itself and thought is kept alive" (LW 4, 182).

The programmatic observations in Section 1 of Chapter 11 of *Ethics* belong to this conceptual framework: the crisis of custom and habit must not trigger a "defense reaction" (MW 14, 91), but must give rise to a *reflective* relationship with the new situation. In the following passage, Dewey clearly describes this connection between crisis and reflection:

> This intellectual search for ends is bound to arise when customs fail to give required guidance. *And this failure happens when old institutions break down*; when invasions from without and inventions and innovations from within radically alter the course of life. *If habit fails*, the sole alternative to caprice and random action is reflection. *And reflection upon what one shall do is identical with formation of ends*. Moreover, when social change is great, and a great variety of conflicting aims are suggested, reflection cannot be limited to the selection of one end out of a number which are suggested by conditions. *Thinking has to operate creatively to form new ends.*
>
> (LW 7, 185, my italics)

I believe that three fundamental ideas derive from this significant passage:

1 Reflective activity in the moral sphere has an experimental character, in the sense that, as is the case for scientific investigation, it is stimulated by a problematic situation to form new ends: "There can be no such thing as reflective morality where there is not solicitude for the ends to which action is directed" (LW 7, 185).

2 Reflective activity, as a formation of ends, in itself has no end, since fixed purposes do not exist and "the acceptance of fixed ends in themselves is an aspect of man's devotion to an ideal of certainty" (MW 14, 162): [...] "Ends are, in fact, literally endless, forever coming into existence as new activities occasion new consequences. 'Endless end' is a way of saying that there are no ends – that is no fixed self-enclosed finalities" (MW 14, 159).
3 Reflection is the way in which the crisis, i.e., the problematic *clash* between expectations and contingency which characterizes human experience, is converted from a threat to an opportunity. Reflective activity not only has the function of re-adapting the individual to a "radically altered" (LW 7, 307) course of life, but it effects a creative transformation of reality in order to give us a richer experience of it.[6]

A History of Conflict: On Thought and Desire

After the first section of Chapter 11 of *Ethics*, Dewey undertakes a philosophical analysis of the way in which moral theory elaborates the relationship between ends and moral good. He constantly refers to the following idea as a contrast to the theories that he is going to analyze: "*The development of inclusive and enduring aims is the necessary condition of the application of reflection in conduct*; *indeed they are two names for the same fact*" (LW 7, 185). We must keep in mind that any philosophical analysis concerning Dewey's moral theories constitutes a development of moral reflexivity. In this sense, theory can never rise above reflection, so as to perform an abstract regulatory function from outside.[7]

The point that Dewey puts at the center of his moral theory is the combination of thought and desire: by putting an end to the activity of desiring, thought makes the human being "aware of *what* he wants." In this case "awareness" means both the anticipation of the result and the prediction of the consequences, which entails the deliberate and intentional adoption of a certain behavior, as well as the drive provided by some urgent need: "A purpose or aim represents a craving, an urge, translated into the idea of an object, as blind hunger is transformed into a purpose through the thought of a food which is wanted" (LW 7, 186).

The end-in-view,[8] the object that the action proposes as its aim, is that which provides unity and continuity to conduct, by making sure that individuals are "intelligently interested in their behaviour and [...] not governed by chance and the pressure of the passing moment" (LW 7, 185). The end provided by reflection is thus neither the mere anticipation or prediction of a result, as otherwise the movement procured by the impulse would be lacking, nor the propulsive force of mere appetite, as in this case the intellectual factor that "gives meaning and direction to the urge" (LW 7, 186) would be absent.

According to Dewey, the challenge is to establish a connection between these two aspects, since the impulse requires immediate action, without any calculation of the consequences of the action, while intellectual deliberation entails the deferral of the action demanded by the impulse: "Craving does not look beyond the moment, but it is of the very nature of thought to look toward a remote end" (LW 7, 186).

How is one to deal with this dilemma? Dewey's main move consists in simply reformulating it. While it is true that "there is a conflict brought about within the self" (LW 7, 187), the idea that this conflict takes place between desire and reason instead proves to be completely false. With an argument that recalls the Freudian idea that "the substitution of the reality principle for the pleasure principle implies no deposing of the pleasure principle, but only a safeguarding of it" (Freud 1911, 223), Dewey asserts that the conflict is between "a desire which wants a near-by object and a desire which wants an object which is seen by thought to occur in consequence of an intervening series of conditions, or in the 'long run'" (LW 7, 187). In this way, the traditional opposition between reason and desire is refuted in its two main aspects: on the one hand, the idea that reason *can* do without desire, because it is capable of autonomously showing us the true and good ends, and on the other, the idea that reason *must* do without desire, because desire is intrinsically bad and offers us only "deceptive goods." In the first case Dewey declares that "no idea or object could operate as an end and become a purpose unless it were connected with some need; otherwise it would be a mere idea without any moving and impelling power" (LW 7, 187); while in the second case he states that "there is nothing intrinsically bad about raw impulse and desire."[9]

The solution, according to Dewey, is not a Manichaean view of the relationship between reason and desire—which corresponds, as mentioned above, to the "compensatory perversion" of an ideal world "without friction"—but a view in which they intermix.[10] For Dewey it is the type of reflection, that is the type of relationship existing between reason and desire, which marks the difference, not the presence or absence of reason: "it is a conflict between two objects presented in thought, one corresponding to a want or appetite just as it presents itself in isolation, the other corresponding to the want thought of in relation to other wants" (LW 7, 187).

It cannot, however, be denied that Dewey assigns a greater moral value to the case in which "this original impulse is transformed into a different desire because of objects which thought holds up to view" (LW 7, 187). He feels that it is the inclusiveness and durability of the consequences, or the ends, that constitute a properly reflexive form of conduct, in which the *Bestimmungsgrund* (to use Kant's words) of moral action lies in the *transformative task* that reason exercises on desire: "what is morally dangerous in the desire as it first shows itself is its tendency to confine attention to its own immediate object and to shut out the thought of a larger whole of conduct" (LW 7, 188). The "inhibitory" action of reason does not therefore have the aspect of a repression or a suffocation of desire, but consists in "transforming a desire into a form which is more intelligent because more cognizant of relations and bearings." Desire is therefore not bad in itself, but only *becomes* so comparatively, that is to say when it is placed "in contrast with another desire whose object includes more inclusive and more enduring consequences" (LW 7, 187).

The idea clearly emerges that reflection, or that which Dewey, using an equivocal expression, halfway between quantity and quality, defines as its "normal function,"[11] constitutes the antidote to the "tendency" of desire toward immediacy. In the passage I cite below, he clearly explains how a moral choice is a preference for the desire of an object that reflection, after making a comparison with other objects, has shown to be more lasting and inclusive. Dewey claims that the only alternative to the removal of desire and to the unreflective inclination toward immediate desire lies within this connection between reason and desire ("thoughtful desire"):

> Reflection has its normal function in placing the objects of desire in a perspective of relative values, so that when we give up one good we do it because we see another which is of greater worth and which evokes a more inclusive and a more enduring desire.
>
> (LW 7, 189–190)

Strength of character or "strength of will" is thus nothing but the fruitful cooperation (or, as Dewey calls it, the "abiding identification") of thought and desire (the above-mentioned thoughtful desire), in which desire provides the impulse while thought "supplies consecutiveness, patience, and persistence, leading to a unified course of conduct" (LW 7, 190). It is no coincidence that Dewey once again underlines how "strength of will" does not coincide with obstinacy or with some kind of repetition compulsion, regardless of the change in the circumstances of the moral action, but with the ability, essentially provided by thought, to be "observant of changes of conditions and [...] flexible in making new adjustments" (LW 7, 190).

"Hedonism Revisited" Reconsidered: Dewey on John Stuart Mill

Sections 3–6 of Chapter 11 of *Ethics* are devoted to a critical examination of different theories of the moral good. Up to this point Dewey has elaborated the criterion for distinguishing the true good from the apparent good. The true moral good (the Good) as an *end* of conduct is, as we have seen, that which satisfies desire and, at the same time, also requires of the agent "rational insight" or "moral *wisdom*." Moral theory therefore has the task of permitting the "discovery of ends which will meet the demands of impartial and far-sighted thought as well as satisfy the urgencies of desire" (LW 7, 191).

Starting from this constructive assumption, Dewey critically examines the moral theories that have unilaterally conceived of the good as capable of satisfying only desire, without also providing the "conditions which alone would enable the end to afford intelligent direction to conduct" (LW 7, 191). This is the case for hedonism.

Hedonists, as is well known, are "those who hold that pleasure is the good" (MW 3, 46). Indeed, it seems self-evident that "what makes any object of desire and attainment good is the pleasure which it gives to the one who has the experience" (LW 7, 191). In the third section, Dewey's controversial goal is John Stuart Mill's ambiguous identification of enjoy*ed* with enjoy*able*. In the fourth chapter of *Utiliarianism* (1861) we read that "the sole proof it is possible to produce that anything is desirable is that people do actually desire it" (Mill 2003, 210).[12] This apparently simple point is in fact rather subtle.

Mill's intention was to establish experience, rather than an abstract construction (for example, that of rational finalism), as a criterion for identifying what is to be desired.[13] From the fact that human beings desire a certain thing it is possible to prove that it is also desirable. In the second chapter of *Utilitarianism* Mill writes, "Of two pleasures, if there be one to which all or almost all who have experience of both give a decided preference, irrespective of any feeling of moral obligation to prefer it, that is the more desirable pleasure" (Mill 2003, 187). What therefore seems to Dewey to be a naturalistic fallacy or a confusion between the desired and the desirable, for Mill is intended to challenge the *Trennung* between *Sein* and *Sollen*.[14]

It is important to understand that Dewey's critique does not simply reveal a logical fallacy, but that it radically replaces a philosophical assumption: not everything that is desired is in fact desirable, since "experience shows that about everything has been desired by some one at some time" (LW 7, 192). There is therefore no relationship of *conversio simplex* between the desired and the desirable, as it is not possible to determine "what *should* be desired [...] until a critical examination of the *reasonableness* of things desired has taken place" (LW 7, 192).

In this distinction that Dewey makes between the desired and the desirable the concept of pleasure plays a fundamental role. While it is true that the experience of pleasure that can be obtained from a certain object means that it is desired, it cannot however be asserted that all that is pleasant is also desirable, or that it *must* be desired. This means that pleasure cannot be considered as a criterion of moral goodness, since it is possible that something desirable, and therefore morally good, does not have pleasure as its end. In other words, it is not desired *because* it is pleasant. This obviously does not exclude the existence of a connection between good and pleasure, but it certainly denies the idea that pleasure constitutes the *Bestimmungsgrund* of the good, or the goal of conduct: "But the statement that all good has enjoyment as an ingredient is not equivalent to the statement that all pleasure is a good"(LW 7, 195).[15]

The passage that follows clearly demonstrates that for Dewey the problematic point is to be found precisely in the connection between desirability and pleasure, and therefore in the distinction between *Good* and *pleasure*: "Our first criticism is devoted to showing that if pleasure is taken as the end, no such cool and far-seeing judgment of consequences as the theory calls for is possible; in other words, it defeats itself" (LW 7, 192–193).

The *reasonableness* that critical analysis seeks, in order to identify—"in the eye of impartial thought" (LW 7, 192)—what is morally good, therefore consists in the critical distance from a mere desire for pleasure. If it is true that desire is moved by pleasure, it is equally evident, Dewey argues, that "pleasures are so externally and accidentally connected with the performance of a deed, that attempt to foresee them is probably the stupidest course which could be taken in order to secure guidance for action" (LW 7, 193). If instead they were not connected with actions in an extrinsic way, they would be nothing but pleonastic complements of one's character, or the indication of a mere congeniality with one's own dispositions. But if this were true, wouldn't the bad actions of an evil person, simply because they are congenial and they therefore bring pleasure to he who performs them, paradoxically be a moral good or a legitimate end?

What then is the criterion that allows us to distinguish good from evil, and a good action from a bad action? As we know, according to Dewey only reflection is capable of *transforming* the urgency that the pleasure of an isolated and immediate object imposes on desire into the calmness of a moral choice that understands the object of desire in the entirety of its present and future consequences and relationships with other desires:

> The important truth conveyed by the relation which exists between enjoyment and good is that we should integrate the office of the judge – of reflection – into the formation of our very desires and thus learn to take pleasure in the ends which reflection approves.
>
> (LW 7, 196)

In the conclusion of the section, it is no coincidence that Dewey returns to Mill, recalling the distinction between quality and quantity in which Mill's revision of Bentham's hedonism consists.[16] Dewey observes that for Mill pleasures are not "alike," differing only in intensity and duration, as most hedonists had claimed, but that they are different due to their "intrinsic quality," since some of them "bear reflecting upon," while others do not. This is a distinction that takes up the ancient argument that human faculties are higher than those of the animals, which consist only of appetites. Herein lies the difference between happiness and fulfillment. The individual who does not lift himself to the use of his higher faculties will find it easier to fulfill his desires: those who are "poorly equipped with capacities for enjoyment," the British philosopher writes, "are more likely to satisfy them fully" (Mill 2003, 245). Instead, the more highly gifted human being will always remain unsatisfied, since the happiness to which he aspires will always be imperfect and never fully attainable. Nevertheless, according to Mill, the imperfect happiness of Socrates constitutes a good with a much greater value than that which satisfies a pig. For this reason, "it is better to be a human being dissatisfied than a pig satisfied; better to be Socrates dissatisfied than a fool satisfied."

But why should we prefer the unhappiness of Socrates to the satisfaction of the pig or of the fool? Mill's thesis, which Dewey considers to be "not wholly clear" and which he then revises, is that "if the fool or the pig is of a different opinion, it is because he only knows his own side of the question." If the fool, in short, *knew* the pleasure of Socrates, however unsatisfied and imperfect, he would prefer it to his own. And the following objection, promptly pointed out by Mill, does not apply: "many who are capable of the higher pleasures, occasionally, under the influence of temptation, postpone them to the lower." Indeed, as Mill asserts, "this is quite compatible with a full appreciation of the intrinsic superiority of the higher (pleasures)." It is only through weakness of character, or through indolence of the will, that gifted human beings "make their election for the nearer good, though they *know* it to be the less valuable" (Mill 2003, 245, my italics).

The problem for Dewey is, however, right here. If the value of a good, and therefore the superiority of the relative pleasure, is determined by the "knowledge" that certain goods are "intrinsically superior," there is a risk that Mill's qualitative hedonism might lead to a theory of fixed ends, which experience would have the redundant task of simply "discovering." In short, the finalism that Mill had pushed out of the door through the identification of enjoy*ed* and enjoy*able* would come back in through the window.[17]

Instead, the only way to make Mill's theory "acceptable" is to specify that "*understanding*" is a "part of the meaning of knowing" (LW 7, 197).[18] By doing so, Dewey emphasizes the difference between "isolation" and "integration"[19] as the foundation of the distinction between "pleasure" and "happiness":[20] a certain object, for example a painting or a book, can be described as *pleasurable* only in relation to a certain *isolated* desire, that is to say, only because they are "congenial to the existing state of a person whatever that may be" (LW 7, 197). In this case, the greater or lesser degree of "pleasant*ness*" of something is established solely on the basis of the greater or lesser intensity of the desire that it occasionally satisfies: "there is something accidental in the merely agreeable and gratifying. They *happen* to us" (LW 7, 198). On the other hand, the *qualitative* distinction between two pleasures, in the way that Dewey revises Mill's hedonism, is a question that concerns neither the intrinsic superiority of one faculty over the other (for example, the pleasures of the intellect over those of the body) nor the pleasure derived from the satisfaction of an isolated and accidental desire.

Dewey reconsiders Mill's distinction between quality and quantity (and also the distinction, closely connected to it, between active pleasures and passive pleasures), connecting it to the distinction between pleasures that satisfy isolated desires and pleasures that satisfy the whole self: the latter are necessarily more lasting and are therefore less accidental than the former; the "happiness" that derives from it, unlike the "pleasantness" of the isolated desire, "is a stable condition, because it is dependent not upon what transiently happens to us but upon the standing disposition of the self" (LW 7, 198). According to Dewey, Mill's argument does not therefore aim to highlight the fact that there are qualitatively different pleasures, but rather to motivate the qualitative difference between pleasures on the basis of the difference between "an enduring satisfaction of the whole self and a transient satisfaction of some isolated element in the self" (LW 7, 197).

Dewey's words are very clear on this point, and it is therefore useful to transcribe the whole passage:

> We conclude that the truth contained in Mill's statement is not that one "faculty" is inherently higher than another, but that a satisfaction which is seen, by reflection based on large experience, to unify in a harmonious way his whole system of desires is higher in quality than a good which is such only in relation to a particular want in isolation. The entire implication of Mill's statement is that the satisfaction of the whole self in any end and object is a very different *sort* of thing from the satisfaction of a single and independent appetite. (LW 7, 197)[21]

"The Negative for the Sake of the Negative": Epicureanism, Capitalism, Asceticism

We have seen how in Section 3 of Chapter 11 Dewey emphasized an important distinction, that between *pleasure* and *happiness*, arguing that happiness is a stable condition (just like the Aristotelian *eudaimonia*), such that the person is led to seek pleasure in "objects that are enduring and intrinsically related to an outgoing and expansive nature"

(LW 7, 198). In this sense, Dewey affirms that "happiness as distinct from pleasure is a condition of the self" (LW 7, 199).[22] The criterion of this distinction is clear, since while isolated pleasures produce interference and conflict, and therefore cause a *disaggregational* effect on the self, the kind of pleasure that brings happiness has a fruitful tendency toward the harmonization of the self, and therefore to its expansion.

In Section 4 Dewey maintains this distinction between the harmonic expansion produced by the "transformed" desire and the disaggregation brought about by the "isolated" desire, using it to conduct an in-depth criticism of another important doctrine: ancient hedonism. In the *Ethics* of 1908, he wrote that the Epicureans, like the Skeptics, "made independence of mind from influence of passion the immediate and working end." Unlike skepticism, however, which "emphasized the condition of mental detachment and non-committal, which is the state appropriate to doubt and uncertainty," Epicureanism preaches the independence of the mind from the external world "because the pleasures of the mind are the only ones not at the mercy of external circumstances. Mental pleasures are equable, and hence are the only ones which do not bring reactions of depression, exhaustion, and subsequent pain" (LW 7, 202).

In *Moral Philosophy* (1894), a short essay published in *Johnson's Universal Cyclopedia* a little over a decade earlier, Dewey undertook an interesting analysis of the points of contact between Epicureanism and stoicism:

> Both are concerned with the question of how the individual, in an environment which is becoming more and more indifferent to him, can realize satisfaction; both answer in terms of a personal detachment from all outward concern, and of an attainment of internal self-sufficiency; both make wisdom the chief means in reaching this end: both, in a word, deal with the problem of the true satisfaction of desire in a world where good is no longer mediated through social organisation, but has to be attained through the individual himself.
> (EW 4, 139)

In the same year, in *The Study of Ethics. A Syllabus* (1894), Dewey also clarified in what sense his own experimental idealism represented an alternative to the traditional opposition between Kant's abstract idealism (as well as that of the Stoics) and the empirical idealism of Epicureanism (as well as of utilitarianism). In both cases, Dewey wrote, we are faced with "the abstraction of one phase of the process of volition":

> Hedonism [...] fails to see that the nature or content of this value [...] depends upon the mediation of reason; while abstract idealism fails to note that the reduction of self to reason or thought leaves the self in the air, with no *individualized* value. [...] The theory of

> experimental idealism (as we term the position here taken), because of its recognition of activity as the primary reality is enabled to give both thought and feeling their due.
>
> (EW 4, 263–264)

In *Human Nature and Conduct* (1922), Dewey homes in even more closely on the target of his polemic, stating that hedonism "strove to center attention upon what is actually within control and to find the good in the present instead of in a contingent uncertain future" (MW 14, 201). Also in the *Ethics* of 1932, Dewey describes Epicureanism as characterized by the opposition between what is "beyond our control" and what is "within our control," between what is "internal" and what is "external." In this sense, for example, "our senses and appetites are concerned with external things, and hence commit us to situations we cannot control" (LW 7, 200). This means, as Dewey points out, that Epicureanism is "a doctrine far removed from that surrender to voluptuous pleasures." On the contrary,

> its maxim is to cherish those elements of enjoyment in the present which are most assured, and to avoid entanglement in external circumstances. This emphasis upon the conditions of security of *present* enjoyment is at once the strong and the weak point in the Epicurean doctrine.
>
> (LW 7, 201)

The most interesting point here is the role of Dewey's criticism of Epicureanism in the context of his thought. He claims that even modern hedonism, that is Utilitarianism, has the merit, just like Epicureanism (since they are both "empirical idealisms"), of making "good and evil, right and wrong, matters of conscious experience," and thus, "they brought them down to earth, to everyday experience" (MW 14, 200). Despite this appreciable effort to humanize otherworldly ends, the error of utilitarianism was to believe that the good was nevertheless a fulfillment in the future, and therefore "sporadic, exceptional, subject to accident, passive, an enjoyment not a joy, something hit upon, not a fulfilling." The experimental idealism of Dewey contests this very principle, namely, that the good "still is separate in principle and in fact from present activity" (MW 14, 201).

Epicureanism, therefore, on the one hand, perfects utilitarianism's critique of abstract idealism, insofar as it gives value to the present activity (and this is its strong point), while, on the other hand, it shows its weakness in the way in which it conceives of this present activity:

> The trouble with it lies in its account of present good. It failed to connect this good with the full reach of activities. It contemplated

> good of withdrawal rather than of active participation. That is to say, the objection to Epicureanism lies in its conception of what constitutes present good, not in its emphasis upon satisfaction as at present.
>
> (MW 14, 201; see also 143)[23]

Epicureanism, according to Dewey, is not only a doctrine of "seclusion and passivity" (LW 7, 201), but essentially "selfish," since "it presupposes that there are others who are doing the hard, rough work of the world, so that the few can live a life of tranquil refinement" (LW 7, 202). It is a form of elitism that interprets the emphasis on the present good in terms of an aestheticizing and apolitical perfectionism, which is completely incapable of feeding the "continual search and experimentation" which "keeps activity alive, growing in significance" (MW 14, 144). The misunderstanding of which, according to Dewey, it is a victim consists in the belief that, since the future is "a source of worry and anxiety, rather than [...] a condition of attaining the good," the solution to every disturbance lies in separating it from the present, just as the interior is separated from the outside, and what is "within" is separated from what is "beyond our control" (LW 7, 200).

But the point on which Dewey's critique of utilitarianism also converges is that "after all, the object of foresight of consequences is not to predict the future. It is to ascertain the meaning of present activities and to secure, so far as possible, a present activity with a unified meaning" (MW 14, 143). If it is true, in fact, that the future result is not certain (as the Epicureans, unlike the utilitarians, understood), it is also true (in contrast to both Epicureanism and Utilitarianism) that the "*tendency* is a knowable matter." We know tendencies "by observing their consequences, by recollecting what we have observed, by using that recollection in constructive forecasts of the future, by using the thought of future consequence to tell the quality of the act now proposed" (MW 14, 143–144). By requesting a "retreat from the scene of struggle in which the mass of men are perforce engaged" the Epicurean doctrine is finally revealed as one that concerns only "those who are already advantageously situated" (LW 7, 202).

In accordance with the opposition suggested by the "political" criticism of Epicureanism, in Section 5 Dewey also examines, albeit briefly, the doctrine that proposes success in "practical affairs" as an end: "business, politics, administration, wherever achievement and failure can be measured in terms of external powers, repute, making money, and attainment of social status" (LW 7, 202). The advantages of this doctrine, Dewey argues, are evident if "one considers the amount of harm done by sheer ignorance, folly, carelessness, by surrender to momentary whim and impulse." In this sense, even the ethics of capitalism, understood as an "enlightened self-interest in external achievement," would appear to be preferable to the soft and brutal indolence of a capricious and incontinent desire. On closer inspection, however, for Dewey the ethics of success and that of immediate desire prove to have the same defect, since they both lack reflection:

> The idea of success in the general sense of *achievement* is a necessary part of all morality that is not futile and confined to mere states of inner feeling. But the theory in question commits itself to a superficial, conventional and unexamined conception of what constitutes achievement.
>
> (LW 7, 203)

In Section 6, Dewey analyzes one more philosophical conception, that of asceticism, on the basis of the same critical principles that he applies to Epicureanism and the doctrine of successful policy. Here Dewey's conception reaches what one might consider its most profound level. The philosophical move of asceticism consists in replacing reflection with the "habit formed by exercise." If "the great thing is to attain command over immediate appetite and desire [...] the moral maxim is then to *practice* the right act till habit is firm" (LW 7, 204). Asceticism means exercise and discipline, and the containment of "ordinary desires" through practice, not through theory and reflection: "The way to subdue them is to engage systematically in exercises which are naturally uncongenial; then we harden ourselves to pain and steel ourselves against the seductions of desire" (LW 7, 204).

Where is this doctrine mistaken? In effect, on the one hand, it seems to correctly understand that the pursuit of ends, and therefore of the good, cannot make use of reflection alone: "Ends contemplated only in thought are weak in comparison with the urgency of passion. Our reflective judgment of the good needs an ally outside of reflection. Habit is such an ally" (LW 7, 205). On the other hand, however, it makes the mistake of understanding the end, or the pursuit of the good, only as the containment of evil, that is to say, *negatively*. The good as an end cannot consist only in the suppression of desire, because for Dewey "to contain" desire basically means "to convert it" from a negative *end* of moral action to a positive *means* for a more inclusive and lasting good. Transforming desire therefore entails the opposite of containing it, because this means that it is taken seriously and "developed." "Instead of making the subjugation of desire an end in itself, it should be treated as a necessary function in the development of a desire which will bring about a more inclusive and enduring good" (LW 7, 206). At the same time, however, the opposite of containment (repression, in Freudian terms) is in no way the expression of desire. Transformation of desire, in short, means neither its expression nor its repression: "The error of the ascetic and the "free-expression" theories is the same" (LW 7, 206).

Conclusion

In the last paragraphs of Section 6, Dewey expounds three fundamental principles of his ethics:

1. Morality is not "a set of special and separate dispositions," and this implies that moral goodness is not "divided off from interest in all the objects which make life fuller" (LW 7, 207).
2. The moral good does not consist in the repression of desire, but in its transformation and development.
3. An ethic that understands the good as the *negation* of evil fosters "a sour and morose disposition": "An individual affected in this way is given to condemnation of others and to looking for evil in them. The generosity of mind which is rooted in faith in human nature is stifled" (LW 7, 207).

We have seen how for Dewey reflection plays a fundamental role in resolving the conflict between the "true" good and the "false" good, and how this type of conflict "is at the heart of many of our serious moral struggles and lapses."[24] The "true" good, in fact, is what the reflection approves, so that "moral wisdom" consists in cultivating "interest in those goods which we do approve in our calm moments of reflection." Morality does not consist in avoiding the "false good" "set up by temporary and intense desire," but has a positive connotation, because, as Dewey writes, "the proper course of action is, then, to multiply occasions for the enjoyment of these ends, to prolong and deepen the experiences connected with them" (LW 7, 208).

In the conclusion of Chapter 11, Dewey highlights a fundamental point: the ends approved by reflection as "real goods" are not *essentially* different from natural goods, so there is no *absolute* difference between "natural goods" and "moral goods," or between goods "which appeal to immediate desire" and goods which are "approved after reflection."[25] "The moral good," Dewey points out, "is some natural good which is sustained and developed through consideration of it in its relations" (LW 7, 207).

This is an important elucidation for two reasons: first, because it allows Dewey to clearly reject the traditional dualism between the moral-spiritual realm and the natural-material realm. Moral goods do not belong to a category of objects that are *different* from natural goods, because they are nothing other than natural goods *chosen* by reflection due to their ability to contribute to the harmonious, total, and lasting development of the personality of the individual. Second, it is significant because in this way Dewey also debunks the idea that only "ideal values," and therefore "reflective values," can be moral, while material values are by definition considered to be non-moral goods: "We cannot draw up a catalogue and say that such and such goods are intrinsically and always ideal, and such and such other ones inherently base because material" (LW 7, 212). For Dewey, the only possible distinction between *ideal values* and *material values* is that between "goods which, when they present themselves to imagination, are approved by reflection after wide examination of their relations, and the goods which are such only because their wider connections are not looked into" (LW 7, 212).

This means that even material values can be reflected values, since the traditional metaphysical correspondence between ideal values and reflected values is broken and reconstructed in non-objective terms. It is only a "*presumption*," based on our past experience, which makes us think that certain ideal goods have an objectively reflected character, and that they therefore constitute a "true" good, like those of "art, science, culture, interchange of knowledge and ideas etc." On the contrary, as Dewey acutely asserts, "there is in fact a place and time—that is, there are relationships—in which the satisfactions of the normal appetites, usually called physical and sensuous, have an ideal quality"[26] (LW 7, 212).

Moral ends are therefore the object of a reflective construction, but there is nothing objective about them. Moral goods are not fixed, but are the creative result of an "endless" reflection on those natural goods that are capable of developing desire in a harmonious and coordinated way:

> The business of reflection in determining the true good cannot be done once for all [...]. It needs to be done, and done over and over and over again, in terms of the conditions of concrete situations as they arise. In short, the need for reflection and insight is perpetually recurring.
>
> (LW 7, 212)

I would like to conclude by quoting a passage from *Human Nature and Conduct*, in which I feel that the main results of Chapter 11 of the 1932 edition of *Ethics* are anticipated in a particularly clear and efficacious way:

> The moral is to develop conscientiousness, ability to judge the significance of what we are doing and to use that judgment in directing what we do, not by means of direct cultivation of something called conscience, or reason, or a faculty of moral knowledge, but by fostering those impulses and habits which experience has shown to make us sensitive, generous, imaginative, impartial in perceiving the tendency of our inchoate dawning activities. Every attempt to forecast the future is subject in the end to the auditing of present concrete impulse and habit. Therefore the important thing is the fostering of those habits and impulses which lead to a broad, just, sympathetic survey of situations.
>
> (MW 14, 144)

Notes

1 See MW 230, 7–12; on conduct as *interaction* between elements of human nature and the environment (see Bohman 2010, 206; Jung 2010, 148).
2 On Dewey's conception of education (see Hansen 2006).
3 On Dewey's political criticism of the dualisms between habit and reflection (see MW 14, 70); about his conception of democracy as "the institutionalization of the experimental method open to the prospect of constant novelty" (see Bohman 2010, 205).
4 On this point (see LW 4, 6–7).
5 See also LW 4, 82. As regards Dewey's way of "rethinking teleology" (see Jung 2010, 151–154).
6 On this point (see also MW 6, 9; MW 14, 163; Pappas 2008, 110).
7 On this point (see Fesmire 2015, 125–128).
8 On this point (see Jung 2010, 150).
9 About the difference between *impulse*, *desire* and *habit* (see Fesmire 2003, 9–26; Pappas 2008, 122–124; Welchman 2010, 169–172).
10 On this point (see LW 7, 219–225).
11 About the concept of function (see EW 1, 243 ff). On this point (see Westbrook 1991, ch. 2; Bernstein 2010, 288–308), on the social (and qualitative) character of morality (see Pappas 2008, 84–87).
12 On this point (see West 2017, 328–341); broadly (see also Donner 1998, 254–292).
13 On this point (see Donatelli 2006, 149–164).
14 On this point (see Bohman 2010, 190).
15 This criticism of Mill on the part of Dewey corresponds to the vice that affects much of hedonism and that Dewey expresses as follows: "As already stated, most hedonists confuse the idea of pleasure as object of desire with pleasure as motive" (EW 4, 271).
16 As regards the quality of pleasure as a criterion, i.e., Mill's qualitative hedonism (see MW 5, 255–256); in particular, on the analysis of Mill's criticism of Bentham (see MW 5, 267–270). Dewey conducts a detailed analysis of modern hedonism in EW 3, 250283.
17 Dewey had already made a criticism of this kind in EW 3, 382, 386–387; MW 12, 182–186. On this point (see also Pappas 2008, 100–101; Putnam 2017, 276–288).
18 On this point (see again EW 3, 388).
19 On this point (see broadly Carden 2006, 28–55).
20 On this point (see EW 4, 265–281).
21 See also MW 5, 259.
22 One should note, therefore, that for Dewey "the good moral character" is ultimately a social character (MW 5, 271). On this point (see also EW 3, 322). On Dewey's critique of the dualisms of modern metaphysics, see, in a summary function, MW 9, 356–370.
23 On this point (see Pappas 2008, 146–155).
24 For the conception of morality as a conflict (see LW 5, 279).
25 On this distinction (see EW 4, 247–249).
26 Dewey's consideration of the circumstances of morality opens up space for a political observation: American life is going through a moment of crisis of reflection, in which the attitude of "love of power over others, of display and luxury, of pecuniary wealth, is fostered by our economic régime." The most important requirement therefore appears to be that of "fostering the reflective and contemplative attitudes of character" (LW 7, 211). This does not, however, indicate a primacy of ethics over politics, but rather their mutual connection.

References

Bernstein, Richard J. 2010. "Dewey's Vision of Radical Democracy." In *The Cambridge Companion to Dewey*, edited by Molly Cochran. Cambridge: Cambridge University Press, 288–308.

Bohman, James. 2010. "Ethics as Moral Inquiry: Dewey and the Moral Psychology of Social Reform." In *The Cambridge Companion to Dewey*, edited by Molly Cochran. Cambridge: Cambridge University Press, 187–210.

Carden, Stephen. 2006. *Virtue Ethics: Dewey and MacIntyre*. London: Continuum.

Donatelli, Piergiorgio. 2006. "Mill's Perfectionism." *Prolegomena* 5, no. 2: 149–164.

Donner, Wendy. 1998. "Mill's Utilitarianism." In *The Cambridge Companion to Mill*, edited by John Skorupski. Cambridge: Cambridge University Press, 255–292.

Fesmire, Steven. 2003. *John Dewey and Moral Imagination: Pragmatism in Ethics*. Bloomington: Indiana University Press.

Fesmire, Steven. 2015. *Dewey*. London: Routledge Press.

Freud, Sigmund. 1911. "Formulations on the Two Principles of Mental Functioning." In *The Standard Edition of the Complete Psychological Works of Sigmund Freud*, vol. XII. London: The Hogarth Press, 218–226.

Hansen, David T. ed. 2006. *John Dewey and Our Educational Prospect. A Critical Engagement with Dewey's Democracy and Education*. Albany: State University of New York Press.

Jung, Matthias. 2010. "John Dewey and Action." In *The Cambridge Companion to Dewey*, edited by Molly Cochran. Cambridge: Cambridge University Press, 145–165.

Mill, John Stuart. 2003. *Utilitarianism and on Liberty*. Hoboken, NJ: Blackwell Publishing.

Pappas, Gregory. 2008. *John Dewey's Ethics: Democracy as Experience*. Bloomington: Indiana University Press.

Putnam, Hilary. 2017. "Dewey's Central Insight." In *Pragmatism as a Way of Life: The Lasting Legacy of William James and John Dewey*, edited by David Macarthur. Cambridge, MA: Harvard University Press, 276–288.

Welchman, Jennifer. 2010. "Dewey's Moral Philosophy." In *The Cambridge Companion to Dewey*, edited by Molly Cochran. Cambridge: Cambridge University Press, 166–186.

Westbrook, Robert. 1991. *John Dewey and American Democracy*. London: Cornell University Press.

West, Henry R. 2017. "The Proof." In *A Companion to Mill*, edited by Christopher Macleod and Dale E. Miller. Oxford: Wiley Blackwell 2017, 328–341.

5 Dewey, Kant, and the Problem of Moral Change

Conor Morris

Overview of Chapter 12

In Chapter 12 of 1932 *Ethics* Dewey argues that the right is a genuine moral factor distinct from the good and virtue. In Section 1 of the chapter he establishes this independence on experiential grounds, focusing on the right's difference from the good. While "the Good is that which attracts; the Right is that which asserts that we *ought* to be drawn by some object whether we are naturally attracted to it or not" (LW 7, 217). In the assertion of right, there is an "exaction" or "demand" (LW 7, 216) that is lacking in the good. In the right we make claims and claims are made on us, and the question is whether these claims are legitimate or not.

In Section 2 Dewey aims to maintain the distinctness of the concept the right, while not isolating it completely—as Kant does—from "the natural desires and tendencies of our human constitution" (LW 7, 217). He meets this aim by arguing that our making claims on each other are natural to beings like us who "live in constant association and interaction" (LW 7, 218). Dewey here makes a social turn, arguing that the legitimate demands that we make on each other spring "from the very nature of the relation that bind people together" (LW 7, 219). Different institutions, the family and friendship, civic society, and the state have their own purposes, which generate distinct demands and corresponding duties. Take, for example, the family. The parental duties that spring from the mostly unspoken claims of their children are not something imposed on them from without. Rather, the responsibility to protect and nurture the child, to provide love and support, is intrinsic to that kind of relationship. Here we have claims of right and corresponding duties, but one's that are not separate from the desires and affections that we have given our inhabiting of that social role. This point applies not only to the family, but also to the more abstract relations that comprise the institutions of modern society.

In Section 3 Dewey undertakes a general critique of Kant's moral theory. Dewey, in line with his Hegelian inheritance, criticizes Kant's dichotomy between reason and sensibility, and he argues that while the right has a different moral grammar than the good, it is still connected to the good. I shall examine these points in detail below.

In Section 4 we get an account of moral wrongdoing, of the refusal to meet legitimate demands. To do wrong, on this account, is to display "faithlessness" (LW 7, 228), to betray the claims and responsibilities internal to the relationships that partly comprise one's identity. In the case of the parent, for example, it is to "degrade the parental office into a means of increasing his own comport and displaying his own whims, satisfying his love of power over others" (LW 7, 229). While Dewey does not accept Kant's point that moral wrongness is due to our contradiction of an "abstract law of reason," he accepts the idea that moral wrongness has to do with our lack of loyalty to the "principle of reciprocity" (LW 7, 230) internal to the specific demands and duties generated by our social relations with others.

In Section 5, Dewey outlines conditions by which subjects can develop a healthy sense of duty, a sense of the genuine "relations and claims involved in any particular situation" (LW 7, 232). The main condition is this: social institutions must inculcate habits of faithfulness to the claims of right internal to them. However, they must do so in such a way as to not reinstall a conventional mode of moral life. Rather, the loyalty that we develop to claims of right must allow for critical self-reflection and creativity in the "creation of new forms of obligation" (LW 7, 233).

In this chapter, I focus on Dewey's criticism of Kant. I argue that there are two major issues here: the connection between the good and the right, and the problem of moral change. Dewey's account of the distinction between the good and the right has to be understood in light of the social development of moral judgments. Concordantly, we will see how Dewey's account of customs and reflective judgments feeds into a larger point about moral theory itself, one that concerns the possibility of explaining moral change. These points, I argue, dovetail into a formidable challenge to Kant's moral philosophy. One important caveat is as follows: I do not take a stand on whether Dewey has an account of moral *progress*. That is a much more difficult and expansive issue. Moral change, however, is a little easier to get a grip on. Through focusing on Dewey's criticism of Kant in the 1932 *Ethics*, I hope to show that Dewey considered change to be an important aspect of moral theorizing. This does not mean defending the claim that morality progresses or is inherently progressive. Rather, I want to stress that Dewey thought of moral change as a significant meta-ethical issue, and that his criticism of Kant turns on Kant's own inability to account for the phenomenon of change.

Dewey's Criticism of Kant

Dewey begins Chapter 12 ("Right, Duty, and Loyalty") by acknowledging a trend in moral philosophy that gives pride of place to "factors in morality which seem to be independent of any form of satisfaction" (LW 7, 214). In fleshing out this trend, Dewey ventriloquizes some of the intuitions that a Kantian might endorse. For instance, Dewey suggests, there are "folk" reasons for thinking of good and right as distinct, since one can think of oneself as, for example, subject to laws that are contrary to one's desires, or subject to responsibilities that, were one given a choice about it, one would reject in favor of satisfying a divergent or anti-thetical desire. When it comes to the Kantian view of morality, though, we find a view that argues that while we cannot exclude questions of goodness from morality per se, we ought to "give 'good' a radically different meaning from the theories previously considered" (LW 7, 214). Goodness need not be the focus of moral theory, and one need not even have "Goodness" in view when thinking about morality. Goodness might be a consequence of rightness, or it may be something divergent from rightness. Or again, goodness might only be an incidental product of those who "submit themselves to that which accords with law and the commands of duty" (LW 7, 214). These Kantian philosophers "admit the existence of *a* good which consists in the satisfaction of desires, but they regard this as a non-moral good; in extreme forms of the theory as even an anti-moral satisfaction" (LW 7, 214). Hence, moral goodness is for these theories what is "Right" "that which accords with law and the commands of duty" (LW 7, 214). These moral theories, according to Dewey, make the following distinction: "The Good is that which attracts; the Right is that which asserts that we *ought* to be drawn by some object whether we are naturally attracted to it or not" (LW 7, 217).

Dewey notes that Kant's moral philosophy makes strong claims about reason and the nature of moral judgment:

> "Reason" is now thought of not as intelligent insight into complete and remote consequences of desire, but as a power which is opposed to desire and which imposes restrictions on its exercise through issuing commands. Moral judgment ceases to be an exercise of prudence and circumspection and becomes a faculty, usually termed, conscience, which makes us aware of the Right and the claims of duty.
>
> (LW 7, 217)

The thesis about reason refers to the constraining role that rationality plays with respect to desire, now reconceived of in terms of hedonism and self-interest. Consequently, moral theory seems to leave "Goodness" in the dust in favor of the duties given by knowledge of what is right. Now, Dewey carefully makes a neat distinction:

> Many theories of this type have not been content to proclaim that the concept of the right is independent of that of Good, but have asserted the Right as the Moral Good is something completely isolated

> *from all natural desires and satisfactions*... [and these theories] look with suspicion upon all the natural affections and impulses.
>
> (LW 7, 217)

Dewey regards this dualism as untenable and aims to show "that it is possible to maintain the distinctness of the concept of right without separating it from the ends and the values which spring from the desires and affections that belong inherently to human nature" (LW 7, 217).[1] This is a familiarly Deweyan move: where one tradition has argued that there is a dualism, Dewey aims to show that there is continuity. What I'll try to show throughout this chapter is that Dewey wants to argue that this continuity between good and right is supported by a claim about the sociality of morality.

Before looking at Dewey's own attempt at bridging this gap, we still need to see how Dewey thinks this effects Kant's famously formidable view. So, the questions for us now are as follows: how is Dewey going to maintain a *distinction* between goodness and rightness without falling prey to a dualism? and, how is Dewey going to develop an account of moral justification based on this? To see this, we need to look more closely at Dewey's criticism of Kant, and try and extrapolate some theoretical claims from it.

Dewey writes:

> [Kant] accepts the hedonistic psychology with respect to desires. From the standpoint of desire, all good is a pleasure which is personal and private... Thus, the moral good is not only different from the natural goods which man experiences in the regular course of living but is *opposed* to them.
>
> (LW 7, 220)

Kant argues that morality not only requires stronger standards of justification than that of practical reasoning (and other "prudential" matters), but also it requires radically different standards of justification. Dewey argues against this by showing that Kant and many other philosophers make psychological assumptions that are simply false. Take, for instance, that claim that pleasures are private and personal. Dewey worries that Kant's theory makes too much of this. In a long passage, Dewey asks:

> Can we find a place for moral authority of the demands to which we are subject, a place which is distinct, on the one hand, from mere coercion, from physical and mental pressure, and which, on the other hand, does not set up a law of duty and right that has nothing to do with natural desires and tendencies of our human constitution?
>
> (LW 7, 217)

The Kantian view is that just having some tendency or just having some feeling does not justify actions undertaken on the basis of those tendencies or feelings. Fair enough. But what happens to this claim when we think of feelings and tendencies in different terms? Dewey argues that the fact that humans are social beings makes a difference to the moral theory that we endorse. Now, issues of justification may not actually look all that different. After all, Dewey is not defending the specious claim that just having a certain physical constitution, or just having a certain feeling, *justifies* one's conduct in any and all cases—far from it. Dewey is simply defending a descriptive claim about the nature of persons and the conceptual poverty of a moral theory that fails to acknowledge that humans are "inherently" social beings, and that our psychology is shaped by being members of communities. And this has stereoscopic effects on the rest of philosophy. Moral philosophy, especially, must fall into step with this beat.

Dewey continues this line of thought with an example: a mother who cares for her child. Dewey wants to show, by taking a close look at Kant's view, that he is not the caricature that he is often made out to be, and that Kant's view is about *motivation* and *justification* in moral cases.

> Natural impulse suggests to a mother care of her infant: but to be *morally good*, the motive of her conduct must be reverence for the moral law which makes it her bounden duty to care for the child. The view has been caricatured by saying that to be truly moral, the mother must suppress her natural affection...But it is no caricature to say that, according to Kant, the parent must suppress the tendency of natural affection to become the *motive* for the performance of acts of attention to offspring.
>
> (LW 7, 220)

So, far from saying that Kant thinks of agents of having to suppress their affections *in any case*, Kant simply urges us to see that to act *morally* we must make sure that the motive of our action is not a natural affection by itself but that any agent "must bring, as far as the moving spring of her actions is concerned, her affection *under* a deliberate appreciation of the *obligatory* nature of what she does" (LW 7, 220). So far so good. Kant seems to be in pretty good shape. If one takes Kant's assumptions about the "unsociable sociability" of agents seriously, then it seems that natural affections—on this model—could not hope to be properly moral. And this is just because the affections, Kant thinks, are matters of personal satisfactions, and not "ought-to-do's." Crucially, and in his defense, Kant does not actually use the term "desire" in *Groundwork*. Rather, Kant uses the term "inclination." Inclination (*Neinung*) is not "desire" (*Begierde*) but rather a much broader term that Kant uses to describe motivations.[2] For instance, Wood (2008, 146) points out that virtuous actions, those that are done *from* duty, are things we *desire* to do since reason itself points out virtuous actions as being worthy in categorical terms. Indeed, Dewey cites Kant's example of making a promise with the intention of breaking it (LW 7, 222). In the case of breaking a promise when "in distress," due to affections, e.g., the fear having to do something untoward, Kant thinks we can easily see that making an exception, though desirable, could never be something that one could "hold good as a universal law," for "with such a law there would be no such thing as a promise. No one should have any faith in the proffered intention" (LW 7, 222). This is the familiar idea that maxims that are unfit do not only engender poor consequences, but they are cases of performative contradictions. That is, qua universal law, they would undermine their own possibility of being actions carried out universally. If lying were a universal law, it would eliminate the possibility of lying, since truth would not have emerged, and thus, lying and dissembling would be practically impossible.

That's the standard Kantian line. And Dewey doesn't at all seem interested in criticizing that line. Rather, Dewey has something else in mind altogether. So, what is the problem with Kant's view from Dewey's perspective? Dewey thinks that Kant has dug too wide a trench between "natural affections" and justified moral judgments. The reason that this is a problem, as we'll see, is that Dewey thinks a core aspect of moral conduct is being able to learn and improve one's "natural affections" in order to act as a *better* moral agent. And this requires re-integrating the "affections" and one's reasons for actions into a more holistic package of moral conduct. Furthermore, Dewey is opening the space to offer a replacement view for the Kantian picture of the connection between the right and the good. And to re-iterate my own aim here, I want to say something about the way that Dewey takes moral change seriously. Dewey's criticism of Kant will simply provide the space to elaborate one way of bringing out that dimension of Dewey's moral philosophy. This seems like a lot. However, I think that there is a tissue of ideas and concepts that lie at the center of Dewey's moral philosophy that Dewey's criticism of Kant will allow us to look at closely. Kant, Dewey worries, proceeds from a faulty psychological claim about the role of feelings and tendencies in moral judgments. Dewey's view, I'll try to show, depends on a tissue of concepts that provides a formidable view about moral judgment as change.

Dewey's major criticism of Kant is that Kant's view fails to properly identify the distinction and relation between goodness and rightness. One thing I have yet to address head-on is Dewey's criticism of Kant's formulations of the Categorical Imperative (CI). Dewey frames his remarks on the CI in the following way: "[Kant] does not blink the fact that the idea of Duty in general is without any particular content of its own" (LW 7, 221). So, when Kant argues that, in the case of a parent caring for their child out of duty rather than their affection, Kant simply wants to show that the CI itself does not have any content, since it does not by itself preclude any act or another. Kant is concerned by the role that states of affairs might play in grounding morality. As Wood points out "the basic value for Kantian ethics is not a state of affairs, but the dignity or absolute worth of rational nature as an end in itself" (Wood 2007, 259). The contingency of possible consequences means that one cannot count on the consequences of a maxim of action to play the correct justificatory role in moral reasoning. Dewey's worry about this will take some unpacking, since it depends on his claim about the nature and origin of morality, and the ultimately social sources of moral thinking and justification.

Dewey's substantial worry about the CI is that the removal of consequences from moral reasoning is a bridge too far, and that Kant *must* have something else in mind. Namely, Dewey suggests:

> [This] method instead of excluding all reference to consequences is but a way of securing impartial and general consideration *of* consequences. It does not say: Ignore consequences and do your duty because moral law, through the voice of reason commands it. It says: Consider as widely as possible consequences of acting in this way; imagine the results if you and others always acted upon such a purpose as you are tempted to make your end.
>
> (LW 7, 223)

This way of interpreting Kant seems to capture the spirit of his work but seems at odds with some rather high-level thoughts about the nature or moral motivation and moral justification. Kant, in his seemingly rationalist mode, often does sound like he wishes to exclude consequences from motivation, since to be motivated by consequences is more like prudential reasoning than it is moral reasoning. So, one way to read Kant is just to think of his arguments as trying to isolate what is essential to moral reasoning and moral justifications by juxtaposing it with prudential or hypothetical reasoning. But Dewey thinks of this as an unfortunate rendering of Kant; of course, Kant doesn't *actually* think that consequences of actions are meaningless or empty. Rather, Kant's view is that consequences are derivative of intentions, and in the case of moral reasoning, intentions are simply primary. However, Kant is not out of the woods. For Dewey, remember, the significant problem posed by Kant's philosophy is the distinction between right and good and the connection between them. Dewey's goal is to draw the correct sort of continuity between them.

Dewey on Customs and Reflection

To grasp Dewey's rejection of the dichotomy between the right and the good we have to examine the distinction that he makes between customary and reflective morality. The distinction appears much earlier in Dewey's *Ethics*, under the heading of "The Nature of Moral Theory." Dewey writes:

> The intellectual distinction between customary and reflective morality is clearly marked. The former places the standard and rules of conduct in ancestral habit; the latter appeals to conscience, reason, or to some principle which includes thought. The distinction is as important as it is definite, for it shifts the center of gravity in morality. Nevertheless, the distinction is *relative rather than absolute*. Some degree of reflective thought must have entered occasionally into systems which in the main were founded on social wont and use, while in contemporary moral, even when the need of a critical judgment is most recognized, there is an immense amount of conduct that is merely accommodated to social usage.
>
> (LW 7, 162)[3]

Instead of accepting a dualism between social customs that are unreflectively adopted by agents, and true moral judgments, Dewey wants to make sense of the interrelation of moral judgments in the philosophers' sense—"critical judgment"—and the concrete effects of moral judgments in the lives of ordinary agents—"conduct merely accommodated to social usage." And, he thinks that this is a way of bringing this empirical kind of claim about the nature of social life to bear on Kant's view. Dewey's view, contrary to Kant's view, is that morality is something totally explicable in terms of ordinary conduct. So, rather than thinking of moral judgments as instances of a special type of reflection, Dewey thinks that "conduct" is key to providing a holistic view that accounts for the continuity between the moral and non-moral: "This idea of conduct as a serial whole solves the problem of morally indifferent acts. Every act has *potential* moral significance, because it is, through its consequences, part of a larger whole of behavior" (LW 7, 169). This bears on the problem just because it allows us to draw down Kant's highly abstract view of morality. The problem for Dewey with Kant's view is that it makes moral actions *too* specialized, so that one cannot bring them into focus with the rest of action and reflection. This aligns with what Dewey is rejecting in his distinction between customary and reflective morality. For Dewey, even the cases of the affective, e.g., love of humanity, have some potential moral content, since they are continuous with moral judgments about the worth of human life. And, conversely, Dewey thinks that the reflective aspect of morality is shot through with affective dispositions to respond to persons, situations, and even objects, as having some potential moral content. It's the formalism of Kant's view that Dewey is arguing against, since Kant's view seems to regard most of conduct "accommodated to social usage" as demonstrably non-moral or immoral. Dewey thinks of this as too high a price to pay, since it fails to connect ordinary customary conduct with reflective judgments. And this is what Dewey thinks we need to get sharp on: the connection between the goods of experience and the right of morality. Kant makes pains to preserve the right from conflation with the goods of experience. But Dewey worries that this has deleterious effects on our moral theory.

Dewey goes on to make several claims about the nature of moral theory. The first claim is that reflective morality is something that ordinary agents come to in the form of developing a "theory" of how they should act (LW 7, 162–163). Now, we need not think that Dewey is committing to the strong claim that morality is a matter of having the correct sort of conceptual knowledge of what one's moral duties are. However, we should be comfortable with thinking that Dewey has in mind a modest claim that moral life involves at least some conceptual and theoretical knowledge of one's commitments and that that is part of what it is to be a moral agent. The difficulty is how we connect this theoretical knowledge of what morality is to concrete situations in which morality becomes salient.

The second related claim is that morality proper, *and* moral theory is restricted to problematic situations. Dewey writes that:

> Moral theory cannot emerge when there is positive belief as to what is right and what is wrong, for then there is no occasion for reflection. It emerges when men are confronted with situations in which different desires promise opposed goods and in which incompatible course of action seem to be morally justified. Only such a conflict of good ends and of standards and rules of right and wrong calls forth personal inquiry into the bases of morals.
>
> (LW 7, 164)

Dewey thinks that moral theorizing is something which occurs in the face of conflicts within some situation. It seems then that Dewey thinks of moral problems as having the structure of dilemmas. Contrary to Dewey's claims about practical reasoning and inquiry into problematic situations, moral theorizing seems to require that are at least two incompatible and yet justified (or justifiable) courses of action. But does Dewey really mean to say that without a dilemma moral theorizing does not exist? The short answer is yes. Dewey thinks that, contrary to much of the tradition, moral theory emerges in and through conduct.

But what about other cases? Are cases in which one witnesses some obviously or intuitively morally good or bad happening morally empty?

In "obvious cases" there is no dilemma. Imagine a case of seeing animal cruelty. Would one really need a dilemma to be in play in order to make some judgment about the wrongness of harming an animal? All one would need is to make the moral judgment, presumably, without having an additional course of action that is also morally justified. There is no dilemma in stopping animal cruelty. This sort of case provides the right sort of contrast that we need to get a grip on Dewey's own view. This might be a case where "customary" morality becomes challenged by reflective morality. If one already has the belief that animal cruelty is wrong, then one need not bring one's reflective capacities to bear. Now imagine the case that animal cruelty is not *customarily* regarded to be wrong, and yet one might see something in that situation that causes one to ask: "is this right?" If there was a society that condoned cruelty to animals, and yet had other injunctions, against cruelty to humans, then it would seem that even if there was no genuine dilemma, one might be caused to reflect on, say, what beings do or do not fall under a certain rule.[4] Dewey writes,

> A critical juncture might occur when a person, for example, goes from a protected home life into the stress of a competitive business, and finds that moral standards which apply in one do not hold in the other. Unless he merely drifts, accommodating himself to whatever social pressure is uppermost, he will feel the conflict. If he tries to face it in thought, he will search for a reasonable principle by which to decide where the right really lies. In doing so he enters into the domain of moral theory.
>
> (LW 7, 164)[5]

So, what Dewey is suggesting that it is in the conflicts of *possibly* incompatible courses of action that moral reflection comes about. And it is only in the face of the fact that the question of "what to do" that one can stand in need of a judgment to resolve this or that situation.[6] In the case of animal cruelty one might feel that the cruelty carried out is "wrong" in some sense, even though one's society may have rules which condone the cruelty. What Dewey is trying to draw out, in cases like these, is that moral judgment is a matter of reflecting on extant standards of action in the case in which one *feels* them to be wanting. It seems a reasonable inference, then, that Dewey thinks that moral theory is the bringing about of moral change according to local needs.

Change from the Ground Up

I ended the last section by talking about Dewey's view on the possibility of moral change, and the claim that one might *feel* the wrongness or rightness of an act before and as a condition of making a full-blown moral judgment. That's an appealing thought, especially given Dewey's commitments elsewhere[7] to the idea that the felt aspects of experience are "continuous" with reflective aspects of experience. But does this hold true for morality too?

How does Dewey connect feeling and judgment in the case of morality? And how can we make sense of crucial issues like moral justification when we draw connections between felt responses and reflective inquiry? Some philosophers might well regard any attempt to do so as being doomed to fail. Kant is a clear example of this; many of his examples in the *Groundwork* revolve around showing how one can be motivated but never justified by one's inclinations to act in some way—even if the action in question is morally worthy. In Chapter 14 of *Ethics*, Dewey poses a question for moral theory about the nature of moral judgments and moral knowledge.

> First, are thought and knowledge mere servants and attendants of emotion, or do they exercise a positive and transforming influence? Secondly, are the thought and judgment employed in connection with moral matters the same that are used in ordinary practical affairs, or are they something separate, having an *exclusively* moral significance?
>
> (LW 7, 262–263)

These are two hands of the same question. On the one hand, Dewey asks whether knowledge *broadly understood* can or does change one's emotional or intuitive perception of a situation. On the other hand, and to some extent on the back of the first claim, is there something like *exclusively* moral knowledge? Both require some unpacking. The reason for raising this problem is that we can make sense of how Dewey carves out a space for the account of situated moral change that starts in *feeling* something to be good or bad as a condition of reflecting on the reasons why something might be good or bad.

For Dewey, a solution to the dualism between reason and emotion emerges in the form of the distinction between reflective and qualitative experience. Dewey thinks that there are, of course, such things as purely emotional responses to situations.[8] But he thinks of this as something that various and sundry theoretical views have intellectualized and distorted. An emotional response is not an intellectual response in disguise, but nor is an emotional response empty. So, Dewey thinks of intuitive, emotional, dispositional responses to situations as being at least parasitic on evaluative responses to situations. As far as Dewey is concerned, the likely case is that emotional, intuitive, and intellectual reflective judgments comprise aspects of the same events. This only gets us partway. After all, denying that there are such things as emotions as a "type" of psychological event does not mean that reflection can change one's emotional reactions: neither theoretically nor practically. Dewey, from an early stage, offered holistic explanations of experience designed to combat empiricist atomism and rationalist intellectualism. In Dewey's *Psychology* (EW 2), he distinguishes three categories in experience: knowledge, feeling, and will. But he is quick to caution us that

> Feeling, knowledge, and will are not to be regarded as three *kinds* of consciousness; nor are they three separable parts of consciousness. They are the three aspects which every consciousness presents according to the light in which it is considered.
>
> (EW 2, 17)

So, Dewey denies the idea, from an early stage, that there is anything like "types" or "kinds" of psychological events that are distinguishable from each other, *except functionally*. That's Dewey's holist answer to both atomism and intellectualism.

Dewey is confident that it's because of the claim about the holistic nature of psychology that we can at least draw continuities between "emotional" or intuitive responses to situations. One's emotional responses can be thought of as proto-evaluative: "We do not content ourselves with a purely external statement about the weather as it is measured scientifically by the thermometer or barometer. We term it fine or nasty: epithets of value" (LW 7, 264). So rather than thinking of knowledge of the weather as evaluatively neutral, Dewey wants us to see that we ordinarily put evaluative and intellectual terms together. And, Dewey thinks, this is because, at bottom, all judgments are evaluative. For Dewey, *the evaluative is unbounded*. This is how Dewey is going to bridge the gap between knowledge in the broad sense and the specifically moral sense.

The second point bears directly on Dewey's criticism of Kant. Dewey writes:

> if conscience is a unique and separate faculty it is incapable of education and modification; it can only be directly appealed to. Most important of all, practically, is that some theories, like the Kantian, make a sharp separation between conduct that is moral and everyday conduct which is morally indifferent and neutral.
>
> (LW 7, 263)

Dewey is suggesting that one can eliminate the discontinuity between moral and "non-moral" conduct and still make room for moral conduct per se. Once we pair that with the claim about the effective unboundedness of the evaluative, we get a compelling view about the connection between affect and reflection, on the one hand, and the connection between affectively enriched reflection and moral reflection, on the other.

This is where moral change and development is going to come in, and it's where Dewey's view is going to differ significantly from Kant's. Briefly, Kant's universalism excludes change from his account. Universalism means, for Kant, that if one makes a moral judgment then it is justified; for to be a moral judgment, in Kant's view, is to be *justified* by virtue of the CI. Therefore, change of the sort that one might want to talk about has to be eliminated from the theory or explained away. I don't want to suggest that Dewey (or anyone else) should take the converse approach. The converse is that there are moral propositions that aren't true moral propositions. Recall that Kant's claim is twofold: there is a claim about the nature of moral judgments and a claim about their justification. For a proposition to be a moral proposition is for it to be justified. Dewey doesn't want to deny this constitutive claim. Rather, what Dewey wants to show is that a deep feature of morality is that our customs are sometimes outran by reality. Moral change is just such a case; our customs cannot account for or resolve this or that problematic situation, and thus, we must reflect. This is one lesson that we can draw from Dewey's account of the distinction between customary morality and reflective morality. Minimally, I want to suggest that, even if Kant himself doesn't have this problem, then, we should see Dewey's criticism of Kant's account of morality as sketching out a problem that moral philosophy *might* end up with. So, for Kant, the problem is that tying justification to the constitution of moral propositions makes it look like the only moral propositions we ever have are justified. Moral change, however, occurs in cases where one's moral propositions are not *unjustified* per se, in the sense of being, e.g., actually morally wrong, or hypothetical imperatives, or results of incorrect reasoning, or whatever. Moral change occurs when our moral concepts and categories are forced into changing. This is why it's important, from Dewey's perspective, to think of change in moral conduct depending on a continuity between our emotional/psychological dispositions and intelligent reflection on rules and principles. Universalism makes morality exhaustive for if there are any moral propositions at all then they are justified moral propositions. The exhaustiveness of Kant's account at the theoretical level precludes change at the practical level.

I've already given a gloss of the way that Dewey's holism affects his own view; that is, how his commitment to a holist psychology allows us to get a grip on the way that emotion, knowledge, and action form a complete package. And, as we saw above, too, Dewey thinks that it's only in the midst of problematic situations that our beliefs about what we ought to do undergo reflective inquiry. It's Dewey's refocusing of the moral life around action and agency that allow him to talk fruitfully about the possibility and actuality of moral change. Worryingly for Kant, Dewey thinks that he may well deny that desires, volitions, and evaluative responses to situations can be improved.[9]

I've been arguing the following. Kant's view has a serious problem when it comes to integrating moral change, never mind moral development and progress. Kant's claim about the universality of moral judgments seems to entail that moral change is simply historical, and not something that philosophers qua moral philosophers need to take seriously. For if one accepts the arguments for viewing morality in terms of universality, then how does change even figure as a feature of a moral theory? One might think that to introduce talk of change into moral theory is just to take seriously the sort of contingency that Kant aimed to eliminate by making universality an essential criterion of moral judgments. Kant has things to say about change and development, and the fact that civilization is becoming more rational and more moral.[10] But this is a claim about political and religious life, *not about moral life*. The problem is this: what role does the phenomenon of moral change play in a moral theory? It seems that moral change is something that Dewey wants us to take seriously. Dewey argues that emotional and reflective lives are continuous, on the one hand, and arguing that we need to understand how our moral "insights" into situations are subject to reflective changes. And this is a view that suggests that moral change, and even moral progress, is possible, and something we need to take seriously as a part of moral theory generally.

Goodness, Right, and Moral Change

I want to return, now, to Dewey's major exegetical point about Kant: how do we differentiate and yet still connect goodness and right? Dewey argued that Kant had provided an answer to that question that resulted in dualism and hierarchy. When Kant argued for the separation of "affectional" aspects of experience from rational capacities to universalize maxims of action, a dualism emerges. As a result of that dualism, one gets an unfortunate hierarchy, in which right in the form of moral law is thought of as superior to the goods of "affectional" experience. What's unfortunate about this is that Kant provides a compelling theoretical answer that, Dewey thinks, makes it difficult to understand the role of agency in moral life. But is Dewey's alternative any better?

Recall Dewey's claim about the connection of goodness and right and the practical effects of moral judgments: "their ultimate function and effect is to lead the individual to broaden his conception of the Good; they operate to induce the individual to feel that nothing is good for himself that is not also a good for others" (LW 7, 225). Combine this with the distinction between customary and reflective morality, and we have an agent-centered view of moral change that emphasizes a practical relation between the right and the good. But this practical relation needs more spelling out. One way to do that is to look at how "principles" are supposed to function on Dewey's view.

Dewey's rejection of the Kantian view on the grounds of its inability to account for the practical requirements of morality to deal with contingency and to generate change *seems* to leave the idea of principles in the cold, in favor of an account that focuses on the generation of particular rules. The problem is that it is difficult to get a grip on how one can connect up various instances of a rule being followed, and the fact that agents respond in like ways to like situations, without begging the question in favor of universalism or absolute moral laws. One might think that, for Kant, one couldn't justify a moral belief just by virtue of the number of agents who had acted in that way in the past: the history of morality cannot justify a particular maxim of action, and one cannot always be sure that it is a CI and not a hypothetical imperative. But, as we've seen, Dewey is concerned with a deeper issue than *just* justification. Dewey is stressing the need to make sense of morality in terms of its effects within the life of an agent who needs to make a judgment in the context of a situation. Furthermore, Dewey thinks of moral agency as located within the broader context of "conduct" (LW 7, 169), the sort of distinctively social milieu which Kant sometimes seems to think is irrelevant to moral philosophy. Principles are indispensable, even if they look very little like their Kantian analogues. Dewey writes that

> through intercommunication the experience of the entire human race is to some extent pooled and crystalized in general ideas. These ideas constitute *principles*... Now a genuine principle differs from a rule in two ways: (a) a principle evolves in connection with the course of experience, being a generalized statement of what sort of consequences and values tend to be realized in certain kinds of situations; a rule is taken as something ready-made and fixed. (B) a principle is primarily intellectual, a method and scheme for judging, and is practical secondarily because of what it discloses; a rule is primarily practical.
>
> (LW 7, 276)

Dewey's rejection of one kind of formalism, therefore, does not entail the rejection of principles. An agent without moral principles would be unable to make intelligent decisions of any kind, since they would lack any evaluative criteria for a given situation. What Dewey rejects is the idea that it is principle that plays the justification role all by itself. Moral judgment, for Dewey, is the development of a course of action that answers the question of "what ought I to do now"? And in the case where one does not reflect upon the question it is likely that one just has a principle on hand.[11] But where there is doubt, Dewey thinks, one needs the use of principles to guide one's reflection, not simply to justify it. If justification is where the only role for principles in moral reflection, then it's hard to see how we could actually capture robust cases of moral change: for example, the kinds of change that involve radically new concepts of gender or race, or of intrinsic human rights, and so forth. If justification is where the only role for principles, then change might end up being short ranged and pretty myopic. A moral principle would then be a straightforward "ought-to-do." But moral principles, Dewey thinks, are long ranged and flexible. And while they might generate rules, it's unlikely that moral principles can be reduced to rules. If one simply enacts principles, one might miss out the part of moral life in which novel problems occasion moral reflection and change.

A Kantian Challenge

I want to briefly consider a Kantian challenge to Dewey's account. The strength of Kant's account is that one can link instances of conduct under universal laws and give those instances a justification on the basis of their both falling under a moral principle and being embodiments of that principle. Actions that fall outside of the principles of morality have to be rejected as engendering moral failures or as somehow non-moral. I've tried to show that Dewey wants to reject pretty much all of this, and yet retain a modified use for principles in guiding moral reflection in such a way that an agent is able to engage in good and right conduct. The Kantian challenge might be the following: if one wants to relax the role of moral principles in moral reflection so that they play a more limited role in providing imaginative or reflective criteria that agents use in action, then one must show that justification can still be made sense of in moral terms. From a Kantian perspective, Dewey's account might look a bit anemic; what, after all, is the role of moral principles if not justification? And if principles do not play this role, how does one account for the ways in which moral judgments according to principles are thought to be uniquely and powerfully binding in a way that, say, a practical judgment just couldn't be?

Dewey's response, I've tried to argue, is by shifting the center of gravity of moral theorizing from principles to acting in situations. If we take Dewey's claim seriously, that morality is engaging in resolving a problematic situation in which the consequences of that action are such that they engender effects on the lives of others, then we've already committed ourselves to the claim that morality is distinctively social. From that point, we have to entertain the idea that our moral principles are artifacts of social interactions in which some action or another might have positive or negative consequences for the lives of other agents, as well as oneself. And, additionally, we have to explain the fact that morality has changed in a non-teleological fashion. For Kant, morality is flat and potentially teleological. If we take the third formulation of the CI seriously, then it seems that Kant had some pretty lofty ambitions in mind for the future moral world. However, Dewey has no such cheery thoughts in mind. Rather, Dewey is simply concerned to show how moral reasoning can be thought of as a perfectly ordinary extension of the kinds of practical reasoning that agents engage in. Dewey has the advantage of explaining the emergence of moral conduct without appealing to rationalist strategies with a very high burden of commitment, and the advantage of accommodating and explaining moral change in a fruitful way.

Conclusion

I began this chapter by looking at Dewey's specific criticism of Kant in *Ethics*. Dewey's central question for Kant and Kantians is as follows: what is the connection and distinction between the moral right and the goods of experience? Dewey thinks that Kant gives a poor answer to the question, and that Kant's moral philosophy is thus open to a kind of dogmatism. I then fleshed out Dewey's broad (but powerful) response to the Kantian project in moral philosophy. This was carried out in two ways: one by appealing to Dewey's account of the sociality of morality, and the other by appealing to Dewey's psychological writings.

In the first case, Dewey argues that morality must be thought of as emerging in light of interactions with other persons. In that case, consequences of actions, even if they do not justify one's intentions *per se*, are a framing concept in moral agency. That is, seeing moral agents as themselves part of the development of morality accounts for one way in which moral judgments can be thought to be binding for those agents.

In the second case, Dewey's psychology provides a means of bridging intellectual judgments/principles and emotional/intuitional aspects of motivation. The virtue of Dewey's account is that it provides a way of explaining the connection between goods and rights without reducing the one to the other. So, on Dewey's account, our psychological dispositions to respond to events and situations are distinctively evaluative. And, as one becomes a full-blooded moral agent, one gains the ability to exert reflective control over this or that disposition in light of some principles that one acquires as a result of inculcation in a social world. That's the connection between the good and the right that is absent from Kant's account (at least as far as Dewey is concerned).

Finally, I tried to say something about the nature of moral change itself. One thing to consider is that Dewey was willing to apply his "master concept," the "problematic" or "indeterminate" situation, to morality. Dewey makes significant claims about the conditions and context of moral *theorizing*. Moral theorizing itself emerges in light of conflicts that are primarily agential, but which have a far wider reach than simply practical judgments. One way of interpreting Kant's distinction between categorical and hypothetical imperatives is that the latter are simply practical judgments which could not be universalized. CIs *could* be practical judgments, and likely *entail* them. But the difference between the two, of course, is moral justification. But for Dewey, moral theorizing can only emerge in light of some occurrent, practical, problematic situation that requires solving. But for Dewey, again, the difference between the two is not in terms of universality; there is a bleeding edge between moral and practical judgments. What Dewey stresses is that moral conduct and moral change are inextricable. This does not require the sort of dualism that Kant might be caught in the grip of. Rather, Dewey's view depends on a tissue of concepts that provide a basis for connecting the right and the good in the context of making a difference to conduct.

Notes

1 It's hard to know if Dewey is serious about there being anything like desires and affections that 'belong inherently' to human nature. After all, Dewey is famously sceptical of the idea that there is fixed human nature. And the suggestion that there are traits that give way to inherent desires and affections seems to run counter to core goals in Dewey's view elsewhere; for example, part 2, section 3 of *Human Nature and Conduct*. Claiming that there are natural desires and affections looks suspiciously like the view that there are "fixed" ends given by virtue of inherent and natural traits of human beings.

2 See the glossary in the Timmerman edition of *Groundwork of the Metaphysics of Morals*.

3 Emphasis added.

4 I am borrowing this example from Kitcher (2012) and modifying it somewhat.

5 It's likely that Kant would find this acceptable, even if the kind of reflection that Dewey has in mind is quite different from the CI. However, that relies on quite a favourable reading of Kant in which he does not have the problems that some Kant scholars (especially Pauline Kleingeld) have suggested he has, namely problems of universalisation that preclude the idea that there is a point in time in which one comes to be a full blooded moral agent, and ceases to live according to what is socially acceptable and embraces morality proper.

6 Cf. these claims about moral judgements and problematic situations with Dewey's argument in "The Logic of Judgements of Practice" in *Essays in Experimental Logic*. Dewey there worries about the questions of "objectivity" in moral judgements when treated as situational, rather than universal or whatever.

7 Especially in "Qualitative Thought" (LW 5).

8 Dewey, in his *Theory of Emotion* (EW 5), rejects the James-Lange theory of emotion that thought of emotions as "outward" expressions according to which specific parts of the body were devoted (e.g. the eyebrows for frowning, etc.)

9 Roth and Formosa (2018). Roth and Formosa want to show that Kant's view precludes this since his view of education is non-moral. Kant does not think that there is no such thing as education; it just doesn't have *moral* relevance—education is likely part of prudence and taste, but morality is rational and universal in a way that these other things are not. Kant does not deny that there is a need and place for education. Roth and Formosa note that Kant even goes as far as saying (in his *Lectures on Pedagogy*) that education is a means to regulation of an "animal nature" and an "innate propensity towards evil."

10 See, for instance Kleingeld (1999). Kleingeld is conspicuously pessimistic about the idea of defending Kant's view of moral development on the basis that Kant's account depends on a pre-Darwinian view of dispositions. However, Kleingeld argues that the concept of moral improvement still needs to play a conceptual role in the overall account.

11 Much of this seems like Dewey is simply stacking up empirical claims and leaving issues of justification and truth to the hounds. In some sense this is so. Justification is a matter, Dewey thinks, of successfully answering the question 'What ought I to do?' That sounds unsatisfying, unless one accepts a range of other pragmatist claims about the open-endedness of inquiry, the rejection of the Quest for Certainty, and the denial of a "fixed" world of truths. See Lekan (2003) for a discussion of these issues in detail.

References

Kitcher, Philip. 2012. *Preludes to Pragmatism.* Oxford: Oxford University Press.

Kleingeld, Pauline. 1999. "Kant, History, and the Idea of Moral Development." *History of Philosophy Quarterly* 16, no. 1: 59–80.

Lekan, Todd. 2003. *Making Morality: Pragmatist Reconstruction in Ethical Theory.* Nashville: Vanderbilt University Press.

Roth, Klas and Paul Formosa. 2018. "Kant on Education and Evil—Perfecting Human Beings with an Innate Propensity to Radical Evil." *Educational Philosophy and Theory* 51, no. 13: 1304–1307.

Wood, Allen. 2008. *Kantian Ethics.* Cambridge: Cambridge University Press.

6 What Exactly Is the Place of Virtue in Dewey's *Ethics*?

Roberto Frega

Overview of Chapter 13

The topic of Chapter 13 titled "Approbation, the Standard, and Virtue" are the virtues, considered as the third independent factor in moral life beside the good and the right. The chapter occupies a central position in the development of Part II of the book. Like the previous two chapters, devoted to the other two independent factors, Dewey' starting point is a major step in the history of moral philosophy, providing a general philosophical interpretation of a central dimension of everyday moral experience. The chapter briefly discusses the moral theories of some of the major representatives of 18th-century British and Scottish philosophy—Anthony Shaftesbury, Jeremy Bentham, Herbert Spencer, Adam Smith, and John Stuart Mill—albeit with a clear focus on utilitarianism. British philosophy is credited for having provided the most complete account of the spontaneity and directness of actions, as manifested in praise and blame. According to this school, what is primitive in moral life are neither desires nor duties, but the sentiments of approval and disapproval are aroused by human actions.

The chapter focuses on the evolution of the notion of virtues in the transition from customary to reflective morality. Whereas customary morality takes the spontaneous reactions of praise and blame as primitive and natural, reflective morality aims "to discover the basis upon which men unconsciously manifest approval and resentment" (LW 7, 235).

Benthamian utilitarianism, the first theory examined by Dewey, locates the source of approbation and disapprobation in utility: it is because they promote social utility that certain actions are praised. Dewey emphasizes the evolution leading from Bentham to Mill as the affirmation of a social utilitarianism freed from hedonistic psychology. With Mill, the idea of virtue refers to the capacity a person has to find happiness in objects and purposes that bring happiness to others as well (LW 7, 243). Accordingly, a virtue-based approach to morality is one which emphasizes the close connection between happiness and character. It contends that to be happy a man must also be good. In other terms, his desire must be in accord with what is right. In this way, good, right, and virtue can be finally reconciled.

Sections 4 and 5 examine the relation of virtue to the other two independent moral factors. Here Dewey explains that the standard of virtue provides a methodological criterion for evaluating actions and purposes from a moral standpoint: it says that diverse forms of pleasure can be morally ranked according to their degree of compatibility with the happiness of others. Section 6 further examines the transition from customary to reflective morality, reasserting a point Dewey made at the opening of the chapter, viz., that this transition transforms the moral function of virtue. Indeed, it is only with reflective morality that praise and blame acquire an objective basis through a more sustained reference to their causes and results. Rather than being taken as ultimate, "approval and disapproval themselves are subjected to judgment by a standard" (LW 7, 254). Reflective morality reveals to moral agent that "in judging, in commending and condemning, we are judging ourselves, revealing our own tastes and desires" (LW 7, 255). The last section lists some general traits that are common to all of the virtues, such as wholeheartedness, persistence, impartiality, and conscientiousness.

Preliminary Remarks

Virtue has played a prominent role in John Dewey's moral philosophy since at least the 1891 *Outlines of a Critical Theory of Ethics*. During the 40 years spanning the *Outlines* and the 1932 *Ethics*, Dewey has constantly updated, reformulated, and significantly modified his conception of moral life. Yet throughout this long stretch of time virtue has occupied an important place, one that, however, has significantly changed over time. In Dewey's moral writings we find at least three different interpretations of the place of virtues in moral experience. While the three answers do not radically diverge, they nevertheless articulate three different explanatory schemes to which Dewey has resorted in order to provide a comprehensive account of morality. Chapter 13 of the 1932 *Ethics*, significantly titled "Approbation, the Standard and Virtue," provides the last stage of Dewey's views, and I suggest that we understand this chapter as an attempt to solve some of the theoretical problems Dewey has been tackling for more than 40 years.

Before entering into a more detailed examination of this chapter's account of virtue, we should first take a look at the structure of Part II of the book. In the 1932 version, virtues stand beside the good and the right as the third main concept of moral theory. This is a significant innovation with respect to almost all of Dewey's previous publications in moral theory, where this privileged position was occupied by the good and the right, and the virtues were assigned a different theoretical function, generally related to the nature of the self.

The innovation introduced in the 1932 version, but already present in the 1930 article "Three Independent Factors in Morals" (LW 5), is conceptually significant. Indeed, till 1930 Dewey conceptualized moral life in terms of a sharp opposition between the good and the right. This opposition is in turn rooted in the even more primitive and irreducible tension that exists between individuality and sociality. Indeed, as I will show in later sections, this ontological distinction provides the ultimate foundation for the dualism of the good and the right. This rather classical theoretical scheme is abandoned in 1930, when the opposition between the right and the good is replaced by the tripartite distinction between the good, the right, and virtue. This distinction, as I will show, introduces major tensions with Dewey's ontology. I then propose to interpret chapter 13 as the result of a new understanding of moral life, with the ensuing difficulties which stem from the attempt to square a threefold distinction—of good, right, and virtue—with a fundamentally dyadic ontology—of individuals and society.

A brief historical overview of Dewey's conception of virtue will help us better understand the philosophical novelty of Chapter 13. My contention is that between 1891 and 1932 Dewey interpreted the moral function of virtue according to three different interpretive patterns. Moreover, what changes in this transition is not merely the definition of virtue but, more significantly, the entire understanding of the moral life. To that extent, the theory of the virtues provides a privileged perspective for understanding the evolution of Dewey's moral theory. Accordingly, it helps us grasp more precisely the philosophical significance of the 1932 *Ethics* in the broader context of his moral theory.

The three conceptions of virtue developed by Dewey throughout his career can be summarized as follows:

1 In the 1891 *Outlines* and in the 1908 version of the *Ethics*, virtues are conceptualized as the connecting link between the good and the right. I will call this the connectionist model.
2 In the 1930 article "Three Independent Factors in Morals," virtue is conceived of as an independent factor, one that is irreducible either to the good or to the right. I will call this the irreducibility model.
3 In the 1932 version of the *Ethics*, virtues provide a synthesis of the other two moral factors based upon an interactionist ontology that aims at reconciling the morality of the good and the morality of the right. I will call this the interactionist model.

A few remarks before I introduce the first model. If we look at materials concerning the good, the right, and virtue, one may be tempted to assert that little changed between 1891 and 1932, insofar as in all the texts here considered we find chapters specifically devoted to these three central categories.

A first glance at the chapters' titles will help visualize the changes in the position occupied by virtue in Dewey's theoretical scheme:

1 1891 *Outlines*. Part 1. Fundamental Ethical Notions: 1. The Good; 2. The Idea of Obligation; 3. The Idea of Freedom. Part 3. The Moral Life of the Individual: 1. The Formation and Growth of Ideals; 2. The Moral Struggle or the Realizing of Ideals; 3. Realized Morality or the Virtues.
2 1908 *Ethics*. Part 2. Theory of the Moral Life: 14. Happiness and conduct: the good and desire; 17. The place of duty in the moral life: subjection to authority; 19. The virtues.
3 1930 "Three Independent Factors": The three factors are explicitly defined as the Good, the Right, and the Virtues.
4 1932 *Ethics*. Part 2. Theory of the Moral life: 11. Ends, good, and wisdom; 12. Right, Duty, and Loyalty; 13. Approbation, the standard, and Virtue.

In all four cases, the order of presentation is somehow the same: it begins with desires or the good; proceeds with an examination of the right, obligation, or duty; and ends with the virtues. It is remarkable that for more than four decades the order of presentation of the three factors has always remained the same. A possible explanation for this fact is that Dewey's method has consistently been shaped by a pragmatic understanding of categories and theories as arising from everyday experience. Consequently, his account of morality reflects this standpoint that he sometimes presents in a quasi-phenomenological way. Moral experience, insofar as it is reflective, as well as morality, must necessarily begin with what Dewey takes to be the primal moral fact, that is to say impulses and desires as they are experienced by individuals.[1] This dimension corresponds to the good. He then proceeds to introduce the social factor as that which imposes constraints upon this otherwise unbound process of individual self-affirmation. Law, duty, and the right correspond to the limitations society imposes upon individual self-affirmation. Third, with an experientially less clear function, starting from 1930 the virtues are introduced as an additional factor, whose phenomenological status is more difficult to grasp. What progressively changes in Dewey's thought is the place (formally and then substantially) assigned to this third factor. From a purely stylistic standpoint, one remarks that in 1891 the virtues are discussed in a different part of the book than the good and the right. Beginning with the first version of the *Ethics*, the virtues are moved into the same part to which the good and the right belong, that is to say the part devoted to the central theoretical notions of moral theory. It is, however, only in 1930 that this formal change becomes substantial, and that the virtues are provided with a radically changed—and much more important—role in Dewey's theoretical scheme.

My hypothesis is that the question of the place of virtues in moral theory should be answered having the experiential background in view, as this is Dewey's methodological starting point.[2] In particular, reference to experience as methodological starting point should be preferred to the kind of historical justification to which Dewey resorts to justify the place of virtues in moral theory. I specifically contend that Dewey's historical claim, based as it is on the historical emergence of virtues at the heart of a philosophical school—the British and Scottish philosophy—should not be taken too seriously as a justification for assigning primitiveness to a factor. The intuition that lies at the bottom of virtue-based theories of morality concerns the relational dimension of moral life, the embodiment of moral norms in others' immediate reactions to our actions. In terms of contemporary moral theory, one could say that the distinctiveness of the virtue-based account amounts to the introduction of a second-person standpoint, whereas the good expresses a first person, and the right a third person standpoint. As Dewey explains, "meritoriousness, deservingness, is measured by the reactions of others" (LW 7, 254). While elements of this idea can be found in Dewey's texts, this is not, however, how he understands the distinctive contribution of virtues to moral theory. As I intend to show, understanding the evolution of Dewey's thought, as the result of his multiple attempts at integrating his own intuitions about the existence of independent moral factors with a pragmatist conception of morality, will prove philosophically more rewarding. Indeed, the philosophical interest of Dewey's errands lies precisely here, or at least this is how I'm proposing to read his texts.

First Model: A Connectionist View of the Virtues

In the *Outlines*, virtue is introduced as an answer to the question of how the moral values, which are good, duty, and freedom, enter the life of individuals. In themselves, the virtues are not basic values or, in Dewey's terminology, sources of moral action (LW 5, 280). Virtues are, rather, the practical embodiment of these values into individual character. The theoretical question that the notion of virtue is called on to answer is, therefore, not: what are the most basic moral values, but, rather, how can the basic moral values be promoted? The answer is found in the idea of an individual self whose interests are oriented toward the *good*, which is also the *right* end (EW 3, 382). This condition is said to correspond to freedom (EW 3, 383).

The account of virtue that we find in the 1908 *Ethics* is in substantial continuity with that developed in the *Outlines*. In both cases, the chapter on the virtues is the last one, is relatively shorter than the others, and is theoretically less refined and articulated. While not confined to a separate part of the book, it follows a much longer chapter on the nature of the self, which it somehow completes. As in the *Outlines*, virtues are introduced as part of a broader theory of moral character and the moral self. The chapter on the virtues in the 1908 *Ethics* begins with the following definition: virtues are "habits of character whose effect is to sustain and spread the rational or common good" (MW 5, 359). To that extent, virtue occupies a conceptual position that is clearly subordinated to that of the good (and the right).

Virtues are then immediately correlated to attitudes of approbation and condemnation, and Dewey clarifies that their intellectual content notwithstanding, approbation and condemnation are not merely intellectual acts, they have a solid emotional and practical basis. As in the *Outlines*, virtues seem to be no more than a vehicle for the realization of those more fundamental values which are the good, now more explicitly related to individual self-affirmation, and the right, now more explicitly formulated in terms of social demands. In other words, the virtues continue to answer the same theoretical question, which is how moral values springing from the two sources of the good and the right can be realized in society, given the potential conflict existing between individual desires and social demands. Like in the previous text, virtue represents the embodiment of social values into the individual self. Hence, virtues are the codification/expressions of social values, and they connect the individual to society by incorporating the latter's standpoint into the former's structure. As such, they embody values conceived as generals and give them effectuality: social values are real insofar as they shape individual conduct. This is, indeed, the function that the virtues fulfill.

From the vantage point of Dewey's later views, this implies that there is not and cannot be talk of three independent factors. Virtues are not an independent factors of moral life. They are that which connect the individual to society, and they mediate, translate, or otherwise operate as a transmission chain from society to the individual. The reason why virtue is not provided with an independent status is not, as Dewey will report later, because at the time he had not read the British moralists yet—a hardly credible explanation. More profoundly, within this social-theoretic explanatory scheme, the theoretical independence of virtue from the good and the right is simply inconceivable, and this is for two reasons. On the one hand, it is because the two sources of moral experience stem directly from the two poles of Dewey's social ontology, that is to say, the individual and the society. On the other hand, the virtues are assigned a different explanatory function, which is to provide the necessary link between society and the individual. Short of such a connecting link, we would have to fall back into some sort of idealism to explain how morality functions.

At this stage, the virtues fulfill a theoretical role that will be later fulfilled by habits: they mediate between social generalities and individual actions. The explanation of the moral meaning of the virtues is functional; through virtues social values obtain reality: "the social esteem, the honor which attend certain acts inevitably educate the individual who performs these acts, and they strengthen, emotionally and practically, his interests in the right" (MW 5, 360). Virtues mediate between personal and social goods, between desire and obligation, or between the good and the right.

Consistent with this perspective, Dewey can define virtues either as the result of individual impulses or as the product of social institutions: "A virtue may be defined, accordingly, either as the settled intelligent identification of an agent's capacity with some aspect of the reasonable or common happiness; or, as a social custom or tendency organized into a personal habit of valuation" (MW 5, 362). He clarifies this point further by saying that "one might catalogue all forms of social custom and institution on one hand; and all the species and varieties of individual equipment on the other, and enumerate a virtue for each" (MW 5: 362).

Second Model: An Independent View of the Virtues

This theoretical scheme is abruptly modified some 22 years later, in an article revealingly titled "Three Independent Factors in Morals." Here Dewey provides an account of the virtues that differs significantly from the one presented in the previous section. Far from assigning virtue a mediating function, Dewey now considers it as a moral factor standing on an equal footing with the good and the right. Virtue acquires, for the first time, the status of a third independent factor in morals, one that is given the same degree of theoretical and experiential independence he had previously attributed only to the good and the right. Taken together, the good, the right, and virtue are now conceived to be the "three independent variables in moral action. [...] Each has a different origin and mode of operation, they can be at cross purposes and exercise divergent forces in the formation of judgment" (LW 5, 280).

The text presents, however, some interesting and perhaps revealing incongruities.[3] To begin with, Dewey sets of his discussion of the three factors by reminding the reader of an irreducible and fundamental distinction among only two factors, which are, unsurprisingly, the good and the right. He writes: "We know that there are two opposing systems of moral theory: the morality of ends and the morality of laws" (LW 5, 280–281). He then continues:

> Now I would like to suggest that good and right have different origins, they flow from independent springs, so that neither of the two can derive from the other, so that desire and duty have equally legitimate bases and the force they exercise in different directions is what makes moral decision a real problem, what gives ethical judgment and moral tact their vitality. I want to stress that there is no uniform, previous moral presumption either in one direction or in the other, no constant principle making the balance turn on the side of good or of law; but that morality consists rather in the capacity to

> judge the respective claims of desire and of duty from the moment they affirm themselves in concrete experience, with an eye to discovering a practical middle footing between one and the other–a middle footing which leans as much to one side as to the other without following any rule which may be posed in advance.
>
> (LW 5, 281)

But two sentences later he writes: "What reasons are there for accepting the existence of these three factors"? How have the two factors become three? Dewey does not provide a justification for this transition, but merely proceeds to describe the three factors.

A few quotations from the text will help appreciate the distance traveled from the 1908 *Ethics*.

About the good he writes:

> No one can deny that impulses, appetites, and desires are constant traits in human action and have a large part in determining the direction conduct will take.
>
> (LW 5, 282)

> Our inheritance from Greek moral theory states one phase of actual human experience of conduct.
>
> (LW 5, 283)

About the right, and shifting reference from the Greek to the Roman world, he explains:

> this theory also corresponds to a fact in moral experience. Men who live together inevitably make demands on one another. Each one attempts, however unconsciously by the very fact of living and acting, to bend others to his purpose, to make use of others as cooperative means in his own scheme of life. There is no normal person who does not insist practically on some sort of conduct on the part of others.
>
> (LW 5, 284)

He then reasserts again, with increased emphasis, the basic irreducibility of these two factors:

> The whole point for which I am contending is simply this: There is an intrinsic difference, in both origin and mode of operation, between objects which present themselves as satisfactory to desire and hence good, and objects which come to one as making demands upon his conduct which should be recognized. Neither can be reduced to the other.
>
> (LW 5, 285)

The passage makes clear that the "whole point" for which Dewey is contending is not only that they are irreducible, but also that they stay in a peculiar functional relation of one to the other. This relation is, more profoundly, that which relates individuals to society, the dynamic relation between individual self-affirmation and social regulation. On the one hand, there is the pull of individual desire calling for satisfaction. On the other hand, there is the "welfare of the community as such" (LW 5, 285). Dewey's social ontology in 1930 does not seem to diverge significantly from that he espoused already in 1891. One gets the impression that an account of morality like the one developed by Dewey would really need only two, not three, independent sources of moral action: the individual and the community. The question then arises as to why Dewey assigns virtue a new and super-ordained role with respect to his previous accounts. The following quotation contains the explanation given by Dewey himself for introducing the third factor:

> Empirically, there is a third independent variable in morals. Individuals praise and blame the conduct of others; they approve and disapprove; encourage and condemn; reward and punish. Such responses occur after the other person has acted, or in anticipation of a certain mode of conduct on his part.
>
> (LW 5, 285–286)

> Resentment, together with a corresponding approbation, are spontaneous and influential empirical phenomena of conduct. Acts and dispositions generally approved form the original virtues; those condemned the original vices. Praise and blame are spontaneous manifestations of human nature when confronted with the acts of others.
>
> (LW 5, 286)

Exactly as in the 1908 *Ethics*, virtues are said to be instinctive, natural, spontaneous, not the work of reason. Yet Dewey now tries to make this factor distinctive, and he does so by juxtaposing it to the supposedly equally basic features of the good and the right. On the one hand, "[t]hey [the Virtues] lack the rational, the calculated character, of ends." On the other hand, they lack "the immediate social pressure characteristic of the right" (LW 5, 286). Spontaneity seems to be the distinguishing trait of the virtues. This difference does not strike me as very significant, nor as very well put, though. Yet Dewey insists:

> as categories, as principles, the virtuous differs radically from the good and the right. Goods, I repeat, have to do with deliberation upon desires and purposes; the right and obligatory with demands that are socially authorized and backed; virtues with widespread approbation.
>
> (LW 5, 286)

The whole text offers only one argument, or rather a sketch of an argument, in support of the primitiveness of virtue. As with the good and the right, the argument traces the primitiveness of virtue to an irreducible fact of experience. Dewey writes that virtue as an independent factor refers to the

> great susceptibility in English society to the reactions of private individuals to one's conduct as distinct from the tendency to rationalize conduct through consideration of purposes, and from that of attaching great importance to the public system of acknowledged demands that form law.
>
> (LW 5, 286)

Let me try to unpack this very quick socio-historical reference to see which kind of "primal" experience it evokes. That the "discovery" of Scottish moral philosophy was that which prompted Dewey to acknowledge the primitiveness of virtue is what he explicitly says in a letter to Horace Fries, written after 1932. Here he says that

> any specific influence in changing my views it was reading more carefully the English moralists. I saw that they determined the good in terms of approbation or identified it with the virtuous; of course I knew already that Kant determined it in terms of obligation. The consequence was that I was led to the idea of three independent factors.
>
> (quoted in Edel 2001, 6)

Here, however, when the moment comes to identify the experiential roots of this way of categorizing experience, what Dewey seems to emphasize are mutual obligations stemming not from the relation of individuals to society, but rather from interactions among individuals. Contrary to society's organized response, which is formal, individuals are moved toward others' actions by spontaneous reactions. Passions such as benevolence or sympathy are said to be independent sources of action in the sense that they are derived neither from an individual's personal drives nor by pre-existing social obligations.

There seems to be, in other terms, a relevant distinction between, on the one hand, demands directly forced by society upon individuals, which take the form of duties, and, on the other hand, demands imposed by individuals upon one another, which take the indirect form of approbation and condemnation. At the same time, Dewey emphasizes the extra-rational nature of virtues, their practical-sentimental value, as he did already in 1908.

In this passage, Dewey seems to be saying that interactions among individuals are a third and independent source of morality, one that differs from individual self-affirmation as well as from social pressure. This may appear as a change in his social ontology, one that would consist in adding an intermediate strata of patterns of social interaction between individuals and society. Such a view is, by the way, consistent with the evolution of Dewey's general philosophy, as it can be inferred, for example, from the fundamental essay on social ontology he published in 1928, "The Inclusive Philosophical Idea."

Indeed, in 1908, society was still conceived by Dewey in decidedly more abstract terms, as a quasi-Durkheimian totality capable of exacting demands on individuals. Thanks to the sustained reflections developed during the 1920s, in 1930 such a view would appear to Dewey as ontologically inadequate, and the consequences of this theoretical evolution are inevitably extended to moral theory too. As a consequence, duties and virtues are now seen as arising from the more fragmented patterns of social interaction, rather than as something that is exacted on individuals by a homogeneous and monolithic "society." Not surprisingly, then, in the 1930 article, duty and law too are reformulated in terms of obligations emerging out of interactions among individuals. The right, he now contends, emerges from the individual attempt to "make use of others as cooperative means in his own scheme of life." This view is reiterated in the 1932 *Ethics*, where Dewey writes:[4]

> Right, law, duty, arise from the relations which human beings intimately sustain to one another, and [...] their authoritative force springs from the very nature of the relation that binds people together. (LW 7, 219)

If this is so, then the interactional dimension is not the exclusive province of virtue, as right too emerges out of interactions among individuals. If things are so, then the autonomy of virtue is not proven. Moreover, whereas in 1908 Dewey considered virtues as the individual side of social sanctions, the habitual interiorization of social norms needed to make them effective, now he seems to endorse a sort of un-Deweyan view, according to which virtues are spontaneous, natural, immediate. This position is hardly tenable for a philosopher committed to the claim, so clearly stated in *Human Nature and Conduct* (Dewey 1922) only ten years before, that "in conduct, the acquired is the primitive" (MW 14, 65). Finally, the idea of a spontaneous sense of approbation of the actions that promote the good of the community would seem to be at the basis of the system of social demands upon which social cohesion is built, too. Here Dewey seems to confound the legal form assumed by social obligations and its experiential source, which are, as he explained, the demands that men who live together make on one another (LW 5, 284). And indeed, what are praise and blame if not means to exact demands on others?

As this brief examination has shown, in this intermediate text Dewey does not really succeed at integrating in an all-encompassing theoretical framework the diverse moral theories he examines, or in giving a genealogical explanation of how each of them has emerged out of ordinary experience. This hypothesis seems to be confirmed by the fact that Dewey never published this paper, and that two years later, in the revised version of the *Ethics*, he significantly softened his perspective: while virtues are here unmistakably singled out as a third factor, in a way more explicit than in the 1908 *Ethics*, there is, at the same time, less emphasis on the irreducibility of the three factors than in the 1930 paper.

Third Model: An Interactionist Account of the Virtues

As I stated at the beginning, the 1932 *Ethics* presents a three-pronged account of the sources of moral action which places virtue on an equal footing with the good and the right. In contrast to the first edition of the book, here Dewey abandons the systematic approach and adopts the historical perspective developed first in the 1930 article. The irreducibility of the three moral sources is first found in the history of moral philosophy, and then explained as the theoretical formulation of the way in which a given society has experienced morality. The 1932 *Ethics* reasserts the basic intuition already developed in the first edition of the book, that virtues incorporate the standpoint of someone's social group. With the support of sympathy, virtues build this concern for others' well-being into an agent's set of attitudes. What distinguishes virtues' from duty's other-regarding quality is the spontaneous, immediate, natural quality of acts of approbation and condemnation, in comparison with the more mediated nature of formal obligations.

Dewey presents a first, preliminary, and very unconvincing argument which tries to assert the primitiveness of the virtues in terms of their spontaneity and naturalness. Obviously, from a Deweyan standpoint this argument is intrinsically problematic. It has therefore to be considered as an indirect statement—the report of what other theories have asserted—but certainly not as Dewey's position. The question is then how Dewey reconciles the historical account with his experience-based account. My contention is that Dewey operates a sort of dialectical "Aufhebung" which will maintain some basic features of the historical positions he considers, while removing aspects that from his own theoretical standpoint appears to be much more problematic. Indeed, after having introduced the historical standpoint, Dewey critically distances himself by the idea of immediacy by saying that "unreflective acclaim and reproof merely repeat and reflect the scheme of values which is embodied in the social habits of a particular group" (LW 7, 236).

This idea is further asserted in the section devoted to justice and benevolence, where the abstract nature of justice as formal obligation indifferent to consequences is criticized in a way that echoes his previous criticism of conventional theories of duty. Benevolence seems to complete and render justice concrete in the same manner in which the virtues materialize duties. This seems to rule out from the start the very possibility of an irreducible origin for the virtues, as they are reduced to the mere expression of accepted social norms, which is to say to the same moral source that finds expression in rights and duties—although in a different form.

In other words, one could say that the social good of a particular group (one of the two sources of moral theory) is promoted in two different ways: through a general system of formal obligations, and through the social practice of praising and blaming. Irreducibility concerns here, therefore, only the phenomenological source of moral action, seen from the standpoint of the individual that faces an external limitation on his claims. According to this view, an individual can be moved to action by three distinct forces: his own desires (the good), what society exacts upon him (the right), and the praise and blame of his fellow human beings (virtue). These three factors are independent in the sense that each can be at odds with the others. Right and praise do indeed sometimes conflict, for example, when groups have moral values at odds with legal norms, such as the mafiosi. Here we see clearly that social blame may prompt an individual to renounce his desire, or to infringe the law, or both. This explanation of the independence of virtue is, however, too simple, and deceptive. Indeed, one senses that the bipartite distinction between the good and the right stands on more solid theoretical grounds than the three-pronged view, and that behind the three factors, what really matters is the dual ontology of the individual and society.

The following paragraphs of the chapter confirm this impression. Still at the beginning of the chapter, Dewey explains that virtue is an independent factor of moral *theory*. His perspective here, it should be noted, is once again that of the historian of philosophy, not that of the theoretician. As he explains, British moralists were trying to make sense of a simple fact of experience, which is the naturalness with which men "show favor or disfavor toward the conduct of others" (LW 7, 235). However, in their search for the moral source of these spontaneous forms of social approbation and reprobation, they had to admit that far from being primitive, reprobation and approbation "repeat and reflect the scheme of values which is embodied in the social habits of a particular group" (LW 7, 236). This analysis is sustained by the distinction between conventional and reflective morality that is one of the leading theoretical assumptions upon which the 1932 *Ethics* is built. And the result is somehow surprising, as it follows a logic that is opposite to that followed in the analysis of the good and the right. Indeed, with respect to virtue, the adoption of the standpoint of reflectivity, far from providing a better articulation of the basic intuition embodied in conventional morality, conduces to its dismissal. As he clarifies,

> The prevalence of a morality based on praise and blame is evidence of the extent to which customary and conventional forces still influence a morality nominally reflective.
>
> (LW 7, 253)

By discovering that virtue, rather than being an original and immediate source of morality merely mirrors established social values, reflective morality deprives it of the status of an independent factor. Consistency with social norms appears as the basis on which virtues are identified within a given community. What remains as a genuine and primitive content of virtue is unsurprisingly a set of intellectual habits which have no direct bearing on conduct, but which prove indispensable for making critical one's attitude toward self, others, and society.

There is then a clear proximity between virtue and right as both establish what "ought" be done as opposed to what is done, or is agreeable to do. Virtue is contrasted with the good in the same manner in which, in the previous chapter, the right was opposed to the good: something is expected from society which counters individual desire. Two major differences distinguish duties from virtues. On the one hand, their external expression differs: a command versus an expression of admiration/resentment. On the other hand, whereas duty appears as a demand exacted by the entire society upon an individual, praise and blame emanate from single individuals. As Dewey explains with respect to rights:

> These demands of others are not just so many special demands of so many different individuals. They are generalized into laws; they are formulated as standing claims of "society" in distinction from those of individuals in their isolates severalty.
>
> (LW 7, 225)

But we find in these descriptions also a clear proximity between the good and virtue, insofar as both express natural tendencies, whereas the right is always the result of a conscious and external mediation.

The relation of virtue to the good and the right corresponds neither to the model of a mediating link nor to that of an irreducible factors. Hence, a third scheme emerges, one in which the virtues provide a sort of dialectical synthesis of the good and the right, one that is expressed by J.S. Mill "social utilitarianism" which combines together individual pleasure and social welfare under the assumption that for thoroughly social being like humans, there can be happiness only insofar as individuals form their desires in agreement with socially shared values. Judgments of praise and blame play a decisive role in bringing the individual morality of the good in line with the social morality of the right, precisely because these judgments are independent from both, but at the same time they must take both of them into account.

The basis of this new synthesis, as I have anticipated above, is provided by the new social ontology developed by Dewey in the previous years, and clearly formulated in "The Inclusive Philosophical Idea" (LW 3). Here Dewey contends that social interactions are the basic fabric out of which the world is constituted, and the principle of association is said to be "the most inclusive philosophic idea." In this text Dewey makes clear that the ultimate constituent of the world are not simple, isolated, and self-sufficient entities but, rather, patterns of social interactions. The shape of individual human beings (the self) and that of societies result from these patterns of interaction. This very broad ontological claim has implications also for moral theory, insofar as it impinges upon the question of the location of the ultimate sources of moral action, and it is indeed from the vantage point of this interactionist ontology that virtues acquire a priority that otherwise could not be stated.

Although Dewey never formulates the idea in this way, by gathering together some of the elements previously discussed we are entitled to say that the good, the right, and virtue differ in terms of their ontological constitution. The good, as Dewey never tires of saying, has its source in the individual and expresses his desires, whereas the right is the expression of "society" as a totality which exacts actions from individuals. From the perspective of Dewey's social ontology, neither entity can be considered as ultimate, both being constituted through associational processes, i.e., through interactions. Society is, indeed, "the process of associating" (MW 12, 198). And, indeed, the moral correlate of social interactions is neither the good nor the right, but the judgments of praise and blame which lie at the root of the concept of virtue. It is indeed through human interactions that moral judgments about the quality of actions are formulated and moral values established, confirmed, negotiated, and transformed in time.

This is a very important fact because reconciling individual and social morality has always been Dewey's theoretical goal. In his previous works, this goal was mainly achieved in the negative, by criticizing those theories which severed the one from the other through reductionist strategies. In the 1932 *Ethics*, Dewey seems finally to have found a positive solution to this problem, which lies in the constructive role of social interactions as the site where individual morality is brought into harmony with social morality. In the *Outlines* this role was assigned to institutions, seen as formative agents. This solution was, however, not entirely satisfying. What was missing was the intermediate level of social interactions, which is now brought within the picture through the play of moral judgments. Judgments of praise and blame play a fundamental role for two reasons. On the one hand, they help individuals to form desires that are in accord with shared social norms. As he explains,

> The significance of the standard [of virtue] is that it involves a conception of the way in which ends that are adopted should be formed;

> namely, that they should be such as to merit approbation because their execution will conduce to the general well-being.
>
> (LW 7, 246)

On the other hand, they are the formative sites where shared social views are formed, which will become the starting point for transforming a society's values and institutions. While this latter point is less emphasized by Dewey in Chapter 13, his general view of social institutions as it can be inferred from Chapters 16 to 17 of the 1932 *Ethics* and from his *Lectures in China* is totally consistent with this theory.

Such a view fits nicely with the Meadian conception of the social self that underpins Dewey's analysis of the virtues. The standard of approbation which defines virtue is in fact said to express the standpoint of social groups, very much like the generalized others which, according to Mead, individuals must incorporate into their selves in order to build their personalities. As Dewey explains,

> The standard says that we should desire those objects and find our satisfactions in the things which also bring good to those *with whom we are associated*, in friendship, comradeship, citizenship, the pursuit of science, art, and so on.
>
> (LW 7, 248, italics mine)

> By personal choice among the ends suggested by desires of objects which are in agreement with the needs of social relations, an individual achieves a kind of happiness which is harmonious with the happiness of others.
>
> (LW 7, 248)

This holds of course only for reflective morality, because in conventional morality judgments of praise and blame are but the reflex of consolidated social customs, whereas reflective morality "involves criticism of prevailing habits of valuation" (LW 7, 255). This critical dimension is that which endows virtue with the transformative function Dewey emphasizes, because it allows the bidirectionality of processes of value formation and institution building which are required to make individual desires and social duties converge.

The morality of virtue is the morality of interactions and social relations, in the sense of finding its origin in social interactions as the site where individual habits and social norms are formed. The ontological discovery of social interactions—the principle of association—as the basis of social life plays here a fundamental theoretical role in reorienting Dewey's interpretation of virtue as a mediating factor. Yet it is capable of incorporating into itself the morality of the good as well as the morality of the right. Virtue transcends the limitations of hedonistic pleasure-based consequentialist moralities, on the one hand, and of deontological Kantian moralities, on the other. Social approbation mediates between individual desire and established social norms. Social interactions is the social locus where morality is constantly created by mediating between individual desires and social constraints.

Whereas the social good as embodied in the law remained abstract and distant, and whereas individual impulses set themselves immediately against those of others, praise and blame set individuals in direct interaction with one another:

> The standard [of virtue] says that we should desire those objects and find our satisfaction in the things which also bring good to those with whom we are associated.
>
> (LW 7, 248)

The principle of association emerges here, unmistakably, as the ultimate ontological category, and virtue appears as the moral concept capable of embodying it. Through praise and blame, individual desires and social norms enter into a ceaseless flux of mediation. The good and the right are therefore maintained, yet they are "resolved" in the idea of virtue as the result of social learning mediated through the participation in social interactions. It is no longer a perspective standing on an equal footing with its rivals, but the result of a dialectical *Aufhebung*.

Conclusion

Chapter 13 provides an account of virtues that at the same time pursues the theoretical move of the 1930 article, while significantly limiting its major claim, which was that virtue reveals a moral fact at the same level as that expressed by the notions of the good and the right. The historical and experiential evolution from customary to reflective morality plays a major part in this transition, as Dewey associates the conventional view of the virtues with conventional morality, and credits reflective morality with a substantial overcoming of this view, particularly in what concerns the status of praise and blame. Reflective morality deprives the virtues of their privileged status in a way that has no equivalent in Dewey's treatment of the other two principles. Yet, at the same time and somehow paradoxically, this move brings the virtues to the fore of ethical life as they now define the epistemic core of reflective morality. Taken together, they denote the "habit of thinking in a reflective way."[5] By replacing the conventional catalog of ethical virtues with the idea of reflective character, Dewey dismisses the conventional conception of a virtue-based ethical life. Virtue now embodies the very idea of reflectivity which is at the heart of modern morality. Yet this new privilege is paid at the price of depriving virtue of the status of independent factor. In this sense, too, Dewey's latest solution to the question of the ultimate sources of moral experience has a dialectical form.

Notes

1 In Chapter 10, where Dewey explains that the revolutionary transition from customary to reflective morality happens at precisely the moment when personal desires and affections are made the true and original source of morality by Greek thinkers and Hebrew prophets. Here one could be induced to think that social norms come before individual desire. This would be however a false start, as the whole point of the book consists precisely in providing guidelines for a reflective morality.
2 See Hildebrand (2011) on the theme of experience as method and starting point in Dewey's philosophical way of proceeding.
3 It should not be forgotten that the available text is the result of a reverse translation from French. Dewey originally wrote the text in English for a conference to be held in France. The text was then translated and published in French, and the original version went lost.
4 Note, however, that he shortly after adds: "These demands of others are not just so many special demands of so many different individuals. They are generalized into laws; they are formulated as standing claims of 'society' in distinction from those of individuals in their isolates severalty" (LW 7, 225). I will come back to this specification in the next section.
5 LW 8, 139. This claim finds independent confirmation in the fact that in *How We Think* Dewey relies on the same list of virtues to define the epistemic attitude of the inquirer.

References

Hildebrand, David. 2011. "Could Experience Be More Than a Method? Dewey's Practical Starting Point." In *Pragmatist Epistemologies*, edited by Roberto Frega. Lanham, MD: Lexington, 41–60.

7 The Interplay between Emotion and Reason

The Role of Sympathy in Moral Judgment

Céline Henne

Overview of Chapter 14

Chapter 14 is divided into five sections and two main parts. In the first part (Sections 1–3), Dewey introduces the question of whether moral knowledge is intuitive or reflective (Section 1), before pointing out the limits (Section 2) and benefits (Section 3) of immediate (or "intuitive") valuings in moral judgment. The second part (Sections 4–5) focuses on the "reflective" side of moral judgment, namely, on deliberation (Section 4) and on the intellectual function of principles in moral inquiry (Section 5).

The first section sets the problem of the whole chapter: what are the relations between immediacy and reflectivity, or emotion and reason, in moral judgment and knowledge? The tendency of past philosophers has been to separate the two and emphasize one or the other. While the British sentimentalists placed the origin and foundation of moral judgment in feelings and spontaneous reactive attitudes, Kant made practical reason the supreme moral guide. Moreover, each side has been tempted to "mark off" moral knowledge from "thought and reasoning as they show themselves in ordinary life and in science" (LW 7, 262). Dewey mentions Kant's "Moral Reason," but his comment is equally applicable to Hutcheson and Shaftesbury's "moral sense." Thus, a second question arises: "are the thought and judgment employed in connection with moral matters the same that are used in ordinary practical affairs" (LW 7, 263)? Dewey links these theoretical questions to important practical concerns, regarding whether "conscience" is capable of education, and whether there is a strictly moral realm distinguished from a non-moral realm.

In line with the didactic style of the book, Dewey proceeds by directly exposing his own view and comparing it with other theories. He starts by spelling out one of the most important distinctions in his practical philosophy, that between "valuing as a direct emotional and practical act" (immediate, spontaneous) and "valuation as judgment" (reflective) (LW 7, 264). The latter involves a process of justification based on the examination of the object's "place and effects, its connections with other things" (LW 7, 265). While many philosophers use the term "judgment" to refer to both acts, Dewey restricts the use of this word to the latter, that is, to the *result* of inquiry.[1]

The second section presents the inherent limits of immediate valuations, based on a genetic account of them. While these can be called "intuitive" in some sense, they are actually the results of "acquired dispositions" (LW 7, 266), and are far from indicating the existence of a separate faculty. Their origin in habits in turn explains why these direct valuations are inherently limited. First, they are often shaped by a misdirected education and/or irrelevant circumstances. Second, that ingrained habits should feel so natural is what makes them problematic, because their immediacy tends to be dogmatically taken as evidence of what is truly right. Third, when they happen to be good habits, they will only be adequate in sufficiently similar and familiar circumstances, but insufficient or even misleading in new and complex situations.

In the third section, Dewey argues that, despite their limitations, these immediate valuations are a necessary condition for moral knowledge. They provide the starting point and data for moral reflection. As we will see more particularly with regard to sympathy, the emotional aspect of moral judgment is inseparable from rational appraisal and deliberation. Besides providing the motivational force as well as the material for moral reasoning, emotion plays a fundamental *intellectual* role—as paradoxical as it may sound.

In the fourth section, Dewey details the deliberative process involved in moral reasoning. In deliberation, the values of means and ends are assessed. One of the specificities of moral judgment as compared with other theoretical or practical judgments is that the value concerned has to do with the self: "The choice at stake (...) is the worth of this and that kind of character and disposition" (LW 7, 274). Dewey describes the process of moral deliberation as the examination of possible consequences in a "dramatic and active" act of the imagination, in which a "direct sense of value" enters (LW 7, 274–275).

In the fifth and last section, Dewey completes his account of moral knowledge by explaining the role played by "general ideas" in moral reflection. The immediate valuations that arise during the dramatic rehearsal are guided by principles and standards. Instead of having a practical role, the latter play a purely instrumental and methodological role, providing a standpoint from which to assess the consequences of an act. Their functional status is distinguished from that of "rules," i.e., fixed prescriptions that command what to do. Dewey criticizes the legalist view of morality, which sees moral judgment as the strict application of rules. According to him, it leads to casuistry and to merely formal and servile conformity to external rules. Such differences in theory have consequences on how moral education is conceived: Dewey's view leads to cultivating a certain *outlook* or *attitude* of "seeking what is good" as well as revising and expanding moral knowledge (LW 7, 282), while the legalist view favors learning by heart dusty cookbooks of moral precepts.

Introduction

Are moral judgments based on emotion or reason? Dewey rejects the alternative presupposed by this question, which was debated by moral sentimentalists and rationalists for centuries. In this chapter dedicated to moral knowledge and judgment, Dewey contrasts his own view with others such as intuitionism, utilitarianism, or legalism, all the while singling out the "permanent element of value" in each of them (LW 7, 268). The result is a unique view in which moral judgments, while being the results of a rational process of deliberation, have emotional reactions as their material.

The chosen topic of this chapter, sympathy—a concept which covers what today we would call "empathy"—perfectly exemplifies the complex interplay between emotion and reason, immediate valuations and reflective deliberations constituting moral judgment according to Dewey. Sympathy poses a familiar problem in moral theory, and in the sentimentalist tradition more particularly. On the one hand, insofar as it connects us with other humans' joys and sorrows, this natural emotional capacity seems to have a fundamental role to play in morality. On the other hand, we are naturally more inclined to share the feelings of those who are "near and dear," which greatly jeopardizes the impartiality and objectivity that (should) characterize moral judgments. David Hume, Adam Smith, and John Stuart Mill all suggested ways in which natural sympathy could be corrected or enlarged. Dewey, who writes that sympathy is the "surest way to attain objectivity of moral knowledge" (LW 7, 270), proposes a different strategy, involving a change in the meaning and function of sympathy in moral judgment. From an instinctive emotional reaction, sympathy becomes an instrument used in the course of moral deliberation as both a data-gathering tool and a pluralized standpoint. The goal of the present chapter is to use the contrast between their respective positions in order to shed light on some crucial and distinctive features of Dewey's view of moral knowledge and judgment.

In the first section, "How Do We Define Sympathy?," I give a classification of the different meanings of sympathy that can be found in the writings of the authors studied and are used throughout the present chapter. In the section "The British Moralists' Views," I then present an overview of Hume's, Smith's, and Mill's accounts of the role of sympathy in moral judgment, highlighting the differences between their respective views. In the section "The Limits of the British Moralist's Views," I present the problems in their views from a Deweyan standpoint. In the last section, "Dewey's View: Sympathy as a Tool for Moral Reasoning," I present Dewey's own account of the role of sympathy in moral judgment.

How Do We Define Sympathy?

The definition of "sympathy," or its contemporary equivalent "empathy," is notoriously difficult to pin down, because of the many meanings covered by the use of the word. Several authors have suggested a classification of these meanings, from which I draw my own, based on what is most relevant for the present discussion.[2]

1 Emotional sharing, which can take two forms:
   a Emotional contagion or imitation. In this first and most basic sense of the word, empathy describes an involuntary psychological mechanism: the sharing of other people's emotions at the sight or at the thought of them. The emotion simply mirrors that of the other.
   b Imaginative emotional sharing: *imagining* feeling what someone else is feeling. This kind of empathy involves more distance, as well as a less acute emotional response than direct emotional contagion.
2 Perspective-taking. It consists in imaginatively placing oneself in someone else's shoes, taking into account her situation. It can be "self-focused" (we imagine what *we* would feel, were we in their situation) or "other-focused" (we imagine what *they* are feeling in their situation).
3 Affinity or agreement. This meaning is closer to the modern use of "sympathy," with "antipathy" as its antonym.
4 Empathic concern, or the urge of caring for other people's welfare.

The first two definitions constitute what we could call the "core meaning" of sympathy or empathy. The two are not always easy to distinguish: for example, perspective-taking (2), insofar as it implies trying to *feel* what it is like to be someone else, also involves imaginative emotional sharing (1b). The third and fourth meanings can be considered as possible *effects* of the general capacity of empathizing with others. Empathic concern (4), for example, will be greatly facilitated by the capacity to put oneself in someone else's shoes (2) and share their feelings (1), although there is no necessary connection between the two[3] (one can take someone's perspective without subsequently wanting the good of that person; conversely, one can care for or feel the drive to help someone without having to take their perspective).

Most authors, including Hume, Smith, and Dewey, employed the term "sympathy" to refer to the first two meanings—although their terminology sometimes gets muddled up between the four different definitions. Mill is the exception of the present chapter, since he employs the term sympathy *primarily* in the fourth sense.

The British Moralists' Views

David Hume and Adam Smith, belonging to the tradition of moral philosophy later called "British sentimentalism," seek to account for the formation of moral judgments,[4] and for morality more generally, by appealing to the natural workings of sympathy, rather than to an innate moral sense, by contrast with early sentimentalists such as Shaftesbury and Hutcheson. John Stuart Mill, while not himself belonging to the sentimentalist tradition, also gives an important (albeit less foundational) role to sympathy in morality. By referring to Hume and Mill on the subject of sympathy in Chapter 13, as well as referencing Smith as the primary source for the topic of "the relation between sympathy and moral judgment" at the end of Chapter 14, and finally by claiming sympathy to be "the surest way to attain objectivity of moral knowledge" (LW 7, 270), Dewey seems to place himself in direct continuity with this tradition. This section will present a brief summary of the three views, so as to later bring out the originality of Dewey's view by contrast.

David Hume: Emotional Sharing as the Constitutive Basis of Moral Judgment

In his *Treatise of Human Nature*, Hume gives an empirical and causal explanation of our feelings of moral approbation and disapprobation, based on the psychological mechanism of sympathy, primarily defined as emotional contagion (1a). This mechanism is itself accounted for by his theory of impressions and ideas (and their association in the mind), the details of which will not be given here (the account can be found in Hume 1739/2007, 206).[5]

According to Hume, our spontaneous approval or disapproval of someone's character can be explained by the fact that we empathize (1) with the pleasure and pain of those affected by their actions: "We approve of a person, who is possessed of qualities *immediately agreeable* to those, with whom he has any commerce; tho' perhaps we ourselves never reaped any pleasure from them" (Hume 1739/2007, 377). In other words, because we share (by association) the happiness of those affected by a particular action, conduct, or character, we approve of that action, conduct, or character. Likewise, disapprobation comes from sharing the negative feelings of those affected.

Since Hume—like Smith—makes sympathy the sole source of our moral judgments, he is concerned with the limits of sympathy and with accounting for the possibility that a naturally partial, narrow sympathy could be the foundation of objective, impartial moral judgments. Thus, we find two aspects in Hume's as well as Smith's accounts: besides the descriptive and genetic account of moral judgments (how spontaneous feelings of approval and disapproval arise) relying on the psychological mechanism of sympathy, they offer a normative account of moral judgments (how we make *impartial, objective, fair* moral judgments), relying on some kind of improvement of immediate sympathy.[6]

Thus, noting the distortion brought about by our own interests (Hume 1739/2007, 377), and the partial and narrow nature of sympathy when it is spontaneously exercised (Hume 1739/2007, 384), Hume explains that this natural mechanism can be corrected by appealing to "some common point of view, from which they might survey their object, and which might cause it to appear the same to all of them" (Hume 1739/2007, 377). This common and impartial point of view can be reached in the survey of particular situations by focusing exclusively on the happiness and sorrow of those directly affected by some action, as well as on the agent, instead of our own interests. This common point of view is also at work in the formation of general rules of conduct, or in the promotion and condemnation of certain typical characters as virtues or vices. In the long run, the same acts, the same characters will come to be judged as virtuous or vicious, while partial judgments will be "canceled out," so to speak.

Adam Smith: Perspective-Taking as a Condition of Moral Judgment

Smith has a more complex and worked-out account of the role of sympathy in moral judgment than Hume's, and represents a bigger influence on Dewey. Instead of reducing sympathy to some kind of emotional contagion (1a), as Hume seems to do, he emphasizes the importance of perspective-taking (2) as the condition of the emotional sharing involved in moral judgments. While we do spontaneously mimic others' emotions at the sight of them, this primitive kind of emotional sharing is not important for morality, and it is not even representative of sympathetic emotions in general. Emotional sharing, according to Smith, is almost always indirect, *resulting from* imagining ourselves in someone else's situation: "Sympathy (...) does not arise so much from the view of the passion [emotional contagion (1a)], as from that of the situation which excites it [perspective-taking (3)]" (Smith 1759/2002, 15).

Smith's account also differs quite substantially from Hume's when it comes to explaining the relation between sympathetic feelings and reactions of approbation or disapprobation. While Smith agrees with Hume that there is a feeling of pleasure involved in approbation, and a negative feeling involved in disapprobation, it does not come from directly sharing the pleasures of those affected by some action, but from the act of sympathizing itself. Thus, just like we enjoy when someone is able to share our feelings, we naturally enjoy being able to *relate* to someone:

> As the person who is principally interested in any event is pleased with our sympathy, and hurt by the want of it, so we, too, seem to be pleased when we are able to sympathize with him, and to be hurt when we are unable to do so.
>
> (Smith 1759/2002, 19)

Notice that Smith also works with the third notion of sympathy as affinity (3), which he connects to the *ability* to enter someone's perspective (2) and share their feelings (1). The pleasure reaped from sympathy (3) is distinct from the feelings that are actually shared (1), otherwise we could not feel pleasure from sympathizing with someone's sorrow or anger.

This particular pleasure felt when we are capable of sympathizing with someone, or the feeling of uneasiness, when we find ourselves unable to do so, forms the basis of our feelings of "propriety or impropriety": "When the original passions of the person principally concerned are in perfect concord with the sympathetic emotions of the spectator, they necessarily appear to this last just and proper, and suitable to their objects" (Smith 1759/2002, 20). For Smith, we approve of someone's motives, feelings, or actions, when we find that they correspond adequately to the situation: that is, when we are able to share and understand their perspective. Note that the *object* of our sympathetic feelings also differs from Hume's account. For Smith, the emotional sharing involved in moral judgment is primarily directed at the *motives* of the agent, as well as the *reactions* of those affected by her actions (we sympathize with their gratitude or resentment). For Hume, by contrast, the direct object of sympathy is the happiness or unhappiness of those affected by some action.

Like Hume, Smith seeks a solution to the problem of partial sympathy. His solution is to introduce the well-known notion of the "impartial spectator," that is, the internalized point of view of an external spectator, perfectly neutral with regard to the situation. This internalized standpoint is primarily indispensable for the judgment of our own conduct: we divide ourselves in two, so to speak, and adopt the point of view of an impartial spectator in order to determine whether or not she would sympathize with our own motives or feelings. But it is also appealed to in a more general manner in order to judge any situation in an impartial way. Hence, for example, passions or feelings appear as "proper and are approved of, when the heart of every impartial spectator entirely sympathizes with them, when every indifferent by-stander entirely enters into, and goes along with them" (Smith 1759/2002, 81). In this sense, Smith's impartial spectator is close to Hume's "common point of view," despite the differences in the way the judgment itself is made.

John Stuart Mill: The Motivational Role of Sympathy

Mill's account of moral judgment, contrary to Hume's and Smith's accounts, is primarily based on the operation of reason rather than sentiment. However, although the mechanism of sympathy does not enter into the formation of (rational) moral judgments, it does retain an important motivational role.

According to Mill, the chief importance of sympathy is to generate what he calls "social feelings" or "moral feelings." These feelings enable the presence of a live concern for human welfare, which is necessary for the application of the utilitarian principle in everyday conduct. The role of sympathy, therefore, does not lie in the genesis or constitution of moral judgments, but in giving a basis in human nature and character to the abstract principle of utility, thereby giving it motivational force. Thus, while the only moral criterion and standard of judgment lies in the welfare of the greatest number, our sympathetic feelings are what actually drive us to make the happiness of others the end of our conduct:

> [T]here is this basis of powerful natural sentiment; and this it is which, when once the general happiness is recognised as the ethical standard, will constitute the strength of the utilitarian morality. This firm foundation is that of the social feelings of mankind; the desire to be in unity with our fellow creatures.
>
> (Mill 1863/1998, 45)

Mill does not exactly have the same concern as Hume and Smith with regard to natural sympathy, since the rational justification of our moral judgments is given by the application of the utilitarian standard—the *content* of our moral judgments is thus safeguarded from sympathy's partiality. However, since the principle of utility is a universal principle based on the equal weight of every individual's happiness, the sympathy that drives the application of the principle in conduct needs to be an "enlarged sympathy," gradually widened so as to include all human beings. Hence, Mill explains how "justice" becomes a properly moral sentiment when the "animal desire to repel or retaliate a hurt or damage to oneself" or those close to us is "widened so as to include all persons, by the human capacity of enlarged sympathy, and the human conception of intelligent self-interest" (Mill 1863/1998, 79).

The Limits of the British Moralist's Views

In this section, I spell out the shortcomings of Hume's, Smith's, and Mill's views from a Deweyan point of view. These will help introduce—in a negative way—Dewey's view, exposed positively in the next section.

Sympathy and the Social End of Conduct: Dewey's Shift from 1908 to 1932

In the first edition of the *Ethics*, published in 1908, Dewey seems to hold a very similar view to Mill's as to the crucial role of sympathy in moral *motivation*. In Chapter 16 (equivalent to the second edition's Chapter 14), one of the main questions he asks is: "Granted that a generalized good, a socialized happiness, is the point of view at which we must place ourselves to secure the reasonable point of view, how does this point of view become an operative method?" (MW 5, 287–288). In Chapter 15 (equivalent to the second edition's Chapter 13), quoting and agreeing with Mill, he criticizes Bentham for thinking that humans are inherently selfish, and hence cannot have a genuine interest in the welfare of others. For Dewey, our "social affections are direct interests in the well-being of others"; hence, the well-being of others can be genuinely regarded as an "inherent object of desire" (MW 5, 268). Dewey explicitly states the crucial importance of sympathy in this respect: despite their limitations, our natural sympathies are "the sole portions of the psychological structure or mechanism of a man which can be relied upon to work the identification of other's ends with one's own interests" (MW 5, 272). Dewey's own solution in order to overcome the partiality of sympathy and transform these "instinctive sympathetic reaction[s]" into a "genuine social interest" is to blend them with other interests and tendencies such as "interest in power, in science, in art" (MW 5, 271–272). In this fusion, instinctive sympathy is given "*perspective and body*," while the other dispositions are given "*social quality and direction*" (MW 5, 273).

These passages completely disappear from the second edition and are implicitly disavowed by Dewey. While general happiness is retained as a standard of approval, it is no longer the "desired end" *as well as* the standard of approval. Instead, Dewey adds the following warning: "The emotion of sympathy is morally invaluable. But it functions properly when used as a principle of reflection and insight, rather than of direct action" (LW 7, 251). It is interesting to note, in light of this warning, that while Dewey extensively revised both Chapters 15 and 16, he chose to retain almost word for word the paragraph in which sympathy is presented primarily as a tool for moral reflection (which will be studied in detail later).[7] We can explain Dewey's choice of rejecting one of the two roles he had previously ascribed to sympathy by appealing to his own view of standards and principles: Dewey is simply being more consistent in the second than in the first edition. Dewey believes that while we can—and must—keep in mind the happiness of others as a standard when we are acting or judging a moral situation, we cannot make it the direct end of our conduct. First, human happiness is a vague notion, just like honesty (Dewey's example). About the Golden Rule in particular, Dewey insists that it cannot be taken as a command or rule of conduct, because it cannot "at once tell everybody just what to do in all the complexities of his relations to others" (LW 7, 280). Second, in taking the happiness of others as our end, we risk imposing our own vision of happiness on others. Instead, when it is taken as an intellectual standard in moral reflection, the Golden Rule provides a "*point of view from which to consider acts*" (id.), calling us to take into account the interests of others (in all their specificity and diversity) as much as our own. Like the Golden Rule (the two are obviously closely related), the role of sympathy is now exclusively restricted to its office as a tool for reflection.

Simple and Complex Situations: The Limits of Hume and Smith's "Common" or "Impartial" Point of View

Despite the intuitive appeal of Hume's and Smith's solution for correcting the partiality of natural sympathy, it is limited and problematic in several respects.

The first problem concerns the scope of this solution. While the adoption of a common point of view could be well-suited to the formation of general moral principles, its utility is seriously diminished when it comes to complex situations. Dewey, on the other hand, is primarily concerned with the latter, in which a straightforward judgment cannot be immediately arrived at. As we have already seen, for Dewey, "moral judgment" does not refer to the immediate act of approbation or condemnation of a character or conduct, but to the practical judgment resulting from a deliberative process. The need for deliberation presupposes a situation that is minimally complex. In fact, in the first edition of the *Ethics*, Dewey explicitly defines the genuine moral situation as a situation "*where the values concerned are so mutually incompatible as to require consideration and selection before an overt action is entered upon*" (MW 5, 194).

This point is important to keep in mind, because Dewey states that sympathy is precisely the "tool, *par excellence*, for resolving complex situations" (LW 7, 270). This suggests that Dewey's account will greatly differ from his predecessors. For both Hume and Smith, corrected sympathy consists in adopting "Mr. Nobody's" view, a completely neutral standpoint that could be shared by "every indifferent by-stander" (Smith 1759/2002, 81); one that allows for the situation to "appear the same to all of them" (Hume 1739/2007, 377). In complex moral situations, such a point of view is impossible to attain. It might even be dangerous to try to go through with this method in such cases: in the effort of trying to find a common or impartial point of view, and confronted with the difficulty or failure of such an attempt, one might be tempted to take the easier route and simply fabricate one that reflects their own beliefs and opinions.

It should be acknowledged that Smith's account is an improvement on Hume's with regard to complex situations. The effort of perspective-taking in order to have a full view of a person's circumstances, motives, and characters suggests that *particular* moral situations are the objects of survey, rather than paradigmatic moral conducts or habits (Hume's virtues and vices). However, it still presupposes that the impartial spectator (1) *either* entirely sympathizes *or* finds herself unable to sympathize with the motives or feelings concerned, and (2) does not equally sympathize with conflicting points of view. This seems to be possible only in a rather simple situation. In a morally complex situation, the impartial spectator might be at a loss to determine whether or not she sympathizes with the agent. Or, if the effort of perspective-taking is followed through, she will find herself sympathizing with several agents with contradicting positions within the moral dilemma. If Smith's solution is taken at face value, we end up at best with several conflicting moral judgments and no possible resolution of the situation.

The Inherent Limitation of Emotional Reactions

Another problem with this solution is that the operation of corrected sympathy remains that of a reactive attitude, benefitting from the higher status of a "moral judgment" only from the change of perspective from which it is issued (the adoption of an impartial standpoint). In this sense, while McCord (2015) is right to remark that Hume and Smith distinguish between (spontaneous) moral approval and (reflective and justified) moral judgment, they do not conceive moral judgments as fundamentally different from the spontaneous reactive attitudes of approval and disapproval sparked by instinctive sympathy. For Hume, we imagine whether anyone would spontaneously share the joys or pains caused by an agent's actions on other people; for Smith, we imagine whether an impartial spectator would spontaneously sympathize with the agent's motives or feelings, once she had a full view of the situation. In both cases, what makes moral judgment supposedly impartial or objective is that it takes place in a kind of thought-experiment, under idealized conditions of observation and judgment.

While in Smith's account, the act of perspective-taking certainly represents an important improvement with regard to the objectivity of moral judgment, compared with the Humean view, the sympathetic reaction of the impartial spectator still stands in need of reflection. Dewey remarks that "There may be no knowledge of *why* a given act calls out sympathy or antipathy, no knowledge of the grounds upon which it rests for justification" (LW 7, 269). Here, Dewey explicitly refers to sympathy (3) as the antonym of antipathy, central to Smith's account. The maintenance of the reactive character of sympathy jeopardizes the supposed objectivity of this corrected sympathy; standing alone, it cannot give rise to a *warranted* judgment.

For Dewey, emotional reactions are not necessarily bad (in the sense that they would always lead to bad moral judgments); but they are inherently limited, as it was pointed out in the overview of the chapter. It takes a "fine and well-grounded character" to be able to "react immediately with the right approvals and condemnations" (LW 7, 271). But in novel and complex situations, "even the good man" cannot trust his spontaneous reactions; he can "trust for enlightenment to his direct responses of values only in simpler situations, in those which are already upon the whole familiar" (id.). The permanent risk is that even Smith's impartial spectator will only give us a ready-made answer, in line with our previous interests or values, or will mistakenly project past judgments onto a novel situation. These emotional reactions, in order to form the basis of a genuine moral judgment, must therefore be subject to critical examination.

The danger attached to reactive sympathy is more particularly linked to the fact that, in the British sentimentalist view, it is given the final word in moral judgment. Indeed, for Smith, the impartial spectator's ability or not to sympathize will directly give rise to the moral judgment of the situation. Far from being a simple observer that helps us get a better view of the situation, the impartial spectator is explicitly characterized by Smith as an "examiner and judge," representing a "tribunal within the breast [and] thus the supreme arbiter of all our actions" (Smith 1759/2002, 152). Considered in light of Dewey's distinction between immediate valuations and reflective judgment in Chapter 14, we already know that the emotional sharing involved in sympathetic feelings will not directly give rise to moral judgment, but will only provide the *material* for moral deliberation.

Dewey's View: Sympathy as a Tool for Moral Reasoning

The main difference between Dewey's view and the British sentimentalists' views is that sympathy's office as "the surest way to attain objectivity of moral knowledge" (LW 7, 270) rests on a functional change in its operation in moral judgment. The logical status of sympathy moves from being the sole source and providing the ultimate standard of moral judgment, to being a functionally indispensable tool for, and hence subordinated to, moral deliberation.

Sympathy as Perspective-Taking

The shift in the functional role of sympathy in moral judgment comes with a change in meaning. In Dewey's account, the emphasis is moved from spontaneous emotional sharing (1a) or sympathizing (3) to perspective-taking (2): "To put ourselves in the place of others, to see things from the standpoint of their purposes and values" (LW 7, 270). While Smith already emphasized the importance of perspective-taking in achieving a sound moral judgment, the key mechanism in reaching that judgment is our ability to sympathize or not (3) with the persons involved in the situation. For Dewey, perspective-taking is an intentional act of the imagination that has little to do with our initial inclination or difficulty in doing so.

In this regard, Dewey's preferred conception of sympathy is probably less influenced by the British sentimentalists than by (relatively) more contemporary sources: Leslie Stephen's *The Science of Ethics*, a book of evolutionary ethics originally published in 1882,[8] and George H. Mead, Dewey's friend and colleague at the University of Chicago. In the pages referenced from Stephen's book, sympathy is treated first and foremost as an instrument of knowledge, before having any relation to ethical considerations. In Stephen's own words: "'*Put yourself in his place*' is not merely a moral precept; it is a logical rule implied in the earliest germs of reason or a description of reasoning itself, so far as it deals with other sentient beings" (Stephen 1882/2011, 230). While sympathy is traditionally opposed to reason, Stephen explicitly links sympathy, here defined as perspective-taking involving emotional sharing, to knowledge and reasoning. According to him, "sympathy is not an additional instinct, a faculty which is added when the mind has reached a certain stage of development, (...) but something implied from the first in the very structure of knowledge" (id.). Just like "representative perceptions of time and space" give us knowledge of the world as a "material whole," "[t]o realize the world of thought and feeling, that world upon which my life and happiness depend at every instant, I must have representative emotions" (id.). Considered in this new light, the opposition between sentimentalism and rationalism, sympathy and deliberation, emotion and reason appears to be arbitrary.

What also makes Dewey's conception of sympathy further away from Hume and Smith, and closer to Stephen and Mead, is that his view of perspective-taking is inherently social. According to Mead, perspective-taking is embedded in the social nature of the human mind:

> Human society endows the human individual with a mind; and the very social nature of that mind requires him to put himself to some degree in the experiential places of, or to take the attitudes of, the other individuals belonging to that society.
>
> (Mead 1934, 300)

Dewey heavily draws on Mead for his social conception of mind, and of communication as implying perspective-taking, in *Experience and Nature* (1925) and other works. In Chapter 14 of the *Ethics*, Dewey also rejects the individualistic theory according to which our knowledge of others is solely based on inference from our sensory impressions (and which we could trace back to Hume), deeming it "absurd" (LW 7, 269). Instead, he claims that "*[e]motional* reactions form the chief materials of our knowledge of ourselves and of others. Just as ideas of physical objects are constituted out of sensory material, so those of persons are framed out of emotional and affectional materials" (id.)—a passage clearly reminiscent of Stephen's words quoted above. With these references in mind, we can have a better understanding of the two functions that Dewey ascribes to sympathy in moral inquiry.

The Two Functions of Sympathy: Data-Gathering and Pluralization of Perspectives

The first role of sympathy as perspective-taking is that of an instrument of knowledge, which can be further described as a data-gathering function. It is indispensable in order to have a full view of a moral situation and its objective conditions, which include—as in every situation but especially in a moral one—other people's interests, feelings, and motives: "there is broad and objective survey of all desires and projects" (LW 7, 270). This differs from Smith's view, in which the primary role of perspective-taking is to deliver the answer we were looking for as soon as the easiness or difficulty in entering into someone's motives is registered into a moral judgment of approval or disapproval. In the Deweyan view, the inability to share someone's feelings should precisely push us to a closer examination and to a greater effort to take that person's perspective. As such, the restriction of the operation of perspective-taking to a process of data-gathering is conducive to greater knowledge and greater impartiality, since the perspectives of those we do not sympathize (3) with are still taken into account in the data of the situation, and hence in the process of deliberation. This does not mean that our initial sympathetic or antipathetic reactions are erased. Instead, they also become part of the material for reflection: they are taken as data to be further analyzed, and as "subject to correction, confirmation and revision" (LW 7, 272), instead of being taken at face value. It is important to note that, even in the case in which their *content* gets ultimately validated by inquiry, their *logical status* is transformed in the process of reflection, as they become the content of warranted moral judgments.

Sympathy does not only tell us *about* the situation, it also tells us *how* to look at a situation: it provides "the most efficacious *intellectual* standpoint" (LW 7, 270) from which to survey the situation, and thus plays a role in the act of judging itself. In the first edition of the *Ethics*, the paragraph on sympathy was the concluding paragraph of the chapter, in the section on the office of principles. This second function of sympathy is therefore to be linked with Dewey's general view of the role of principles in moral deliberation, as providing instrumental standpoints for reflection. Insofar as it implies the effort of entering into *everyone*'s feelings, interests, and values, and giving them equal consideration, sympathy as the intellectual standpoint of moral inquiry switches from seeking a "common point of view" to a pluralization of perspectives. Dewey's conception of objectivity and impartiality thus differs from Hume's or Smith's, and appears much better-suited to complex moral situations: it is not a universal point of view, or a view from nowhere, but a pluralized view. This is how I believe we should understand Dewey's claim that "the only truly general thought is the generous thought" (LW 7, 270). Generality is here to be opposed to the particularity of the agent's interests, while generosity consists in giving equal weight to the interests of others. It is interesting that Dewey mentions Smith's "impartial spectator" only with respect to *one* of the functions described by Smith: not that of a final judge, nor that of providing the appropriate standpoint to survey the moral situation, but as a way to "humble (...) our own pretensions and claims" (id.).

This intellectual function of sympathy can be linked to the principle of the "Golden Rule," mentioned in the last section. The Golden Rule, from Dewey's perspective, is best described as a sympathetic outlook or standpoint that "suggests the necessity of considering how our acts affect the interests of others as well as our own," and "tends to prevent partiality of regard" (LW 7, 280–281). The sympathetic standpoint is slightly different from other principles. It does not give us an idea of the worth of an action from a certain point of view (contrary to other standards such as justice and human welfare), but it tells us that we should give equal consideration to the claims and interests of everyone involved in the situation. Its office is properly "intellectual," in the sense that it gives guidelines as to the way in which the situation should be surveyed, namely, in a manner as impartial and as objective as possible. The special status of the sympathetic standpoint might explain why the paragraph was initially placed at the end of Chapter 16 in the first edition, with Dewey declaring sympathy to be "the general principle of moral knowledge" (MW 5, 303), thus giving it prime importance.

The Conjoined Role of Emotion and Reason in Moral Judgment

Most philosophers choose to found morality on either emotion *or* reason: Hume and Smith, who belong to the tradition that what was later called "moral sentimentalism," give a descriptive and normative account ultimately based on emotions and sentiments, while for Mill, the justification of moral judgments is solely based on the calculation of the amount of pleasure and pain resulting from a particular act. Dewey could be taken to belong to the second group of moral theories, since he defines moral judgment properly speaking as the result of a reflective process or "deliberation." As such, Dewey does present it as the work of reason (although he prefers the term "intelligence"). In his view, however, there is no strict separation between emotion and reason in the process of moral deliberation—both are equally necessary and depend on one another for the issuing of a good moral judgment.

The role of sympathy is a perfect example of this close interplay between emotion and reason.[9] While Dewey calls sympathy an "*intellectual* standpoint" (LW 7, 270, his emphasis), it is important to note that it is the opposite of a cold and detached standpoint. Thus, the perspective-taking that Dewey has in mind differs from what some contemporary authors call "cognitive empathy," defined as a purely intellectual, non-emotional process of knowing what it would be like to be someone else—the only kind of empathy that psychopaths are capable of (Decety and Cowell 2014; Kauppinen 2014). In Dewey's view, genuine perspective-taking necessarily involves affective states: it means vividly imagining oneself in someone else's situation. Sympathy's process of data-gathering, therefore, is not a purely cognitive process of gaining knowledge of cold facts about people. The fact that it is called an "intellectual" standpoint is due to the new methodological status given to sympathy in the process of moral reflection, as we have already seen.

In fact, the affective aspect of the sympathetic standpoint is fully instrumental in attaining objectivity of moral judgment. The kind of "information" gathered by sympathy could not be replaced by propositions describing the states of the agents involved in the situation, which I could entertain in my mind while reasoning about them. For example, it is very different to register the fact *that* some people are dissatisfied with the government, and to *imagine being them*, seeing how their anger relates to their condition, values, etc. For Dewey, without this affective component of perspective-taking, different interests could not be given proper weight and consideration in moral deliberation: "It is sympathy which saves consideration of consequences from degenerating into mere calculation, by rendering vivid the interests of others and urging us to give them the same weight as those which touch our own honour, purse, and power" (LW 7, 270). In the process that Dewey calls "imaginative rehearsal" (LW 7, 275), when several courses of action are imagined during deliberation, sympathy renders alive the consequences that some action would have on all the interests involved in the situation.

While Dewey's views on the relation between motivation and sympathy evolve between the two editions (as we have seen, in 1932 sympathy no longer provides the direct motive and end of a moral act), sympathy still has a role to play in moral motivation in the second edition. By rendering vivid the claims of others, sympathy makes us more compelled to act according to our moral judgments—more than if reason alone had reached the same conclusion: "'Cold blooded' thought may reach a correct conclusion, but if a person remains anti-pathetic or indifferent to the considerations presented to him in a rational way, they will not stir him to act in accord with them" (LW 7, 270). The major difference between the two editions is that in 1932, Dewey is insistent on the fact that emotional reactions, including sympathy, should not directly provide the content of the final moral judgment, which is instead reached by (rational) deliberation, working *with the help of* the material provided by emotional reactions.

Conclusion

Like Hume, Smith, and Mill, Dewey thinks that sympathy has an important role to play in moral life, despite being prone to bias and partiality in its natural operation. The specificity and originality of Dewey's "solution" to the limits of sympathy is that it goes beyond the mere enlargement of natural sympathetic responses to the whole of humankind. Sympathy, redefined as perspective-taking, is taken in its close connection to knowledge and reason, instead of being reduced to the realm of spontaneous feelings and reactions. In moral judgment, our social capacity to put ourselves in the place of others is intentionally used as a data-gathering tool and an intellectual standpoint for moral reflection—a pluralized perspective from which to survey the different motives, feelings, interests, and values involved in the situation. For Dewey, the destitution of sympathy from its status of mighty judge to a subordinate but indispensable tool for moral reflection is the only way for it to be the "tool, *par excellence*, for resolving complex situations" (LW 7, 270), and the "surest way to attain objectivity of moral knowledge" (id.).

Notes

1 This is the case for all judgments, practical or theoretical: for Dewey, all genuine knowledge is the product of a more or less rudimentary kind of reflection.
2 My classification is inspired in particular by Decety and Cowell (2014) and Kauppinen (2014).
3 See Prinz (2011, 218–221), for an argument based on empirical studies.
4 It is important to note that their notion of "moral judgment" is different from what Dewey is willing to properly call judgment. As we have noted in the chapter overview, for Dewey, the term "moral judgment" is reserved for that which terminates a moral inquiry into a particular situation. It does not refer to attitudes of approval or disapproval, nor to general moral principles such as "charity is good" or "torture is bad" (the primary examples of moral judgments in Prinz 2011).
5 All references to David Hume's *Treatise of Human Nature* are indicated by the abbreviation "T" followed by book, part, section, and paragraph numbers.
6 As Sayre-McCord puts it, Hume and Smith "move from an account of moral approbation to an account of moral judgment" (Sayre-McCord 2015, 210).
7 He even made it doubly important, in a way, by (mistakenly) inserting it in both Chapters 13 and 14.
8 Stephen's book appears as Chapter 14's second bibliographical reference under the heading "the relation between sympathy and moral judgment," after Smith's *Theory of Moral Sentiments*.
9 From the first to the second edition of the *Ethics*, the paragraph on sympathy is moved from the last section of the chapter, focused on the topic of principles, to the section "Sensitivity and Thoughtfulness," on the importance of immediate valuations and emotional reactions in moral judgment.

References

Decety, Jean and Jason Cowell. 2014. "Friends or Foes: Is Empathy Necessary for Moral Behavior?" *Perspectives on Psychological Science: A Journal of the Association for Psychological Science* 9 no. 4: 525–537.

Hume, David. 1739/2007. *A Treatise of Human Nature.* Oxford: Clarendon Press.

Kauppinen, Antti. 2014. "Empathy, Emotion Regulation, and Moral Judgment." In *Empathy and Morality*, edited by Heidi Maibom. Oxford: Oxford University Press, 97–121.

Mead, George Herbert. 1934. *Mind, Self & Society.* Chicago, IL: University of Chicago Press.

Mill, John Stuart. 1863/1998. *Utilitarianism.* Oxford: Oxford University Press.

Prinz, Jessie. 2011. "Is Empathy Necessary for Morality?" In *Empathy: Philosophical and Psychological Perspectives*, edited Amy Coplan & Peter Goldie. Oxford University Press, 211–229.

Sayre-McCord, Geoffrey. 2015. "Hume and Smith on Sympathy, Approbation, and Moral Judgment." In *Sympathy: A History*, edited by Eric Schliesser. Oxford: Oxford University Press, 208–246.

Smith, Adam. 1759/2002. *The Theory of Moral Sentiments.* Cambridge: Cambridge University Press.

Stephen, Leslie. 1882/2011. *The Science of Ethics.* Cambridge: Cambridge University Press.

8 The Identity of Self and Act

Pluralism, Growth, and Our Social Interest[1]

Steven Levine

Overview of Chapter 15

Chapter 15 of Dewey's 1932 *Ethics*, "The Moral Self," is the final chapter of the book's middle section, "Theory of the Moral Life." In the prior chapters of this section Dewey utilized the concept of the self in several important ways. For instance, in Chapter 10, Dewey argues that the self cannot be understood independently of what it does insofar as character and conduct are "strictly correlative" concepts, and in Chapter 13 he gives an account of the virtues, of the character traits necessary for the self to develop what he calls complete interests. In Chapter 15 Dewey addresses the topic of the self directly. He does so, however, by examining a number of seemingly disparate topics: choice, motivation, interest, egoism and altruism, responsibility, freedom, and growth.

In briefly outlining the chapter, we can begin to see the interconnection of these topics. In the first section of the chapter Dewey develops a line of thought that he first broached in Chapter 10, where he argued that a correct moral theory depends on grasping that there is a kind of identity between the self, its acts, and the consequences of such acts. In this section he examines the role that choice plays in this identity, arguing that the choice and execution of an act contributes to the development of the character of the self who chooses and acts. In the second section, Dewey examines the concept of motivation, and argues that it cannot be accounted for by either external stimulus or by inner psychological states like desires. He instead argues that motivation is best understood through the concept of a self's interests. On Dewey's view, interests are neither subjective nor objective, but are expressive of an active union of self and object grounded in habits. In the following two sections, Dewey discusses moral motivation. He begins by analyzing the concepts of egoism and altruism, which are the concepts usually cited to account for moral motivation. He criticizes the moralistic argument that the conscious regard for self is always bad and that consideration of others is always good, and he tries to neutralize the egoistic argument that because all action is expressive of the self's interests that all action is selfish. He then argues that egoism and altruism are not sources of motivation at all, but are attitudes by which certain objects and consequences come to notice. In line with his general view of motivation, moral motivation needs to be seen as a product of one's cultivated interests. Our most basic interest, he argues, is in the good of the social groups of which we are a part, for instance, the family. Our social interest mediates the development of our conscious regard for self and other. In the last section of the chapter, Dewey discusses responsibility, freedom, and growth. He argues that we hold people responsible for their actions to help them change their future behavior, not to punish past behavior. This assumes that the agent can change their behavior, that agents are plastic to some degree. Dewey's account of freedom takes its cue from this fact. To be free requires not only that one can change, but that one actively pursues opportunities to grow by developing social relations that allow for more varied yet integrated interests. To finish, Dewey considers the concept of growth, and attempts to determine its place in moral theory.

Two Questions

What I want to do in this chapter is to further bring out the interconnection of these topics by examining two questions about Dewey's account of the self. Both questions concern the relationship between the notion of the self at play in the 1932 *Ethics* and the notion found in Dewey's earlier ethics of self-realization, where he first worked out his account of the self.

Most scholars take it that by the time he wrote the 1932 *Ethics* Dewey had long given up the ethics of self-realization of his youth.[2] This happened in two stages. First, in the early 1890s Dewey came to reject the idea, put forward by T.H. Green, that there is a split within the self between the empirical or finite self and the absolute or infinite self, and that the goal of the empirical self is to instantiate the absolute self. Dewey came to see that this view is neo-Kantian rather than Hegelian insofar as it posits as its ideal a unified self that always ought to be realized but never in fact is.[3] In contrast, Dewey puts forward a view in which there is no ideal self that sets the standard for self-realization, rather the standard for self-realization is immanent to the ongoing practices of the self. Self-realization on this new account "does not mean...act so as to fill up some presupposed ideal self. It means to act at the height of action, to realize its full meaning" (EW 4, 49).

Second, Dewey came to reject the primacy of the good altogether, and so the idea that all other moral concepts can be derived from the good of self-realization. In the 1932 *Ethics* this idea takes the form of a pragmatic pluralism in which the good is seen as one moral principle alongside two others, namely, the right and virtue. Dewey's view is pragmatic because it posits that these moral concepts, and the theories which take them as their objects, are tools to help agents solve moral problems; it is pluralistic because it claims that these principles cannot be reduced to one another insofar as they each have independent sources in natural features of human life (desire, social demands, and attitudes of approval and disapproval). As becomes clear in Chapters 12 and 13, obligation is based in the demands of others, not desired ends, while virtues as traits of character that ought to be approved cannot be determined by ascertaining the ends for which we in fact act. Thus, neither right nor virtue can be derived directly from the good. The persistent tendency in Western ethical thought to base moral theory on a single principle is decisively rejected.[4]

But as Axel Honneth points out, in Chapter 15 of the 1932 *Ethics* Dewey seems to endorse the idea that there *is* a kind of ultimate moral good for the self, i.e., freedom understood as growth.[5] This concept is a clear descendent of the concept of self-realization that is left over after Dewey's rejection of Green's neo-Kantian account of self-realization. But if Dewey continues to use this concept of growth, and if growth is the ultimate moral telos for the self, how is that compatible with Dewey's pragmatic pluralism? This is my first question. Honneth argues that it is not compatible, that there is here an unresolved conflict in Dewey's moral theory. I argue, in contrast, that if we understand the concept of growth correctly then we can see our way to a position in which there is no conflict between it and Dewey's pragmatic pluralism.[6]

My second question concerns Dewey account of the self's interest in and regard for the welfare of others. In the ethics of self-realization of Green and Bradley the self has an interest in the good of others because one's own realization depends on the social relations that enable the free development of one's capacities and potentialities. The self does not develop apart from other selves, but in relation to others in the family, in friendship, in civil society, and in the state. One must cultivate these relationships to realize oneself fully. In this sense, one's own good is bound up with the good of others. But in his early work Dewey spotted a deep problem with this strategy: the fact that my realization depends on others to whom I am socially related does not mean that I must be concerned for their intrinsic good, it may just mean that I am concerned with their good *only to the extent* that they are a means to my end, to my self-realization. As Dewey asks pointedly, is it really "better to act to *get* goodness *for* the self, than it is to get pleasure for the self" (EW 4, 51)? Is not an ethic of self-realization structurally as egoistic as hedonism? If so, how then can it account for the self's interest in the intrinsic good of the other? Dewey's answer in the 1932 *Ethics* has two parts. First, Dewey argues that our interest in the good of others cannot be accounted for by the concept of altruism. This interest, what he calls the social interest, is rooted in a more basic relation between self and other. Second, Dewey does not think that he can give a freestanding philosophical justification of this relation; he can only give a pragmatic justification.

Here is how this chapter will unfold. In the next two sections I lay out Dewey's account of action, focusing on the identity of self and act and on the idea that motivation is to be accounted for by the concept of interest. This puts us in position, in the section "Egoism, Altruism, and the Social Interest" section, to understand Dewey's claim that the self's interest in the good of others is more basic than that captured by the concept of altruism, and to show, in the section "Freedom as Growth", how freedom as growth is consistent with Dewey's pragmatic pluralism.

The Self and Its Acts

In line with his earlier thought, Dewey in the 1932 *Ethics* claims that there is an "identity of self and act," and that this identity is the "central point in moral theory" (LW 7, 296).[7] Expanding on this, he says:

> It is not too much to say that the key to a correct theory of morality is the recognition of the *essential unity of the self and its acts,* if the latter have any moral significance; while errors in theory arise as soon as the self and acts (and their consequences) are separated from each other, and moral worth is attributed to one more than the other.
>
> (LW 7, 288)

In saying that there is an identity between the self and its acts, Dewey is not claiming that there is a strict identity between them, but rather that there is, to use Hegel's term, a "speculative identity." For Hegel, two items are speculatively identical when (1) the concepts of those items cannot be thought of independently of each other, and (2) when, through a certain type of process, they reciprocally constitute each other's being. As Dewey puts it, when we consider two speculatively identical items "[a]t whatever end we begin we find ourselves intellectually compelled to consider the other end. We are dealing not with two different things but with two poles of the same thing" (LW 7, 173).[8]

In Chapter 10 and in the first section of Chapter 15 Dewey focused on the first part of the speculative identity claim, the one concerning the interdependent nature of our concepts. His goal is to show that our moral judgments about an agent depend on our judgments about what they do and bring about in the world over time, their conduct, and that our judgments about their conduct depend on placing it within the context of an ascribed character. On the one hand, Dewey argues that the "self reveals its nature in what it chooses. In consequence a moral judgment upon an act is also a judgment upon the character or selfhood of the one doing the act" (LW 7, 287). But one can't glean the character of an agent right away, for character can only be ascertained by taking note of what an agent does over time in a series of acts. This is because, as Dewey notes, different acts express a person's character to varying degrees. At certain moments, we "are not ourselves," and do things that are "out of character." We can only formulate a baseline to judge whether an act is *characteristic* of the agent, or not, in the context of that agent's prior acts.

> *This* act is only one of a multitude of acts. If we confine ourselves to the consequences of this one act we shall come out with a poor reckoning. Disposition is habitual, persistent. It shows itself therefore in many acts and in many consequences. Only as we keep a running account, can we judge disposition, disentangling its tendency from the accidental accompaniments.
>
> (MW 14, 34–35)

But while we must keep a running account of an agent's acts to ascertain their character, we must, on the other hand, develop a conception of their character to interpret and evaluate these very acts. For it is only by placing an act in the context of an ascribed character that we are able to understand how it coheres with that agent's other actions. Generally the acts of an agent are not comprised of a "succession of disconnected acts," rather "each thing done carries forward an underlying tendency and intent" (LW 7, 168). But how can we discern this underlying tendency, which binds an agent's acts together in an intelligible fashion? The answer is given by "rendering explicit the allusions which have been made to disposition and character" (LW 7, 170). Expanding on the point, Dewey says: "Continuity, consistency, throughout a series of acts is the expression of the enduring unity of attitudes and habits. Deeds hang together because they proceed from a single and stable self" (LW 7, 172).

We are here in a circle in which we evaluate an agent's actions in light of their character, and we evaluate their character in light of their conduct. In this way the concepts of "character and conduct are strictly correlative" (LW 7, 172). What one *is* and what one *does* are not two things but two poles of the same thing. But if this is true then, Dewey argues, the main moral positions found in late modernity, Kantian deontology and utilitarianism are damagingly one-sided. While Kant thinks that only inner motives have moral worth, and so that the "self, apart from what it does, is the supreme and exclusive moral end" (LW 7, 285), the utilitarian thinks that moral worth can only be ascribed to actions and their consequences in the world. But if the only way to make sense of the moral meaning of conduct is by reference to character, and vice versa, then ascribing moral worth exclusively to one or the other does not make sense. For Dewey, the utilitarian is right that the moral worth of an action involves its consequences and bearings in the world, but they overlook the key point that the most important of these consequences will be its "making a difference in the *self*, as determining what one will *be*" (LW 7, 274). Indeed, for Dewey an act can be counted as moral only if, through a kind of feedback loop, its consequences change the nature of the self who performs the act. Dewey's theory therefore

> gives both self and consequences indispensible roles...[N]either one can be made to be merely a means to the other. There is a circular arrangement. The self is not a *mere* means to producing consequences because the consequences, when of a moral kind, enter into the formation of the self and the self enters into them. Similarly, conduct and consequences are important, but instead of being separate from the self they form, reveal, and test the self.
>
> (LW 7, 286)

It is because of this circle that at whatever end we begin, self or act, character or conduct, we "find ourselves compelled to consider the other end."

Habit, Interest, and Motivation

In Section 2 of Chapter 15 Dewey focuses on the second part of the speculative identity claim, on the process by which self and act reciprocally constitute each other's being. This reciprocal constitution is based in his theory of *habits* and *interests*, which are the ultimate ground for the identity of the self and its acts.

Let us start by considering how action constitutes the self who acts. The actions that a self performs not only reveal their character, they constitute it in the sense that the "attainment of consequences reacts to form the self" (LW 7, 287). It does so because one of the consequences of these actions is to confirm or weaken certain of one's habits and dispositions.

> [O]ur actions not only lead up to other actions which follow as their effects but they also leave an enduring impress on the one who performs them, strengthening and weakening permanent tendencies to act. This fact is familiar to us in the existence of *habit*.
>
> (LW 7, 170)

In performing certain acts we reinforce the susceptibilities that make us the type of person who performs those very acts. One's character is comprised of habits, so much so that Dewey says in *Human Nature and Conduct* that they "constitute the self" (MW 14, 21). This would be a nonsensical thought if we considered habits to be simply the susceptibility to repeat prior actions. But Dewey's conception of habit is far richer than this:

> [W]e are given to thinking of a habit as simply a recurrent mode of action, like smoking or swearing...But habit reaches even more

> significantly down into the very structure of the self; it signifies a building up and solidifying of certain desires; and increasing sensitiveness and responsiveness to certain stimuli, a confirmed or an impaired capacity to attend to and think about certain things... And this aspect of habit is much more important than that which is suggested merely by the tendency to repeated outer action, for the significance of the latter lies in the permanence of the personal disposition which is the real cause of the outer acts and of their resemblance to one another.
>
> (LW 7, 171)

Conversely, how does the self constitute their actions? Dewey approaches this question through a consideration of motivation, a consideration of the factor that brings about an action. Dewey distinguishes his view of motivation from two others, one in which action is motivated by external environmental stimuli and one where it is motivated by inner states, beliefs and desires. The first view, which is adopted by philosophers who take a physiological approach to human behavior, including the reflex-arc theorist, is incorrect because it views human selves as passive, as having to be moved from the outside, whereas in fact humans as creatures of impulse and habit are intrinsically active. The second view, which is the view of those who take a psychological view of human behavior, argues that certain inner mental states, beliefs and desires, motivate us to act insofar as they cause distinct bodily movements. This view, standard in much contemporary philosophy of action, is incorrect because it "separate[s] a unified deed into two disjointed parts, an inner called motive and an outer called act" (MW 14, 33). Dewey, as we shall see, argues that motives are not to be found in "states that happen to exist in consciousness," in "personal feeling," but rather in one's "set disposition" (LW 7, 174), which can only be ascertained, even by the acting agent, through its actualization in action.

To understand Dewey's view we must see that for him the self is not *merely* a habit-self. When our habits come into conflict because it is unclear which act will best cope with the situation, reflection and deliberation arise in which we consciously weigh the value of different courses of action by imaginatively rehearsing them and their potential consequences. In this situation action does not flow automatically from our habits but from deliberation and explicit choice. We should not think of the capacity for deliberation and choice as detached from our habits. As Dewey argues in Chapter 14 "Moral Judgment and Knowledge," our pre-standing habits, dispositions, and bodily skills structure the immediate intuition or perception of salience and value that make certain actions seem eligible and others not. But while intuition is immediate the habits upon which they are based are not. This is because the "results of prior experience, including previous conscious thinking, get taken up into direct habits, and express themselves in direct appraisals of value." So while "most of our moral judgments are intuitive" they are nonetheless "the result of past experience funded into direct outlook upon the scene of life" (LW 7, 266). But while deliberation is guided by intuition that is funded by habits, deliberation itself, in turn, informs the habits that fund future intuition. For once a decision is made about what action to take, this choice leaves an enduring impression on our habits, predisposing us to act in certain ways in the future. In other words, in choosing a course of action we are also choosing our future self.

> Now every such choice sustains a double relation to the self. It reveals the existing self and forms the future self. That which is chosen is that which is found congenial to the desires and habits of the self as it already exists.... The resulting choice also shapes the self, making it, in some degree, a new self.... In committing oneself to a particular course, a person gives a lasting set to his own being. Consequently, it is proper to say that in choosing this object rather than that, one is in reality choosing what kind of person or self one is going to be.
>
> (LW 7, 287)

This picture, in which the self is formed through feedback relations between habit, intuition, and the reflective use of reason, puts the psychological view of motivation into doubt because according to it we are not motivated to act by given states of ourselves, our inner desires, but by propensities or dispositions that are *informed by what has been learned from the outcomes and consequences of past experiences and actions.* Dewey does not deny that desires must be part of the story about motivation, but, as we are about to see, they are not self-standing internal mental states that cause action.

Dewey's thesis is that the term "motive" can mean either (1) "those *interests* which form the core of the self and supply the principles by which conduct is to be understood," or (2) "the *objects*, whether perceived or thought of, which effect an alteration in the direction of activity" (LW 7, 290). The first way of characterizing motives could be misleading because of Dewey's use of the term "principle." But in *Human Nature and Conduct* Dewey says that the "word 'principle' is a eulogistic cover for the fact of *tendency*" (MW 14, 37). In other words, when we try to understand what motivates the conduct of an agent, what their "principles" are, what we are really trying to do is to understand the tendencies of their character, what they are *predisposed* to do. So by interest Dewey means far more than what we standardly mean by it, for instance, when we say that a tax break is in our interest. Rather, for Dewey, any

> concrete case of the union of the self in action with an object and end is called an interest ... An interest is, in short, the dominant direction of activity, and in this activity desire is united with an object to be furthered in a decisive choice.
>
> (LW 7, 290)[9]

What does it mean to say that there is a union of self and object in action? If one is interested in something, for example, music, one will have the tendency to pursue opportunities to perform, listen, or discuss music. These objects are internal to this interest. If one does not pursue these objects, if this interest is not "manifested in action," then "it is unreal" (LW 7, 291). The interest is "objective" we could say because it involves actualizations of tendencies to act toward certain objects. But the interest is also "subjective" insofar as these objects would not be objects of one's interest were one indifferent to them, if one did not *care* about them. For one to have an interest in an object "impulse and desire" must therefore be "enlisted" (LW 7, 290). But impulse and desire should not be thought of as discrete psychological states that push us to act. Rather, our caring for objects, their mattering to us, is embedded in our affective and bodily way of responding to an object or class of objects, embedded in our bodily habits.

If interests account for motivation, and if interests are habitual predispositions, embodied in action, toward certain objects, then a motive

> is not then a drive *to* action, or something which moves *to* doing something. It *is* the movement of the self as a whole, a movement in which desire is integrated with an object so completely as to be chosen as a compelling end.
>
> (LW 7, 291)

In other words, to be motivated is not to be driven to act by an inner psychological state, a want or desire, rather it is to be in a state of *motivatedness* in which desire is already, through habit, integrated with an object. As Dewey says:

> The hungry person seeks food. We may say, if we please, that he is moved by hunger. But in fact hunger is only a name for the tendency to move toward the appropriation of food. To create an entity out of this active relation of the self to objects, and then to treat this abstraction as if it were the cause of seeking food is sheer confusion. The case is no different when we say that a man is moved by kindness, or mercy, or cruelty, or malice. These things are not independent powers which stir to action. They are designations of the kind of active union or integration which exists between the self and a

> class of objects. It is the man himself in his very self who is malicious or kindly, and these adjectives signify that the self is so constituted as to act in certain ways towards certain objects. Benevolence or cruelty is not something which a man *has* ... it is something which he *is*; and since his being is active, these qualities are *modes of activity*, not forces which produce action.
>
> (LW 7, 291)

Because there is an active union of subject and object in an interest we can now understand why Dewey says that objects themselves can directly motivate us to act. Objects can directly motivate us to act because one has become the type of self who directly responds to such objects through the prior cultivation of interests. Dewey illustrates: "The avaricious man is stirred to action by objects which mean nothing to a generous person, a frank and open character is moved by objects which would only repel a person of a sly and crafty disposition" (LW 7, 291). So while we can say that the objects that move one to act determine our motivations, and so that the "inner" is determined by the "outer," we can also say that the "inner" determines the outer insofar as we take this object and perform this act because of the kind of self that we have become.

Egoism, Altruism, and the Social Interest

Getting Dewey's account of motivation right allows us to get the question of *moral motivation* right. Traditionally the issue of moral motivation has been considered as part of the debate between egoism and altruism, between those who argue that selves are only motivated by their own advantage and those who argue that selves are also motivated by benevolence, and that this is the only morally justifiable motive for action. The debate is misconceived, according to Dewey, because it is based on the assumption that self-love and altruism are "original ingredients in our psychological make-up," when in fact they are "acquired dispositions" (LW 7, 293). Here Dewey follows James who argues that a child's impulses are neither egoistic nor altruistic but "are rather direct responses to situations" (LW 7, 293). When a child is considered selfish, for example, when it does not want to share a toy with another child, it is *the toy* itself that is the object of their attitudes rather than themselves. This kind of response does not yet have moral quality because the child does not yet have its own good as part of the *conscious aim* of their act. But while the child's action is not motivated by conscious self-regard, the *result* of the action, which can be noted by an adult, does show disregard for the valid claims of other children. Based on this the adult will approve or disapprove of the child's behavior and will respond to the child in such a way as to reinforce proper behavior. In this way

> the child gradually becomes conscious of himself and of others as beings who are affected for good or evil, benefit and detriment, by his acts. Conscious reference to one's own advantage and the good of others may then become definitely a part of the *aim* of an act.
> (LW 7, 294)

But the fact that conscious regard for self or other is acquired does not undermine the egoist's main argument, namely, that all "action is selfish because it manifests an interest, since every interest involves the self" (LW 7, 295). Even if one's interests are acquired, the egoist argues, in acting out of them one is still doing what one wants, and so is acting selfishly. Though he does not cite him, Dewey's response to this argument is in essence Butler's. Butler says:

> If, because every particular affection is a man's own, and the pleasure arising from its gratification his own pleasure...such particular affection must be called self-love; [then] according to this way of speaking, no creature whatever can possibly act but merely from self-love...But...this is not the language of mankind: or if it were, we should want words to express the difference between the principle of an action, proceeding from cool consideration that it will be to my own advantage; and an action, suppose of revenge or of friendship, by which a man runs upon certain ruin, to do evil or good to another. It is manifest the principles of these actions are totally different, and so want different words to be distinguished by.
> (Butler 1990, 536–537)

The point is that even if we concede that all actions are egoistic in the sense that they are an expression of what the self wants to do we still need to make a distinction between actions that take as their object one's own advantage and actions that are undertaken on behalf of others for their own sake.

Dewey agrees with this, but puts the point in the language of interests. For Dewey the idea that all action "springs from and affects a self," and therefore is self-interested, is trivially true, for "interest defines the self" (LW 7, 295). The difference between selfish and unselfish action is not that the former is interested while the latter is not. Those acting to advance the welfare of others are not "uninterested." Those who act benevolently have a deep and abiding stake in what they do. If they did not then their action would be "apathetic, dull, routine, easily discouraged" (LW 7, 296). The difference between those who act selfishly and those who act unselfishly lies rather in the quality of the interests they both have and the "kind of self that is being furthered and formed" (LW 7, 295) by those interests:

> Whether one obtains satisfaction by assisting friends or by beating competitors at whatever cost, the interest of the self is involved. The notion that therefore all acts are equally 'selfish' is absurd. For 'self' does not have the same significance in the different cases; there is always a self involved but the different selves have different values. A self changes its structure and value according to the kind of object it desires and seeks; according, that is, to the different kind of objects in which active interest is taken.
>
> (LW 7, 295–296)

The question of whether action is selfish or unselfish concerns whether the objects of one's interests are wide, inclusive, and enduring, having to do with the good of those that comprise the myriad and overlapping groups of which one is a part (including oneself), or narrow, exclusive, and short-lived, having to do just with oneself. Since self and act are speculatively identical breadth of interest entails a broad self, while narrowness of interest entails a self that is cut off from the wealth of goods that are necessary for their well-being. We shall come back to this point below.

Those who think that acting out of one's interest is *equivalent* to acting selfishly overlook the identity of the self and its acts. Specifically, they suppose that there is a difference between self and the object or ends of action, so that the object is always only a *means* to the self's advantage, that being the self's true end. But while the object of one's action can of course be a mere means to one's advantage, *even in that case* the object enters into the formation of the self who acts. "To use a somewhat mechanical analogy, bricks are means to building a house, but they are not *mere* means because they finally *compose* a part of the house itself" (LW 7, 286). Just as the bricks are not *external* means to the building of the house but *constituents* of it, the objects of our action are not just external means to our advantage but constituents of the character of the one who pursues those objects. This applies equally to those who act selfishly and those who do not. It is the quality of the objects internal to one's interests, and the kind of self that they help to constitute, which is the central moral issue.

But if the distinction between egoism and altruism ultimately depends on the kind of self that is constituted by their interests, the distinction, Dewey argues, is itself secondary. It is secondary because the self's most basic interest, and hence most basic object, concerns the groups to which it belongs, which cuts across the divide between self and other. As Dewey puts it, "regard for self and regard for others are both of them secondary phases of a more normal and complete interest: regard for the welfare and integrity of the social groups of which we form a part" (LW 7, 299).[10]

Dewey begins his justification of this point by noting that the distinction between egoism and altruism is a product of the individualism found in the early and modern period, which posits that isolated selves are primary and natural while social arrangements are "secondary and artificial" (LW 7, 299). On this view, self and other regarding attitudes are seen as *given* features of the self, features to be managed one way or another by society. For Dewey, in contrast, "selfhood is not something that exists apart from association and intercourse. The relationships which are produced by the fact that interests are formed in this social environment are far more important than are the adjustments of isolated selves" (LW 7, 298–299). Dewey accepts the Meadian point that one's very character, one's habits and interests, is bound up with the attitudes that others have toward us.[11] When one initially comes to take one's own or another's good as part of the conscious aim of one's acts, one therefore does so in a context where one already *identifies* with the interests and ends of the social groups with which one is associated. Dewey, of course, recognizes that people often use others as means to their ends and that people develop selfish characters. But even in these cases, the selfish person can draw upon a "memory" of their social interest in, and identification with, the group of which they are (or were) a part.

For Dewey, the self's interest in the welfare of the social groups of which they are a part is more basic than what philosophers call egoism or altruism. Egoism and altruism are not for Dewey original powers that motivate one to act, rather they are tools that we develop to help us "*think* of objects and consequences that would otherwise escape notice" (LW 7, 300). It is these "objects and consequences" that "constitute the *interests* that are the proper motive of action. Their stuff and material are composed of the relations which men actually sustain to one another in concrete affairs" (LW 7, 300). In other words, one is motivated to act by one's interests, and the content of those interests is developed through relations to others in the social groups to which one belongs.

For instance, take the family. The family is

> an enduring form of association in which the members of the group stand from the beginning in relations to one another, and in which each member gets direction for his conduct by thinking of the whole group and his place in it, rather than by an adjustment of egoism and altruism.
>
> (LW 7, 299)

This is perhaps an overly idealized image of the family. It sometimes happens, for good or bad reasons, that a family member becomes indifferent to the claims of the other members of the family. But we would not say, as a matter of descriptive fact, that this is the norm. What is more common is that family members are interested in the good of the family, which is at the same time an interest in their own good. Conscious regard for another's good is possible because one is already interested in the good of one's social group, and conscious regard for one's own good depends on the fact that one oneself is a member of the group for which one is concerned.[12] Here we have another kind of speculative identity: in being interested in the welfare of the group one is interested in one's own welfare, and in being interested in one's own welfare one is interested in the welfare of the group.

It is important to note that when Dewey talks about social groups other than the family there is a shift in his presentation. For instance, right after discussing the family Dewey says this about industry and business:

> From the moral standpoint, the test of an industry is whether it serves the community as a whole, satisfying its needs effectively and fairly, while also providing the means of livelihood and personal development to the individuals who carry it on...In a justly organized social order, the very relations which persons bear to one another demand of the one carrying on a line of business the kind of conduct which meets the needs of others, while they also enable him to express and fulfill the capacities of his own being. Service, in other words, would be reciprocal and cooperative in their effect.
>
> (LW 7, 299)

There are two shifts here. The first concerns the fact that the family is a different kind of group than that of the business or industrial enterprise. While the family directly identifies the welfare of self and that of the group, the business or industrial enterprise mediates the relationship between self and social groups beyond the enterprise. The second shift concerns the fact that Dewey's account of the family is a *description* of how agents, from their own point of view, do in fact identify their good with the good of the group of which they are a part, while the account of industry and business is *prescriptive*, a story about how industry and business *would* mediate the reciprocal good of self and social group in a justly organized social order. Is this move from description to prescription evidence of confusion? I don't think so.

To explain why, we have to briefly discuss Dewey's account of ideals. Dewey was always wary of abstract moral ideals "that set up vast and vague aims in separation from a basis and leverage in existing conditions" (LW 7, 344). To posit just social arrangements that lack purchase in social reality is to posit ends that are not connected to possible means. Dewey, in contrast, argues that ideals must have purchased in social reality. An ideal is a feature of social reality that is found to be good, and which is projected by the imagination to its limit. Our conception of how things ought to be therefore takes its lead from certain of the way things are, but we use this conception as a tool to go beyond the way things currently are. What is important for our purposes is that interest in the social group of which one is a part is an existing feature of self-identity and social reality. It is not an ideal set up out of heads. It is *found* in the family and in the other relational complexes that comprise the social environment, but is not *fully actualized* in all of these complexes. As such, it is an ideal that *ought* to be more fully actualized, for example, in industry and business. What ought to be actualized here is nothing less than what Dewey famously calls the *democratic ideal*:

> From the ethical point of view...it is not too much to say that the democratic ideal poses, rather than solves, the great problem: How to harmonize the development of each individual with the maintenance of a social state in which the activities of one will contribute to the good of all the others. It expresses a postulate in the sense of a demand to be realized: That each individual shall have the opportunity for release, expression, fulfillment, of his distinctive capacities, and that the outcome shall further the establishment of a fund of shared values. Like every true ideal, it signifies something to be done rather than something already given, something ready made.
>
> (LW 7, 350)

Dewey does not think that he can give a freestanding philosophical account of the goodness of the democratic ideal, an account that grounds it on non-question begging premises. So he does not think that we can *directly* answer the second question that we posed in the introduction, the question of why each of us should be interested in the intrinsic good of those who comprise the groups of which we are a part. What we can do, and what Dewey does do in the 1932 *Ethics*, is show, through a kind of *denotative* method, that selves in fact take their good to be bound up with the good of the groups of which they are a part, and so *already accept* the goodness of the democratic ideal.

This is one of the main goals of the three historical chapters of the 1932 *Ethics*, for all three chapters—on the good, the right, and virtue, respectively—demonstrate that the most advanced moral theories, which are based on features of everyday moral experience, point to the goodness of the democratic ideal. While these chapters are meant to give a genealogy of the three moral factors, and so have a pluralistic function within the text, they also have a unifying function insofar as they are meant to show that the three main moral traditions in the Western tradition are working out the same insight: that the good of the self depends on the good of the selves who comprise the groups of which they are a part, and that the good of these groups depends on the good of the selves of which they are comprised. The chapter on the good shows us that the true rather than the specious good involves the cultivation of wide rather than narrow interests, interests that depend on our relations to others; the chapter on the right shows us that the ultimate effect of the rightful claims of others on us is to "lead the individual to broaden his conception of the good; they operate to induce the individual to feel that nothing is good for himself that is not also a good for others" (LW 7, 225); and the chapter on virtue shows us that the general criterion for the moral worth of an action concerns its effects on the general welfare, which includes one's own welfare. While the democratic ideal poses rather than solves the problem of how to harmonize the good of the self with that of others, the problem is posed in a moral context where the ideal already has purchase. Because this is so, the text gives us a pragmatic justification to act experimentally so as to make this ideal more fully actual.

Freedom as Growth

But the question naturally arises: what *is* good, for either self or other? The answer given in Chapter 15 is *growth*. But if growth is the good then the first question we asked in the introduction comes back, namely, whether this idea is compatible with the pragmatic pluralism of the 1932 *Ethics*. But before answering this question I must lay out Dewey's account of growth, which in the *Ethics* is part of an account of responsibility and freedom.

Very often it is said by philosophers that to hold an agent responsible for an action requires that the agent could have done otherwise than they in fact did. To make sense of responsibility we need an account of freedom of the will in which the agent is seen as having the unmotivated power of choosing between different options. What Dewey argues is that we get a different account of freedom if see responsibility as prospective rather than retrospective. We don't need an account of how an agent could have done otherwise in the past in order to make sense of our holding them responsible in the present because the point of holding them responsible is to *modify their future behavior*.

> A man might have 'acted otherwise than he did act' *if* he had been a different kind of person, and the point in holding him liable for what he did do (and for being the kind of person he was in doing it) is that he may *become* a different kind of self and henceforth choose different sorts of ends.
>
> (LW 7, 305)

Dewey points to the fact that we hold young children responsible for their behavior even though we don't assume that they have acted intentionally. We do so, so that

> *in the future* he may take into account bearings and consequences which he has failed to consider in what he *has* done. Here is where the human agent differs from a stone and inanimate thing, indeed from animals lower in the scale.
>
> (LW 7, 303)

We hold the child responsible because they can *learn*, and can therefore

> modify and—to some extent—remake his prior self... With every increase of capacity to learn, there develops a larger degree of accountability. The fact that he did not deliberate before the performance of an act which brought injury to others, that he did not mean or intend the act, is of no significance, save as it may throw light upon the kind of response by others which will render him more likely to deliberate next time he acts under similar circumstances. The fact that each act tends to *form*, through habit, a self which will perform a certain kind of act, is the foundation, theoretically and practically, of responsibility.
>
> (LW 7, 304)

What account of freedom follows from this?[13] Just as the ability to do otherwise is necessary for a retrospective account of responsibility, the capacity to learn, grow, and modify character is necessary for a prospective account. This is the key to Dewey's account of freedom. One has the potential for freedom because one has the capacity for growth. One has "actual" or "positive freedom" when one becomes "aware of possibilities of development" and is "actively concerned to keep the avenues of growth open." Humans *are* continually remaking themselves through action, whether they wish it or not. But it is only to the extent that "we fight against induration and fixity, and thereby realize the possibilities of recreation of ourselves, [that] we are actually free" (LW 7, 306).

In Chapter 15 Dewey puts the point in a way that makes explicit reference to the view of the self found in the ethics of self-realization.

> Practically all moralists have made much of a distinction between a lower and higher self, speaking of the carnal and spiritual, the animal and the truly human, the sensuous and the rational, selves which exist side by side and which war with one another.
>
> (LW 7, 307)

Dewey too posits a lower and a higher self. But he does not think that the distinction between the two is fixed or static. The lower self is not the animal self, but simply the self that is resting on its laurels, content with the actions facilitated by their pre-existing habits, while the higher self is not an unattainably unified and infinite self, but simply a self that is attempting to grow. We are free when we consciously attempt to move past our "static self," the self of habits already formed, and become a "dynamic self"—a growing, enlarging, and liberated self that "goes forth to meet new demands and occasions, and readapts and remakes itself in the process" (LW 7, 307). When one takes the step from static to dynamic self one "enters into an experience of freedom" (LW 7, 308).

Again making explicit reference to the ethics of self-realization, Dewey argues that this experience of freedom in growth has social conditions of possibility:

> The kind of self which is formed through action which is faithful to relations with others will be a fuller and broader self than one which is cultivated in isolation from or in opposition to the purposes and needs of others. In contrast, the kind of self which results from generous breadth of interest may be said alone to constitute a development and fulfillment of self, while the other way of life stunts and starves selfhood by cutting it off from the connections necessary to its growth.
>
> (LW 7, 302)

For example, to discover and to develop my capacity to enjoy and play music, capacities that through cultivation become interests, I must open myself to relations with others, to musical peers, role models, mentors, teachers, etc. To cut oneself off from these relations is to cut oneself from this process of discovery and potential growth. Furthermore, for my interest to be as rich as it can be, I can't let my musical interests stunt other of my potential interests, for example, painting. While excellence in a practice like music requires a kind of single mindedness, one's capacities to appreciate and play music can only be enhanced by an interest in an art like painting, which itself requires being open to the social relations that enable that interest. To have a varied yet integrated self, one must let one's interests, and the associations, relations, and groups that foster those interests communicate and cross-pollinate.

But as I mentioned in the introduction, Dewey spotted a problem with the way that the ethics of self-realization articulates this point, for could it not be the case that one is interested in social relations only to the extent that they are a means to one's own end, one's fullness of self or self-realization? Here, the problem of egoism comes back. Dewey addresses this problem in two ways.

First, as we saw above, Dewey develops the theory of social interest in which selves are shown, prior to their conscious regard for self or other, to already have non-instrumental and constitutive relations to others who comprise their groups. Second, and more importantly in this context, Dewey argues that *growth is not an end at which we can aim*, and so one's relations to others cannot be a mere means to *this* end. This point is not obvious because Dewey says: "We set up this and that end to be reached, but *the* end is growth itself" (LW 7, 306). But we must clarify what this means.

Growth is not an end that is external to the action that is a mere means to it. Rather, growth is something that happens *in* acting. But nor is growth what Dewey calls an end-in-view, which from the agent's point of view is a foreseen consequence of action that is consciously adopted, and which, looking back, is an internal pivot point within a larger course of conduct. Growth cannot be an end-in-view because to make growth "a conscious aim might and probably would prevent full attention to those very relationships which bring about a wider view of the self" (LW 7, 302). In other words, for a self to make growth a conscious aim will lead to the kind of narrowing of interests that puts genuine growth out of reach. To be genuinely interested in the welfare of others, for instance, requires developing habits in which certain acts flow *directly* from the needs of others. So if one has the right habits then one will not act in order to grow but to meet the needs of the other. But then what sort of end can growth be?

Growth is "the outcome and limit of right action" (302), meaning that it is the *by-product* of a course of action that is done well or excellently, whether for its own sake or not. "It is," Dewey says, "in the *quality* of becoming that virtue resides" (LW 7 306). The virtue or excellence of a course of action depends on the *way* we act toward ends, whatever ends we happen to have. It depends on whether action displays the kind of flexibility—between habit and intelligence, means and ends—that facilitates the movement from the static to dynamic self. On the one hand, an excellent or virtuous course of action is one which there is an open and ongoing feedback loop between habit and reflection—where our habits become more varied, flexible, and meaningful through incorporating what has been learned through past reflective problem-solving, and where our reflective problem-solving activity is more flexible and creative through being funded by these enriched habits. And it is, on the other hand, one in which there is a reciprocity between means and ends, where the specification of the end of our action is continually revised in light of changing conditions and means of realization, and where the means to our end are constituents of the end rather than merely instrumental to it. Because of the speculative identity of self and act, a course of action that has these characteristics leads to the growth of the self who performs them, even though it is not undertaken for the sake of growth. It is rather done for the sake of the ends internal to the interests that motivate the course of action in the first place.

In light of this, let us now come back to Honneth's claim that there is an unresolved conflict in Dewey's moral theory. Honneth's argument is that Dewey's concept of growth as *the* end of human action is inconsistent with the idea, found in reflective morality, that we can only be concerned with the plural procedures that we use to solve moral problems, procedures reflected on by the moral frameworks centered on the three moral factors, the good, the right, and virtue. Reflective morality is concerned with understanding, in a more general and systematic way, the different factors that go into deliberation and moral decision-making given a particular context—not with identifying the final end toward which such deliberation and decision-making ought to be aimed. Given the collapse of the notion that there is an objective hierarchy of value, Dewey does not think it possible for moral philosophy to identify such an end (and the ends naturally subsidiary to that end); rather, moral philosophy is a tool to help first-order agents identify the good, or the right, or the virtuous thing to do in a particular situation. But, instead of sticking to this insight, Dewey, Honneth argues, "withdraws to the premises of a naturalist teleology, which are incompatible with the intentions of his proceduralism" (Honneth 1998, 704). In other words, he withdraws to the view that regardless of the moral framework one calls upon to cope with a moral problem, moral action in fact has a single end, the growth of the self who acts.

But we must make a distinction between growth as *the good* and *what it is good to do*, which is determined by reasoning and moral perception utilizing the framework of the good, just as what it is right to do, or virtuous to do, is determined by reasoning and moral perception utilizing those frameworks. The concept of growth concerns *how* one ought to comport oneself, not *what* one ought to do in being so comported. What one ought to do can only be determined by *acting agents* utilizing these frameworks as tools to solve particular problems in particular situations. A course of action that is genuinely good to do, or right to do, or virtuous to do, will be conducive to growth, but this course does not *aim* at growth as its end but rather at the ends internal to one's interests. So while it is true that growth as the good is *brought about* by a course of good, right, or virtuous action, it is not the *telos* of action, much less the teleological principle to which the other moral factors are reducible. Here the pluralism of the three moral factors is maintained.[14]

It is true that growth can function as a kind of second-order teleological principle in the sense that we as first-order agents can come to grasp the importance of growth, and accordingly set our "thought and desire upon the *process* of evolution instead of upon some ulterior goal" (LW 7, 306). This, Dewey argues, will allow selves to "find a new freedom and happiness" (LW 7, 306). But setting our thought and desire on the process by which we grow still does not determine *what*, in a given situation, we should do. This question, and the particular framework of moral perception and reasoning used to address it, can only be answered contextually in reference to a particular situation. But whether the cycle of perception, reasoning, and action is flexible and conducive to the production of the dynamic self, or mechanical and conducive to the reproduction of the static self, is not determined by these frameworks, it is rather determined by whether the good of growth is present—a good that Dewey, throughout his long career, never rejected.

Notes

1 I would like to thank all of the members of the workshop on "Rethinking Dewey's Ethics." I single out Roberto Frega for special thanks, as he gave me detailed and extremely helpful comments on this paper.
2 For instance (see Welchman 1995).
3 For Dewey's claim that Green's view is neo-Kantian (see EW 3, 159; EW 4, 53; EW 5, 25n3).
4 For much more on the interrelation of the three moral factors, see Frega this volume.
5 See Honneth (1998). While many other commentators have noted the importance of growth, and it's being in potential tension with Dewey's pragmatic pluralism, Honneth's paper is unique in focusing solely on the 1932 *Ethics*.
6 In his book *Pragmatism and Political Theory*, Festenstein argues that Dewey never relinquished the idea that growth is a kind of ultimate good for the self. But Festenstein also argues that the 1932 *Ethics* is not pluralist. While Festenstein accepts that Dewey did advance moral pluralism in his 1930 paper "Three Independent Factors in Morals," he interprets Dewey as retreating from this view in the *Ethics*. (See Festenstein 1997, 205–206.) I agree with Festenstein that Dewey never relinquished the concept of growth. But I disagree with the claim that Dewey retreated from the moral pluralism espoused in "Three Independent Factors in Morals." Rather, I argue that Dewey in the 1932 *Ethics* tries to find a way to hold onto both of these doctrines.
7 Dewey made this point in different ways throughout his career. For example, in *Outlines of a Critical Theory of Ethics* (1891) Dewey says: "Character and conduct are, morally, the same thing, looked at first inwardly and then outwardly. Character, except as manifest in conduct, is a barren ideality...conduct is merely mere outward formalism excepting as its manifests character" (EW 3, 246); in "Self-Realization as the Moral Ideal" (1893) Dewey argues that we should see the "self as always a concrete *specific* activity" and that there is an "identity of self and realization" (EW 4, 43); and in the 1908 *Ethics* Dewey claims that philosophers often make an error "in trying to split up a voluntary act which is single and entire into two unrelated parts, one termed 'inner,' the other 'outer'" (MW 5, 218).
8 In using the Hegelian term "speculative identity" I do not mean to commit myself to the idea that Dewey in his later work accepts Hegel's speculative logic. I simply mean to claim that Dewey accepts in his mature thought the idea that many phenomena are only graspable through interdependent concepts and are reciprocally co-constitutive. If one wished to call this a "practical identity" that would be fine, as long as the reciprocal movement at play here is not forgotten.
9 Dewey first developed the concept of interest in his theory of education. See his short monograph from 1895, *Interest in Relation to Training of the Will* (EW 5), as well as his 1913 *Interest and Effort in Education* (MW 7). For a far more comprehensive account of the concept of interest, see Santarelli, this volume.

10 It is important to point out that Dewey does not have the view that there is a single group, "the community" or "society in general" that stands against the individual. He rejects the very idea that there is *a* community, instead arguing that what we call the community is comprised of many groups, for example, one's family, one's peers, one's classmates, one's church, one's firm, one's professional group, one's community association, one's city, state, etc.

11 See Frega's paper in this volume for how Dewey's account of both right and virtue incorporate this thought at different levels.

12 For Dewey it is important that "there can be no effective social interest unless there is at the same time an intelligent regard for our own well-being and development" (LW 7, 300). Indeed, this interest has a kind of primacy for Dewey. For when "selfhood is taken for what it is, something existing in relationships to others and not in unreal isolation, independence of judgment, personal insight, integrity and initiative, become indispensible excellences from the social point of view" (LW 7, 300).

13 Dewey is here interested in freedom's "practical and moral sense" (LW 7, 305), not its metaphysical sense.

14 As Stéphane Madelrieux pointed out to me, there is a sense of pluralism with which the concept of growth is most definitely in tension. Dewey takes it that growth requires both the differentiation and unification of the self, a process in which their interests develop and change yet increasingly cohere. Indeed, Dewey accounts for the pathologies of the self in terms of processes that either block differentiation or forestall unification. But one could, as Madelrieux put it to me, conceive of growth "as a process of continuous diversification without the need to unify or integrate all these realms of experience in a single unified whole." Here we would have a different kind of pluralism than that found with the three moral factors—an unrestrained pluralism of the self.

References

Butler, Joseph. 1990. "Fifteen Sermons." In *Moral Philosophy from Montaigne to Kant: An Anthology*, edited by Jerome B. Schneewind. Cambridge: Cambridge University Press, 525–542.

Festenstein, Matthew. 1997. *Pragmatism and Political Theory.* Chicago, IL: University of Chicago Press.

Honneth, Axel. 1998. "Between Proceduralism and Teleology: An Unresolved Conflict in Dewey's Moral Theory." *Transactions of the Charles S. Peirce Society* 34: 689–711.

Welchman, Jennifer. 1995. *Dewey's Ethical Thought.* Ithaca, NY: Cornell University Press.

9 Democracy and the Problem of Domination

A Deweyan Perspective[1]

Justo Serrano Zamora

Overview of Chapters 16 and 17

Chapter 16 "Morals and Social Problems" and Chapter 17 "Morals and the Political Order" are the opening chapters of the third and last part of the *Ethics*, titled "The World of Action." Chapter 16 introduces readers to Dewey's social and political theory as a constitutive part of his moral theory.[2] The first section explores the transition from moral life to the world of social problems, which include political, economical, industrial, and family-related problems. While a detailed characterization of the moral import of social problems is provided in the first section of Chapter 17, Dewey points here to the specific condition concerning individuals belonging to modern societies: individual decisions have become so dependent on social conditions that questions regarding social transformations have become morally pressing. This involves the need for expanding individuals' capacity for moral judgment to include the evaluation of social questions. This contrasts with traditional societies where the moral dimension of individual lives consisted in abiding to existing norms and institutional arrangements. Taking this characterization as a point of departure, Section 2 points to a difference of schools in their approach to social problems, viz., that of the individualists and that of the collectivists. While for the former existing problems must be approached by freeing the individual from her. social bonds, for the latter collective solutions, must have primacy in seeking social reform. Both schools assume the existence of a conflict between the "individual" and the "social" that Dewey considers to be a false opposition between two abstract notions. Section 3 links social problems to the notion of social conflict, which is understood in terms of a conflict between groups as well as between social institutions and forms of thinking. This section also presents a particular form of conflict: the struggles for recognition of social groups that suffer under conditions of domination. Section 4 briefly points to the experimentalist and democratic method as the most appropriate way of dealing with social conflicts. The ideas formulated in Sections 3 and 4 will be developed in more detail in the course of the present chapter. Finally, Section 5 focuses on the difficulties generated by the historical and institutional embodiment of individualistic views in modern societies and argues for a contextualist approach, where "individualist" or "collectivist" solutions may be provided according to their consequences. Here again Dewey points to the experimentalist method from which to approach social life, in contrast to the basic normative criterion for evaluating social institutions, which is explored in detail in the next chapter.

In the first section of Chapter 17, Dewey presents a compelling argument for affirming that social conditions have a moral import—thereby making them a central object for the *Ethics*—namely, they play an essential role in the formation of our moral character and will. They do so by determining opportunities that shape our intentions and desires, by stimulating different individual powers, by defining the system of obligations towards others, as well as by influencing any of our plans of changing society. Again, our approach to the value of social conditions must be experimental, and it must use past experiences and present conditions as a source of suggestions and as a rule for action. The second section of the chapter explores the central question of the criterion we should use in order to evaluate the normative quality of "social institutions and in projecting plans of social change" (LW 7, 345). Here Dewey's notion of "growth" appears as the focal point of his normative analysis, which introduces notions such as "community," "common good," "enlargement of experience," "equality," and the "ideal of democracy" that stand in contrast to social relations of "privilege" and "inequality of power." Section 3 considers the current problems of democracy as a form of government as well as their connection to economic issues. In a nutshell, the actual problems of democracy must be met by adapting existing political institutions to current social conditions, which prominently include economic developments. Accordingly, the latter must be considered as having moral and public relevance. Section 4 explores the idea of liberty of thought and of expression which he characterizes both as the liberty to communicate knowledge and ideas as well as the freedom to inquire in order to generate (socially valuable) knowledge. These freedoms realize the democratic ideal since they are necessary for the free articulation needs and aims of individuals as well as for the enhancement of the rational quality of these needs and aims. In addition, they are considered as essential conditions for education and cultural growth. Finally, Section 5 briefly explores the phenomenon of nationalism in its ambivalent role for modern societies. On the one hand, love of one's own nation has become a necessary condition for the social integration of modern states. On the other hand, it is easily placed at the service of hostile action against other nations. Due to the persistent precariousness of existing feelings of peace, we need an "objective" organization of peace, which can be achieved only by eliminating the existing legal sanction of war or by reinforcing mediating institutions such as the League of Nations.

Introduction

Out of the many different and interesting paths that can be explored based on Chapters 16 and 17 of the *Ethics*, here I propose to focus on the idea that democracy in its social form (in contrast to its individualistic form) represents the best method of approaching social problems involving situations of economic, cultural, and political privilege or domination. Social problems, according to Dewey, must be the object of study of any moral inquiry since they provide—particularly under modern conditions—the "material" (LW 7, 342) of moral questions. For Dewey, social problems can and very often involve situations of structural inequality or, in his own terms, of an "unequal distribution of power" (LW 7, 347)[3] where the members of one social group are able to take advantage of current institutional arrangements and ways of thinking at the expense of the members of other groups. In line with Dewey's own use of the concepts, here I propose to call these kinds of situations social "privilege" or "domination."[4]

Dewey's "pro-democratic" ideas are not obvious to those contemporary critiques of democracy which emphasize the domination-reproductive effects of democratic institutions and practices. So, for example, many authors have pointed to how some forms of civil societal participation tend to overrepresent the interests and views of a mobilized middle class against the interests of less well-organized social groups that are social-structurally underprivileged (Blühdorn 2013, 2018; Nachtwey 2017). From this background, the aim of my chapter is to explore how Dewey is able to respond to the challenges posed by such a skeptical view in a way that the ideal of democracy can be saved (once again) for an emancipatory project that aims at challenging unequal distributions of power.[5] Dewey's strategy is particularly productive, since it is able to acknowledge the domination-(re)productive effects of existing democratic practices, which he links to a form of politics embodying individualistic patterns of action. In line with the distinction between old and new liberalism,[6] Dewey contrasts this "old," individualistic way of organizing democratic practices and institutions with a more "socialized" ideal, one by which the practice of democracy represents a truly social activity, one in which individuals genuinely cooperate in the identification, definition, and resolution of social problems. For him, socializing democracy represents the most adequate political and social response to the normative goal of challenging any kind of existing class or group privilege.

In contrast to other texts where Dewey develops his social and political philosophy such as *The Public and Its Problems* (1927) and the *Lectures in Social and Political Philosophy* (2015), the 1932 *Ethics* stands in a privileged position since it provides a systematic connection between the phenomenon of social domination and the reformist proposal of socializing democracy in all of its different dimensions that cannot be found anywhere else in Dewey's work. In the following sections, I will first (1) explore Dewey's theory of group privilege as it can be found in the *Ethics*. For Dewey, social problems always incarnate conflicts among concrete social instances such as social groups, institutions, and ways of thinking. At the same time, conflicts can and often involve relations of unequal power between different social groups.[7] These relations of domination have both a social-structural and an ideological dimension. Given that one of the main tasks of democracy is the identification, definition, and solution of social problems, we can redefine one of democracy's main tasks as consisting in the identification, definition, prevention, and challenging of relations of domination—a goal that, in turn, itself represents a constitutive part of the larger ideal of a democratic form of life. In a second step (2), I will present Dewey's notion of democracy as involving three different dimensions: (a) a habitualized and institutionalized but always evolving method of collective inquiry, (b) an ethical ideal of domination-free organization of social life, and (c) a particular way of promoting and organizing (unavoidable) social struggle against existing relations of domination that complements (a) in a complex way. In a third and final step (3), I will explore how two different forms of democracy—individualistic and socialized, or better: "socializing"[8]—provide two contrasting approaches to the problem of domination. In this context, I will focus on both the first and third dimensions of Dewey's notion of democracy: how should we organize collective problem-solving and social struggle such that existing relations of group-domination can be challenged and, in the best case, abolished? As I aim to show, while individualistic democracy is at the source of the generation and reproduction of relations of domination, a socializing democracy seems much better prepared for confronting them. Exploring why this is so represents a pressing task in times where the ability of democratic institutions to challenge existing inequalities and structures of domination is put into question.

Problems, Conflicts, Domination

For Dewey, modern, industrialized societies are characterized by the pivotal role played by social conflicts. This role is made explicit in the *Ethics* in at least three different senses. First of all, (a) conflicts represent the general form of what members of modern societies often identify as social problems that need to be solved. In other words, most social problems citizens identify can be articulated in terms of the existence of a tension or opposition between conflicting social instances. This conflict can be implicit or explicit for social agents, and it can concern social instances of different kinds such as "social classes or groups," "institutions," "traditions," or "ways of thinking."[9] But in Dewey's analysis, the notion of "conflict" (b) also concerns the different, incompatible ways in which people believe social problems—and this means, in turn, social conflicts themselves—should be approached. This second kind of conflict, which represents second-order conflict—i.e., a conflict concerning the way conflicts should be conceived of and resolved—can be described as the confrontation between individualistic versus collectivist approaches to the task of resolving social problems. As will be shown, at these two first levels of analysis, conflict often involves the presence of relations of domination, understood as the relation by which one group (the dominant) is able to realize—through different ways—its interests and powers or capacities at the expenses of other groups (the dominated).[10] Finally, in a third sense (c) social conflicts can take the form of open struggles against existing relations of domination on the side of oppressed groups. In this latter case, conflicts represent the open confrontation between two groups, the dominant and the dominated. Struggles are meant to lead to the emancipation from what the dominated first identify as an "unjust" situation involving lack of due recognition of the group's own interests and powers,[11] a process that also involves the struggle around the question about how existing social developments should be framed, viz., as involving unjust relations of domination.

In this first section I will explore each of the three senses of social conflict and their connection to Dewey's understanding of privilege or domination. Before examining the notion of conflict in the first sense, Dewey starts his exploration by focusing on second-order conflicts, those regarding the ways in which members of modern societies tend to approach social conflicts "concerning all phases of life, education, politics, economics, art, religion" (LW 7, 321). These two opposing approaches are "individualism" on the one side, and "collectivism," on the other.[12] The conflict regarding the best way to approach the question of "marriage" represents a good example of what Dewey has in mind:

> [t]here are those who think the maximum amount of liberty should be accorded to individuals in their sex relations; that marriage should not be a fixed institution but rather a voluntary contract, to be broken at will provided the interests of the offspring are duly protected. There are others who regard such opinions as a form of moral anarchy, entertained only because of desire for satisfaction of lawless appetites, and destructive of the basic stability of social life. With respect to property and the economic situation, the strife between the upholders of private property as sacred and those in favor of communal ownership is to well known to need more than a reference.
>
> (LW 7, 321)

For individualists, social problems must be described as affecting the freedom of the individual—understood in isolation from others—and as having the dependence of individuals on social relations at their source. Therefore, social problems should be approached through individual initiative and have an individualistic solution, i.e., one that weakens the connection of individuals to their social ties so that the highest value, the good of the individual, can be preserved. For collectivists, existing social problems concern individuals in their (too weak) connection to their social relations. What is needed, according to this group, are collective solutions since merely promoting the good of atomized individuals represents an obstacle to the pursuit of the common good, which represents the highest value to be preserved. While Dewey denies both the theoretical and practical adequacies of such an alternative, he attributes its origin to a way of framing problems that is shared by both fronts of the conflict, namely, as involving the irreconcilable opposition between two abstractions: the individual and the social. For Dewey, the very opposition of the individual and the social as abstract entities represents an absurdity since

> [i]ndeed, *no* question can be reduced to the individual on the one side and the social on the other. As it is frequently pointed out, society consists of individuals, and the term 'social' designates only the fact that individuals are in fact linked together, related to one another in intimate ways. 'Society,' it is pointed out, cannot conflict with its own constituents; [...]. On the other hand, individuals cannot be opposed to the relations which they themselves maintain. (LW 7, 323)

This passage leads us directly to the first understanding of conflict, namely, as the general form social problems often take in modern societies. Hence, Dewey affirms that the common (and wrong) form of framing conflicts—namely, as involving the opposition of the individual versus the social—should be replaced by a very different approach. Hence, for the author, conflicts exist only

> between some individuals and some arrangements in social life; between groups and classes of individuals; between nations and races, between old traditions embedded in institutions and new ways of thinking and acting which spring from those few individuals who depart from and who attack what is socially accepted. (LW 7, 324)

According to this brief characterization, social conflicts take place between concrete instances and not abstract entities, which include not only groups of individuals, such as groups or social classes, but also existing traditions, institutions as well as other kinds of social arrangements and ways of thinking. Interestingly, concerning the question about the way in which we should understand these conflicts, the *Ethics* almost immediately points to the existing connection between them and the presence of relations of social domination. Hence, according to Dewey, existing conflicts between these different sorts of social instances often involve, albeit in different ways, a relation of domination between two social groups: the dominant and the dominated.[13]

Relations of domination do not only directly concern "groups and classes of individuals," but they are also often in the background of the collision or incompatibility between new and old institutions, traditions, or ways of thinking. Hence—and this is a central interpretative thesis of this chapter—conflicting institutions, traditions, and ways of thinking can always be put (and are indeed very often put) at the service of different social groups promoting their advantage against the advantage of other groups such that the permanence, substitution, or transformation of the former goes often hand in hand with the transformation of existing power constellations.

Now, in what terms should we describe this relation of domination? According to Dewey, society is organized in "social units" of many kinds.[14] Analysis shows that these social units have common traits (LW 7, 325) and that they

> [...] compete vigorously against one another. They unite in nations and the nations war with each other; workers combine in trade unions and employers in trade associations and association intensifies struggle between opposite interests.
>
> (LW 7, 324)

Competition among "opposite interests" characterizing conflict seldom takes place on equal terms. In this context, domination means a superior position of power or economic wealth which determines the groups' capacity to satisfy their collective interest at expenses of other groups in the context of social competition or conflict. The notion of "interest" is in the present context particularly important. In the context of Dewey's philosophy, interests cannot be taken as merely given and fixed (LW 7, 345, see also Santarelli's contribution to this volume). On the contrary, they are articulated not only in everyday social practices—or "habitual patterns of interaction" (Frega 2015; Testa 2017)—but also in the very social struggles in which the question about the social satisfaction of collective interests is at play (Serrano Zamora 2017). At the same time, the notion of interest cannot be separated from that of "powers," in the aforementioned sense of "capacities."[15] Hence, in Chapters 16 and 17 of the *Ethics* the interest of a social group is directly related to the social conditions that promote the realization of the group's own powers. Or negatively formulated, the suppression of interests that is present in relations of "domination," "group privilege" or "unequal competition" has as a consequence the incapacity of a dominated group to realize its own powers.[16] At the same time, the development of new powers represents a source for the emergence of new interests so that both interests and powers must be seen in a mutual relation of influence. This is the sense in which I believe Dewey's early quote can be read: "I believe that interests are the signs and symptoms of growing power, I believe that they represent dawning capacities" (EW 5, 92) In the larger context of Dewey's social and political philosophy, powers represents the normative core of any emancipatory view of society, since it is through the realization of one's potentialities that growth—a core value of Dewey's social and moral philosophy[17]—takes place.

From this brief characterization it seems justified to affirm that Dewey defends what one can call a "social-structural" understanding of domination (Mitgarden 2012), one that identifies an unequal distribution of power-positions by which groups become unequally unable to secure their interests and hence the realization of the potentialities of their members. Following Dewey, we can call this relation one of "domination" since it involves the existence of social arrangements by which one group is able to realize its interests and powers *at the expenses* of other groups. This represents the background from which we can understand the following passage, which puts particular stress on the negative effects of an "inequitable distribution of power":

> A very considerable portion of what is regarded as the inherent selfishness of mankind is the product of an inequitable distribution of power—inequitable because it shuts out some from the conditions which evoke and direct their capacities, while it produces a one-sided growth in those who have privilege.
>
> (LW 7, 347)

Here we should consider that, in contrast with other views of social-structural domination, however, a Deweyan notion includes at its base an open social ontology, according to which interests and powers are not merely given in social life, but are progressively articulated during social intercourse.[18] Furthermore, Dewey does not only characterize relations of domination in pure social-structural terms. The latter have an essential symbolic or cultural dimension. Hence, a situation of domination involves the capacity of the powerful group to identify what it takes to be its particular interests with the general interests of society (LW 7, 325, Dewey 1973, 2015). In contrast to the powerful, the members of the dominated group are often not able to articulate their own interests since they lack the symbolic and institutional resources for it. And even in those cases where they are able to articulate their interests and views in the context of social struggles,[19] these are at first dismissed and rejected by the rest of society as going against what is commonly accepted as the general interest. The capacity of the dominant group to hold a "hegemonical" position in society and the counter-hegemonical attempts and strategies of the dominated are present in many Deweyan texts and have been studied from a social-theoretical perspective.[20] More will be said about this Deweyan motive in the coming sections since the ideological dimension of domination must be included in any consideration of the workings of a democratic society: democratic institutions and practices must be able to counter-act this sort of ideological formations—that is, those promoting the identification of the interests of dominant groups with the general interests of society—if it is to contribute to social emancipation.

Up to this point we have seen that for Dewey in modern societies social problems involve conflict, and conflict often involves relations of domination between social groups. These relations may take the form of direct and unequal competition for resources in order to satisfy interests that promote the realization of a group's powers, but they can also be institutionally mediated by a conflict between old and new social arrangements, traditions, and ways of thinking. In other words, many social problems must be seen as conflicts between social instances (such as institutions or ways of thinking) which are often entangled with relations of domination between groups since they can be put at the service of some of their interests. Furthermore, in an indirect sense, we can also affirm that the conflict between individualistic and collectivist approaches to social problems we have described at the beginning is entangled with relations of domination since, by giving priority to one of both strategies of framing and implementing solutions to social problems, some groups may be able to profit from the one-sidedness involved in this dichotomy at expenses of the other one. So, for example, regarding the problem of the conduction of economic affairs, Dewey explains how an individualistic understanding of economic freedom "meant *in effect* the legally unrestrained action of those advantageously placed in the existing distribution of power, through possession of capital and ownership of the means of production" (LW 7, 334).

After these considerations, we come finally to the third sense of "social conflict" that we can identify in the *Ethics*, namely, that of social struggle. In social struggle, the dominated group, starting from a situation of implicit or explicit acceptance of the existing relation of domination, begins to develop a consciousness of *unjust* relations of oppression that goes hand in hand with the development of what Dewey calls a "sense of powers" (Dewey 2015, 23). Social struggle consists, according to Dewey's description, in a multi-faceted learning-process that involves at least two main dimensions: oppressed groups learn, first of all, to articulate their claims in social or general terms—i.e., in terms of the contribution that the serious consideration of their claims would make to the whole of society. But, second, oppressed groups also learn to innovate and enhance the quality of the practices of inquiry through which they collectively formulate alternative views of social reality that shows the "unacceptability" of the current distribution of power, becoming thereby innovators able to challenge the prevalent identification of the interests of the dominant group with those of society. Corresponding to this, struggle against domination has both an ideological and a social-structural dimensions.

As I mentioned in the introduction, this three-dimensional theory of conflict and social domination constitutes the background from which democracy must often draw its problem-solving task. Taken as a method of identification, definition, and resolution of problems as well as an intelligent form of organizing social struggle, democracy must be seen as—though not reduced to—a method to prevent, challenge, and reduce relations of domination both in their social-structural and ideological dimension. However, as we will see in the following sections, the capacity to satisfy this double task depends on the particular form—individualistic or social—in which democracy has been historically institutionalized and the particular way in which it needs to be reformed.[21]

The Three Dimensions of Democracy

In the 1932 *Ethics* Dewey provides a three-dimensional characterization of democracy that needs to be spelled out before turning to the contrast developed in the third and last part of this chapter, namely, that between the domination-effects of individualistic democracy[22] and the emancipatory effects of what I have called a "socializing" democracy.[23] Dewey characterizes democracy, first of all, (a) as "share in the duties and rights belonging to control of social affairs" which consists in the exercise of a collective, experimental, and habitualized method of identification, definition, and resolution of social problems; second, (b) as a particular way of organizing social life that makes possible and promotes social and individual growth[24]; and, finally, (c) as a particular form of institutionalizing (unavoidable) social struggle.

The two first dimensions of democracy can be identified in the way Dewey characterizes what he calls the "democratic ideal:"

> For democracy signifies, on one side, that every individual is to share in the duties and rights belonging to control of social affairs, and, on the other side, that social arrangements are to eliminate those external arrangements of status, birth, wealth, sex, etc., which restrict the opportunity of each individual for full development of himself.
> (LW 7, 349)

For Dewey, democracy represents, in a first sense, the institutionalization of an experimental method of collective inquiry into social problems that takes the form of political will-formation and decision-making—i.e., of "control of social affairs." In Chapter 16 of the *Ethics*, Dewey characterizes the experimental method in its application to social affairs in the following terms:

> The alternative method may be called experimental. It implies that reflective morality demands observation of particular situations, rather than fixed adherence to a priori principles; that free inquiry and freedom of publication and discussion must be encouraged and not merely grudgingly tolerated; that opportunity at different times and places must be given to trying different measures so that their effects may be capable of observation and of comparison with one another. It is, in short, the method of democracy, of a positive toleration with amounts to a sympathetic regard for the intelligence and personality of others, even if they hold views opposed to ours, and of scientific inquiry into facts and testing of ideas.
>
> (LW 7, 329)

The first dimension of democracy is largely explored in his famous political-theoretical work *The Public and Its Problems*. In this book, the institutionalization of the experimental method takes place through the emergence of democratic publics, which, once they come to perceive social consequences as affecting them collectively, are able to self-organize at different level as communities of inquiry and decision-making. To this extent, state-institutions must play the instrumental role of implementing collective decisions while at the same time promoting intelligent collective inquiry at different levels of the public inquiry process (LW 2, 253–258). Here it should be noted that this process of institutionalization, just as in the second and third senses democracy, does not need to be limited to what many often call the "political" sphere, that is, the sphere of state action, transnational governance, or the "sphere of democratic will-formation" (Honneth 2011). Hence, the democratic method can be institutionalized in many other spheres of life, such as in the family, in schools, and at workplaces, representing thereby a reflexive, self-governing movement that can be present at different spheres of social life (Frega 2019).

Dewey describes the second dimension of democracy more specifically in terms of an ideal to be reached, that of the full development of each individual in the context of social cooperation, an ideal that can only be achieved through the abolition of "privilege and monopolistic possession," i.e., of the relations of domination between groups:

> As an ideal, it expresses the need for progress beyond anything yet attained; for nowhere in the world are there institutions which in

> fact operate equally to secure the full development of each individual, and assure to all individuals a share in both the values they contribute and those they receive.
>
> (LW 7, 349)

A more detailed characterization of this social ideal as well as its direct connection to the question of domination as an obstacle to the "full development of individuals" can be read in the following passage of the *Ethics*:

> The tenor of this discussion is that the conception of common good, of general well-being, is a criterion which demands the full development of individuals in their distinctive individuality, not a sacrifice of them to some alleged vague larger good under the plea that it is "social." Only when individuals have initiative, independence of judgment, flexibility, fullness of experience, can they act so as to enrich the lives of others and only in this way can a truly common welfare be built up. The other side of this statement, and of the moral criterion, is that individuals are free to develop, to contribute and to share, only as social conditions break down walls of privilege and of monopolistic possession.
>
> (LW 7, 348)

Finally, even if, as we said before, the task of the democratic method is to generate the conditions for the full development of individual potentialities, Dewey is aware that, in many cases, democracy as an institutionalized method of controlling social affairs might not be sufficient—especially if we take into account that the prevailing historical form of institutionalizing democracy is particularly prone to the reproduction of social domination. In light of this, he considers, third, social conflicts in the form of social struggles initiated by dominated groups as a constitutive part of his idea of democracy. Here it should be noted, first of all, that under democratic conditions social struggles should not necessarily be less common than under other forms of political and social organization; on the contrary, democratic social life should promote the conditions for the formation of struggles on the side of those suffering under (always unavoidable) relations of domination. Second, even if social struggles very often display something that we could call a "disorganized" character, democratic social life should be able to make of struggle a collective learning-process where initial disorganization[25] is able to generate intelligent forms of inquiry which generate alternative ways of framing social reality as well as collective strategies for action. In this learning-process struggling groups should progressively adopt the experimental method of democracy as an intelligent form of collective action.[26] In fact, it is wrong to think that democracy as institutionalized experimental method for the control of social affairs and democracy as struggle signify two fully separated dimensions of democracy. On the contrary, both dimensions of democracy are so entrenched that they undergo mutual influences and learning-processes.

Let's recall Dewey's view before turning to our last two sections: For Dewey, democracy represents (1) the set of habits and institutions aiming at the identification, definition, and resolution of social problems, i.e., the control of social affairs; (2) the set of social institutions and habits promoting individual and social growth and, therefore, embodying the reduction of "privilege" and of "monopolisitic possession" (LW 7, 324), this is, of relations of domination; and, finally, (3) the intelligent organization of struggle against domination that emerges from existing privilege that cannot be countered by commonly institutionalized forms of "control" of social affairs.

In the following last two sections my aim is to focus on democracy's capacity to generate methods of collective problem-identification, -definition, and -solution (first dimension of democracy) and of organizing intelligent struggle (third dimension of democracy) as the two complementary and interacting ways of dealing with the relations of domination that stand in the way of the free and cooperative development of individuals' and groups' powers (second dimension of democracy). This is surely not the only way the relation between the three dimensions of democracy could be framed in this context. Hence, it is obvious—also for Dewey—that certain conditions regarding equality and the absence of social domination need to be met if democracy as an institutionalized method and as way of organizing social struggle is to have any existence at all. James Bohman among others has called the attention to the particularities of this problem for a deliberative-dialogical understanding of democracy.[27] In his turn, Axel Honneth has pointed to Dewey's ideal of democracy as "reflexive cooperation" to stress the mutual dependence at least of the first and second dimensions, namely, political will-formation and economic organization.[28] In the present context, focusing on the first and third dimensions of democracy in their capacity to deal with the problems that emerge in the second dimension seems to be in line with Dewey's own prioritization of "democratization" in his emancipatory idea of social reform: since the problem of domination is to be solved democratically, social reform should focus on promoting and ameliorating democratic methods and creating the conditions for intelligent social struggles. However, as it will be shown, this reformist project must first confront a difficulty concerning the institutionalization of democracy itself. Hence—advancing my conclusion—*social-structural domination and ideological formations of the kind previously described can only be confronted if existing democracy goes through a "socializing process" both as an institutionalized method and as a way of organizing social struggle.* Otherwise, in line with current criticisms, existing democracies will only either create new relations of domination or contribute to the perpetuation of existing ones (Hogan 2015). Let's see first in what sense this can be so.

Individualistic Liberal Democracy and the Reproduction of Domination

According to the division between two main understandings of liberalism and their derivative values that are at work in Dewey's text, individualistic and social, Dewey makes a distinction between two main forms of institutionalizing democracy that correspond to each of these understandings. While the first one mainly corresponds to really existing democracies and has its historical roots in the first liberation struggles from feudal society, the second one, while having roots in some forms of social life, represents for Dewey rather an ideal to be realized. Very briefly, in individualist liberal democracies[29] political practices and institutions are such that the method of solving social problems, the generation of social conditions for individual growth, and social "struggle" are understood in terms of individuals interacting with each other in atomistic or non-transactional terms: parting from an isolated process of generating individual ends and strategies, individuals *only* gather in order to aggregate pre-formed preferences, seal contracts, and come to compromises. A typical institution of individualistic democracy is the aggregation of pre-given preferences by secret voting and majority rule. In contrast, in a socializing democracy, political and social practices and institutions must be seen as institutionalizations of relations of cooperation among individuals, concerning both the process of formation and implementation of their political views and preferences (LW 7, 358, see also Honneth 2014, ch. 6.3.).

In many of his works, including the *Ethics*, Dewey is unambivalently critical about the historical institutionalization of individualistic democracy, whose insufficient understanding of freedom he takes to be the at the root of many of the problems of modern democratic societies, starting with political apathy and the extended preference for expertocratic forms of government—elements which, interestingly enough, also characterize current political developments (see, for example, Geiselberger 2017). Thus, my aim is to stress that, for Dewey, individualistic liberal democracy has a domination-productive and -reproductive effect: instead of representing a method of resolving social conflicts, individualistic democracy is unable to respond to the normative challenges posed by the transformation of institutional realities as well as to the re-distribution of power relations which go hand in hand with those transformations, and to the ideological challenges related to them.[30] On the contrary, according to the *Ethics* as well as other major social-political and epistemological works,[31] individualistic democracy contributes to the structural and cultural solidification of relations of domination in, at least, four different ways.

First of all, individualistic liberal democracy, its institutions and practices, represent a deficitary institutional form of collective inquiry since by reducing political practice and communication to a minimum – namely, the aggregation of pre-given preferences (LW 7, 358–366) – it undermines the conditions for the formation of collective intelligence necessary for challenging relations of domination. By reducing political communication, it makes particularly difficult the necessary tasks of collecting relevant facts, share experiential inputs and innovative insights that allow for an adequate identification and framing of problems and generation, implementation and testing of solutions in political inquiry. Regarding the possibilities of struggle, an individualistic understanding of democracy undermines the communicative conditions for the very collective articulation of grievances that are necessary for social struggles to come about at all (see Honneth 2007).

Second, individualistic liberal democracy understands the necessary "intelligence" for political matters as the ability of some particularly well-educated individuals instead of the ability of an inquiring collective. To this extent, it undermines epistemic cooperation at different levels of political life, thereby making particularly difficult the communication between experts (social scientists, journalists, politicians, etc.) and those who directly experience the effects of social developments (LW 2, 364–365). Democracy can easily become an expertocratic regime under individualistic conditions (LW 7, 363). In other words, under individualistic premises, knowledge concerning what needs to be done in a political community can be generated without cooperation with common citizens, it is rather the product of the intellectual work of an elite.[32] Finally (and ironically), individualism fosters social homogeneity by "discouraging" or "preventing" the free expression and articulation of individuality in political practices. This is the direct effect of the so called "majority-rule," which represents the paradigmatic rule guiding political practice under individualistic premises:

> The conception of majority rule, determined by counting of individual ballots has, to take only an example, tended to work out in the opposite direction to that which was anticipated. It rested upon a kind of quantitative individualism, but *it often operates to set up a new kind of despotism, in that ideas uncongenial to the majority are discouraged and their expression not only frowned upon but often prevented by violence.*
>
> (LW 7, 355, my italics)

In short, individualistic liberal democracy, as far as it institutionalizes political practices isolating individuals from each other, is unable to fulfill its problem-solving task—by which here I mainly focused on problems regarding domination or privilege as a method of inquiry, as form of organizing social struggle and promoting mutual learning, as a bridge between experts and the knowledge of those concerned with social problems as well as a method of articulating political options and taking collective decisions. On the contrary, by discouraging communication and collective organization, by maintaining a limited understanding of collective action and political practice, by separating experts from the knowledge of citizens, and by promoting homogeneity of thought and the imposition of a majority against a minority through an unmediated exercise of the majority rule, individualistic democracy (re-)produces domination both in its social-structural and ideological dimensions.

It is well known, however, that, while Dewey was particularly critical of existing individualistic democratic institutions—to the extent that he characterized liberal democracy as a political order that generates the conditions of its own destruction—he was convinced that the solution to the problems of democracy is more democracy, but of another kind (LW 2, 325). Democracy should, as we already mentioned, embody the ideal of the new, social liberalism. We should now explore in what sense a socialized—or better said: a "socializing"—democracy represents a very different approach to the problems of social domination as they are depicted in the *Ethics*.

The Need for Socializing Liberal Democracy

In the spirit of the *Ethics* we can define a "socializing" liberal democracy as the set of institutions, customs, and habits characterizing a whole society that embodies, to different degrees, values, and norms that can be seen as expression of social cooperation. In its political sense, members of a socializing democracy see each other as partners in a cooperative activity of problem-solving (Honneth 2014, ch. 6.3). This includes not only a purely epistemic dimension—that of the identification, definition of problems as well as the implementation and testing of hypothesis—but also the fulfillment of the very conditions for political cooperation which involve epistemic and political habits such as that of openness to other's arguments, empathy, and willingness to listen (LW 7, 329). At the same time, we should not understand a socializing democracy as a fixed institutional and practical arrangement. On the contrary, the list of possible socializing institutional and practical forms of democracy must be thought of as open-ended and discoverable by the experimental method. In a central sense, to socialize liberal democratic societies means expanding social forms of democracy to spheres of life that remained previously out of its reach (Frega 2019). Hence, as we have seen, democracy, in all of its three dimensions (as an institutionalized method of will-formation and implementation, as a way of organizing social life and as intelligent social struggle), can be expanded to other spheres of social life thereby becoming a full form of life (see also Honneth 2014). Regarding the pervasive problem of group privilege or domination, which is the main object of my analysis, a socializing democracy has at least three main advantages in contrast to its individualistic counter-model which runs parallel to the previous four critical points:

First of all, the practices of a socializing democracy promote the cooperative participation of individuals in intelligent, experimental inquiries in which more facts and experiences are gathered, more perspectives are taken into account, collective creativity is enhanced and social complexity can be better dealt with.[33] Experimental inquiry represents, if we follow Dewey's logical characterization, the method that is able to establish a fluid relation between factual and ideal content in an inclusive atmosphere (LW 12, ch. 25). The fluidification of the relation between facts and ideas has, similarly to Theodor W. Adorno's notion of non-reified thinking,[34] anti-ideological function: hence, it promotes the critical revision of well-established ideas and meanings in light of the experiences of all those affected by the consequences of social interaction—including its victims, who are able to reframe situations of domination and inequality in ways that promote collective emancipation.

As I mentioned before, a socializing democracy in the Deweyan sense is one that does not dissolve conflicting positions in a harmonious community of inquiry. On the contrary, it promotes the conditions for (intelligent) social struggle understood primarily as the resistant and opposing action of the dominated against the social phenomena (distribution of power-positions, institutional arrangements, ideologies) that perpetuate relations of domination. If we define democracy as the set of social conditions that facilitate intelligent, experimental, and democratic pursuit of collective interests on the side of the dominated, we can distinguish at least four ways in which intelligent struggle is promoted: (1) *Participation in social life*: according to the underlying expressivist premises of Dewey's social theory, collective powers cannot become fully articulated without the existence of "channels" for participation in social life[35] (Dewey 2015, 9). A socializing democracy promotes breaking barriers to social participation, thereby opening the possibility for the dominated group to come out of their state of cognitive "dumbness" (Dewey 2015, 1 bis) and develop a "sense of powers" that is at the base of their normative claims, their framing activities as well as the formation of collective identities. (2) *Cooperation and communication*: in a socializing democracy, people can meet and share their experiences, which is a condition for the articulation of individual and collective views. By fostering cooperation, activities are generated that promote relations of sympathy and epistemic confidence (LW 7, 329; see also Fricker 2009, ch. 7). (3) *Generation of non-dominant views*: as I just mentioned, due to its logical features, experimental inquiry can play an anti-ideological function, one by which the cultural hegemony—that is, its capacity to impose definitions and solutions for social problems such that the interests of the dominating groups can be systematically identified with that of the whole society—of the dominant group can be challenged: problems can be re-defined, new problems can be identified, new solutions can be articulated, etc.

Second, a socializing democracy fosters a reciprocal relation between experts and citizens that promotes mutual learning-processes. This idea is particularly well developed in *The Public and Its Problems* (LW 2, 364–366). Dewey's main idea is that intelligence is a collective enterprise where the necessary division of intellectual labor between experts and common citizens is not incompatible with mutual sharing and testing of ideas and experiences. This means, on the one hand, that in socialized political practice experts have better chances to not to reproduce hegemonic patterns of thought that justify existing relations of domination, since what counts as publicly relevant problems and solutions needs to be defined without exclusion of those potentially affected by problematic social interactions.[36] On the other hand, according to this view, the desirability of an expertocratic government—one where only a reduced set of knowers inquires and takes binding decisions for all citizen—is denied as a way of getting to better political solutions without negating the functional need for experts in modern societies. Hence, socializing democracy does not mean that a set of experts gets to think for the rest, but rather that all, experts and citizens, think together in a division of epistemic labor that involves cooperation on both sides.

Third, a socializing democracy is better prepared to avoid the despotism of the majority against minority views and positions since it does not reduce political practice to individualistic procedures such as vote aggregation and majority rule but it is rather embodied in strongly communicative practices which promote the heterogeneity of individual lives and views against the uniformity promoted by individualism (LW 7, 355). The articulation of heterogeneity and plurality in political practices is a central value for intelligent public inquiry since it enhances the quality of problem-definitions, the creative search for solutions, and their practical implementation. As a consequence of valuing heterogeneity and plurality, socializing democracy puts especial emphasis on freedom of thought and the expression of ideas in ways an individualistic democracy does not. Hence, the latter represent the necessary conditions for the articulation of plural lives and options in the larger context of social life (LW 7, 358–366).

Concluding Remarks

In his *Ethics*, Dewey turns to social problems as a constitutive dimension of morality. This represents for him a specially pressing task, since in modern times individual decisions concerning normative issues have become particularly dependent on social conditions. Dewey characterizes social problems as involving conflicts, which in their turn often come to (re-)produce relations of privilege or domination between social groups. Problems involving domination can be said to be reduced when members of oppressed groups get the possibility of articulating and realizing their interests and powers in a context of inclusion and equality in the different dimensions of social life. Liberal democracy, in its individualistic form, is unable to adequately identify and challenge existing relations of domination. According to the lines of argument we can find in the *Ethics*, the individualistic understanding of democracy involves deficient forms of democratic practice and institutions concerning different levels of analysis: it generates fixity of ideas, the disconnection of ideas from experiences (and hence, it promotes the reproduction of ideological justifications of domination), it also blocks opportunities for the emergence and development of intelligent social struggle as well as the mutual epistemic and practical cooperation between experts and citizens, and finally, it promotes individualistic practices of problem-solving and decision-making that reproduce the domination of majoritarian groups through the repression of social and intellectual heterogeneity. On the other hand, a socializing democracy is one where relations of domination can be approached at least at three different fronts: first of all, socializing democracy creates the conditions for those affected by relations of domination to identify problems, articulate normative claims, and pursue intelligent struggle. It thereby sets the conditions for inclusive and intelligent, public problem-solving at the general level of interacting public spheres. Second, socializing involves the active communication of natural and social scientists as well as other experts with citizens experiencing the effects of domination thereby promoting mutual learning-processes. Finally, it values and fosters heterogeneity making it particularly suitable to avoid the domination-promoting effects of individualistic political practices, such as the unfamous tyranny of the majority. Domination in its structural and ideological forms is certainly nothing we can get fully rid of in any conceivable social order. Dewey was fully aware of this. However, it is so not only because of its inclusive aspects and intelligence-promoting aspects but also because of its ability to extend the sense of inclusion and intelligence in always deeper senses that socializing democracy represents a plausible project of emancipation, namely, the set of social conditions that promote the methods, collective strategies, and forms of life by which we can best deal with pervasive problems of social domination.

Notes

1 I would like to thank all the participants at the Berlin Workshop on John Dewey's 1932 Ethics, most particularly to Brendan Hogan, Torjus Mitgarden, Gregory Pappas, Roberto Frega, Steven Levine, and Matteo

Santarelli. I also would like to thank specially Kurt Mertel for his always useful comments. This chapter has been written with the support the DFG-ANR research project DEMOFUTURES (Prof. Lisa Herzog & Prof. Jan Spurk).

2 He characterizes it as the "material" in contrast to the "formal" moral theory of Part 2 of the Ethics. By "material," Dewey understands the "content" of moral ideas such as the "Good, Right, Duty, Approvation, Standard, Virtue, etc." (LW 7, 314). This content does not come from the inner nature of the individual but is provided by the social environment. Hence, one can affirm that the social world provides the "material" of morals. As such, it must be the object of study of the *Ethics*.

3 Along the two chapters, Dewey understands "power" and "powers" in the sense of "power to" (Hildreth 2019) or capacities. This sense will be respected throughout the present chapter.

4 See for example LW 7, 325.

5 The negative prospects for such an attempt are discussed in Blühdorn (2018).

6 See LW 5.

7 For Dewey, problems do not always involve the presence of a relation of domination even if they always involve conflict between social instances. See below.

8 The adjective "socializing" will be used to underline the fact that democratic practices and institutions can be always made more deeply social or made social in different ways.

9 See below.

10 For a different, though not fully incompatible view of this interpretation of Dewey's theory of domination (see Frega 2015).

11 For the discussion about Deweyan view of social struggles as struggles for recognition as well as the relevance of the notion of "injustice" (see Särkelä 2013; Renault 2017).

12 An example that shows the meaning of this opposition may be useful here, so concerning marriage,

> [t]here are those who think the maximum amount of liberty should be accorded to individuals in their sex relations; that marriage should not be a fixed institution but rather a voluntary contract, to be broken at will provided the interests of the offspring are duly protected. There are others who regard such opinions as a form of moral anarchy, entertained only because of desire for satisfaction of lawless appetites, and destructive of the basic stability of social life. With respect to property and the economic situation, the strife between the upholders of private property as sacred and those in favor of communal ownership is to well known to need more than a reference.
>
> (LW 7, 321)

13 According to Dewey we can distinguish

> [t]hree angles from which a social problem may be analyzed in detail in order to decide upon the moral values involved. First, the struggle between a dominant class and a rising class or group; secondly, between old and new forms and modes of association and organization; thirdly, between accomplishing results by voluntary private effort, and by organized action involving the use of public agencies.
>
> (LW 7, 328)

While Torjus Mitgarden proposes to read this in terms of the different phases of the development of social problems, here I propose a more literal, however "weak" reading of Dewey's statement: while not all conflicts do de facto involve domination, they represent potential sources for the (re-) organization of group privilege, and hence, of domination.

14 They include trade unions, parties, nations, the "state," the "church," as well as any kind of association such as friendships, professional organization, or criminal bands (see LW 2, 278).

15 See note 2.

16 In fact, as Dewey points out in several passages, this also affects the dominant group. Hence, unequal distribution of power goes hand in hand with a lack of communication with other groups and hence with a significant reduction of the possibilities for mutual learning and the realization of new experiences. Dewey also refers to this fact as "one-sided growth" of the privileged (LW 7, 347).

17 See "Overview of Chapters 16 and 17."

18 As Santarelli rightly points in his contribution to this volume, Dewey's political texts such as "Imperative Need: a New Radical Party" (LW 9) also point to the articulative, i.e., ontologically open nature of social interests.

19 See below.

20 See, for example, Hogan (2015), Frega (2015) and Serrano Zamora (2017).

21 Apart from the *Ethics*, readers can find in *The Public and Its Problems* (LW 2) and in *Individualism Old and New* (LW 5) a more detailed version of Dewey's historical reconstruction of democracy in its individualistic form as well as a compelling defense of the need of "socializing" current liberal democracy.

22 By "individualistic democracy" I will understand in this chapter the set of democratic institutions and practices incarnating the principles of what Dewey calls "old individualims" (see LW 5), i.e., an (artificial) understanding individuals as isolated from each other (see below).

23 This expression might sound redundant, since for Dewey democracy is precisely the most social form of organization. However, the label contributes to understand the contrast between the individualistic historical realizations of democracy and the need for an open-ended, "socializing" reform.

24 For detailed analysis of this "ethical" dimension of democracy (see Pappas 2008).

25 "At a certain stage of such conflicts, the inferior but growing group is not organized, it is loosely knit; its members often do not speak for a group which has achieved recognition, much less for social organization as a whole" (LW 7, 325).

26 The idea that "inferior" or "oppressed" groups develop intelligent methods of inquiry as a condition for the generation of alternative perspectives to the ones of the dominant groups is developed in his lectures delivered in China (Dewey 1976, 2015). However, in the *Ethics* we find the idea that the oppressed group makes some innovative and counter-hegemonic "epistemic work" by re-framing the meaning of the current social order in different terms as the dominant ones:

> There are also cases in which the troubles of the present are associated [by the inferior group] with the breakdown of a past order, while existing evils are capable of being remedied only by organized action. [...] Those who profit by the existing régime and who wish to have it retained are now the "individualists," and those who wish to see great changes brought about by combined actions are the "collectivists." These latter feel that institutions as they exist are repressive shell preventing social growth. They find disintegration, instability, inner competition to be so great that existing society is such only on outward appearance.
>
> (LW 7, 327)

27 See Bohman (1997).
28 See Honneth (1998).
29 Dewey usually uses the expression "old liberalism" (LW 5) to refer to what I call in this chapter "individualistic liberal" democracy.
30 A similar critique to current democracies has been recently formulated in Blühdorn (2013). However, Blühdorn's diagnose clearly differs from Dewey's in regarding democracy's crisis as the result of the exhaustion of its normative potentials in times of a third modernity.
31 Even if most of the elements to be mentioned are to be found in the *Ethics*, here I propose to expand the reach of the literature to capture a more general picture of Dewey's contrast between individualistic and, proper, socializing democracy. For this task I consider Dewey's 1908 *Ethics*, *The Public and Its Problems* (LW 2), *Liberalism and Social Action*, *Individualism Old and New*, *Logic: A Theory of Inquiry*, and the *Lectures in Social and Political Philosophy* delivered in China to be essential.
32 To this extent, what Miranda Fricker has called "epistemic injustice" (Fricker 2009) tends to take place since those who occupy positions of symbolic power (such as experts) are detached from the testimonies of those who suffer from domination. Under these conditions, experts tend to reproduce ideological frames that make invisible the effects of domination and thereby contribute to its reproduction (see LW 7, 362).
33 For an actual Deweyan "epistemic" view of democracy (see Anderson 2006).
34 Adorno (2015). Even if important differences exist between Adorno's notion of dialectical thinking and Dewey's notion of inquiry, the idea of a fluidification between facts and ideas against the reification of thinking seems to be common essential trait of both notions.
35 It should be noted that the idea of "channels" for social participation as a condition for the realization of one's own powers is already present in Dewey's *Ethics* from 1908 (see MW 5, 388).
36 "Ultimate authority is to reside in the needs and aims of individuals as these are enlightened by a circulation of knowledge, which in turn is to be achieved through free communication, conference, discussion" (LW 7, 358).

References

Adorno, Theodore. 2015. *Einführung in die Dialektik*. Berlin: Surhkamp.

Anderson, Elizabeth. 2006. "The Epistemology of Democracy." *Episteme* 3: 8–22.

Blüdorn, Ingolfur. 2013. *Simulative Demokratie: Neue Politik nach der postmodernen Wende*. Berlin: Suhrkamp.

Blühdorn, Ingolfur. 2018. "Rethinking Populism: Peak Democracy, Liquid Identity and the Performance of Sovereignty." *European Journal of Social Theory* XX: 1–21.

Bohman, James. 1997. "Deliberative Democracy and Effective Social Freedom: Capabilities, Ressources, and Opportunities." In *Deliberative Democracy. Essays on Reason and Politics*, edited by James Bohman and William Rehg. Cambridge: MIT Press.

Dewey, John. 1973. *Lectures in China 1919–1920*. Honolulu: The University Press of Hawaii.

Dewey, John. 2015. "Lectures in Social and Political Philosophy." *European Journal of Pragmatism and American Philosophy* 7, no. 2: 7–44.

Frega, Roberto. 2015. "John Dewey's Social Philosophy: a Restatement." *European Journal of Pragmatism and American Philosophy* 2, no. 7: 1–27.

Frega, Roberto. 2019. *Pragmatism and the Wide View of Democracy*. London: Palgrave.

Fricker, Miranda. *Epistemic Injustice: Power and the Ethics of Knowing*. Oxford: Oxford University Press.

Geiselsberger, Heinrich. 2017. *The Big Regression: An International Debate*. Cambridge: Polity Press.

Hildreth, Roudy W. 2019. "Reconstructing Dewey on Power." *Political Theory* 37, no. 6: 780–807.

Hogan, Brendan. 2015. "Pragmatic Hegemony: Questions and Convergence." *The Journal of Speculative Philosophy* 29, no. 1: 107–117.

Honneth, Axel. 1998. "Democracy as Reflexive Cooperation." *Political Theory* 26, no. 6: 763–783.

Honneth, Axel. 2007. *Disrespect. The Normative Foundations of Critical Theory*. Cambridge: Polity Press.

Honneth, Axel. 2014. *Freedom's Right. The Social Foundations of Democratic Life*. New York: Columbia University Press.

Mitgarden, Torjus. 2012. "Critical Pragmatism: Dewey's Social Philosophy Revisited." *European Journal of Social Theory* 15, no. 4: 505–521.

Nachtwey, Olivier. 2016. *Die Abstiegsgesellchaft: Über das Aufbegehren in der regressiven Moderne*. Berlin: Suhrkamp.

Pappas, Gregory. 2008. *John Dewey's Ethics*. Bloomington: Indiana University Press.

Renault, Emmanuel. 2017. *Reconnaissance, Conflit, Domination*. Paris: CNRS Editions.

Särkelä, Arvi. 2013. "Ein Drama in Drei Akten: Der Kampf um öffentliche Anerkennung nach Dewey und Hegel." *Deutsche Zeitschrift für Philosophie* 61, no. 5–6: 681–696.

Serrano Zamora, Justo. 2017. "Articulating a Sense of Powers." *Transactions of the Charles S. Peirce Society: A Quarterly Journal in American Philosophy* 53, no. 1: 53–70.

Testa, Italo. 2017. "Dominant Patterns in Associated Living: Hegemony, Domination, and Ideological Recognition in Dewey's Lectures in China." *Transactions of the Charles S. Peirce Society* 53, no 1: 29–52.

Part III

Historical and Systematic Perspectives

10 Dewey's Fully Embedded Ethics

Roberta Dreon

Compared to any aprioristic treatment of morality, Dewey's *Ethics* (both in its 1908 edition and in the 1932 revised version) stands out for its emphasis on the fact that reflective and intelligent evaluations, as well as individual decisions, do not come first, i.e., they are not made in a vacuum. Rather, they arise out of a background of largely pre-personal, habitual, qualitatively, affectively, or aesthetically configured ways of reacting to environmental circumstances and the conduct of other people, which have to be taken into account as the source of reflective behavior, intelligent and voluntary decision-making, appraisal and judgment, as well as their ultimate point of arrival.

In my opinion, this position was enhanced and became more coherent in the shift from the first to the second edition of Dewey and Tufts' *Ethics*, because in the meantime Dewey was able to develop a conception of human nature and behavior according to which both habitual features and the qualitative or aesthetic characters of experience are seen as pervasive and structural in each phase of human conduct, including moral acts. Morality can be considered neither a linear process of emancipation of more conscious and reflective individuals from inherited social customs, nor an evolutionary progress of civilization from mainly conservative and traditional communities to more progressive societies where individuals are supposed to act and choose autonomously (Edel and Flower 1985, xii, Edel 2001, 99). In Dewey's words, "Conduct is complex" (LW 7, 235) not only because it cannot be reduced to a single principle—whether the good, the right, or even virtue, as becomes clear in the 1930 paper, *Three Indeterminate Factors in Morals* (LW 5). Conduct is also complex because the transitions from customary behaviors to more reflective acts are continuous and bidirectional: reflective decision-making and comparative appraisal grow out of habitual responses, affectively oriented likings, and dislikings when situations become troubled and indeterminate. By means of reflective acts, individuals try to disentangle the different primarily qualitative elements involved in a specific context when needed. Nonetheless, the new meanings and values provided by theoretical or practical inquiries return to qualitative experience and become sedimented as habitual dispositions, where they contribute to nourishing a shared sensibility as well as one's sense of what is primarily felt to be valuable and dear or dangerous and morbid.

Therefore, while sharing Edel's preference for an anthropological treatment of ethics (Edel 2001), I will endorse the thesis that such an approach is not rooted only in Dewey's theory of habits, as systematically presented in *Human Nature and Conduct* (MW 14). A further crucial source for Dewey's mature ethical thinking is his idea of the primarily qualitative, aesthetic, or affective meanings of experience, which was explicitly expounded in *Experience and Nature* (LW 1). In that work, he fully developed his idea that any reflective kind of experience is anchored in primarily qualitative, affective, or aesthetic interactions with the natural as well as naturally social environment; reflective experience responds to the troubles and problems originating in human beings' primary engagement with the word as a living organism rather than as a knowing subject.[1] In the meanwhile, the relational or mediated results of our more reflective acts return to ordinarily qualitative, affective, or aesthetic experience, by enriching (or impoverishing) it with new meanings and values which can in their turn be directly felt or had, praised, and prized.

This idea of a continuous and circular shift from customary morality to reflective morality, from affectively as well as habitually based valuing and praising to comparative appraising and evaluating, does not simply represent a relevant point for scholars interested in the different phases of Dewey's thought. In my view, this sort of approach reveals how Dewey's position strongly contrasts with the traditional divide between ethics and aesthetics that characterizes modern thought (Gadamer 1960/1990), insofar as it highlights a common source between the ethical and the aesthetic dimensions of human experience. According to Gadamer's interpretation of Kant's transcendental project, aesthetics is still dominated by Kantian moral philosophy, which is based on the attempt to purify ethics from any aesthetic and sentimental factors (Gadamer 1960/1990, 46). By reading Dewey's *Ethics* together with his *Experience and Nature* and his *Art as Experience* (dating back to 1934, that is only two years after his 1932 *Ethics*), his approach seems to be welcoming toward a new aesthetic and ethic non-differentiation, based on an anthropological framework. This involves a criticism of the traditional claims to autonomy of aesthetics, on the one hand, and of morality, on the other, characterizing our relatively recent philosophical past.

Dewey's ethical account acknowledges the crucial role of affective, qualitative, or aesthetic features in human conduct while avoiding moral emotivism as a form of reductionism, as well as moral subjectivism. This is possible because Dewey strongly opposed any methodologically individualistic and mentalistic approach to affectivity, emotion, and feeling, and considered them to be an integral part of human behavior in a naturally social environment (Dreon 2019a, 2019b). At the same time, Dewey avoided any rigid opposition between qualitative experience and cognition, as well as any kind of foundational order governing the two. On the ethical level, this approach translates into a basic continuity between qualitative and cognitive aspects in moral judgments, as well as between the act of valuing, i.e., of feeling something to be precious and worthy of care, and the act of appraising, i.e., of making comparisons.

To briefly sum up the content of my inquiry, the first section will focus on the pervasive as well as structural role of qualitative experience in morals. Primarily aesthetic/affective reactions to events and persons as well as the sense of belonging, mutual interdependence, and the aspiration to a satisfying life are a natural source of moral reflection that, in its turn, is largely based on the sympathetic imagination and the capacity to perceive a situation through the eyes of others. In the second section, I will explore the connections between the idea of aesthetic qualities in primary experience developed in *Experience and Nature* and Dewey's conception of valuing as the act of considering something precious and dear to oneself: my contention is that in the *Ethics* he focused particularly on those aesthetic qualities of human behaviors that rest on their being living organisms belonging to a naturally social environment. Later, I will use Dewey's conception of the circular relations between so-called primary experience and cognition as a model for understanding the intertwining of customary morality and reflective morality as well as of valuing and appraising in human conduct in a non-foundational way.

The third section will be devoted to briefly drawing a balance of Dewey's ethics with reference to the typically modern "compartmental conception of fine arts" (LW 10, 14) and the complementary ascription of morals to a separate sphere of values. Finally, I will argue that Dewey's emphasis on the role of aesthetic or affective qualities in experience can be interpreted as involving neither a form of moral subjectivism nor a reductive naturalism. Even moral sentimentalism as a label risks capturing just one part of Dewey's conception and disregarding some basic differences.

The Place of Affectional Facts in Morals

It has been observed that classical pragmatists—not only James and Dewey but also Peirce—emphasized the role of feelings, affectivity, and emotions in thought. Among the first philosophical statements made by James was his claim in favor of "the aesthetic sphere of the mind, its longings, its pleasures and pains, and its emotions" (James 1884, 188). In James' view, this sphere suffered from a lack of attention among both psychologists and philosophers, who had been traditionally concerned with cognitive processes.[2] Calcaterra rightly pointed out that the anti-intellectualism of James—and of the pragmatists, more generally—does not involve a form of irrationalism. On the contrary, it is intended to shape a less simplified picture of rationality (Calcaterra 2003, 86), capable of including a variety of qualitative features that contribute to the development of thought and cognition.

I argue that Dewey's approach to ethics extended this kind of assumption to the field of human moral conduct, and that this trend was more fully developed in the 1932 edition of the volume.[3] As stated by Abraham Edel and Elisabeth Flower in their *Introduction* to the book,

> The change in the theory of virtue from 1908 to 1932 reversed the position of the cognitive and the affective. In the 1908 *Ethics,* the good determines which character traits are conductive of the social good, and this determination legislates for our affective reactions of appreciation, praise, blame, etc. In 1932 these affective reactions are conceived as prior and independent. They are psychological reactions under social influences, and so in a changing world have to be constantly scrutinized since they may reflect older habits that require alteration.
>
> (Edel and Flower 1985, XXX)

The introduction, from 1930 onward, of virtue as a third independent factor in morality together with the good and the right involves a marked attention to approval and disapproval, praise and blame, sympathetic encouragement and resentment: in brief, "favour or disfavour toward the conduct of others" (LW 7, 235) as a primitive source of moral judgments. These are all characterized as "*natural*" reactions which occur "without conscious reflection"; as "original," "instinctive," and "immediate"; as "spontaneous" and "direct." It could be said that primary praise and blame work as a sort of proto-evaluation of others' behaviors, preceding reflective judgment and serving as their basis (either to be confirmed or to be denied). Furthermore, they consist in an entanglement of habitual dispositions and affective, emotive, qualitative, or even aesthetically oriented attitudes. Dewey goes so far as to say that "they are so deeply engrained in human nature, that the whole business of reflective morality and of moral theory is to determine a rational principle as the basis for their operation" (LW 7, 236–237).

However, "valuing as a direct, emotional and practical act" (LW 7, 264) is not exhausted by praise and blame as the first source of moral reflection and judgment, but also concerns the field of moral good and right. When dealing with the good and happiness, Dewey focuses on the difference between, on the one hand, what humans desire or shun, what they actually enjoy or suffer, what pleases them or annoys and disgusts them, and, on the other hand, what should be considered enjoyable and desirable or what should be rejected and avoided from a wider, less self-centered and shared perspective.

Similarly, when tackling the issue of what is right, Dewey strongly emphasizes our feeling of human interdependence as the natural basis of our sense of duty. Mutual dependence is not primarily an intellectual argument for defending a common law. Primarily, it manifests itself on an affective or qualitative level as a sense of vulnerability or an impulse to control others' actions and thoughts; it shows itself in our need for belonging as well as in our need to exclude foreigners, in our need to be guided by a strong man or to exercise our power on others—as Dewey was to observe in his *Freedom and Culture* a few years later (see LW 13).

Reflective morality does not represent a sort of banishing of all qualitative and emotive factors from our conduct, because it has to scrutinize these affective reactions through the use of intelligence as well as of sympathy and an affectively based capacity to imagine alternative paths and to feel others' disposition toward our actions (Fesmire 2003, 2015; Pappas 2008).

These last considerations on moral judgments show that the latter do not consist in a transition from primarily emotively based behaviors to cold decision-making, which excludes any affective, qualitative, or aesthetic component. On the contrary, moral judgments are conceived of as involving a kind of extension of human sensitivity to other persons, other groups and ideally the whole of humanity, as well as the common environment all humans belong to. To put it in a formula, the difference between "esteem and estimation," "prizing and appraising," (LW 7, 264) or customary and reflective morality does not amount to the difference between brute emotive reactions and cold cognition. On the contrary, according to Dewey,

> The obvious difference between the two attitudes is that direct admiration and prizing are absorbed in the object, a person, act, natural scene, work of art or whatever, to the neglect of its place and effects, its connections with other things.
>
> (LW 7, 264–265)

By contrast, reflection means thinking and "to think is to look at a thing in its relations with other things, and such judgments often modify radically the original attitude of esteem and liking" (LW 7, 265).

Moral Life as a Qualitative Circle

In my opinion, the last distinction drawn by Dewey between prizing and appraising is a crucial one and can help us understand the problem of the relationship between immediate and mediated values, or between the non-cognitive and the cognitive, to quote Morris Eames' formulations of the issue (Eames 2003, 41, 55). In the following years, Dewey will also suggest a similar distinction in his *Theory of Valuation* (LW 13, 195), where he will stress the emotional quality of prizing, while valuation as appraisal involves an explicit focus on the relational properties of an object. However, my suggestion is that it might be more helpful to look back at *Experience and Nature* (LW 1), rather than turn to Dewey's later writings.

In his landmark 1925 book, Dewey depicts human beings' primary experience of the environment as qualitatively or aesthetically characterized, and repeatedly says that they are first absorbed by things and events for what they can do directly to us or against us.

> Empirically, the existence of objects of direct grasp, possession, use, and enjoyment cannot be denied. Empirically, things are poignant, tragic, beautiful, humorous, settled, disturbed, comfortable, annoying, barren, harsh, consoling, splendid, fearful; are such immediately and in their own right and behalf. If we take advantage of the word esthetic in a wider sense than that of application to the beautiful and the ugly, esthetic quality, immediate, final, self-enclosed, indubitably characterizes natural situations as they empirically occur. (LW 1, 82)[4]

However, even if this is the way humans first and for the most part feel the environment around them, they also experience things as signs of something else, by responding to them "for the sake of ulterior results": that is, they experience a thing or an event not in and by itself but as a reference "to something that may come in consequence of it" (LW 1, 105). According to Dewey's naturalistic account of thought (Dreon 2019c), this basically occurs because humans are moving animals that can defer the consummation of an end in view as well as being linguistic organisms that share certain practices. In any case, it is important to note that aesthetic qualities, meanings, or values are qualities of the direct relations that persons, things, and events have with our existence, because according to Dewey they are structurally dependent living organisms. In other words, these are not simply subjective properties, but refer to the existential conditions humans really suffer or enjoy: they feel a specific situation or interpersonal relation as dangerous or welcoming because it can really hurt them or help and satisfy them.[5] Moreover, it is clear that this kind of primary perception of the environment is not at all meaningless or simply descriptive: on the contrary, it involves a kind of proto-valuation connected to the impact of something on our own lives. It is, in other words, a kind of quasi-biological, affectively anchored form of value.

I would argue that, whereas in *Experience and Nature* Dewey was focusing on the primarily qualitative or aesthetic meaning of things and events, in *Ethics* he shifted his focus to the affective or qualitative meanings and values that other persons have in relation to our living conditions, before becoming the object of moral judgment, reflection, and intelligence. This fact has evident consequences, particularly as regards the enduring debate on intersubjectivity and the so-called problem of others people's minds. In the chapter devoted to "Moral Judgment and Knowledge," Dewey qualifies as "absurd" (LW 1, 269) the theory according to which I would "infer by analogy that a particular physical body is inhabited by a sentient and emotional being" by perceiving merely sensorial information regarding another body. On the contrary, "Emotional reactions form the chief materials of our knowledge of ourselves and of others" (LW 7, 269).

By considering the implication of this assumption with reference to goodness and virtue, more specifically, it could be argued that our natural disposition to praise and blame others' actions, as well as one's own, depends on the basic feeling of mutual dependence among human beings: the attitudes of others in shaping my own dispositions are so influential for customary behavior because of the direct impact of their actions on my own life.[6]

Furthermore, I believe that a comparative reading of Dewey's *Ethics* and *Experience and Nature* might help us to understand the relationship between customary and reflective morality, or between valuing as prizing and taking something to be precious and dear to us, on the one hand, and valuing as esteeming and appraising, on the other hand. I have already mentioned Edel's thesis that in the second edition of the *Ethics* Dewey renounced any linear conception of morality as a transition from the silent approbation of already existing customs to a more conscious individual use of intelligence and reflection both in the life of the individual and in the historical development of human societies. For sure (Edel 2001, 1), historical events played an important role in leading Dewey to recognize that the distinction between customary and reflective morality "is relative rather than absolute," although "clearly marked" on the intellectual level, and that both in societal life and in individual behavior "there is an immense amount of conduct that is merely accommodated to social usage" (LW 7, 162). Another reason can be found in the influence of cultural anthropology (Edel and Flower 1985, xiv–xv): Dewey collaborated with Franz Boas at Columbia and his book *The Mind of Primitive Man* features prominently the bibliographical references of *Experience and Nature*.[7] However, I think that Dewey's conception of the relations between primary experience and knowing as reflective analysis in *Experience and Nature* constituted a model for understanding the relations between prizing and appraising as well as between customary and reflective morality in a more complex, non-foundational, and open way.

In his 1925 book Dewey understood the transition from primary experience to more analytic or cognitive interactions with a problematic situation as a circular one: of course, for him a primarily qualitative experience constitutes the source of a reflective experience which reconsiders a previously holistically experienced situation when individuals do not know what to do, when there is a crisis in habitual modes of behavior and in common sensibility. However, from a phenomenological perspective, the American pragmatist considered that the meanings and values produced by analytic reflection must return to ordinarily felt experience so as to be deposited and even absorbed in it. In other words, I think that Dewey's theory of experience should be read as involving a kind of loop effect or feedback action of our inquiries on our generally holistic experience (Dreon 2018), notwithstanding some hesitations that can be found in his texts (Eames 2003, 29, 41, 55). Conscious individual acts become part of one's own habitual moral dispositions and sensitivity, and Dewey goes as far as to argue that they become part of the self, in the sense that they contribute to shaping one's own individuality. At the same time, they contribute to nourishing a common sensitivity and routine habits that influence individual acts and are continually reformulated by our personal choices as well as intelligent habits.[8] From this point of view, moral reflectivity is but a phase in human conduct, albeit a crucial one, and should be considered embedded in a continuous flow that is, primarily, the flow of acting and undergoing of a living being, and not the product of a merely cognitive subject.[9]

Ethical and Aesthetic Non-differentiation

By adopting this kind of approach to Dewey's *Ethics*, it becomes clearer why he says that in the pre-modern world both the Greeks and the Romans perceived a strong similarity between judgments of good and bad and those on beauty and ugliness in conduct, while "the modern mind has been much less sensitive to esthetic values in general and to these values in conduct in particular" (LW 7, 271).

Thirty years before Hans-Georg Gadamer, Dewey appears to have been critical of the typically modern trend toward the autonomization of ethics, as well as of aesthetics. This is a phenomenon he depicted as the process of compartmentalization of human lives in *Art as Experience*, a phenomenon due, first of all, to material existential conditions—the arising of nationalisms at the turn of the 20th century, as well as the disrupting impact of industrialization on social, political, and moral aspects, as well as on aesthetic sensibility. The institution of museums as specific places where works of art are expected to be experienced through pure contemplation nurtured the idea of art as a separate realm that is supposed to be valued only on the basis of its own criteria and independent principles. Art with a capital A and as a singular universal concept (Kristeller 1951, 1952; Shiner 2001) became something "ethereal" (LW 10, 26) and foreign to ordinary interactions and to everyday aesthetic practices and human needs—that is, to the doing and undergoing of living creatures within the environment they belong to. This process has had very important ethical and political consequences: on the one hand, it led to the marginalization of the arts from politics—except in those cases where the artistic heritage is seen as a cultural deposit to be economically exploited and where the arts are used for political propaganda; on the other hand, art, conceived as independent from any external tribunal—from religious, moral, or political values as well as from any utility issue—was easily appropriated by the market (see Cometti 2012, 2016). This phenomenon is not alien but complementary to the process that has eliminated any sentimental, aesthetic, and natural feature from the allegedly independent faculty of pure practical reason and transformed the natural human disposition toward affectively as well as intelligently evaluating what is going on in their surroundings into a separate realm of transcendental values (Johnson 2014, 15). These values, in turn, are expected to subsume our specific actions by means of determinative judgments, where an only universal, a priori norm is already given.

By contrast, Dewey's emphasis on the continuity of eminently artistic interactions with aesthetic features in ordinary experience reflects the continuum between reflective morality and the naturally sensitive as well as habitual conduct of human beings, making a plea in support of a new aesthetic and ethical non-differentiation, to quote Gadamer's later words (Gadamer 1995).[10]

The common roots of aesthetic and moral sensitiveness may be found in primary, unreflective, and qualitative human experience, which has its roots in the peculiar bio-cultural structure of human beings. First, human organisms happen to feel situations, things, and events to be sweet or bitter, joyful or painful, comfortable and welcoming, or adverse and dangerous. At the same time, for the most part, they feel other people and their acts to be repulsive or attractive, disgusting or fascinating; other people make them feel either good or bad or even embarrassed. In Dewey's cultural-naturalistic account, this happens because human organisms are peculiarly vulnerable beings at birth, much more dependent from their natural environment as well as from our naturally social environment than any other animal, owing to their marked immatureness at birth and to the acute interdependence characterizing any typically complex human activity or practice (see MW 14 and see also Mead 2001/2011). This is the reason why it is misleading to consider their primary experience of the environment, including other human beings, as mere representations of a fact to be charged with meanings and values only afterward, by adding an intellectual evaluation to allegedly merely descriptive givens.[11] On the contrary, human beings perceive situations and other persons around them in terms of the direct impact they have on one's own life. Hence, humans' first and most significant experience of the social environment is affective, qualitative, or aesthetic, if we adopt Dewey and James' usage of this adjective as that which is related to sensitivity.

Understanding Dewey's Understanding of Sensitivity

From the previous section, it became clear that Dewey's approach to ethics involves a form of moral naturalism[12] with a specific emphasis on the role of affective factors in morality[13]—both aspects being rooted in his anthropological assumptions about the kind of beings that humans have become in a completely contingent although irreversible way (cf. Margolis 2017). However, in assessing affective, qualitative, or aesthetic factors as a natural source of morality (as Johnson 2014, Pappas 2008 and Fesmire 2003 and 2015 have done), I think it is important to stress the difference between Dewey's position and a series of labels that would sound misleading if applied to his approaches, such as ethical non-cognitivism, moral emotivism, and ethical expressionism. Even moral sentimentalism should be handled with care.

Most importantly, Dewey's acknowledgment of affective, qualitative, or aesthetic factors in experience as a primary source of moral judgment should be connected with his long-lasting reflection on emotions and affectivity. From very early on, he refused to consider feelings and emotions from a primarily individualistic and mentalistic perspective: from his first papers on emotions (EW 4), he clearly rejected the idea of emotions and feelings as mental states primarily taking place within one's own interior theater. This kind of approach to human affective life is deceptive because it engenders noxious artificial problems, such as that of understanding how a private psychic state could be expressed and communicated in the public sphere—not to mention the never-ending problem of other people's minds. Differently, the classical pragmatists (Dreon 2019a) developed a conception of emotions as constitutive parts of organic interactions as well as structural elements in the mutual coordination of conduct within a basically shared environment. They also saw a constitutive continuity between emotion, cognition, and action, by conceiving emotions as dispositions to act, involving a kind of affective-based proto-valuation of the specific situation as well as the impact of our own behaviors on those of others, and vice versa.

Returning more specifically to the so-called "esthetic qualities" in primary experience, as a natural source of both more refined aesthetic practices and ethical judgments, it might be recalled that, in *Experience and Nature*, Dewey refused to consider such qualities according to the interpretative grid of classical empiricism—according to which they should be ascribed to the knowing subject rather than to the known object because of their resistance to any clear-cut definition or quantification. By contrast, for Dewey these qualities are not properties of an isolated subject or of an equally isolated object: they are real modes of interaction between living organisms and the real environment—a material and social, as well as cultural environment—which they belong to and of which they are an important part, insofar as they are capable of altering it.

In *Theory of Valuation*, two sections are particularly interesting for our current purposes—the one on "Value-Expression as Ejaculatory" and the following section on "Valuation as Likings and Dislikings." Dewey focuses on the active role played by emotions and affective factors in moral judgments while considering the ambiguities of philosophical usages of the word "feeling." He firmly denies that we should ascribe a private or inner state to the individual mind of our interlocutors, when considering, for example, the communicative connection of a baby's cry with the response of its mother. For sure, a cry in a broader linguistic context is a first source of value, although in the sense that it says something to someone else, and it is "affective-motor" because it leads the interlocutor to respond in one way or another. "An emotion, as the word suggests," says Dewey in his *Ethics*, "moves us, but an emotion is a good deal more than bare 'feeling'; anger is not so much a state of conscious feeling as it is a tendency to act in a destructive way towards whatever arouses it" (LW 7, 174).[14] Consequently, when recognizing that moral values have roots in our primitive unarticulated utterances, likings, and dislikings, there is a risk of confusing Dewey's position with the above-mentioned positions—moral emotivism, ethical expressionism, ethical non-cognitivism, or moral sentimentalism. The point is that Dewey did not share some of the basic assumptions underpinning that complex family of ethical positions. Very synthetically, he decisively gave up an approach to feelings and the emotions considered as merely subjective—and consequently as having no objective import (Ayer 1936)—reinterpreting them as dispositions to act in shared context. He even rejected a conception of them as foreign to cognition, endorsing an idea of emotions as involving a kind of proto-evaluation of the circumstances that should be further reconsidered when facing a situation of crisis.

Moreover, as I argued in "Moral Life as a Qualitative Circle" section, it is important from Dewey's perspective to take this claim for sensitivity in moral conduct and judgment neither as the exclusive component of morality nor in a foundationalist sense. Reflective analysis, discriminative intelligence, and explicit considerations of alternative paths of actions by means of imaginative rehearsal are at the core of Dewey's concept of responsibility, conceived almost literally as the capacity to respond to a situation that has become troubled, because ordinary modes of behavior based on habits and sensitiveness have entered into crisis and do not work anymore.

> Dewey thus poses a continuity between processes of intuitive judgments, on the one hand, and, on the other hand, more deliberative, reflective, critical processes of thought that are required if we are to intelligently address our most complex moral problems arising in our interpersonal and cultural contexts.
>
> (Johnson 2014, 87–88)

However, there is a further crucial aspect that should be taken into account from a Deweyan perspective, in my opinion. The point is that his claim in favor of a primarily sensitive engagement with the environment is not to be understood as a kind of foundationalism. Human intelligence and the capacity to interact reflectively with specific circumstances are not simply rooted in qualitative experience. The practical results of a previous reflective inquiry—one's own decisions, changes in both the organic and cultural conditions of a situation—return to primarily qualitative experience and contribute to re-shaping its largely habitual fabric as well as the implicit feeling of one's own role in society, a shared sensibility for what individuals have in common with other people and what they consider alien, and the quality of their sense of satisfaction, fairness, and recognition. In other words, insofar as human sensitivity lies at the basis of reflective judgments in the artistic field as well as in transactions of moral significance, it is not a fundamental datum, but is rather continually and dynamically reconfigured by means of our reflective and justificatory practices in a naturally social and cultural world.

To me, this is but a consequence of Dewey's cultural naturalism, which takes into account the peculiar socially shared and linguistically practiced environmental niche characterizing the human animal.

Conclusion

As argued at the beginning of this chapter, I have privileged an approach to Dewey's ethics focusing on the background of largely pre-personal and habitual, qualitatively, affectively, or aesthetically configured ways of reacting to environmental circumstances and other people's conducts as the source of more reflective behaviors, intelligent and voluntary decision-making, evaluations and judgments. Nonetheless, this does not at all involve an underestimation of the role of human intelligence and individual responsibility in human behavior. In keeping with the pragmatist tradition, I think that it should cultivate a non-naïve and non-dogmatic belief in both of these elements as affordable, albeit limited, resources for engaging with the complex sphere of human affairs.

From this perspective, a pluralistic, contextual, and contingent approach to morality (cf. Fesmire 2003, 2015 2016; Pappas 2008, Calcaterra 2015), capable of including a lucid awareness of some structural indeterminacies in human conduct, is not foreign to a naturalistic, yet non-reductive, point of view. On the one hand, Dewey endorsed the idea that our reflective conduct is rooted in our being primarily living creatures who are structurally dependent on—and interact with—a natural and a naturally social environment, which provides primarily affective meanings and values. On the other hand, this statement must be qualified by the assumption that our reflective evaluations and intelligent practices contribute to reshaping our aesthetic and ethical sensitivity through education, expositions to alternative paths—as is often the case with literary fiction and the arts—as well as through examples, whether inspiring or disruptive ones. This, in my view, is the non-foundational, anti-dogmatic side of Dewey's view of human experience. At the same time, the essential permeability of human sensitiveness to human cultural practices—whether moral or political or economic—does not always mean an enrichment or a broadening of human possibilities. On the contrary, it often involves an impoverishment, a stronger sense of self-identity and of the identity of one's own group, entailing a more intense feeling of exclusions of others. This, I would argue, is the non-naïve side of Dewey's conception of democratic life, which should be seriously taken into account nowadays.

Notes

1 On this aspect (see Frega 2010, 592–593):

> The judgment of practice—assumed by Dewey as the general paradigm of reasoning—is defined according to the following trait: 'propositions exist relating to agenda—to things to do or be done, judgments of a situation demanding action' (MW 8, 14). The holistic understanding of the situation as a complex whole that includes the agent and his deeds sets the stage for the refusal of a purely representative conception of judgment in favour of a transformative conception of judgment as being itself part of the situation it is supposed to settle.

2 Dewey followed James' usage of the term "aesthetic" (or "esthetic") to characterize the sensitive-affective features of our experience, in addition to using the word to refer to eminently and more refined artistic practices. He thereby admitted two different meanings of the term, which nonetheless are connected and form a continuum in his philosophical framework (see LW, 16). I think that a line of thought running from James to Dewey mainly through the influence exercised on *Experience and Nature* by the *Essays on Radical Empiricism* was decisive for the development of Dewey's emphasis on qualitative, affective, and aesthetic features in human experience. Of course, while he distanced himself from the Kantian conception of pure practical reason, Dewey was deeply interested in the English sentimentalist tradition and engaged very seriously with Mill and Smith. Nonetheless, I believe that an original pragmatist trend—probably dating back to some Peircean insights and even to Alexander Bain—should be regarded as the primary source of his approach to sentiment in morals and, more generally, to sensitivity in ordinary experience. On the influence of James' philosophy on Dewey's conception of aesthetics (see Shusterman 2011). On Dewey's engagement with English moral sentimentalism, see Henne in this volume.

3 The words "ethics," "morals," "morality," and related adjectives will be used almost interchangeably in this chapter, as Tufts and Dewey did in both edition of their *Ethics*. In his *Introduction* (MW 5, 9; LW 7, 9), Tufts points to the basic convergence between the terms, given by their common origin in the idea of *ethos*, *mores*, or *Sitten*. For sure, Dewey was aware of the distinction so strongly emphasized by Hegel. However, I think that his apparently more informal use of the terms reflects the basic assumption that human individual consciousness and action always arise from already

socially shared practices, modes of conduct, and norms. I even think that, despite—or perhaps because of—his apparent lack of concern with Hegel's distinction, Dewey gave a naturalistic reading of Hegel's idea that individual morality *per se* is just an abstraction of the intellect that should be viewed, in its truth, from the holistic perspective of the societal life in which it is rooted.

4 This quotation from *Experience and Nature*, like other passages from *Art as Experience*, confirms Dewey's usage of the word "esthetic" as something primarily connected with human sensitivity, as opposed to the enduring understanding of the aesthetic as something that regards merely formal or aspectual relationships between the different components of an object, a work of art, or anything else. This latter understanding is clearly indebted to the Kantian tradition—although it should also be noted that in the first section of Kant's *Critique of Judgment*, a judgment is considered "aesthetic" because it is focused on the feeling (*Gefühl*) of pleasure/displeasure felt by the subject himself when engaging with the mere representation of an object. See note 2.

5 My idea is that Dewey's account of aesthetic qualities can be connected to Peirce's category of Secondness, which, differently from Thirdness, is linked with knowing and making signs as making reference to something else by suspending or deferring its direct effect on our lives. This hypothesis involves a transition in Secondness from merely causal relations to the affective or qualitative impact of something or someone on someone else (see Maddalena 2014).

6 Of course, one could refer here to Mead's development of this issue—Mead was working on the very idea that humans have the capacity to refer to themselves through the eyes of others. Nonetheless, I think it is worth mentioning the fact that William James had already sketched out this thesis in his 1884 essay *The Theory of Emotion* (later included in a revised form in his *Principles of Psychology*). Here he clearly states:

> The most important part of my environment is my fellow-man. The consciousness of his attitude toward me is the perception that normally unlocks most of my shames and indignations and fears. The extraordinary sensitiveness of this consciousness is shown by the bodily modifications wrought in us by the awareness that our fellow-man is noticing us *at all*. No one can walk across the platform at a public meeting with just the same muscular innervation he uses to walk across his room at home. No one can give a message to such a meeting without organic excitement.
> (James 1884, 195)

7 I have explored the connections between Dewey and cultural anthropology in my book on Dewey's aesthetics (Dreon 2012/2017) both from a textual-historical and theoretical perspective.

8 On the difference between routine and intelligent habits (see MW 14, 51). A partially convergent distinction can be found in LW 10, 47, where Dewey characterizes experiences as "anesthetic" when they lack unity and care, as well as when they are merely routine and unable to become "an" experience.

9 The influence of Hegel's teaching on Dewey can be perceived in this sort of dialectical interpretation of the relationship between the different phases of experience as involving different forms of valuing—so that the results of more reflective or mediated process are incorporated and become part of our immediate experience, namely of our largely sensitivity-based and habitual conduct. From this point of view, I agree with Steven Levine that Dewey is "a type of left-Hegelian naturalist" (Levine 2015, 632).

10 We could also add a third claim to this kind of approach endorsed by Dewey with regard to the continuum between logic and our existential as well as cultural matrix (LW 12), a claim involving the need for a natural history of logic (Dewey 2004) in order to recover the continuum between the apparently separate realm of logical norms and practical human thought and intelligence.

11 Of course, this aspect lies at the root of the pragmatists' criticism of the fact/value dichotomy (see Marchetti and Marchetti 2018).

12 On the many oscillations of the term "naturalism" as a label in moral theories (see Cremaschi 2007). In Dewey's case, at the very least it should be said that it deals with a kind of cultural naturalism that assumes a basic continuity between nature and culture, and is consequently foreign to any form of reductionism. For a new formulation of cultural naturalism in moral theory (see Johnson 2014, 2 and ff).

13 See Johnson (2014, 84): "Human moral appraisals have deep affective roots."

14 As I mentioned before, Dewey's first inquiries into emotions date back to the last decade of the 19th century. Nonetheless, it is from the 1920s onward that we can fully consider the wider consequences of his view on emotions as dispositions to act.

References

Ayer, Alfred Jules. 1936. *Language, Truth and Logic*. New York: Penguin Books.

Calcaterra, Rosa M. 2003. *Pragmatismo: i valori dell'esperienza. Letture di Peirce, James e Mead*. Roma: Carocci.

Calcaterra, Rosa M. 2015. "Constructing on Contingency: William James from Biology to Ethics and Politics." *Cognitio* 16, no. 2: 219–232.

Cometti, Jean Pierre. 2012. *Art et facteurs d'art. Ontologies friables*. Renne: Presses Universitires des Rennes.

Cometti, Jean Pierre. 2016. *La nouvelle aura. Économies de l'art et de la culture*. Paris: Questions théoriques.

Cremaschi, Sergio. 2007. "Naturalizzazione senza naturalismo: una prospettiva per la metaetica." *Etica & Politica* IX, no. 2: 201–217.

Dewey, John. 2004. *Essays in Experimental Logic*. Mineola, NY and New York: Dover Publication.

Dreon, Roberta. 2012. *Fuori dalla torre d'avorio. L'estetica inclusive di John Dewey oggi*. Genova: Marietti.

Dreon, Roberta. 2018. "Is There Any Room for Immediate Experience? Looking for an Answer in Dewey (and Wittgenstein) via Peirce and James." *Pragmatism Today* 10, no. 2: 59–73.

Dreon, Roberta. 2019a. "A Pragmatist View of Emotions. Tracing Its Significance for the Current Debate." In *Emotions for Knowledge*, edited by Laura Candiotto. London: Palgrave: 73–99.

Dreon, Roberta. 2019b. "Gesti emotivi e gesti verbali. L'eredità di George Herbert Mead sulla genesi del linguaggio umano." *Sistemi Intelligenti*, 1/2019: 115–133.

Dreon, Roberta. 2019c. "Framing Cognition. Dewey's Potential Contributions to Some Enactivist Issues." *Synthese*, Radical Views on Cognition: 1–22.

Eames, S. Morris. 2003. *Experience and Value: Essays on John Dewey and Pragmatic Naturalism*. Carbondale and Edwardsville: Southern Illinois University Press.

Edel, Abraham. 2001. *Ethical Theory and Social Change: The Evolution of Dewey's Ethics, 1908–1932*. New Brunswick-London: Transaction Publishers.

Edel, Abraham and Elizabeth Flower. 1985. "Introduction." In *The Later Works of John Dewey, 1925–1953*, Volume 7: 1932 *Ethics*. Carbondale: Southern Illinois University Press: vii-xxxv.

Fesmire, Steven. 2003. *John Dewey and Moral Imagination: Pragmatism in Ethics*. Bloomington: Indiana University Press.

Fesmire, Steven. 2015. *Dewey*. London and New York: Routledge Press.

Frega, Roberto. 2010. "From Judgment to Rationality: Dewey's Epistemology of Practice." *Transactions of the Charles S. Peirce Society* 46, no. 4: 591–610.

Gadamer, Hans Georg. 1960/1990. *Wahrheit und Methode. Grundzüge einer philosophischen Hermeneutik, Gesammelte Werke I*. Tübingen: J.C.B.Mohr (Paul Siebeck).

Gadamer, Hans Georg. 1995. *Die Aktualität des Schönes. Kunst als Symbol, Spiel und Fest, Gesammelte Werke VIII*. Tübingen: J.C.B.Mohr (Paul Siebeck).

James, William. 1884. "What is an Emotion?" *Mind* 9, no. 34: 188–205.

Johnson, Mark. 2014. *Morality for Humans: Ethical Understanding from the Perspective of the Cognitive Sciences*. Chicago, IL and London: Chicago University Press.

Kristeller, Paul Oskar. 1951. "The Modern System of the Arts: A Study in the History of Aesthetics. Part I." *Journal of the History of Ideas* 12, no. 4: 496–527.

Kristeller, Paul Oskar. 1952. "The Modern System of the Arts: A Study in the History of Aesthetics. Part II." *Journal of the History of Ideas* 13, no. 1: 17–46.

Levine, Steven. 2015. "Hegel, Dewey, and Habits." *British Journal of the History of Philosophy*, 23, no. 4: 632–656.

Maddalena, Giovanni. 2014. "'Non far violenza a nessuna parte dell'anima umana.' Peirce, l'estetica e la sintesi." *Cuadernos de Sistemática Peirceana* 6: 103–117.

Marchetti, Giancarlo and Sarin Marchetti (eds.). 2018. *Facts and Values. The Ethics and Metaphysics of Normativity*. London and New York: Routledge.

Margolis, Joseph. 1974. "Works of Art as Physically Embodied and Culturally Emergent Entities." *The British Journal of Aesthetics* 3, no. 14: 187–196.

Margolis, Joseph. 2017. *Three Paradoxes of Personhood. The Venetian Lectures*. Milano: Mimesis International.

Mead, George Herbert. 2001/2011. *Essays in Social Psychology*. New Brunswick, NJ and London: Transaction Publishers.

Pappas, Gregory. 2008. *John Dewey's Ethics. Democracy as Experience*. Bloomington: Indiana University Press.

Shiner, Larry. 2001. *The Invention of Art: A Cultural History*. Chicago, IL and London: Chicago University Press.

Shusterman, Richard. 2011. "The Pragmatist Aesthetics of William James." *British Journal of Aesthetics* 51, no. 4: 347–361.

11 Psychology, Moral Theory, and Politics

Dewey's Mature Theory of Interest in the 1932 *Ethics*[1]

Matteo Santarelli

In Dewey's work, references to the concept of interest are numerous and significant. They cover different disciplines—psychology, pedagogy, social and political philosophy, theory of evaluation, aesthetics—and they appear at important passages in some of his most crucial texts, such as *Democracy and Education* and *The Public and its Problems*. However, secondary literature has not devoted specific studies to the subject.[2] There are probably two reasons for this omission. First, finding a unified and unequivocal conception of interest in Dewey seems problematic, given the variety of disciplinary fields in which he uses the term. Second, Dewey is never mentioned in the historical and philosophical accounts of the concept of interest.[3]

This chapter aims to partially fill this gap by discussing the theory of interest developed by John Dewey in the 1932 revised version of *Ethics*. Specifically, we intend to show how in this text Dewey reorganizes and re-elaborates the conceptualizations he proposed in his previous work in the domains of psychology, pedagogy, and moral theory. These contributions will be briefly summarized in the first section of the chapter. In the second part, the 1932 *Ethics* will be analyzed. We will attempt to show how Dewey's theory of interest is based on two precise theoretical bets: he conceives the close link between interest and self without reliance on the paradigm of self-interest; he develops a pragmatic understanding of interest. This reconstruction will be organized around three separate but interrelated definitions of interest: psychological, moral, and political.

The choice of these three disciplinary domains is not random. Psychology, morality, and politics are the three main fields covered by the most relevant modern and contemporary conceptualizations of interest. In Western tradition it is not uncommon to find authors who discussed the concept of interest simultaneously from the standpoint of two of these three dimensions. Just to mention some examples: 16th-century Italian political theorist Francesco Guicciardini provided seminal insights on the concept of interest from a political—and in a way moral—standpoint, but he did not contribute to the psychological discussion in this regards; 17th-century French moralist François La Rochefoucauld decisively contributed on the moral side, by taking somehow into account the psychological dimension, but without almost any reference to the political level; finally, 20th-century French sociologist Pierre Bourdieu discussed at length the political and sociological dimension of interest and he hinted at the psychological background of his conceptualization, and yet he completely overlooked the moral side of the discussion.

On the contrary, Dewey positions himself to some extent in that liberal tradition that has endeavored to conceive the concept of interest by keeping the psychological, moral, and political levels together. However, there is a crucial difference between Dewey and its predecessors in this regard. While authors like Bernard de Mandeville, Jeremy Bentham, and Adam Smith conceptualized the entrenchment of the psychological, moral, and political dimensions by understanding interest essentially in terms of self-interest,[4] Dewey's criticism explicitly targeted this equation. More radically, it can be argued that the criticism of the liberal theorization of self-interest is the focal point of Dewey's theory of interest.

The threefold sub-organization of the present reconstruction of Dewey's 1932 theory of interest follows two main goals. First, it aims at showing how Dewey's concept of interest is plural, and yet unitary. There is an ongoing interaction between the different uses of the term "interest" in the various disciplinary domains, which share a number of precise common features, such as the refusal to equate interest with self-interest, and the pragmatic and contextual definition of interests. This means that Dewey's plural uses of the concept of interest lead to a unitary and integrated conceptualization, rather than expressing heterogeneous meanings which can be only juxtaposed. Second, it highlights how Dewey's concept of interest provides original contributions in each of these domains. On the psychological level, it entails and it is deeply related to new understandings of concepts such as self and motivation. On the moral level, it paves the way to the overcoming of the long-standing dichotomy between egoism and altruism. On the political level, it exemplifies and at the same time it helps in articulating Dewey's refusal of conceiving the social and the individual as two opposed entities.

The Entanglement of Psychology, Pedagogy, and Moral Theory: The Origins of Dewey's Criticism of Self-interest

Between the last decades of the 19th century and the first two decades of the 20th century, Dewey wrote several essays which dealt with the problem of interest. This section aims to show how these essays develop a unitary conception of interest, despite they belong to different disciplinary domains—psychology, moral theory, pedagogy.

The first important contribution in this regard is probably represented by Dewey's *Psychology* (1887). This essay contains two intuitions which will be fully developed in the successive works: the close connection between interest and self, and the dynamic conception of the self. If the first assumption seems to suggest that interest reduces to self-interest—i.e., selfishness,—the second assumption questions the inexorability of this reductive gesture. If the self is to be conceived as an activity, rather than as "something which acts" (EW 2, 216), then the plurality of the activities involving the self will reflect on "a differentiation of interests" (EW 2, 248) and on the resulting impossibility of reducing this variety to a single kind of interest. In 1887s *Psychology,* this intuition, which will play a key role in Dewey's concept of interest, is still incomplete and limited by his endorsement of a subjectivist definition of interests—i.e., interests as things which have value for the subject, regardless of the nature of the objects of interest (EW 2, 108). During the following years, Dewey would continue to develop and articulate this conception, and subjectivism would eventually disappear from his texts. The main examples of this development are the 1891 essay *Outlines of a Critical Theory of Ethics* and his pedagogical articles composed in the last years of the 19th century.

Outlines of a Critical Theory of Ethics quite moves away from the subjectivist definition of interests endorsed four years before:

> Interest is the union in feeling, through action, of self and an object. An interest in life is had when a man can practically identify himself with some object lying beyond his immediate or already acquired self, and thus be led to further expression of himself.
>
> (EW 3, 305)

This quote suggests that interests cannot be easily defined as either purely subjective or purely objective experiences. Rather, they should be located in that intermediate dimension in which subject and object identify each other, and in which the subject is absorbed in an object, whose nature is modified and partially reshaped by the interested activity of the subject. Interests take place in an affectively characterized activity. They are transitional in nature.[5] This transitional definition does not rule out the strict connection between interest and self already outlined in his *Psychology.* Rather it further highlights how flawed the interest-self-interest equation is. This identification is debatable for several reasons: first, we can posit cases in which the subject identifies herself with an external object—she may be interested in a cause, another person, an injustice. It is undeniable that in some specific cases interests could push us to act immorally and without any concern for others. At the same time, we can be devoted to interests which involve the self in direction, but whose ultimate outcomes are experiences of "self-transcendence" (Joas 2000). If a scientist is completely devoted to his mission and his job, we should consider him moral, as long as "he does his work for its own sake, from interest in this cause which takes him outside his 'own miserable individuality,' in Mill's phrase" (EW 3, 312).

An analogous thread of argumentation can be found in a different disciplinary domain: Dewey's pedagogical essays written during the last decade of the 19th century and the first decades of the 20th century. In these essays and articles, interest becomes the specific focus of attention. In spite of the disciplinary shift, in *Interest in Relation to the Training of the Will* (1896), Dewey further develops his critique of the reduction of interest to self-interest anticipated in his 1891 moral essay:

> It is true that the term interest is also used in a definitely disparaging sense. We speak of interest as opposed to principle, of self-interest as a motive to action which regards only one's personal advantage; but these are neither the only nor the controlling senses in which the term is used. It may fairly be questioned whether this is anything but a narrowing or degrading of the legitimate sense of the term. However that may be, it appears certain that controversy regarding the use of interest arises because one party is using the term in the larger, objective sense of recognized value or engrossing activity, while the other is using it as equivalent to a selfish motive.
>
> (MW 7, 160)

Interests always involve a self, but their selfish nature cannot be taken for granted. The self is not a private locus, self-contained, and perfectly autonomous. If we conceive of it as an activity, the self exists also in the external world and enters into relationships with objects. As the etymology endorsed by Dewey suggests, interest has a transitional nature. "Inter-esse" means "to be between," and thus, it "marks the annihilation of the distance between the subject and object; it is the instrument which effects their organic union" (EW 5, 122).

The dismissal of the paradigm of self-interest finds a mature formulation in Dewey's 1916 pedagogical and philosophical manifesto *Democracy and Education*. Here Dewey makes clear how the idea according to which every action is by definition self-interested, and that human beings are motivated to act only when we think that there is "something in it" for ourselves (MW 9, 335) is fallaciously grounded on a narrow definition of the self, and on a consequent misunderstanding of the strict relation between self and interest. This misunderstanding vanishes once a social and dynamic definition of the self is adopted. Interests mark out the affectively charged and pragmatic merging of a self and an object. This pragmatic understanding of the self implies a specific psychological and epistemological move: the abandonment of introspectionism, and of its psychological and philosophical implications.

> If the self is something fixed antecedent to action, then acting from interest means trying to get more in the way of possessions for the self—whether in the way of fame, approval of others, power over

> others, pecuniary profit, or pleasure. Then the reaction from this view as a cynical depreciation of human nature leads to the view that men who act nobly act with no interest at all.
>
> (MW 9, 361)

"Self and interest are two names for the same fact": this sentence could be an effective recap of Dewey's psychological, moral, and pedagogic definition of interest (see Hansen 2005). However, this definition requires a profound rethinking of the concept of the self. This is the core of Dewey's theoretical challenge: we must consider the deep connection between self and interest, without reducing interest to self-interest.

Developing the Entanglement of Psychology and Moral Theory: The Concept of Interest in Dewey's *Ethics* (1932)

In his 1932 account of interest Dewey reconnects and reconstructs several positions and intuitions already presented in his works from previous decades in the domains of psychology, pedagogy, political, and ethical theory. I propose to undertake the reconstruction of Dewey's 1932 definition of interests in three parts: the psychological framework, the moral understanding of interests, and the political understanding of interests. The deep interconnections between these domains show how Dewey's conception of interests is plural, and yet unitary.

The Psychological Bedrock

Dewey's discussion of interest in the 1932 *Ethics* leans directly on two key assumptions of his psychological theory: the understanding of psychological processes as phases of an organic circuit, and anti-introspectionism. This entanglement of psychology, epistemology, and ethics is neither accidental nor the result of methodological confusion.[6] Rather, it forms a necessary part of Dewey's crystal clear strategy: he aims to show how the paradigm of self-interest in ethics cannot be adequately put in question without critically discussing its psychological and epistemological presuppositions:

> The same Cartesian starting point that in epistemology leads to the problem about the epistemic states of other knowers, leads in ethics to the problem of accounting for emotional, direct, and genuine interest for other things—including other persons—that are outside the self.
>
> (Pappas 2008, 213)[7]

Dewey begins the discussion like he had 50 years before in his 1887 *Psychology*. His argument hinges on the assumption of a tight connection between self and interest. A key role is played again by Dewey's pragmatist definition of the self. This definition is explicitly portrayed as a third alternative to the dichotomy opposing Kantian and utilitarian understandings of ethics. The well-established dichotomy between "ethics of selves" and "ethics of consequences" loses its appeal, once it is acknowledged that "[t]he self is not a mere means to producing consequences because the consequences, when of a moral kind, enter into the formation of the self and the self enters into them" (LW 7, 286). Unless we understand the self and the consequences of action into the framework of this circuit, we fail to grasp the key presupposition of a correct theory of morality, namely "*the essential unity of the self and its acts*" (LW 7, 288).[8]

The acknowledgment of this identity is a necessary step toward a proper understanding of "motivations." Motivations, a crucial concept in ethical and moral discussions, are often conceived of as inner or external drives pushing the self to act. Being motivated to do something means thus starting to act. Once the relation between self and action is understood as a circuit, motivations can be described in an alternative way. The self is not passively waiting for external or inner sources of motivation to prompt it to act. On the contrary, the self is an organism which is constantly acting. Rather than something that brings action into being, and which thus connects the allegedly heterogeneous dimensions of the self and the action, motivations play a role of organization and direction of an already existing conduct. Therefore, there is no use in looking for specific motivations—such as the search for pleasure—understood as primary sources of conduct. Conduct is already acting when motivations appear.

In order to portray the psychological background of his rethinking of motivation, Dewey reconnects with an early and long-standing intuition of his own. In the groundbreaking article "The Reflex Arc Concept in Psychology" (1896) he represented stimulus and response as two phases of the organic circuit of conduct.[9] This means that the organism is not brought into action by an external stimulation calling for a response. Rather, the stimulus should be understood as a redirection and potential reorganization of the conduct of an already acting organism:

> The function of a stimulus is – as the case just cited illustrates – to change the direction of an action already going on. Similarly, a response to a stimulus is not the beginning of activity; it is a change, a shift, of activity in response to the change in conditions indicated by a stimulus.
>
> (LW 7, 290)

Therefore, the connection between self and action, organism and environment, does not need to be explained. Rather, it is a constitutive dimension of the human conduct and experience of an organism whose action is ongoing. Into this wide psychological and anthropological picture, Dewey introduces one of his most articulated definitions of interest:

> Any concrete case of the union of the self in action with an object and end is called an interest. (...) An interest is, in short, the dominant direction of activity, and in this activity desire is united with an object to be furthered in a decisive choice. Unless impulse and desire are enlisted, one has no heart for a course of conduct; one is indifferent, averse, not interested. On the other hand, an interest is objective; the heart is set on something. There is no interest at large or in a vacuum; each interest imperatively demands an object to which it is attached and for the well-being or development of which it is actively solicitous.
>
> (LW 7, 320–321)

Interests consist of an integration between subjective and objective dimensions of experience and conduct. There is no interest unless someone is interested in some object or activity. Lack of desire or impulse does not increase the purity of interest. Rather, it is incompatible with its very existence. And yet, desire and impulse are necessary, but not sufficient conditions for the establishment of an interest. According to Dewey, interests present an objective dimension:

> There is no interest at large or in a vacuum; each interest imperatively demands an object to which it is attached and for the well-being or development of which it is actively solicitous [...] Interest is regard, concern, solicitude, for an object; if it is not manifested in action it is unreal.
>
> (LW 7, 290–291)

In order to express themselves in an interest, desires and impulses must be able to organize conduct. Interests represent an articulation of impulses, desires, and wishes into organized conduct. No one would say that someone has a real interest in something, unless this interest organizes and shapes her conduct in some way. Being interested means caring, and caring means doing something with a certain continuity and organization:

> If a man says he is interested in pictures, he asserts that he *cares* for them; if he does not go near them, if he takes no pains to create opportunities for viewing and studying them, his actions so belie his words that we know his interest is merely nominal. Interest is regard, concern, solicitude, for an object; if it is not manifested in action it is unreal.
>
> (LW 7, 321)

All the characterizing features of the Deweyan understanding of interest presented in his previous contributions are at work in the 1932 definition: the strong connection between self and interest, a pragmatist redefinition of the self, the understanding of interest as an affectively charged and pragmatic identification of the self with an object. At the same time, in the revised version of *Ethics,* objectivity plays an even more decisive role. There is no interest, unless the "interestedness" of a subject is able to organize a stable course of conduct. Otherwise, there would be a mere wish, that is, a merely subjective desire which is incapable of articulating and organizing practice.

Neither Self-interest nor Disinterestedness. Interest as a Moral Concept

This pragmatic definition of interest, self, and motivations is the starting point of Dewey's further attack against the reduction of interest to self-interest—i.e., egoism, selfishness—in the moral domain. The focus of his criticism is the fallacy which holds that since interest always involves the self, it must always be reducible to self-interest. As appealing as it may seem, this assumption is partial, since it in turn implies a debatable definition of the self. Once one endorses the pragmatist definition of the self—dynamic, social, pragmatic—the connection between self and interest appears as a truism. However, the self is not necessarily selfish. The self can be fully absorbed in an action totally devoted to others. According to Dewey's dynamic and pragmatic definition, the self is what the self is doing in a specific situation.[10] Once the self-interest connection has been rephrased within the framework of the pragmatist definition of the self, there is no longer a need to tie morality and disinterestedness together. Indeed, attempts to do so can end up assuming a sort of comical flavor:

> It is absurd to suppose that the difference between the good person and the bad person is that the former has no interest or deep and intimate concern (leading to personal intimate satisfaction) in what he does, while the bad person is one who does have a personal stake in his actions. What makes the difference between the two is the quality of the interest that characterizes them. For the quality of the interest is dependent upon the nature of the object which arouses it and to which it is attached, being trivial, momentous; narrow, wide; transient, enduring; exclusive, inclusive in exact accord with the object.
>
> (LW 7, 296)

In order to avoid the paradox of assuming that good persons are dull, shallow persons, devoid of any attachment to the world, a social definition of both selves and interests should be adopted: "Selfhood is not something which exists apart from association and intercourse. The relationships which are produced by the fact that interests are formed in this social environment are far more important than are the adjustments of isolated selves" (LW 7, 298–299). Ten years before, in his 1922 psychological essay *Human Nature and Conduct* Dewey introduced a distinction which could integrate the thread of argument developed in 1932s *Ethics*. Dewey explains how many words and expressions—e.g., interest—"get spoiled when the word self is prefixed to them" (MW 11, 96). This pejorative connotation of the prefix "self" is not inevitable. Specifically, it could and it should be avoided by means of the distinction between acting *as* a self and acting *for* self:

> The fallacy consists in transforming the (truistic) fact of acting *as* a self into the fiction of acting always *for* self. Every act, truistically again, tends to a certain fulfilment or satisfaction of some habit which is an undoubted element in the structure of character. Each satisfaction is qualitatively what it is because of the disposition fulfilled in the object attained, treachery or loyalty, mercy or cruelty. But theory comes in and blankets the tremendous diversity in the quality of the satisfactions which are experienced by pointing out that they are all satisfactions.
>
> (MW 11, 95)

The dilemma of altruism versus egoism vanishes in a sort of Wittgensteinian way once we abandon the individualistic conception of the self, and the dichotomies which arise from it. We can act *as* a self, embedded in a web of social relationships, without necessarily acting *for* ourselves. After the emergence of the self as an ontogenetic phenomenon, the shadow of selfhood becomes almost impossible to overlook in human action. It is hard to find an area of human conduct which remains unrelated to the domain of selfhood, especially since the latter encompasses both the reflexive and the pre-reflexive dimensions of conduct. This is why we often act *as* selves. But there is no logical contradiction in saying that we get involved *as* selves in social actions which contribute to the well-being and happiness of the others, that is, social actions which do not involve acting *for the* self.

Dewey's original definition of interest is reflected in the originality of his discussion of virtues. In Chapter 13 Dewey enters into a debate which played an important role in modern philosophical and moral discussion: the issue of the relation between interest and virtue—even if he does not mention any of the participants in this debate, except for a short reference to Bernard Mandeville. This debate hinged on two different answers to the question: is self-interest compatible with virtues? As studies such as Hirschman (1977), Force (2003) and Holmes (1995) have reconstructed in a detailed way, during the 17th and 18th century, authors who tended to give a negative answer to this question (La Rochefoucauld, Mandeville, Rousseau) coexisted and argued with authors who were inclined to a more reconciliatory attitude (Saint-Lambert—i.e., the author of the headword "interest" in the Diderot-D'Alembert *Encyclopedia*—and Adam Smith).[11]

Dewey's position cannot be reduced to coincide with either of these lines of thought. Rather, it implies reframing or even dismissing the discussion outright by considering the opposition between self-interest and allegedly disinterested virtues fictitious. In Dewey's definition, virtues are not disinterested habits of conduct. Rather, they express "an interest in objects and institutions" (LW 7, 255).[12] Therefore, the definition of something as a virtue depends on its connection with a specific kind of interest, which Dewey calls genuine, or complete interest. There are three criteria according to which an interest can be defined as genuine. The first feature is wholeheartedness, in the sense of a sincere and integrated absorption of a subject into an object. This means that genuine interests cannot be understood as purely subjective intentions of doing something good for the others. Rather, they require the merging of subjective inclinations and feelings into the specific object which directs and organizes the virtuous conduct. The second feature of genuine interest, namely, continuity and persistency in time and action. Differently from immediate enthusiasm, a virtuous interest requires "consistency, continuity, and community of purpose and effort" (LW 7, 256).

The third characterization, impartiality, deserves some additional attention. This reference to impartiality in the framework of Dewey's theory of interest appears puzzling. Once the appeal to disinterestedness has been dismissed as unnecessary and misleading, on what basis could an interest be understood as impartial? Moreover, impartiality seems to involve an equal distribution of interest which is simply at odds with real functioning of interested conduct in everyday life (LW 7, 257). However, Dewey does not understand impartiality as a form of disinterestedness. Impartiality means here a specific organization of interests:

> Equity demands that when one has to act in relation to others, no matter whether friends or strangers, fellow citizens or foreigners, one should have an equal and even measure of value as far as the interests of the others come into the reckoning.
>
> (LW 7, 257)

To sum up, virtues as genuine interests are specific kinds of integrating interests acting at three levels: affectively charged integration between self and object—wholeheartedness; integration into a habit—continuity and persistency; integration between the perspective of the self and the perspective of the others—impartiality. Briefly, virtues are related to what Dewey calls "complete interest" (LW 7, 257). A complete interest embodies a full development of all the various dimensions which characterize Dewey's concept of interest, with special attention devoted to their integrative capacity: integration of the affective and the intelligent dimension, and integration of conduct into the capacity to pursue an interest despite every obstacle.

Contingency and Organization. The Political Definition of Interests

In Chapters 15 and 16 Dewey applies his criticism of self-interest and his overall pragmatic redefinition of interests to the domain of political interests. In this specific context, Dewey's dismissal of the interest-self-interest equation is not intended to merely demonize the interests of the individual and to affirm the inherent superiority of social interests. It is meaningless to contrast individual interests with social interests in themselves, because the meanings of "individual" and "social" shift according to different historical and social contexts. Thus, the appeal to individual interest may play an emancipatory or a conservative role, depending on current social and political conditions.

Here Dewey is creatively reusing the criticism of individualism which he introduced in *Individualism, Old and New* and other writings from the early 1930s. In these essays Dewey acknowledges that the appeal to the individual played a positive and liberating function during the 17th century, an historical period in which institutions like the state and the church were broadly oppressive toward individuals and social groups. The significance of this appeal changed dramatically once society had shifted towards a new organization dominated by powerful private industrial and financial enterprises. In this new context, *laissez-faire* appeals to "rugged individualism" involved the refusal of any kind of democratic and social control of these hegemonic private interests. Paradoxically enough, this lack of control contributed to the creation of a situation of insecurity which undermined the development and full realization for millions of individuals: "Fear of loss of work, dread of the oncoming of old age, create anxiety and eat into self-respect in a way that impairs personal dignity. Where fears abound, courageous and robust individuality is undermined" (LW 5, 68). The individualistic refusal to place limits on self-interest damaged the very existence of the majority of individuals.

This criticism of individualism, however, does not necessarily imply unreserved praise for collective interests. Like the appeal to "self-interest," the outcome of an appeal to "collective interests" varies based on historical context. In a context of "rugged individualism," collective interests can play a progressive role in defense of poor and marginalized individuals and groups. Conversely, in a period in which new interests and needs emerge, this appeal can serve to justify the conservation of existing asymmetrical social relations.

> No single formula signifies the same thing, in its consequences, or in practical meaning under different social conditions. That which was on the side of moral progress in the eighteenth and early nineteenth centuries may be a morally reactionary doctrine in the twentieth century; that which is serviceable now may prove injurious at a later time.
>
> (LW 7, 336)

In some concrete instances of social conflicts,[13] the importance of context and social position in determining the meaning of the terms "social" and "individual" becomes apparent. On the one hand, dominating groups tend to portray themselves as the defenders of social interests and shared values, and present emerging rival groups "as rebels against constituted authority, as seeking for the satisfaction of their personal appetites against the demands of law and order" (LW 7, 325). On the other hand, emerging groups will often tend to criticize the oppressive role of extant social institutions. But this is not the only shape taken by social conflicts. In other historical contexts, the parts may be reversed: "Those who profit by the existing regime and who wish to have it retained are now the 'individualists', and those who wish to see great changes brought about by combined action are the 'collectivists'" (LW 7, 327). To sum up, expressions like "individual" and "social" have a contextual meaning and a strategic use. In fact, real conflicts never oppose two entities such as the individual and the social, but always groups against other groups, individuals against other individuals (LW 7, 325).[14]

There is a further sense in which the meaning and value of the interests involved in social conflict are contingent and dynamic. This sense is strictly related to one of the main assumptions in Dewey's psychological and pedagogic theory: interests are not given. Rather, they are the emerging manifestation of a dynamic process of expression and articulation. As early as 1897, in his essay "My Pedagogic Creed," Dewey wrote: "I believe that interests are the signs and symptoms of growing power. I believe that they represent dawning capacities" (EW 5, 92). Given their emerging nature, interests are defined by means of a process of growing organization. On a political level, this means that social conflict does not always oppose clear-cut, well-defined interests. On the contrary, social conflict often opposes well-established and clearly defined interests, on the one hand, against marginalized, emerging, and vaguely expressed interests, on the other hand.

The key role of this process of expression and organization of interests is not new in Dewey's social theory. One may argue that the issue of the public, as depicted by Dewey in his major work *The Public and Its Problems* (1927), boils down to the problem of organizing a shared concern into a common interest. The public is a social group which takes shape starting from a situation in which the members of this emerging group find themselves affected by the consequences of a specific social event. This shared concern must be articulated by means of collective inquiry via a two-step process. First, the problematic situation which concerns the public needs to be defined and articulated. Second, the problematic situation must be framed as a problem. During the first step, the most urgent issue is that of articulating the shared concern into the definition of an interest common to a plurality of the individuals and groups involved: "The prime difficulty, as we have seen, is that of discovering the means by which a scattered, mobile and manifold public may so recognize itself as to define and express its interests" (LW 2, 327).

In the 1932 *Ethics* Dewey rephrases and develops these intuitions. Since interests are not given, a key role is played by the process of organization of emerging interests. Emerging interests have two serious obstacles to overcome. The first difficulty is basic organization. Organization requires energy, strength, and symbolic resources. The lack of any one of these factors could prove fatal to the process of expression and organization. The second difficulty is the fact that new interests often emerge from situations of conflict. This means that emerging groups have to articulate and organize their interests in a situation in which their interests are portrayed by privileged groups as intrinsically antisocial. The emerging, partially indeterminate structure of these interests unwittingly facilitates this ideological representation. In Bourdieu's jargon, this process of organization and expression takes place in a social context characterized by an asymmetrical distribution of symbolic resources.

It is interesting to compare these theoretical reflections with Dewey's contributions to the political debate of the time. During the first years of the 1930s, Dewey was an active member of both *The People's Lobby* and the *League for Independent Political Action* (Lee 2015; Midtgarden 2019). As a prestigious and productive member of the two associations, Dewey took an active part in the public discussion, expressing his positions in a variety of media, from newspaper articles to public speeches and pamphlets. But how should we analyze this production in light of his two main lines of reasoning in *Ethics* as discussed above: the fallacious nature of the opposition between individual and collective interests, and the key role played by the process of organization of emerging interests?

The first assumption appears to contradict Dewey's incessant call for social control of private interest which we find in articles such as "The Irrepressible Conflict" (1931), "The Need for a New Party" (1931), and

"Democracy joins the Unemployed" (1932). The first lines of "The Irrepressible Conflict" are quite explicit in this regard:

> Our League [the League for Independent Political Action] was formed because of a realization that our existing political parties in the conduct of government are more concerned to serve the selfish and financial interests of the few than the human needs of the many. (LW 6, 149)

In these essays the private interests of the few are incessantly contrasted with the interest of the people, the interests of the many, and the interests of the common man (LW 6, 157). "The need for a new party" is grounded on the incapacity of both the Republican and the Democratic parties to take the side of "human interests" in their clash with "property interests" (LW 6, 159). And again, the only suggested remedy to the crisis is "new political action based on social interests and realities" (LW 6, 163). This begs the question: is there a tension between the moral philosopher Dewey's refusal of the individual interests versus social interests dichotomy, and the public intellectual Dewey asserting the primacy of social interests?

This possible contradiction or ambiguity vanishes once we recall Dewey's commitment to contextualism. The assumption that the meaning of terms such as "individual" and "social" depends on context is perfectly consistent with the fact that, within certain specific social contexts, these terms may in fact have very precise meanings. While appeals to social interests are not considered characteristically progressive, they can nonetheless play a progressive function in specific situations. Dewey believes that the economic and political crisis of the 1930s is exactly this kind of situation. His call for greater sharing of social control, for a democratic participation in the definition of social interests is not a moral or a political axiom. It is rather a contingent response to the big political issue of that time: the colonization of social life by means of private groups, and the individual and social suffering generated by this colonization. In an era in which economic issues played a prominent role, supporting social control of unrestricted private interests on behalf on "social interests" was a necessary step toward a better social organization, one which doesn't require individuals to make sacrifices, but rather provides them better living conditions. Therefore, Dewey's theoretical reflections are not in contrast with the spirit of his political convictions of the time. Rather, they help contextualize his political involvement without transforming it into a source of broad-ranging and inflexible moral and political rules.

But, of course, the mere appeal to social interests is not enough to resolve the second key issue regarding the organization and expression of interests. The relevance of this issue emerges clearly again in Dewey's political writings. In "The Need for a New Party," one of the essays in which the appeal to social and human interests against the hegemony of private interests is most emphatic, Dewey makes it clear that the group of potential voters for the hypothetical new party will necessarily be sociologically multifaceted: the middle class, laborers, agrarian workers, and the unemployed. Still, this audience is not totally heterogeneous.[15] These social groups may share a number of problems and desires which need to be articulated into common interests.

A passage in Dewey's "Address to the National Association for the Advancement of Colored People" (1932) hits exactly this point. Dewey appears cautiously optimistic about the fact that the Great Depression, despite its disrupting and devastating effects, could offer minority groups "a better opportunity to express themselves, their needs, their wrongs, their demands for greater freedom, a larger opportunity and a wider field than they had in the past" (LW 6, 225). But still, how shall these minorities groups come to perceive their situation as a collective problem? Why should black workers be interested in the problems of white workers and vice versa, when these two groups live in two different social situations? Dewey's answer to his rhetorical question is a compendium of his understanding of the process of organizing and expressing emerging interests. Through the process of articulation and integration of shared issues, a plurality of individuals and groups can develop a common interest:

> the depression has also disclosed a community of interest among all the minority, repressed and oppressed groups of the country. It has made clear that all of these groups that are suffering, while they are not suffering in exactly the same way, are after all fundamentally the victims of the same causes. I do not mean that I think this lesson of the community of interest among all these different groups of whatever race or color has been very fully learned as yet or that the consciousness of it has sunk very deep or spread very wide. But I think that, the fact that all of them are suffering in greater or less degree from the same causes has been made clear and that the recognition of that fact is going to grow with increased rapidity, sink deeper from now on.
>
> (LW 6, 225)

In Dewey's democratic framework, the problem of organization emerges both at the level of the single group and at the level of the relation between groups. The plurality of groups and of interests in society does not rule out the possibility of articulating a wider common interest. This latter activity should be the core business of any political organization attempting to democratically move forward out of a political, economic, and social crisis such as the huge and devastating crisis which the USA experienced while Dewey was in the midst of writing the new version of *Ethics*.

Conclusions: A Plural Yet Unitary Theory of Interest

The 1932 *Ethics* is arguably Dewey's richest and most exhaustive representation of his theory of interest. For starters, this work demonstrates the application of the concept across three different theoretical domains: psychology, moral theory, and political theory. However, this plurality of meanings should not be misconstrued: Dewey's use of the term interest is not equivocal. The different meanings of "interest" in *Ethics* share the following common features:

1. *The refusal to equate interest with self-interest*: if it is true that every interest involves the self, it does not follow that every interest is selfish. In fact, this latter conclusion presupposes an individualistic conception of the self which is explicitly challenged by Dewey.
2. *The refusal of the subjective/objective dichotomy*: interests involve both a subjective and an objective dimension of experience. Interests involve concern and involvement, and at the same time they are always embodied in conduct.
3. *The meaning of an interest is context-dependent*: it is impossible to attribute a fixed meaning to a specific kind of interest. This meaning will depend on the kind of interactions and consequences which derive from this interest. Appeals to "individual interest" in the Papal States during the 17th century have a different meaning than appeals to "individual interest" in the USA in 1929.

As late as 1932—that is, almost 50 years after his first systematic reflection on this subject—the circuit connecting the different disciplinary uses in Dewey's line of reasoning was still evolving. The theoretical output from one disciplinary domain—e.g., psychology—was still working as an input signal for other disciplinary domains—e.g., politics. This plural, and yet unitary conception of interest is a major theoretical contribution by Dewey (although it is often overlooked). And yet the 1932 version of *Ethics* does not close the circuit. There was a key aspect regarding the definition of interests which was yet to be assessed by Dewey: the problem of valuation. Given their pragmatic nature, and given the contextual nature of their meanings, interests are not provided with a fixed meaning and with a fixed value. Sometimes these must be ascertained by means of a process of valuation. But what does "valuating" an interesting mean? Is it a purely cognitive and intellectual action? Is it a purely affective process? Or does "valuating" mean judging an interest with respect to a pre-fixed system of given values? These latter questions will be dealt with by Dewey in the last tile of the mosaic of his theory of interest: *Theory of Valuation* (1939). But of course, the path to this last step was already paved by Dewey's reflection on interest in the 1932 *Ethics*. Since interests are not given, and since they are neither purely subjective, nor purely objective, intelligent valuation of interests—in Dewey's 1939 jargon: evaluation will not be reduced to a simple intellectual definition, nor to the mere expression of a purely subjective feeling. Rather, it will consist in a process of pragmatic re-definition and reconstruction, whose results will be challenged by new emerging problematic situations.

Notes

1 I would like to thank all the participants of the Berlin workshop on Dewey's 1932 *Ethics* for their comments, especially Torjus Midtgarden for having discussed the first draft of this chapter.
2 Partial exceptions are Jonas (2011) and Pennacchini (2015), which focus specifically on Dewey's pedagogical works. Without focusing directly on this issue, both Midtgarden (2012) and Frega (2015) highlight significant features of Dewey's concept of interest with regard to social philosophy. Pappas (2008) discusses Dewey's criticism of self-interest from a moral standpoint. Finally, Levine has recently contributed to this subject (see his essay in this volume).
3 See, for instance, Swedberg (2005).
4 See Force (2003), Swedberg (2005) and Santarelli (2019).
5 The term "transitional" is used here in analogy with the definition of the term introduced by Winnicott (1971). According to Winnicott, the transitional space is the space situated between the subjective and objective dimensions of experience. In this sense, the idea of the transitional presents similarities with the Deweyan concept of transaction. But since the latter concept is only used systematically by Dewey in the late phase of his career—see *Knowing and the Known* (LW 16)—the term "transitional" was preferred in order to avoid chronological confusion.
6 On the role that this entanglement plays into the pragmatist framework (see Calcaterra and Dreon 2017).
7 More generally speaking, see Pappas (2008) for an interesting reading of the connection between Dewey's criticism of self-interest and his anti-introspectionism.
8 On the identity of self, interest, and action, see Levine in this volume.
9 On the genesis and the definition of the concept of organic circuit (see Garrison 2003).
10 The concept of situation plays a crucial role in Dewey's epistemology and social theory. For a full account of this concept, see Dewey's 1938 *Logic: Theory of Inquiry.*
11 See Force (2003). For a discussion of the modern debate on interest (cfr. Hirschman 1977; Swedberg 2005).
12 See Frega's contribution in this volume for a detailed discussion of Chapter 13.
13 For a detailed analysis of Dewey's discussion of social conflicts in *Ethics*, see Serrano's essay in this volume. More generally speaking, see Serrano (2017) for an account of Dewey's concept of expression.
14 The idea that social conflict is essentially a conflict between groups clearly emerges in the *Lectures in China* 1919–1920, especially in the recently published original notes (see Frega 2015).
15 In a recent unpublished article written with Just Serrano (Santarelli and Serrano 2019), we tried to show how the issue of heterogeneity is a crucial point of disagreement between Dewey's and Laclau's perspectives on the genesis of political identities.

References

Calcaterra, Rosa and Roberta Dreon eds. 2017. *Pragmatism and Psychologism (Special Issue). European Journal of Pragmatism and American Philosophy* 9, no. 1.

Force, Pierre. 2003. *Self-Interest before Adam Smith. A Genealogy of Economic Science.* Cambridge: Cambridge University Press.

Frega, Robero. 2010. "From Judgment to Rationality: Dewey's Epistemology of Practice." *Transactions of the Charles S. Peirce Society* 46, no. 4: 591–610.

Frega, Roberto. 2015. "John Dewey's Social Philosophy." *European Journal of Pragmatism and American Philosophy* 7, no. 2: 98–127.

Garrison, Jim. 2003. "Dewey's Theory of Emotions: The Unity of Thought and Emotion in Naturalistic Functional 'Co-Ordination' of Behavior." *Transactions of the Charles S. Peirce Society* 39, no. 3: 405–443.

Hansen, David. 2012. "Dewey's Book of the Moral Self." In *John Dewey and Our Educational Prospect: A Critical Engagement with Dewey's "Democracy and Education"*, edited by David Hansen. Albany: State University of New York Press, 165–188.

Hirschman, Albert O. 1977. *The Passions and the Interests: Political Arguments for Capitalism before Its Triumph.* Princeton, NJ: Princeton University Press.

Holmes, Stephen. 1995. *Passions and Constraints: On the Theory of Liberal Democracy.* Chicago, IL and London: University of Chicago Press.

James, William. 1890. *The Principles of Psychology.* New York: Henry Holt and Company.

Joas, Hans. 2000. *The Genesis of Values.* Chicago, IL: University of Chicago Press.

Jonas, Mark E. 2011. "Dewey's Conception of Interest and Its Significance for Teacher Education." *Educational Philosophy and Theory* 43, no. 2: 112–129.

Lee, Mordecai. 2015. *The Philosopher-Lobbyist: John Dewey and the People's Lobby, 1920–1948.* Albany, NY: SUNY Press.

Midtgarden, Torjus. 2012. "Critical Pragmatism. Dewey's Social Philosophy Revised." *European Journal of Social Theory* 4: 505–521.

Midtgarden, Torjus. 2019. "Dewey's Conceptualization of the Public as Polity Contextualized: the Struggle for Democratic Control over Natural Resources and Technology." *Contemporary Pragmatism* 16: 104–131.

Pappas, Gregory. 2008. *John Dewey's Ethics. Democracy and Experience.* Bloomington and Indianapolis: Indiana University Press.

Pennacchini, Maddalena. 2015. *L'interesse in John Dewey e l'educazione dell'anziano.* Roma: Armando Editore.

Santarelli, Matteo. 2019. *La vita interessata. Una proposta teorica a partire da John Dewey.* Macerata: Quodlibet.

Santarelli, Matteo and Justo Serrano. 2019. "Articulating the People: The Genesis of Political Identities between Inquiry and Rhetoric." Draft.

Serrano, Justo. 2017. "Articulating a Sense of Powers: An Expressivist Reading of John Dewey's Theory of Social Movements." *Transactions of the Charles S. Peirce Society: A Quarterly Journal in American Philosophy* 53, no. 1: 53–70.

Steiner, Pierre. 2017. "Pragmatism in Cognitive Science: From the Pragmatic Turn to Adverbialism." *Pragmatism Today* 8, no. 1: 9–27.

Swedberg, Richard. 2005. *Interest.* Berkshire: Open University Press.

Winnicott, David. 1971. *Playing and Reality.* London: Tavistock.

12 Duties and the Ethical Space of Claims in Dewey's 1932 *Ethics*

Mathias Girel

Introduction: Three Questions

If we take *Three Independent Factors in Morals* as a roadmap for the second part of the 1932 *Ethics*, Chapter 12, on duties and moral obligations, has a clear function: accounting for the specificity of the Right, after the Good, and before the Virtues. Still, the same chapter leaves the reader with three different but related perplexities, which will be the subject-matter of the present chapter: (1) Why would Dewey say, quite early in his career, that James's treatment of obligation was "the simplest and best" and never use it again in his own writings, and in particular, in this chapter?[1] (2) Since we have previous versions of Dewey's treatment of obligation in 1891 and 1908, what is relatively new in 1932, and are there some groundbreaking arguments or new concepts in the "new" analysis of duty and the Right? (3) Why is Chapter 12's ending so "dark"? Why would Dewey devote a chapter to duties to conclude that "the new forms of lawlessness and the light and loose way in which duties are held cannot be met by direct and general appeal to a sense of duty or to the restraint of an inner law" (LW 7, 234)?

The first question is a puzzle for the Dewey reader: how can we understand Dewey's praise, in 1891, and the fact that he would never refer explicitly to James's arguments and to this particular paper? My claim, here, is that Dewey's contribution, in the 1932 *Ethics* (hereafter E 1932), is actually the closest to James's statement, much more so than the *Outlines of a Critical Theory of Ethics* (1891), written before James's text, and the 1908 *Ethics* (hereafter E 1908), even if there is no direct textual reference to it in 1932. There are interesting variations on Bain, Spencer, and Kant, but the main novelty is the "claim-talk," much more prominent in 1932. To make things clear, my intuition is that there is a new account of the social dimension of ethics in 1932. That would be the groundbreaking, positive, novelty, and this new account would bring Dewey closer to James. The third question is related to the first and the second: being responsive to the ethical claims of others, which becomes a shared concern for Dewey and James, presupposes some minimal requirements, and these social and moral conditions, in Dewey's account and in his mature works, seem to become more fragile than ever.

"The Best and Simplest Statement"

In this section, I document Dewey's early interest in James's seminal text, identifying two cardinal points mentioned in a 1891 letter to James, where Dewey expresses his admiration. In that paper, far from formulating a formal theory of ethics, and even less a monograph, James enumerates minimal conditions for the ethical regime to exist: (1) a differentiated and distributed space where agents raise competing claims, (2) a relationship between moral obligation and specific and concrete claims raised by concrete beings, rather than a reference to an abstract purpose, a structure of Reason, or an alleged encompassing social interest.[2] The starting point is therefore an undecided situation, where moral claims clash, and the experimental and perfectionist dimension of ethics begins truly when we try prioritizing these claims and articulate these ideals, in a way that remains fallible and must be responsive to the failures of ethical experimentation.

Just after Dewey had published his *Outlines*, he wrote to James about this paper, "The Moral Philosopher and the Moral Life," just published in April in the *International Journal of Ethics* and later retrieved in *The Will to Believe*.[3] He singled two particular interrelated issues out, the discussion of obligation and that of rules:

> ...although I had read your ethical article [Philosophers and the Moral Life] once & recommended it to my class to read, I wanted to read it again. The article rejoiced me greatly—if possibly, two things more than others, [...] your statement that any desire, as such, constitutes a claim & any claim an obligation, and your discussion of rules. I was only sorry that the discussion of obligation, in particular, had not appeared before I wrote my Ethics. I think it is the best & simplest statement I have ever seen.[4]

In that text, as we mentioned, James does not offer a substantive ethical theory—even if there are substantive arguments in the paper—but rather an approach to morality. Sarin Marchetti convincingly claims that James's interest

> ...is rather that of showing the shape moral reflection should take to meet the difficulties of the moral life it should address instead of castling itself behind a moral theory or some metaphysical picture of human beings. Moral reflection, according to James, should have an exhortative character, its point being that of gesturing toward the varieties of ways in which we can be – or fail to be – touched by situations that prompt our sensibility and understanding to respond ethically.[5]

In my own terms, I would say that James, in particular in the section devoted to the "metaphysical" problem of morality, states what is to his eyes the minimal "grammar" necessary to give moral descriptions of a situation and, certainly, to belong to a circle of morality. There must at least several least agents, their desires or ends, their claims, and, which is as important, the way they respond to the claims of others. It is tempting to think that, at that time, Dewey had perceived the gist and novelty of the paper, since his letter mentions two crucial points in James's argument.

1 Dewey's first acknowledgment concerns James's view about obligation. James had rephrased the moral discussion in terms of *claims*: there is no obligation without a concrete claim, and, more radically still, every claim implies obligations:

> ...we see not only that without a claim actually made by some concrete person there can be no obligation, but that there is some obligation wherever there is a claim. Claim and obligation are, in fact, coextensive terms; they cover each other exactly.
> (James 1979, 148)

As often with James, the subtlety of the argument could easily be missed: he did not imply, of course, that any foolish claim made by a mad tyrant commands the same obedience as a sensible demand (insofar as it would lead us to overlook other claims, for instance). His concern, rather, was that we can easily be blind and deaf, unresponsive, to actual moral claims raised by our contemporaries, in particular to weaker voices, and that one of the challenges for ethics is to "hear" these voices.[6] One cannot decide in advance if any particular claim carries with it an actual obligation on our part. Even if we "deflect" a claim, we *still* address it and understand it as a moral claim and an obligation, perhaps weaker than another one:

> Take any demand, however slight, which any creature, however weak, may make. Ought it not, for its own sole sake, to be satisfied? If not, prove why not? The only possible kind of proof you could adduce would be the exhibition of another creature who should make a demand that ran the other way.
> (James 1979, 149)

2 James also endorsed a view of moral rules in which they have to be revised and, so to speak, incessantly reconstructed, when they become "too narrow":

> In point of fact there are no absolute evils, and there are no non-moral goods; and the highest ethical life-however few may be called to bear its burdens-consists at all times in the breaking of

> rules which have grown too narrow for the actual case. There is but one unconditional commandment which is that thou shalt seek incessantly with fear and trembling, so to vote and to act as to bring about the very largest total universe of good which thou canst see.
>
> (James 1979, 158)

This opened a perspective where, since the actual moral situation is a field of competing claims, and since no rational or a priori reconciliation of them is at hand, we have to prefer the "richer" articulation of ideals:

> He knows that he must vote always for the richer universe, for the good which seems most organizable, most fit to enter to complex combinations, most apt to be a member of a more inclusive whole. But which particular universe this is he cannot know for certain in advance; he only knows that if he makes a bad mistake the cries of the wounded will soon inform him of the fact.
>
> (James 1979, 158)

Such an articulation is always fallible and must be handled with care. In view of Dewey's later experimentalism regarding values,[7] it is interesting that James's paper would have "rejoiced" him so greatly. But his leaves us with a puzzle: why would Dewey not even quote it in his treatment of moral obligation in 1908? Why would it "the best & simplest statement [Dewey had] ever seen" and not even deserve passing mention? Of course, it would be possible to use James's arguments without quoting from him, but we don't really find, in 1908, a neat equivalent of James's arguments in the chapter devoted to duties and moral obligation in general.

Moral Obligation in 1891 and 1908: The "Standard View"

If the *Outlines* were written before James's text, as Dewey claims, there can obviously be no reference in it to the 1891 paper, but it is also very clear that Dewey's treatment of obligation was, at that time, quite different from James's. Using James's paper would not have implied a minor mention but, probably, more substantive revisions.

We can find Dewey's treatment of obligation in the first part of the *Outlines*, on "Fundamental Ethical Notions," where three main ideas are discussed: The Good, the Idea of Obligation, and the Idea of Freedom. It also resurfaces in the third part, when Dewey discusses the "Moral Struggle and the Realizing of Ideals." Reading that book in light of the mature Dewey, it is tempting to say that, in the *Outlines*, we have a standard account of duty—standard for the contemporary literature—where internal impulses meet external resistance, and where this external, brutal, authority is gradually "internalized." When it is still external, we have obligation as in the sentence "I was obliged, forced, to do so," whereas when it becomes more internal, we have obligation as in "I felt obliged." This appears quite well in the restitution of Bain's ideas on the subject, and in the analysis of the problem posed by obligation to "hedonistic" theories, where it is often perceived as an internalization of social coercion, through the fear of punishment and unpleasant consequences:

> On the model, however, of the action of this external authority there grows up, in time an internal authority—"an ideal resemblance of public authority," or "a facsimile of the system of government around us."
>
> (EW 3, 329)

This kind of public authority, in most cases, has interesting effects: it makes us aware of our social bonds. Duties express first of all the relations of the Self, which are in good part social relations. When they are well understood, that is, when they are no longer felt as mere external coercion and when they become the subject-matter of moral reflection, they indicate the dimensions along which the self can fully "realize" its individuality.

> The community, in imposing its own needs and demands upon the individual, is simply arousing him to a knowledge of his relationships in life, to a knowledge of the moral environment in which he lives, and of the acts which he must perform if he is to realize his individuality.
>
> (EW 3, 339)

If we sum up, at that time, we could say that Duty is second to the Good (it is a means for the flourishing of individuality), and the Social is so to speak second to the Self (it "arouses" it to the perception of its dimensions of realization). Obligation, the "ought," is only one "aspect" of our relationships to ends, to our visions of the Good:

> In other words, obligation or duty is simply the aspect which the good or the moral end assumes, as the individual conceives of it. From the very fact that the end is the good, and yet is not realized by the individual, it presents itself to him as that which should be realized—as the ideal of action. It requires no further argument to

> show that obligation is at once self-imposed, and social in its content. It is self-imposed because it flows from the good, from the idea of the full activity of the individual's own will. It is no law imposed from without; but is his own law, the law of his own function, of his individuality. Its social content flows from the fact that this individuality is not mere capacity, but is this capacity acting, and acting so as to comprehend social relationships.
>
> (EW 3, 336)

Things are not totally different 17 years later. In E 1908, the Chapter 17 of the second part, Theory of the Moral Life, is devoted to "The Place of Duty in the Moral Life." It offers another "standard" treatment of duties, where the Kantian approach is opposed to the utilitarian one, and where both one-sided views are reconciled in Dewey's "Final Statement." The formulation is more precise than in 1891 though. Duty is mainly the opposition between present inclinations of the Self and constraints ("Duty as a conscious factor means constraint of inclination") (MW 5, 307). This contrast can lie between my present desires and "what meets the demands, the necessities, of the situation in which it takes place" (MW 5, 306), and then it is very close to the Roman "offices" (the "external" obligations of the previous paragraph). It can also lie between the present Self and its ideals, whether it is the universal and rational self, in the Kantian theory, or "social institutions and demands," in the utilitarian theory. It will not come as a surprise that, to Dewey's eyes, both approaches are one-sided: the Kantian one because it entertains an abstract view of Reason and the Self, as opposed to all our inclinations and habits, the utilitarian one because, paradoxically, it endorses an autonomous view of the Self, where, because of the latent hedonistic psychology of that movement, it is seen as independent in some ways of social institutions, which are then merely constraining it.

In 1908, we have, more clearly than in 1891, a double dialectic: between the Self, as identified with its existing habits, and the projected Self that exceeds the comfort of its habits, and between the individual dimension of reflection and the social dimension of customary loyalties. The solution is "dynamic": in order to "grow," the self must identify all of its relationships and social relationships are for it as many ways to stimulate or control this full growth of the Self.

There are new elements in the picture: as we can see, habits now play a prominent role. Without them, there would be no tension at all between our settled tendencies, and other possibilities and other lines of conduct. A totally plastic self would be in the same situation as the solipsistic agent in James's paper,[8] there would be no "should" contrasting with our impulses, any line of action would be equi-possible. Since the sense of duty is only another name for the felt difference between what we tend to do, very often actions compatible with the customary and parochial morality, and other ends, there would be no sense of duty at all:

> A self without habits, one loose and fluid, in which change in one direction is just as easy as in another, would not have the sense of duty. A self with no new possibilities, rigidly set in conditions and perfectly accommodated to them, would not have it.
>
> (MW 5, 310)

Edel and Flower are certainly on the right track when they contrast E 1908 and E 1932 on the basis of the "sociocultural dimension in ethical theory," absent in the first, present in the second (LW 7, *x*). They construe Dewey's first approach as "linear": "morality had evolved from customary group morality to a reflective individual morality." This was true of the *Outlines*, and it is also true of E 1908. Our "offices," external duties, can remain forever dead habits, customary loyalties, but when they are better understood (through individual reflection), they are as many stimuli to control and foster this realization of a richer individuality. I would still call this approach "Self-centered" because the social aspect, the "Community," is here again reduced to a mere function. Even if the perspective is now dynamic—the Self and its ongoing reconstruction being at the center of the stage—the overall pattern remains the same. "Social influences" ... are influences, that is to say they are so many ways to lead the Self in the process of his fuller realization, and they help distinguishing between our tendencies:

> Social influences enable an individual to realize the weight and import of the socially available and helpful manifestations of the tendencies of his own nature and to discriminate them from those which are socially harmful or useless.
>
> (MW 5, 325)

And the center of gravity is and remains the Self, in its process of reconstruction:

> The phenomena of duty in all their forms are thus phenomena attendant upon the expansion of ends and the reconstruction of character. So far, accordingly, as the recognition of duty is capable of operating as a distinct reenforcing motive, it operates most effectively, not as an interest in duty, or law in the abstract, but as an interest in progress in the face of the obstacles found within character itself.
>
> (MW 5, 327)

Duties (moral obligations) are by-products of the "reconstruction" of character and of our "ends." The "Social," here, has no real thickness, and it is and remains quite abstract.

1932: The Justification of Moral Claims

In a 1927 letter to Scudder Klyce, and in particular in a paragraph where he comments upon *Experience and Nature*, Dewey has this tantalizing remark about conflicting claims:

> Generalizing a little, there is no branch of social facts more important than social claims, and no humanistic problem of greater importance than determination of the validity of such claims—every legal controversy, every moral and political and economic issue is one sense a matter of adjudicating conflicting claims. Every philosophy, historically speaking, is a claim of some sort, and the social consequences of accepting and giving general currency to unjustified claims are serious—again as matter of perceived fact.[9]

In a sense, this is pure Dewey in the emphasis of the relationship between claims and consequences, but it is also very close to James's standpoint in the *Will to Believe*, in particular the idea that any philosophy is "a claim of some sort" and that we are always faced with a conflict of claims that we have to "adjudicate."[10] Be it as it may, "claims," as in this letter, seem to be more prominent in Chapter 12 of E 1932 than in the previous equivalents. Even if a philosophical evolution is never settled by a mere mention of occurrences, the fact is that the term is used about 40 times in our chapter, compared to 9 times in Chapter 17 of E 1908. It might be said that there is nothing new here. After all, the content of each normative discipline or practice is by definition uttering normative statements, is it not the same thing as raising claims? I think the difference lies in the description we provide of these normative disciplines and statements: ends, standards, and even values can remain quite abstract, while claims are raised by individuals, in front of concrete situations, addressed to particular groups or individuals. The grammar of our descriptions of moral situations becomes highly different. A claim is raised by someone over something to someone else with a certain view in mind and, when it is not the sheer exercise of brute force, refers to a standard or rule. In the field of knowledge, when I claim that something is the case, I state or assert that something is the case, typically without providing evidence or proof, I'm addressing an audience and asking them to accept the authority of the statement. In moral and social issue, when I raise a claim, I raise a demand for something that I think I have a right to. Recasting the problem of duties in terms of claims helps stressing that the issue is undecided, that another particular claim can be opposed to the first one, and that even the authority to which we appeal is uncertain, as regards the issue of the exchange. The idea developed in this section is that the social dimension of duties has a new texture in E 1932, quite in line with Dewey's letter to Klyce.

Chapter 12 of E 1932 deals with "Duty" and articulates Right, Duty, and Loyalty, while providing distinctions between the Good and Duty—proving that they are "independent factors" in morality, before turning to Virtue in Chapter 13—and showing that Duty is no mere external coercion. We have the following distinction, quite in line with previous texts:

> The Good is that which attracts; the right is that which asserts that we ought to be drawn by some object whether we are naturally attracted to it or not.
>
> (LW 7, 217)

Our chapter maintains the distinction between Good and Right, while showing too that the Right is nevertheless related to desire and affections, ends and values. Dewey's goal is to find a source of moral authority distinct from mere coercion and still related to impulses, affections, and desires, and this exactly where we find his analysis of "claims."

Of course, Dewey still has a strong criticism of abstract views of the individual: they go against the brute fact of survival and subsistence (which involve the help of others), but even more subtle facts involve the social. Thinking, even when one is alone, always implies "a language that is derived from association with others" and independence of judgment "is something displayed in relation with others." This is also true for philosophic thought: we inherit our problems, we share our conclusions with others, and we try to "win their assent."

> Such facts are familiar and commonplace. Their meaning is not always so definitely recognized: –namely, that the human being is an individual because of and in relations with others. Otherwise, he is an individual only as a stick of wood is, namely, as spatially and numerically separate.
>
> (LW 7, 227)

So far, this is in line with previous texts, but another element stands out now. The "Claim-Talk" is now at the forefront of the analysis and deeply rooted in Dewey's naturalism. We are now, so to speak, *claim-making creatures*. If we allow that there are two types of claims, claims made by society on individuals, and claims made by individuals upon each other,[11] Dewey, while focusing the second meaning, pays closer attention to the "horizontal" claims, the concrete demands, often conflicting, that we raise upon each other. It is *natural* for us to do so:

> The way out is found by recognizing that the exercise of claims is as natural as anything else in a world in which persons are not isolated from one another but live in constant association and interaction.
>
> (LW 7, 218)

Some of these relations assign duties (expose us "to the expectation of others and to the demands in which these expectations are made manifest" (LW 7, 218)), and Dewey is not thinking of abstract or virtual duties in general, he has actual claims in mind, as raised by fellow creatures:

> Others do not leave us alone. They actively express their estimates of good in demands made upon each one of us.
>
> (LW 7, 224)

In their illuminating introduction to volume 7 of LW, Edel and Flower have their own reading of the major change concerning duty between E 1908 and E 1932:

> Such a picture of every individual living in a network of relations is a far cry from the individual's inner tension of long-range ideal and established value of 1908, or from the widely prevalent contractualism of wills in individualist ethics.
>
> (LW 7, xxix)

This might be true, even if we have seen that the social factor was not absent in 1908, but it is true because the nature of the social has changed. It is now fully perspectival.

As often with Dewey, it is difficult to find clear breaks and discontinuities in his vision, but his picture of agents as claim-creatures is definitely older than E 1932. In addition to the *Letter to Klyce*, the clearest account of it, if not the earliest, is certainly in *Logical Method and Law*. Dewey gives there a genealogy of logic, and, if he's quite cautious ("highly probable," "quite conceivable"), even formal logic would be a remote consequence of the more basic need of justifying one's actions and decisions:

> It is highly probable that the need of justifying to others conclusions reached and decisions made has been the chief cause of the origin and development of logical operations in the precise sense; of abstraction, generalization, regard for consistency of implications.
>
> (MW 15, 73)

So far, this might seem quite abstract, but Dewey has in mind the way we concretely answer to concrete claims raised over our conduct and acts by others. Our justifications are embedded in the conflictual and perspectival setting that we have just described: we elaborate them *because* others press us to account for them. Because there is a moral pressure, an exchange of claims, and the expectation that we must justify ourselves, we form the habit of justifying the method through which we reach a conclusion, and this paves the way for epistemology, such would be the quite radical argument. That is a very bold move indeed, and, whether we accept it or not, it is rooted in this natural-anthropological account of selves as "claim-making":

> It is quite conceivable that if no one had ever had to account to others for his decisions, logical operations would never have developed, but men would use exclusively methods of inarticulate intuition and impression, feeling; so that only after considerable experience in accounting for their decisions to others who demanded a reason, or exculpation, and were not satisfied till they got it, did men begin to give an account to themselves of the process of reaching a conclusion in a justified way.
>
> (MW 15, 73)

The social, here, is not the collective, the intersubjective, not even the public in the standard, pre-Deweyan or pre-Meadian, sense, and this is the reason why I think that we are getting closer to the conflictual field of claims that James was describing than to E 1908. This stands out clearly in the summary Dewey provides of the chapters as a whole, after having referred to the social relations of the moral agent:

> These relations are expressed in *demands, claims, expectations.* One person has the conviction that *fulfillment of his demands by others is his right*; to these others it comes as an obligation, something owed, due, to those who assert the claim. Out of the interplay of these claims and obligations there arises the general concept of Law, Duty, Moral Authority, or Right.
>
> (LW 7, 308)

We can get a sense of the pervasiveness of this perspectival background that if we pay attention to Dewey's description of the "non-conformist" in morals in E 1932:

> The justification of the moral non-conformist is that when he denies the rightfulness of a particular claim he is doing so not for the sake of private advantage, but for the sake of an object which will serve more amply and consistently the welfare of all.
>
> (LW 7, 231)

1 Dewey's description implies a distributed space of competing, and possibly incompatible, ends and claims: the non-conformist is not only making his own claims, he is also denying "the rightfulness of particular claims."
2 It cannot be the description of an exotic character, in the same way as we would have descriptions of "cranks" and lunatics. If

conformism cannot command obedience, as Mill and Emerson had already shown well before Dewey, and if it is often another face of coercion, every new claim, every criticism of a prevailing institution, every proposed experimentation, must, in the first times at least, be "non-conformist." I take it that when Dewey describes the "non-conformist," he is also describing, by inclusion, the attitude of radical, moral, criticism, and any experimentalist approach to values.[12]

3 This hunch is further backed by the reasons urged by the non-conformist, which are basically the same as moral claims *in general*: he objects to claims "for the sake of an object which will serve more amply and consistently the welfare of all." So far, the difference between the "non-conformist" and more moderate moral thinkers lies not in the general line of reasoning, but perhaps in the goal, in the object aimed at.

I don't think that the first and third claims are controversial; the second one is more speculative, but not extravagantly so when we read Dewey. Opposing dominant moral claims comes with certain duties though, let's call them "methodological" or "procedural" duties:

> The burden of proof is upon him. In asserting the rightfulness of his own judgment of what is obligatory, he is implicitly putting forth a social claim, something therefore to be tested and confirmed by further trial by others. He therefore recognizes that when he protests he is liable to suffer the consequences that result from his protesting; he will strive with patience and cheerfulness to convince others.
>
> (LW 7, 231)

The non-conformist cannot be content to differ, he has to convince others "with patience and cheerfulness," he has to play the game of "giving and asking for reasons," to use a Sellars-Brandom phrase.

> Toleration is thus not just an attitude of good-humored indifference. It is positive willingness to permit reflection and inquiry to go on in the faith that the truly right will be rendered more secure through questioning and discussion, while things which have endured merely from custom will be amended or done away with.
>
> (LW 7, 231)

One caveat must be made. Dewey does not think though that discussion will be enough, because public debates can also silence weaker claims, as more recent scholars of "epistemic injustice" have seen. In addition, he does not think that we can reach a consensus over ethical matters, and in particular over duties. A "cooperative inquiry," as in science, can perfectly take into account a disagreement, which allows for a plurality of perspective. The search for consensus is, on the other hand, more a political program of coercion than a moral ideal, and it will not be much better if it takes the disguise of the "method of discussion," as Dewey will stress in *Liberalism and Social Action*:

> The idea that the conflict of parties will, by means of public discussion, bring out necessary public truths is a kind of political watered-down version of the Hegelian dialectic, with its synthesis arrived at by a union of antithetical conceptions. The method has nothing in common with the procedure of organized cooperative inquiry which has won the triumphs of science in the field of physical nature.
>
> (LW 11, 251)

Discussion can be "corrupted," and we can make sense of this corruption only if we allow that, under the surface of polite discussions, claims do persist:

> The crisis in democracy demands the substitution of the intelligence that is exemplified in scientific procedure for the kind of intelligence that is now accepted. The need for this change is not exhausted in the demand for greater honesty and impartiality, even though these qualities be now corrupted by discussion carried on mainly for purposes of party supremacy and for imposition of some special but concealed interest.
>
> (LW 11, 51–52)

Even if the discussion comes to an end, there is still the possibility that underlying conflicts of duties persist, and that our moral (and political) discussions do not exhaust what there is to be said:

> The mass usually become unaware that they have a claim to a development of their own powers. Their experience is so restricted that they are not conscious of restriction. It is part of the democratic conception that they as individuals are not the only sufferers, but that the whole social body is deprived of the potential resources that should be at its service. The individuals of the submerged mass may not be very wise. But there is one thing they are wiser about than anybody else can be, and that is where the shoe pinches, the troubles they suffer from.
>
> (LW 11, 218–219)

Dewey, as Cavell later, has a clear perception that there are certain "dispensations" of society in which we can become unintelligible to ourselves, and that discussions and the search for consensus can obscure things, and need to be supplemented by other kinds of experiences.

The Eclipse of Duty?

But that is not the end of the story, since raising claims is not enough: we also have to respond to them and to assess their legitimacy; we have to articulate them and sometimes to hierarchize them, as James had suggested.

We have to assess duties, since, after all, coercion is also a social phenomenon, and does not command the same duties and loyalties as "intimate" relations, the new term Dewey is now using. Here is the criterion: duties arise from enduring relations: "the duties which express these relations are intrinsic to the situation, not enforced from without" (LW 7, 227–228). I shall come back to this stability-requirement, but, on the face of it, it does not seem to be enough too: relations of domination, of symbolic violence, even slavery, can be desperately enduring and "intrinsic to the situation." It might be the case that duties can supervene only on enduring relations, rather than episodic ones, but this stability cannot be the main ground for reverence and obedience.

If duties arise "from the relations which human beings intimately sustain to one another," if they "spring from the very nature of the relation that binds people together" (LW 7, 219), how are we to tell them from more coercive relations, such as brutal domination? There are two lines in the argument here: Dewey provides a test, but he also mentions a condition for the test.

The test implies that we are in capacity to answer the following question:

> Reflective morality asks: What about the rightfulness of specific claims and demands that are put forth by society, especially by those in authority? Are they, in the concrete forms in which they are put forth, claims and expectations which should be exercised?
>
> (LW 7, 225)

It is worth remarking, in line with the previous section, that that question is phrased in terms of actual situations ("concrete forms," "specific claims"). The test offered by Dewey is also more complex than the previous versions: it involves a demand, a vision of the good, and my own stance about this vision of the good:

> Does the conduct alleged to be obligatory, alleged to have the authority of moral law behind it, actually contribute to a good *in which the one from whom an act is* demanded will share?
>
> (LW 7, 230)[13]

But the test also seems to presuppose that, when we appeal to someone's sense of duty, we have to do it on the basis of shared valuations (or at least a mutual understanding of the good we'll share and of our respective situations in this share). Other voices need to have a moral standing. We can find a confirmation that such a condition is pressing for perfectionism in the fact that such an Un-Deweyan perfectionist as Cavell would stress exactly the same point:

> Moral standing is pushed to the center of the stage in perfectionism. Where the morally good is calculated, say in a revised tax code, or where the morally right is derived from Kant's categorical imperative, say in the case of abortion or capital punishment, if an act is bad or wrong, then it is bad or wrong period; that is, no matter who you are. But if you tell me "Neither a borrower nor a lender be" or "To thine own self be true," you had better have some standing with me from which you confront my life, from which my life matters to you, and matters to me that it matters to you.
>
> (Cavell 2004, 50)

This background condition for the test, in Dewey's text, seems to be more problematic than the general question or, to rephrase James's argument mentioned in the section "The Best and Simplest Statement," the equivalence claim-obligation itself presupposes background conditions that are fragile.

Let us try to explain why. Oddly enough, Dewey devotes an entire chapter to duties and to the justification of moral claims, and concludes with these words:

> In countless ways the customary loyalties that once held men together and made them aware of their reciprocal obligations have been sapped. Since the change is due to alteration of conditions, the new forms of lawlessness and the light and loose way in which duties are held cannot be met by direct and general appeal to a sense of duty or to the restraint of an inner law. The problem is to develop new stable relationships in society out of which duties and loyalties will naturally grow.
>
> (LW 7, 234)

Of course, the whole second part of E 1932 diagnoses a transition between customary morality and reflective morality and a natural objection would be that this transition, and this transition only, is at stake here. I think that the previous quote casts light on another aspect: the problem is not that customary rules and loyalties are threatened because that general change would apply to modernity as a whole.[14] I read it as saying that ordinary valuations, exactly the kind we might submit to reflective examination, become problematic. It is tempting to think that Dewey, here, is diagnosing an "eclipse" of duty that might be a counterpart to the eclipse of the public analyzed in *The Public and Its Problems*. Being aware of the "should," as contrasted with the Good, presupposes a background both of stable and reciprocal obligations which are essential to our moral claims, when we try to convince others about the objects where they should find their good or when we subject them to criticism. To Dewey's eyes, these very conditions are missing, or at least are becoming highly problematic.[15] We thus face a kind of dead-end: (a) the justification of claims presupposes specific social conditions (stable and "intimate" relations); (b) these conditions are missing and we can explain why in light of recent transformations of society; but (c) the justification of claims is just what makes the difference between duties and mere coercion. The chapter ends with a "problem," but the resolution, or transformation of the problematic situation, is not given, here, in Dewey's contribution.

Even if the 1932 *Ethics* can be read as a textbook on ethics, it is natural to try and see if Dewey's views, as expressed in major works from the "mature" period, influence his analysis of Ethics. I shall leave to others, or to future inquiries, comparisons between *Human Nature and Conduct* and Dewey's views on habit and character, and between *Experience and Nature* and the 1932 views on the moral self. In the remaining of this last section, I shall confine myself to a brief comparison between our chapter, Chapter 12, in particular the treatment of the justification of moral obligation, and *The Public and Its Problems* and *Individualism, Old and New*. The rationale for this comparison is the following: these are major works written and published just before E 1932, and both offer a treatment of moral "attachments" that resurface in the E 1932, as preconditions of moral relations, of our awareness and acknowledgment of duties.

In *The Public and Its Problems*, in the chapter "The Eclipse of the Public" as well as in other parts, Dewey had already addressed what he thought was a precondition for our responsiveness to the claims of others, which he described as a kind of "attachment." These attachments are instrumental in the emergence of publics, insofar as they help feeling concerned with the indirect consequences of associated action. They are themselves dependent upon our environment: when things move too fast, when "mobility" disturbs these attachments "at their root," publics become ghost-like, because they cannot identify themselves anymore. Or, in other terms, agents cannot identify themselves with the indirect consequences of associated action.

> [Attachments] are bred in tranquil stability; they are nourished in constant relationships. Acceleration of mobility disturbs them at

> their root. And without abiding attachments associations are too shifting and shaken to permit a public readily to locate and identify itself.
>
> (LW 2, 323)[16]

In E 1932, the issue is not the existence of publics anymore, but attachments are also crucial, when we respond to the claims of others, even to if we deflect them. This precondition in no way decides in favor of the validity of such claims, but helps making us aware of claims, when they are raised:

> A sense of a common value and interest binding persons together is therefore the normal support and guide. But we are all of us subject to conditions in which we tend to be insensitive to this value, and where the sense of what is due others is weak in comparison with the force of a contrary inclination. The claims of others then find a valuable ally in a generalized sense of right and obligation which has been growing up because of previous appreciations of concrete relations.
>
> (LW 7, 233)

For the same reason as in *The Public and Its Problems*, these shared "previous appreciations of concrete relations" become unstable:

> Nevertheless, changes in domestic, economic, and political relations have brought about a serious loosening of the social ties which hold people together in definite and readily recognizable relations.
>
> (LW 7, 234)

Another version of the argument can be found in "The Lost Individual." The second part of the chapter, which is essential in the economy of *Individualism, Old and New*, focuses on the "relaxation of traditional moral codes" (LW 2, 73). Dewey addresses a common misunderstanding: thinking that this loosening is the consequence of individual deeds, of a few writings and works by artists and academics. But this is confusing causes and effects: literary persons and academic thinkers "reflect and voice the disintegration which new modes of living, produced by new forms of industry and commerce, have introduced" (LW 2, 74). This latter state of affairs is a major concern for the new individualism Dewey is formulating, since without a minimal stability in the ties that allow individuals to shape their lives, to exert their self-control, there is no individual at all, or, to repeat the title of the chapter, the individual is "lost." The negative part of Dewey's argument is quite clear and quite obvious: this rebuilding, this "reconstruction," is not at hand. It is an ongoing task.

Conclusion

I have claimed that, as such, Chapter 12 is in some ways aporetic. For reasons that were already developed in *The Public and Its Problems*, the practical justification of moral claims seems threatened, because its background condition, the sharing of ordinary values, is missing. That is the main problem not only for Dewey's theory of duty but also for his theory of democracy. Is the solution or the transformation of the problem given elsewhere in the book and, for that matter, in the chapters authored by Dewey? Chapters 16 and 17 deal with the "material side" of the problem and not the "formal" characterization of moral attitudes, i.e., with their "content," as "provided by contemporary organization of life" (LW 7, 314), so much so that we might expect a more detailed treatment of the eclipse of duty described in Chapter 12. Such an examination would be the natural sequel for the present chapter. From that perspective, Chapter 16, "Moral and Social Problems," has a more general scope: the need for an experimental approach to institutions in a context where they "lose their quasi-sacredness and are the objects of moral questioning" (LW 7, 315). As such, it can start providing alternative approaches to the inquiry on the Good, and on Values, as *The Quest for Certainty* had done. But concerning the weakening of duties and attachments, we find a more detailed treatment in chapter 17, "Morals and the Political Order." My hypothesis here is that this last chapter is an epitome of *The Public and Its Problems*, and in particular of the challenges to democracy Dewey was then surveying, but this would be the subject-matter for another paper.

On the more positive and constructive side, Dewey seems to be closer to James's 1891 text in 1932: the context is not that of the "growth" of the Self anymore but that of the articulation of conflicting ethical stances. Contrariwise to some readings, Dewey was not blind to the "tragic" dimension of ethical life, in particular when the opposition is not between Self and World but the Self and a multitude of Selves. The "claim-talk" puts a decisive stress on the discussion of singular ethical situations. The relevant question is not "What is Right?" anymore, but "Is *this* Right?" (LW 7, 163). Our chapter definitely paves the way for a perfectionist ethics, where the particular dimension of ethical cases becomes prominent; it is by no means "only" a textbook chapter, and it should be a required reading for any treatment of Dewey's ethical thought.

Notes

1 There are some passing mentions of it, but mainly in lists of references, see *The Study of Ethics, A Syllabus*, in EW 4, 227, and in the *Ethics* LW 7, 283.

2 James lists these conditions in the "metaphysical" section of the paper (James 1979, 145 *sq.*), after the "psychological" question, about the origin of

our moral ideas, and before the "casuistic" question, about the "measure of the various goods and ills that men recognize": "The next one in order is the metaphysical question, of what we mean by the words 'obligation,' 'good,' and 'ill'." A Wittgensteinian might talk of a "grammatical" elucidation.

3 James (1979, 141–162). The present chapter deals mainly with Dewey and commenting in detail upon this tremendously important text by James is not possible here, see Sarin Marchetti's fine piece, Marchetti (2010).

4 J. Dewey, *Letter to William James*, June 3, 1891, in: James (1992–2004 vol. 7, 165).

5 Marchetti (2010, §2).

6 I had tried to show how that program was fulfilled in other texts by James in the 1890s in Girel (2007).

7 See LW 4, ch. 10.

8 "In such a moral solitude, it is clear that there can be no outward obligation" (James 1979, 146).

9 John Dewey to Scudder Klyce (1927.05.18; Dewey and Hickman 1997 #04696).

10 See, for example, the analysis of the "claims" of absolutistic philosophies in James (1977, 29). Or the analysis of materialistic philosophies, in James (1979, 99–100).

11 See Roberto Frega's paper in this volume.

12 See also, for example, Dewey (2015, 26).

13 My emphasis.

14 Even in that case, it should be added that Dewey does not say that the change has to be read as demarcating two historical periods:

> Some degree of reflective thought must have entered occasionally into systems which in the main were founded on social wont and use, while in contemporary morals, even when the need of critical judgment is most recognized, there is an immense amount of conduct that is merely accommodated to social usage.
>
> (LW 7, 162)

15 Similar things happen to the Good and to Virtue and the reconstruction of character (LW 7, 260–261), but these phenomena, even though they evidence a similar shrinking of the good and of standards of virtue, should be explored for their own sake.

16 See at the end of *Freedom and Culture,* Dewey's own commentary on these lines, where, ten years after *The Public and Its Problems*, this problem is still pressing: "But the problem of harmonious adjustment between extensive activities, precluding direct contacts, and the intensive activities of community intercourse is a pressing one for democracy" (LW 13, 176–177).

References

Cavell, Stanley. 2004. *Cities of Words*. Cambridge, MA: Harvard University Press.

Dewey, John. 2015. "Lectures in Social and Political Philosophy." *European Journal of Pragmatism and American Philosophy* VII, no. 2. http://ejpap.revues.org/404

Dewey, John and Larry A. Hickman, ed. 1997. *The Correspondence of John Dewey, 1871–1952*. Charlottesville: InteLex Past Masters (Electronic Database).

Girel, Mathias. 2007. "Pragmatisme et éducation morale. Philosophie et conduite de la vie chez Peirce, James et Dewey." *L'art du comprendre* 16 (June): 49–79.

James, William. 1977. *A Pluralistic Universe, Works of William James.* Cambridge, MA: Harvard University Press. Original edition, 1909.

James, William. 1979. *The Will to Believe and Other Essays in Popular Philosophy, The Works of William James.* Cambridge , MA: Harvard University Press. Original edition, 1897.

James, William. 1992–2004. *The Correspondence of William James.* Skrupskelis, Ignas K., Berkeley, Elizabeth M. (eds.). Charlottesville: University Press of Virginia.

Marchetti, Sarin. 2010. "William James on Truth and Invention in Morality." *European Journal of Pragmatism and American Philosophy [Online]* II, no. 2. http://journals.openedition.org/ejpap/910

13 Moral Theory and Anti-Theory in Dewey's 1932 *Ethics*

Sarin Marchetti

Introduction: Dewey between Theory and Practice

What is moral philosophy good for?—and how should we understand and practice it accordingly? In attempting an answer to these vexed metaphilosophical questions about the very nature and point of ethical thinking, the multi-layered position advanced by Dewey in his 1932 *Ethics* represents a rich source for reflection, pragmatist and otherwise. What we find in this text, in fact, is both an elaboration of a number of ethical insights sketched in earlier works—most notably, in the *Outlines of a Critical Theory of Ethics* (1891), *The Study of Ethics: A Syllabus* (1894), *Human Nature and Conduct* (1922), and *The Quest for Certainty* (1929), as well as in "Moral Theory and Practice" (1891), "Self-Realization as the Moral Ideal" (1893), and "Three Independent Factors in Morals" (1930) —and an attempt at systematization. This is quite understandable, since the *Ethics* was originally written as a textbook, whose first edition came out in 1908, and hence Dewey, in the parts he wrote for the renewed edition—an almost different work altogether—attempted to make his views cohabit with an overview of the state of the art of philosophical ethics.[1]

This operation, although instructive and largely successful, brought to light a tension within Dewey's own philosophical and ethical outlook—a tension very well visible throughout the text. What we find in this work, or so I shall claim, is, in fact, the productive yet somewhat problematic coexistence of a *midwifery* conception of moral philosophy as piecemeal criticism of conduct from within moral practice, and as a *directive* device for moral education and growth governing practice from without. While the former aims at self-transformation via a rearrangement of what we know and yet tend to overlook about ourselves, the latter's goal is self-direction by means of considerations extrinsic to the problematic situation we find ourselves in. Although the formulation of aspects of the two understandings of moral matters is sometimes hardly distinguishable, mostly because of the significant pragmatic bent given by Dewey to moral reflection, once read in light of what happened to philosophical ethics at the dawn of the 20th-century after the demise of the moral systematizations of early and late modernity, we would be able to appreciate the coexistence, in the text, of rather different insights about how to best approach and eventually assist the moral life: what we might call a *therapeutic* conception of ethics and a *substantive* one.

This very duality lies—in spirit as well as in letter—at the core of pragmatist moral thinking, and hence Dewey's text can be seen as a source of both *anti-theoretical*—as in *midwifery* and *therapeutic*—approaches to ethical matters, and *theoretical*—as in *directorial* and *substantive*—ones within this philosophical tradition. The present chapter aims to explore this tension in Dewey's *Ethics*: in particular, this duality of philosophical methods and ethical purposes will be investigated by comparing how Dewey speaks about virtue and the virtues in Chapters 10 and 13 of the *Ethics*, where we find outlines of, respectively, an anti-theoretical and a theoretical approach to the moral life. Virtue and the virtues are in fact depicted by Dewey as *both* what allow the subject to successfully extricate herself from the troubling site she finds herself in by bringing to light the sources of her own understanding of the situation in need of practical healing—a movement which sources lie in the very subject undergoing this transformative activity—*and* what is needed to resolve the felt tension between conflicting factors to which establishment she has not contributed—amounting to an almost mechanical shift in moral focus. This is but an instance of the oscillation palpable in Dewey's work overall—and, as said, in pragmatism as a whole seen as an instance of an ever wider metaphilosophical contrast at the heart of contemporary moral philosophy—which reverberates in the other chapters of the *Ethics* as well, in which we can appreciate the alternation of chapters leaning more to an anti-theoretical reading (namely, Chapters 10 and 15), and chapters betraying a stronger theoretical purpose (Chapters 11–14).[2] Whether the two aspects can be reconciled, and how, can be answered only once their respective contours are properly acknowledged.

Moral Theory and Anti-Theory: Mapping the Ground

Philosophical ethics is currently characterized by two radically different pictures of the moral life, and hence of the latter's need for reflective guidance. On the one hand, it has been claimed how the business of defining the very shape of ethics is deeply intertwined with our most intimate moral outlooks as well as with our views about the methods and goals of moral philosophy as a reflective inquiry into the moral life. That is to say, according to this view it would be highly problematic, if not utterly impossible, to disentangle our commitments to, and involvement with, the moral life from the activity of critical reflection on what we take ethics to be and on the philosophical tools to investigate and possibly improve it. On the other hand, it has been claimed that, to avoid moralizations and moral preaching, the activity of critical reflection on our moral outlooks should be able to distance itself from the moral life it investigates with the goal of bettering it from without, as one might say. If we in fact think that the distancing from the singularity of the troubling situation we currently inhabit is crucial to the effectiveness of moral reflection, we would then be moving away from moral practice and rely on theoretical models of the good life in order to resolve such troubles; while if we think that reflective morality does not consist in the stepping outside of customary one but rather in its deepening or clarification, we would then need to breathe fresh air into customs themselves by means not so much of theory but rather of strokes of further practice. Moral philosophy, the moral life, and the moral inquirer seem then to be three legs of a table whose dependability relies on their capacity for overall balance, when too much or rather too little distance between them marks the difference between a stable yet unserviceable table and an accessible yet wobbling one.[3]

This is, in a nutshell, the situation moral philosophy has been facing in the 20th and now 21st century.[4] The so-called theory versus anti-theory quarrel over the nature and point of moral philosophizing and its relationship with the moral life which has been mounting with renewed force since the 1980s revolves around the feasibility and opportunity of emancipating moral practice from moral theory, and how.[5] The clash originated in the registration of a distance between different pictures of the moral life, and built up into a divide over how the moral life could and should be handled philosophically.[6] According to the moral theorists, the moral life consists in the facing of moral conflict—over goods, duties, and evaluation more broadly—which moral philosophy should alleviate by means of directive devices through which finding solutions to such moral problems, meta-ethical or normative alike. Contrarily to this picture, for the anti-theorists the moral life consists in the very capacity to, and responsibility in, raising moral issues—and hence to participate to the quest over goods, duties, and evaluation in the first place—with moral philosophy performing the therapeutic activity of helping us checking our very own credentials in moral matters. For the moral theorists, philosophical ethics should strengthen the moral life by supplying it with a foundation and structure through which remaking practice from without, while for the moral anti-theorists ethics should strengthen the moral life by clearing the way from misconceptions of how moral practice proceeds from within. The moral theorist is said to be governing the erratic moral life by means of devices not themselves subject to confusion and delusion—most notably, moral concepts and principles regulating the practice from the above of its contingencies—while the moral anti-theorist sees herself as assisting the moral life by means of midwifery reminders about the very unfolding of the moral practice under critical scrutiny—that is signposts potentially redirecting the self from within its contingencies which are themselves subject to change and rearrangements.[7]

Confronted by the anti-theorists, the theorists—when sensible to the challenge at all—tried to present their principled directives with a keener sight on the unfolding of moral practice, although their attempts have been often rebutted as mere cosmetic readjustments of a hopeless foundational model hindering, rather than empowering, the moral life, generating a new wave of anti-theoretical protest.[8]

Pragmatism did not shy away from the debate over the statute of philosophical ethics, and offered its own version of things.[9] However, the answer was not unitary, as pragmatism proved to be equally torn between an understanding of moral philosophy as a therapeutic, midwifery activity—along a Jamesian-Rortian line—and an understanding of moral philosophy as a substantive, directive task—along a Lewisian-Misakian line. The issue of whether pragmatist ethics should be read as theoretical or rather a therapeutic piece of philosophical activity revolves around the nature of the alleged practical character of moral reflection itself, and its bearings on the moral life. To see what pragmatism can contribute to this nagging debate we should acknowledge the distinctive pragmatist metaphilosophy with its radical understanding of philosophical theorizing—and, as a consequence, of anti-theorizing. If, for pragmatism, to use James's famous line, "*theories become instruments, not answers to enigmas, in which we can rest*" (James 1975, 32), then moral theories will equally be "limbered up" and work as tools thanks to which to plough and rework the moral terrain they purportedly cover. If this is the case, then, pragmatist moral theorizing should look like an activity of resolution of ethical troubles via bottom-up—as against top-down—interventions of philosophical conceptions. Still, theories so conceived do retain an aspect of moral directivity which would remake moral experience and conduct in light of considerations exceeding the problematic situation at hand.

As a contrary to this pragmatist, theoretical thrust, pragmatist anti-theory variously thinks of moral philosophy as an activity in which the only appropriate tools are the ones under-labored by the subjects involved themselves. Anti-theoretical pragmatist approaches are in fact equally skeptical of both bottom-up and top-down directive approaches in so much as they aim to lift subjects out of the problematic situations they occupy from without. To quote James again, pragmatism should be understood as that particular attitude "*of looking away from first things, principles, 'categories,' supposed necessities; and of looking towards last things, fruits, consequences, facts*" (James 1975, 32). The point of philosophical ethics, on this score, is not so much that of handling subjects tools through which ameliorating their position—say, by looking at the consequences of the various competing rules and principles—as the pragmatist theorists think, but rather showing subjects how to handle the tools they already possess and yet overlook so to ameliorate their own self-understanding and hence moral condition—say, by taking care of their perception of, and reaction to, the moral landscape.[10]

One significant outcome of this clash, inside and outside of pragmatism, has been the re-discovery of the language of the virtues as a way to center moral philosophy back on the moral self and away from abstractedness. That of virtue is in fact at once a descriptive and an evaluative term, its point being that of tracing morality back to human beings and their makeup—actual or possible alike. In this regard, the insistence on the virtues, as opposed to norms and principles both in their deontological and consequentialist varieties, have been often taken as the mark of an anti-theoretical approach, so much that virtue ethics—drawing back to such Classics as Aristotle and Hume—has since become one of the preferred venues along which to vindicate the primacy of practice over theory. Yet, lots hinge on our conception of the virtues, as, once again, both a theoretical and an anti-theoretical understanding of them is possible. According to a theoretical understanding, the virtues are the excellent traits of what we might call human nature—our metaphysical or natural constitution—and hence they show how human beings should think, speak, and act independently of the particular position they currently occupy. According to anti-theoretical understanding, instead, virtues hinge on a reflective capacity of human beings—indeed a practical possibility—to review the particular position they happen to occupy.[11] While, according to the former, what the virtues deliver is a safe route to our duties and obligations—as is, e.g., the case with Plato and Kant—for the latter, the virtues signal our distinctive positioning in the moral realm and hence our very accountability—e.g. for Hume and Nietzsche.[12]

Virtue ethics has since played the double role of either a more nuanced moral theory or rather as an example of moral anti-theory, and this depends on the metaphysical or rather practical understanding of its very nature and mission. Now Dewey, in the *Ethics*, seems to have endorsed a distinctive version of both understandings of the virtues, contributing in this way to the clash between theoretical and anti-theoretical conception of moral philosophy I have been presenting in this section. While his contribution to this quite intricate debate cannot be reduced to his conception of virtue and the virtuous life, this is what I will be mostly occupied with in the remaining of this chapter, as I take his views on the virtues as representative of his broader understanding of philosophical ethics and its relationship with the moral life. To show the relevance of Dewey's understanding of virtue to the metaphilosophical debate about the nature and point of ethical thinking, a few words more on how Dewey understood moral theory—and hence anti-theory—are in order.

Ethics and Metaphilosophy in the *1932 Ethics*

Dewey is a particularly interesting figure as in his work we can find traces of both ethical theory and therapy, pragmatically understood. In his many ethical writings we can appreciate several endorsements of both theoretical and anti-theoretical conceptions of moral inquiry. Not only, in fact, Dewey changed his mind about single ideas or even overall themes over time thanks both to philosophical discoveries and to mutation in cultural climate—think about the waning of the role of perfection as a moral ideal or the affirmation of habit as a central moral category and dispositive—but he also couched these variations in terms of their contribution to either pragmatic moral theory or pragmatic moral practice.[13] Here's a sample of Dewey's early, middle, and late statements:

> **Dewey as Theorist:**
> The difficulty, then, is to find the place intermediate between a theory general to the point of abstractness, a theory which provides help to action, and a theory which attempts to further action, but does so at the expense of its spontaneity and breadth. I do not know of any theory, however, which is quite consistent to either point of view.
>
> (EW 3, 155)
>
> Theory located within progressive practice instead of reigning statically supreme over it, means practice itself made responsible to intelligence; to intelligence which relentlessly scrutinizes the consequences of every practice, and which exacts liability by an equally relentless publicity. As long as morals occupies itself with mere ideals, forces and conditions as they are will be enough for "practical" men, since they are then left free to their own devices in turning these to their own account.
>
> (MW 4, 48)
>
> A moral principle, such as that of chastity, of justice, of the Golden Rule, gives the agent a basis for looking at and examining a particular question that comes up. It holds before him certain possible aspects of the act; it warns him against taking a short or partial view of the act. It economizes his thinking by supplying him with the main heads by reference to which to consider the bearings of his desires and purposes; it guides him in his thinking by suggesting to him the important considerations for which he should be on the lookout.
>
> (LW 7, 280)

Dewey as Anti-theorist:

I am certain that moral science is *not* a collection of abstract laws, and that it is only in the mind of an agent as an agent. It is his perception of the acts that need doing, – that is, his perception of the existing world of practice in all its concrete relationships [...]. Moral theory, so far as it can exist outside of the particular agent concerned with a special act, exists in the mind of him who can reproduce the condition of that agent.

(EW 3, 99)

Growth of present action in shades and scope of meaning is the only good within our control, and the only one, accordingly, for which responsibility exists. The rest is luck, fortune. And the tragedy of the moral notions most insisted upon by the morally self-conscious is the relegation of the only good which can fully engage thought, namely present meaning of action, to the rank of an incident of a remote good, whether that future good be defined as pleasure, or perfection, or salvation, or attainment of virtuous character.

(MW 14, 194)

A moral philosophy which should frankly recognize the impossibility of reducing all the elements in moral situations to a single commensurable principle, which should recognize that each human being has to make the best adjustment he can among forces which are genuinely disparate, would throw light upon actual predicaments of conduct and help individuals in making a juster estimate of the force of each competing factor. All that would be lost would be the idea that theoretically there is in advance a single theoretically correct solution for every difficulty with which each and every individual is confronted.

(LW 5, 288)

While in the first list of quotations moral theory is thought of as what enlightens moral practice *by making it* reflective and intelligent, in the second list moral practice is best pictured when emancipated from moral theory *at pains to* losing its reflective character. While a theoretical understanding of moral reflection focuses on the task of *resolving* conflict—hence placing reflectivity within moral theory—a practical one revolves deals with the issue of how to *discriminate* conflict in the first place—hence placing reflective within moral practice itself.

Now, both registers seem to be simultaneously at play in the *Ethics*, where we find a juxtaposition of an understanding of philosophical ethics as concerned with the implementation of reflective tools—which have the shape of the key concepts of the good, duty, and the virtues—to direct the moral life, and an understanding of philosophical ethics as the inquiry of our very positioning—that is our character and paths of habituation—from which a moral situation is faced as such. Both options are pragmatic reconfigurations of the metaphilosophical categories I have been presenting in the previous section. Dewey's chief ethical questioning, epitomizing the pragmatist mindset, revolves around the issue of how moral philosophy can be effective—that is affecting our thinking and conduct—without being prescriptive—telling us what to think and do. Moral philosophy, for Dewey

> does not offer a table of commandments in a catechism in which answers are as definite as are the questions which are asked. It can render personal choice more intelligent, but it cannot take the place of personal decision, which must be made in every case of moral perplexity.
>
> (LW 7, 166)

In walking this rather narrow path, Dewey, on the one hand, leans toward a thoroughly therapeutic strategy, while, on the other, he attempts a rescue of moral theorizing as one such form of practice. One way of presenting this clash is in terms of a difference between the analysis of *ordinary moral problems* and the analysis of the *problems of moral theory*. While according to the anti-theoretical understanding, once philosophical ethics successfully deals with the former, the latter might happily go, for the theoretical understanding the two inquiries go hand in hand, and the question becomes that of the practical import of the reflection on moral theorizing. Pragmatist moral theorists and anti-theorists disagree over the nature and place of moral reflection in our moral lives: while according to the theoretical understanding moral philosophy is what *spurs* moral reflection by handling the subjects the instruments (principles, rules, standards) to effectively choose among competing values, goods, and duties of which the moral life is paved, according to the anti-theoretical understanding moral reflection consists in the critical survey of what lead moral practice to become problematic in the first place by investigating the kind of selves we became *so to have* such doubts about how to go on living morally.[14]

Dewey opens the part of the book he wrote with a chapter on the very methodology and metaphilosophy of ethics, making a strong statement for an anti-theoretical understanding of moral reflection. In Chapter 10 the distinction drawn between customary and reflective morality is one in depth in self-understanding rather than in actions performed—or at least most importantly so. A change in conduct is in fact depicted as a reassessment of the customary self in light of the new situation—with this explaining why the distinction between customary and reflective morality is "relative" rather than "absolute." Dewey writes in this direction that

> The difference between customary and reflective morality is precisely that definite precepts, rules, definitive injunctions and prohibitions issue from the former, while they cannot proceed from the latter. Confusions ensue when appeal to rational principles is treated as if it were merely a substitute for customs, transferring the authority of moral commands from one source to another.
>
> (LW 7, 165–166)

The key features of moral reflexivity thus lie in the "enabling a perplexed and doubtful individual to *clarify* his own particular problem by placing it in a larger context...[and] render personal reflection more systematic and enlightened, suggesting alternatives that might be otherwise *overlooked*" (LW 7, 166, emphases mine). Dewey's focus is here on what the individual might do of, and for, her own understanding of the moral situation, with philosophy playing a therapeutic, clarificatory role. As this part of the book unfolds, however, we have Chapters 11–14 on the three "working theories of morals" and their contribution to, and combination in, moral knowledge in which Dewey shifts the focus from moral understanding to moral resolution of conflict, with philosophy turning into a directive device for sorting out action, closing it with Chapter 15 on the moral self in which the two conceptions cohabit in the idea of the "*essential unity of self and its acts*" (LW 7, 288).[15] This progression is not explicitly acknowledged by Dewey, who apparently saw the two understandings on a continuum.

The preface to the first edition of the text, which was kept for the second edition and only supplemented with a much shorter and rather uninformative one indicating the changes which have occurred, opens with a statement which equally sits between the two understandings, suggesting both the idea according to which the task of moral philosophy is to facilitate self-understanding, and the idea according to which there would be moral problems to be decided via reflective procedures with the aid of philosophical theories. We read:

> The significance of this text in Ethics lies in its efforts to awaken a vital conviction of the genuine reality of moral problems and the value of reflective thought in dealing with them.
>
> (LW 7, 5)

Now the student of morals, whom will enter the scene but a few lines down and to whom the book—a textbook indeed, although a rather peculiar one— is explicitly addressed, is the moral inquirer—whom one eventually thinks or rather hopes has an impact which is much wider than the library and seminar room— facing the dilemma about how to square her moral life with moral philosophy, and *vice versa*. The idea is that the book aims not so much at giving philosophical answers to moral problems, but rather to awaken (or perhaps re-awaken) the connection between moral reflection and practice, empowering us in the critical handling of their coupling. Yet, this goal admits two readings, and what Dewey writes right afterward can be interpreted accordingly. On the one hand, the point of such awakening is to (re-)direct one's attention to one's conduct and its moral quality—our habits and their (re-)formation—always under our eyes and yet, because of this, often disregarded. We read in this regard:

> Experience shows that the student of morals has difficulty in getting the field objectively and definitely before him so that its problems strike him as real problems. Conduct is so intimate that it is not easy to analyze. It is so important that to a large extent the perspective for regarding it has been unconsciously fixed by early training [...]. To follow the moral life through typical epochs of its development enables students to realize what is involved in their own habitual standpoints; it also presents a concrete body of subject-matter which serves as material of analysis and discussion.
>
> (LW 7, 5)

Being conduct so pervasive and intimately related to our sense of self, we tend to reduce our habitual responses to what is commonly felt—to which we have been trained—in such situations, disregarding our personal contribution in moral matters. According to this understanding, moral progress takes the shape of a work of the self on the self, in which we are called to mobilize ourselves. On the other hand, yet presented in continuity with the former, Dewey praises, with qualification, the role of a theoretical understanding of moral principles as practical guides to the moral life, which however should not be mistaken with what they try to cast a critical light on—that is, moral experience. We read:

> The classic conceptions of moral theory are of remarkable importance in illuminating the obscure places of the moral life and in giving the student clues which will enable him to explore it for himself. But there is always danger of either dogmatism or a sense of unreality when students are introduced abruptly to the theoretical ideas. Instead of serving as tools for understanding the moral facts, the ideas are likely to become substitutes for the facts [...]. Theories are treated not as incompatible rival systems which must be accepted or rejected *en bloch*, but as more or less adequate methods of surveying the problems of conduct.
>
> (LW 7, 5–6)

The moral life is then to be enlightened by devices that have a certain degree of autonomy from the problematic situation under scrutiny, giving clues to the subject involved in how to resolve the inbuilt tension in it. Here moral progress consists in the settling of the unsettled situation, thanks to the tools handled to us by reflective theories.

If it is true that Dewey is consistent in presenting moral problems as problems of meaningful conduct, the key issue is that we find, in the text, at least two understandings of conduct indeed: what we might call self-conduct—that is what we make of ourselves so to face moral situations the way we do—and conduct as overt action—that is deliberation about what is morally appropriate in the first place.[16] While the former calls for checking of oneself as the very source of moral significance, the latter tends to present the moral situation such self faces as already morally loaded before any contribution from her part. While self-conduct invites moral midwifery, that is the prevention from getting "morally discouraged" (LW 7, 306) at remaking oneself and fostering growth in meaning in so doing, overt action is a matter of moral directivity, that is the "guidance for the unsolved problems of life which continually present themselves for decision" (LW 7, 15).

In Chapter 10, Dewey speaks of two kinds of moral struggles, both having to do with a conflict in goods, standards, and rules: one has to do with the "conflict which takes place when an individual is tempted to do something which he is convinced is wrong" (LW 7, 164), while the other with "a conflict between incompatible values presented to him by his habits" (LW 7, 165). Now while the former, although practically important, does not occasion moral theory as it is a mere case of weakness of will which does not cloud our conception of what is right to do,[17] the latter prompts critical reflection about which values one has to let go by rearranging her end in this way. While the former consists in a problem of personal consistency, the latter is an instance of practical conflict: only the latter, but not the former, will then be genuine moral problems. Now, in addition to these, another case of moral struggle worth singling out is that in which what is at stake is our very capacity to fix ends in the first place, to which Dewey refers only in passing when he relates moral activity to character formation later into the book but which is of the highest moral significance as it constitutes an alternative picture of the moral work on the self. Now, this case of moral struggle does not so much raise the need to resolve the conflict by butchering the source(s) of trouble or instability, but rather to resolve the self by checking it and reconfiguring it otherwise. What is actively exercised in the latter, and given for granted in the former case, is the capacity to discriminate a given situation *as* moral, *and hence* one possibly in need of being reworked through deliberation and choice.

In this third kind of moral struggle virtue is equally called in cause, although very differently so. To see how, I shall now pass to the rather different treatments we find, in the *Ethics*, of this feature of both moral philosophy and the moral life.

Virtue and the Virtues: Habituation as Insight and as Choice

Although Dewey is not ranked among the greats of virtue ethics, and the works specifically dedicated to this aspect of his moral thought constitute a tiny yet quality niche,[18] it is simply impossible to miss—far less to understand—his multiple references to this moral option as well as the discussion of its past embodiments. The concept of virtue is in fact internally related to those of character, habit, and growth, which in turn represent the very backbone of Dewey's moral outlook and approach. It is then rather curious, one might notice, that so little has been written directly on it, despite it is often referred to when dealing with Dewey's moral philosophy. If it is true that the focus of the scholarship is often on the mentioned kindred concepts, virtue would have deserved much better publicity as the way we read this cluster notion would affect the most notable ones associated with it as well. And, as I shall argue in this section, plenty hinges on how we read it.

What strikes the reader of the *Ethics* is the difference in characterization, treatment, and use of virtue in Chapters 10 and 13, although, to my knowledge at least, this has been overlooked by the literature—or at least underappreciated. What is even more curious is that in Chapter 10.3, titled "Conduct and Character," virtue does not even feature as a word despite the whole section is a detailed discussion of its working and consequences. Indeed, the term virtue makes its day-view only very late in the chapter, when in Chapter 10.6 Dewey presents the contents of the forthcoming chapters. Two more entries in Chapters 10.1 and 10.5 play no significant role as virtue is mentioned in passing as one feature of morality among others—hence closer, if possible, to how Dewey will be understanding it in Chapter 13. We then face the somewhat paradoxical situation in which virtue, despite bearing much of the load of Chapter 10, is barely mentioned, although many singular virtues—that is examples of the stable traits and dispositions of a well-crafted character—are occasionally listed. This absence possibly constitutes the reason why the understanding of virtue put forward in this chapter—and especially in the pivotal Chapter 10.3—has been neglected by the literature.

The two different ways in which Dewey thinks of virtue is exemplary of the metaphilosophical contrast I have been mounting in the previous sections. On the one hand, Dewey in fact depicts virtue now as one aspect of (or factor in) moral judgment—having to do with the approval and disapproval of actions and characters seen in social contexts—which harmonize the opposite pulls of (inner) intentions and (outer) consequences. On the other hand, Dewey also presents virtue as the very capacity of the subject to appreciate the situation at hand as one requiring undertaking or rather retraction—that is, having to do with the fostering or rather with the hindering of selected reflective habits of thought and conduct. Virtue is what allows the subject to *relate* the goods and duties involved *in* the problematic situation, but virtue is also—and perhaps most importantly—what allows one to *see* the goods and duties which make the situation *as* problematic in the first place. According to the first understanding, virtue is a part of what makes us morally skilled to judge and choose, while according to the second understanding, virtue consists in those moral habits which skillfully select morally significant situations. If so, the clash would not be between virtues as intuitive and as reflective devices—as often portrayed by non-pragmatist virtue theorists—but rather between the exercise and the direction of one's subjectivity.

The chapter by Roberto Frega in this volume carefully reconstructs the progress in Dewey's understanding of the virtues from an early "connectionist," to a middle "irreducibility," to a late "interactionist" model. If my reconstructive hypothesis is sound, the "interactionist," theoretical model Dewey eventually defends in Chapter 13 of the *Ethics* is only half of the story, to be complemented—perhaps contrasted—with what we might call an "expressivist" or "sensibilist," anti-theoretical model put forward in Chapter 10.

The anti-theoretical understanding in Chapter 10.3 reprises several such themes from (and entire passages of) *Human Nature and Conduct*, of which it is in all respects a brief yet effective digest. In this picture the context for morality is the presence of a self with a character won by strokes of habitual responses: conduct is portrayed as the active expression of this sedimented character, always reinforced or rather challenged by the choices it lives by, or fails to. Action or inaction is to be valued from the point of view of their consequences on the self, that is their "effects upon character, upon confirming and weakening habits" (MW 14, 35). A consideration becomes morally relevant or irrelevant in the measure in which it touches the self and its stratified habits. In turn, what is so valuable can be told only from the point of view of the end they bring about.

Virtue is the capacity to raise a moral issue, or rather abstracting from so doing, and so to discriminate what makes a situation moral in the first place, that is one in which our individual contribution is called for. Dewey writes:

> *Potentially* conduct is one hundred percent of our conscious life. For all acts are so tied together that any one of them may have to be judged as an expression of character. On the other hand, there is no act which may not, under some circumstances, be morally indifferent, for at the time there may be no need for consideration of its

> relation to character. There is no better evidence of a well-formed moral character than knowledge of when to raise the moral issue and when not. It implies the sensitiveness to values which is the token of a balanced [virtuous] person.
>
> (LW 7, 170)

In *Human Nature and Conduct* we find a similar formulation of this challenge:

> The mutual modification of habits by one another enables us to define the nature of the moral situation [...]. To know when to leave acts without distinctive moral judgment and when to subject them to is itself a large factor in morality. The serious matter is that this relative pragmatic, or intellectual, distinction, between the moral and the non-moral, has been solidified into a fix and absolute distinction, so that some acts are popularly regarded as forever within and others forever without the moral domain. From this fatal error recognition of the relations of one habit to others preserves us. For it makes us see that character is the name given to the working interactions of habits, and that the cumulative effect on insensible modifications worked by a particular habit in the body of preferences may at any moment require attention.
>
> (MW 14, 31)

This discriminative task is open-ended and ultimately individual, as it showcases our very involvement with morality. To ask what counts as moral amounts to asking what kind of people we are and will be. The reflective capacity to distribute moral value, and to tell moral from non-moral situations, is indeed prospective, as it foretells which self I will become.[19] What is at stake, when our virtues are exhibited, is not so much the capacity to resolve *the* problematic situation by means of (pragmatized) theory—as a tool for dealing with a difficulty in choice—but rather the capacity to see the situation *as* problematic in the first place through the aim of (pragmatized) practice—as a reminder of our habitual constitution leading to such difficulty. While the goal of the former is growth itself, the point of the latter is resolution.

When Dewey, in Chapter 13, discusses virtue, it suddenly becomes the centerpiece of the triad of notions that rule our conduct as directive devices also listing the good and the right. In particular, virtues redirect our judgments of goodness and rightness by showing how we do, as a matter of fact, praise both duties and consequences as diverse aspects of our reflective moral practices about what to do. Virtues so understood are what allows subject to accommodate both motives and outcomes in moral judgment, hence reforming the two schools of deontology and utilitarianism presented in Chapters 11 and 12. No chance than that in

Chapter 14, dedicated to moral judgment, Dewey presents sound moral deliberation (involving both intentions and outcomes) as that best performed by the experienced (that is virtuous) agent. Here's Dewey:

> Deliberation involves doubt, hesitation, the need of making up one's mind, of arriving at a decisive choice. The choice at stake in a moral deliberation or valuation is the worth of this and that kind of character and disposition [...]. Deliberation is actually an imaginative rehearsal of various courses of conduct. We give way, *in our mind*, to some impulse; we try, *in our mind*, some plan. Following its career through the various steps, we find ourselves in imagination in the presence of the consequences that would follow: and as we then like and approve, or dislike and disapprove, these consequences, we find the original impulse or plan good or bad.
>
> (LW 7, 275)

In Chapter 13 virtue is depicted as the immediate or original capacity to approve or condemn (as vices) the motives and deeds of others—and our own at earlier times—thus offering the standards of judgment. This spontaneous capacity for praising or blaming must be systematized and made itself reflective, in a movement from what is valu*ed* to what is valu*able*—from idiosyncrasy to objectivity—which would, in turn, constitute a standard for what is to be done. Once stabilized, these responses become self-reflective and start feeding back on their own applications. As Dewey writes, "approval and disapproval themselves are subjected to judgment by a standard instead of being taken as ultimate" (LW 7, 254). A virtuous person is then someone whom not only judges according to standards of approval or disapproval, but is herself subject to such standards in the measure in which such approbations and reprobations reveal who we are. Writes Dewey:

> In judging, in commending and condemning, we are judging ourselves, revealing our own tastes and desires. Approval and disapproval, the attitude of attributing vice and virtue, becomes itself a vice or virtue according to the way in which it is administered.
>
> (LW 7, 255)

If this is the case, then, the virtues represent that device through which we judge what to do, and shape who we will likely be, by weighting both the demands of individuality and those of society. The goal and value of the virtues are that of exploring the moral complexity of the situation, and harmonize conflicts generated by the opposite pulls of individuality and sociality through the insight about what might resolve the generated tension. In so doing we would be settling the dispute between individual appetites and environmental considerations and see both as different routes leading to the realization of a common good, where the ends actively pursued are those which are praised by the constraints of societal bounds.

Conclusion: Towards a Unified Picture?

These being the two occurrences and understanding of virtue, which in turn betray as many metaphilosophical understandings of the relationship between moral philosophy and the moral life, one might ask whether the two understandings are ultimately irreconcilable. This issue goes beyond strict Deweyan scholarship—for which it is indeed relevant in its problematizing the standard view of how character and conduct, or self and act, necessarily go together[20]—and poses a genuinely philosophical problem about where to place reflectivity in moral practice which exceeds the scope of this chapter. I shall close with a few brief considerations about what might invite to think them in continuity or rather in discontinuity with each other.

On the one hand, we might be tempted to opt for their essential irreconcilability, as they suggest different overall pictures of the moral life and the opportunity of a philosophical intervention on it, and of which kind. If virtue is depicted as the practical ability—to be constantly negotiated as one goes along—to discriminate moral salience by re-making the self, then there would be no room or need for a further directive device for choice: taking care of one's moral landscape is already to take action in distinctive ways. In this case, what I have called a midwifery conception of ethical thinking occupies the entire spectrum of philosophical activity, as to (still) raise the directive question about how to resolve conflict in choice would mean to miss the idea of how something becomes a problem altogether. But if we take virtue as concerned with those particular choices about the next self we will turn into by so choosing among competing options, then any depiction of moral insight beyond this activity of discrimination and resolution, enlightened by moral theorizing, would look like a rather suspect survival of teleological or metaphysical capacities to seize the moral realm. This interpretation of Dewey is the most intriguing as, at least to my knowledge, it points to a tension between moral discrimination and action often if not systematically underplayed by the literature.

On the other hand, a possible reconciliation might go in the direction of acknowledging these two aspects as performing different tasks and eventually completing each other by transforming each other: self-transformation makes direction thicker, while direction makes self-transformation practical and effective. Vision creates the site for moral action, which in turn certifies and validates such vision. As Stéphane Madelrieux claims in his contribution to this volume, for Dewey "the purpose of moral reflection is to solve specific moral problems not just to perfect oneself," and hence any moral thinking stopping short of action would be simply ineffective. On the other hand, what would be the point if a moral resolution was not, first and foremost, a betterment of the self? If this is indeed the case, perhaps then the difference between the two understandings of virtue, although present, should not be overdramatized—the distinction should not be built into a divide, at pains of falling into the very dichotomic thinking alien to the Deweyan spirit—as they jointly contribute to the very same quest of making sense of our practices as we go along. This option would be the one more in line with the scholarship, as it would present the two movements (clarification and choice) as aspects of the larger moral activity of self-constitution.

Irreconcilable or not, the task of this chapter has been that of registering the co-presence of the two moral registers in the *Ethics*, showing their wider metaphilosophical stakes, and, in so doing, evoking a possible tension within Dewey's ethical thinking which can be instructive for non-Deweyans moral philosophers as well.[21]

Notes

1 For a highly informative presentation of the origins and structure of the text, as well as of the methodological and substantive differences between the two editions, see Edel and Flower (1985), who also offer a brief yet compelling reading of the cultural and intellectual background against which the new edition has been written. Three recent, finest overviews of Dewey's moral philosophy putting the *Ethics* in connection with the wider body of his ethical work are Welchman (2010), Fesmire (2015, ch. 4) and Anderson (2018).

2 It is important to notice how the "Preface" and Chapter 1 feature aspects of both, and how, more generally, even the chapters I have indicated as falling within one of the two camps admit occasional exceptions, betraying Dewey's duality about the matter and, in the end, perhaps, his attempt to bring the two understandings together.

3 See Putnam (2004) for an illuminating version of this contrast.

4 For an early classical statement (see Prichard 1912). For an even earlier, pragmatist pronouncement (see Dewey's "Moral Theory and Practice" (EW 3: 93–109); James 1978[1891]). For an influential recounting of the unfolding of the events told from the point of view of moral theory, but with an eye to anti-theory as well (see Darwall, Gibbard and Railton 1992).

5 For the terms of the contemporary anglophone debate over the scope and stakes of moral philosophizing, see the by now classical Clarke and Simpson (1989) and Louden (1992), and the recent attempt at a synthesis by Fotion (2014).

6 The text that almost single-handedly brought the clash to the forefront of the philosophical discussion is Williams (1985), on which see Hooker (2012). For a forceful presentation of the wider stakes of the divide (see Rorty 2007).

7 Some of these issues have been variously touched upon by Jörg Volbers's contribution to this volume, with whom the present chapter shares more than a diagnosis, even if not all of the remedies.

8 Needless to say, the anti-theorists vary even more than the theorists in their assumptions, strategies, and goals—if only because they variously reacted

to what they saw as the various theoretical varieties of moral theory. For a recent genealogy of moral anti-theory (see Robertson 2017). Some possible synergies between Wittgensteinian and pragmatist anti-theorist varieties have been explored by Frega (2014) and Marchetti (2016).

9 For the best efforts to showcase pragmatist's reconstructions in philosophical ethics to date (see Lekan 2003; Wallace 2009). For specifically Deweyan versions (see Fesmire 2003).

10 On this way of ordering the various joints collectively bearing, or claiming, the title of pragmatist ethics, see Marchetti in progress.

11 I have addressed this point, if only briefly, in Marchetti (2013). For a contrast between metaphysical and practical aspects of the virtues with reference to the pivotal issue of moral exemplarism (see Marchetti 2018).

12 The literature on virtue ethics is vast and uneven, as it is the tradition accounted for. For an overview (see Russell 2013; van Hooft 2014).

13 The best overall survey of Dewey's moral philosophy, in which theoretical and (what I call) anti-theoretical aspects are investigated in their communal quest to enlighten moral experience, is Pappas (2008).

14 I owe thanks to Roberto Gronda for having suggested this alternative formulation.

15 In his contribution to this volume, Steven Levine excavates the Hegelian roots of Dewey's composite conception of growth as act and as end along lines which are congenial to my reading of Dewey as undecided, and possibly torn apart, between a constitutivist and a proceduralist conception of moral inquiry.

16 Goodman (2007) traces a similar distinction, in Dewey, between action as "intelligent bodily activity" and action as "growth," "self-expression," or "finding one's way," opposing both to the Peircean purely logical-inferentialist understanding.

17 One might indeed question, from an internalist point of view, if in such cases of "obstructed will," to use a Jamesian expression dear to Dewey, the moral force of the conviction is intact, or whether it is not itself jeopardized and radically questioned by such inaction.

18 See Gouinlock (1986), Alexander (1993), Rosenbaum (1994), Teehan (1995), Carden (2006) and Frega, this volume.

19 This anti-theoretical reading of virtue resonates with McDowell's (1996) thesis about the uncodifiability of ethical responses. Differently from Dewey, however, McDowell does not seem to make any room for personal transformation. On the opportunity of this lack (see Donatelli 2018). On Dewey and McDowell on ethical training (see Welchman 2008).

20 Thanks to Roberto Frega for bringing this to my attention.

21 My warmest thanks to Roberto Frega and Steven Levine for having lured me into this project and for their extended patience. I am also grateful to the participants to the workshop on Dewey's Ethics held at the Centre Marc Bloch in December 2018, and especially to Jörg Volbers for a thorough commentary to an earlier version of this chapter, which put me on a much more profitable path – a path reinforced by further precious comments by Roberto Frega, Roberto Gronda, Steven Levine, Federico Lijoi, and Stéphane Madelrieux.

References

Alexander, Thomas M. 1993. "John Dewey and Moral Imagination: Beyond Putnam and Rorty toward a Postmodern Ethics." *Transactions of the Charles S. Peirce Society* 29, no. 3: 369–400.

Anderson, Elizabeth. 2018. "Dewey's Moral Philosophy." *Stanford Encyclopedia of Philosophy*. https://plato.stanford.edu/entries/dewey-moral/

Carden, Stephen D. 2006. *Virtue Ethics: Dewey and MacIntyre*. London and New York: Continuum.

Clarke, Stanley G. and Evan Simpson, eds. 1989. *Anti-Theory in Ethics and Moral Conservatism*. Albany: State University of New York Press.

Darwall, Stephen, Allan Gibbard, and Peter Railton. 1992. "Toward *Fin de siècle* Ethics: Some Trends." *The Philosophical Review* 101, no. 1: 115–189.

Donatelli, Piergiorgio. 2018. "Moral Perfectionism and Virtue." *Critical Inquiry* 45, no. 2: 332–350.

Edel, Abraham and Elizabeth Flower. 1985. "Introduction." In *The Later Works of John Dewey, 1925–1953*, Volume 7: 1932 *Ethics*. Carbondale: Southern Illinois University Press, vii–xxxv.

Fesmire, Steven. 2003. *John Dewey and Moral Imagination*. Bloomington: Indiana University Press.

Fesmire, Steven. 2015. *Dewey*. London and New York: Routledge Press.

Fotion, Nick. 2014. *Theory vs. Anti-Theory in Ethics: A Misconceived Conflict*. Oxford: Oxford University Press.

Frega, Roberto. 2014. "New Voices for Expressive Pragmatism: Bridging the Divide between Pragmatism and Perfectionism." *Metaphilosophy* 45, no. 3: 399–421.

Goodman, Russell. 2007. "Two Genealogies of Action in Pragmatism." *Cognitio: Revista de Filosofia* 8, no. 2: 213–222.

Gouinlock, James. 1986. "Dewey, Virtue, and Moral Pluralism." In *Frontiers in American Philosophy*, edited by Robert W. Burch. College Station: Texas A&M University Press, 175–181.

Hooker, Brad. 2012. "Theory versus Anti-theory in Ethics." In *Luck, Value, and Commitment: Themes from the Ethics of Bernard Williams*, edited by Ulrike Heuer and Gerald Lang. Oxford: Oxford University Press, 19–40.

James, William. 1975. *Pragmatism: A New Name for Some Old Ways of Thinking*, edited by Frederick H. Burkhardt. Cambridge, MA: Harvard University Press.

James, William. 1978. "The Moral Philosopher and the Moral Life." In *The Will to Believe and Other Essays in Popular Philosophy*, edited by Frederick H. Burkhardt. Cambridge, MA: Harvard University Press, 141–162.

Lekan, Todd. 2003. *Making Morality: Pragmatist Reconstruction in Ethical Theory*. Nashville, TN: Vanderbilt University Press.

Louden, Robert B. 1992. *Morality and Moral Theory: A Reappraisal and Reaffirmation*. Oxford: Oxford University Press.

Marchetti, Sarin. 2013. "Review of Le etiche della virtù by Alessio Vaccari." *Hume Studies* 39, no. 1: 119–123.

Marchetti, Sarin. 2016. "The Quest for Moral Progress: Lessons from Diamond and Rorty." *Iride. Filosofia e discussione pubblica* 29, no. 78: 347–359.

Marchetti, Sarin. 2018. "Two Varieties of Moral Exemplarism." *Etica & Politica / Ethics & Politics* 20, no. 2: 105–122.

Marchetti, Sarin. in progress. *Ethics after Pragmatism*.

McDowell, John. 1996. "Virtue and Reason." In *Mind, Value, and Reality*. Cambridge, MA: Harvard University Press, 50–73.

Pappas, Gregory. 2008. *John Dewey's Ethics: Democracy as Experience*. Bloomington: Indiana University Press.

Prichard, Harold A. 1912. "Does Moral Philosophy Rest on a Mistake?" *Mind* 21, no. 81: 21–37.

Putnam, Hilary. 2004. *Ethics without Ontology*. Cambridge, MA: Harvard University Press.

Robertson, Simon. 2017. "Anti-Theory: Anscombe, Foot and Williams." In *The Cambridge History of Moral Philosophy*, edited by Sacha Golob and Jens Timmermann. Cambridge: Cambridge University Press, 678–691.

Rorty, Richard. 2007. "Kant vs. Dewey: the Current Situation of Moral Philosophy." In *Philosophy as Cultural Politics*. Cambridge: Cambridge University Press, 184–202.

Rosenbaum, Stuart. 1994. "A Virtue of Dewey's Moral Thought." *Southern Philosophy Review* 19, no. 1: 35–59.

Russell, Daniel C. (ed.). 2014. *The Cambridge Companion to Virtue Ethics*. Cambridge: Cambridge University Press.

Teehan, John. 1995. "Character, Integrity and Dewey's Virtue Ethics." *Transactions of the Charles S. Peirce Society* 31, no. 4: 841–863.

van Hooft, Stan, ed. 2014. *The Handbook of Virtue Ethics*. London and New York: Routledge Press.

Wallace, James D. 2009. *Norms and Practices*. Ithaca, NY and London: Cornell University Press.

Welchman, Jennifer. 2008. "Dewey and McDowell on Naturalism, Values, and Second Nature." *The Journal of Speculative Philosophy* 22, no. 1: 50–58.

Welchman, Jennifer. 2010. "Dewey's Moral Philosophy." In *The Cambridge Companion to Dewey*, edited by Molly Cochran. Cambridge: Cambridge University Press, 166–186.

Williams, Bernard. 1985. *Ethics and the Limits of Philosophy*. London: Fontana Press.

14 Rationality as a Moral Problem

Dewey and Williams on the Role of Theory in Moral Reflection

Jörg Volbers

Introduction

Ethical thinking is concerned with questions such as "How should I live?" and "How should I act?" Life can be lived in many different ways, of course, but questions such as these bring to the fore the fact that there are choices to be made. These choices range from the quite ordinary to the rather momentous; nonetheless, they have to be made. Now moral philosophy, broadly conceived, insists on the idea that any worthwhile answer to such a question calls for the use of reason. This assumption is constitutive for much philosophical as well as non-philosophical reflection on morality, particularly at times when religious answers to ethical questions seem out of place. Whatever we strive to do or to be—it seems a good idea to examine it, in particular if the matter is of some importance. In this broad sense, living a good life is a thoroughly *rational* affair.

But what exactly does that mean—to decide something "rationally"? As the history of moral philosophy since Socrates has aptly shown, both content and extension of the concept of reason is contested. The fundamental challenge, which was forcefully articulated by Nietzsche, runs deeper. He did not just scrutinize the possible models of ethical rationality, but challenged the mainstream philosophical consensus that rationality itself is of value, that it should guide our actions (Schacht 2008). Is it really the case, Nietzsche forcefully asks, that leading a rational life, with its focus on truth and justification, is actually *morally* preferable and thus of greater value than leading other kinds of lives? In this way, Nietzsche is not simply suggesting that rationality might be of no use for the solution of some ethical issues. More radically, he undermines the very idea that rationality should guide our ethical lives. He suggests that the "use of reason" might *itself* be an ethical problem, e.g., if living "rationally" amounts to suppressing all that makes one's own live worth living. Hence, with Nietzsche, the possibility opens up to seeing rationality itself as an ethical problem.

In this chapter, I want to discuss a contemporary variation of this Nietzschean theme. It has to be seen against the backdrop of the widespread modern assumption that ethical reflection—if it is to be rational—must take a theoretical form. Ethical reasoning, on this view, is something which can and must be done "scientifically," and "theory" is taken to be the hallmark of scientific thought. Under such premises, the Nietzschean doubts about the moral value of reason quite naturally turn against this use of "theory." In light of this, an anti-orthodox current has developed in modern philosophy that rejects this scientific understanding of ethical rationality, and this for ethical reasons. Prominent examples are Charles Taylor (2007), Elizabeth Anscombe (1958), or Martha Nussbaum (1990).

In the following, however, I focus on examining Bernard Williams (2006), who is often classified as an "anti-theorist" in ethics (cf. Fotion 2014; Chappell 2015). For an anti-theorist like Williams, the very idea of looking for a *theory* in moral philosophy is simply wrong from the beginning. According to this position, any theoretically guided approach to ethical thinking will inevitably miss its real subject, that is, ethical life with its subtleties and complexities. But note that this criticism does not amount to a simple rejection of ethical rationality. Rather, Williams does not accept the modern scientist identification of "reason," or rationality, with "theory." Following the lead of Wittgenstein and Nietzsche, Williams' criticism of modern moral philosophy thus targets the widespread background assumption that ethical thinking *should* assume a theoretical form. For these authors, there is something intrinsically wrong with the modern preoccupation with theory and theoretically guided rationality.

But what exactly is the meaning of "theory" in these claims? The central argument of this chapter is that this anti-theoretical criticism, as it can be found in Williams, barks up the wrong tree. More precisely, it suffers from a misunderstanding of the nature of theory.[1] The following criticism thus fully agrees with the skeptical motive of the anti-theorist approach. Anti-theory rightly opposes an overly formalized and intellectualized understanding of ethical thought, such as it can be found still today in mainstream moral philosophy. In particular, it rightly emphasizes the perils of systematic thinking and conversely stresses the ethical importance of intuitive responses which cannot be formalized.[2] Yet in taking issue with systematical ethical theorizing *as such*, it throws the baby out with the bath water. Such a broad rejection of "theory" not only leaves ethical thinking rather helpless, taking away from reasoning all the powers that justify its traditional high esteem; it also concedes way too much to the very modern, scientistic understanding of rationality it seeks to distance itself from. In treating a reduced, actually positivist understanding of "theory" as the sole possible realization of "systematic reflection," it indirectly reaffirms this problematic conception, instead of attacking it.

Dewey's mature ethical philosophy, such as it is formulated in his 1932 *Ethics*, offers an alternative view. Dewey's thinking grew in an intellectual climate not yet fully dominated by the positivist ideal of science that had come to rule anglophone philosophy by the middle of the 20th century, and which is still widely held today. Accordingly, his writings developed a philosophical outlook which allows us *both* to criticize certain strands of an overly rationalistic modern morality, and to still acknowledge the distinctive value of theory in general. One indication for Dewey's possibly unorthodox position is that we find, in the chapter of the *Ethics* dealing with "The Nature of Moral Theory," a section entitled "Present Need of Theory" (LW 7, 176), as well as the antithetical remark therein, that moral theory "does not offer a table of commandments" (LW 7, 166). Dewey's philosophy is deeply sensitive to the Nietzschean problem raised above, and his *Ethics* can thus be profitably read as an original reflection on the problem of how theory and rationality, if it is to be of moral worth, should be conceived of. Despite his occasional scientistic language, Dewey actually presents an account of reasoning which is nothing like the insensitive and pedantic philosophic rationalism against which Nietzsche and the anti-theorists justly revolt.

The goal of that chapter, therefore, is to present Dewey as a sympathetic alternative to the anti-theorist discourse, the latter exemplified by the works of Williams. To frame that discussion, I will focus on the ways the notion of *generality* is understood on each side, since I take this to be the underlying issue. We are talking about ethical reflection after all, and I suggest that in a fundamental sense, ethics is concerned with how we should respond to each other, and to our own motives and desires, *in general*. Given that understanding, the differences between the two positions contrasted here—that of Dewey and that of the anti-theorists—can be reconstructed in terms of their respective understanding of this ethical generality. The anti-theoretical approach, I claim, unwittingly sides with the very modern scientism it seeks to oppose by understanding "theory" as the only binding articulation of general, or even universal, rules and insights. Theory is thus set over against the particular situations of ethical life, and problematically so, as I will show.

Dewey, on the other hand, locates the binding force of generalizing thought in the ongoing situation in which the subject is entangled—in short, in "experience." This key concept of Dewey's whole philosophy also frames his ethical philosophy. Locating thought in experience, on this view, means to submit it to a steady dialectical movement of resistance and adjustment. For Dewey's experimentalist conception of thought, any claim to generality can therefore be challenged by further experience and thus eventually transformed. But more importantly, being exposed to change in this way is not antithetical to the general nature of such a claim. Dewey understands the particular and the general as reciprocally determining one another, rather than being simply opposed. Ethical generality, therefore, is not won *against* the particular, but rather exists in an ongoing interaction with it. Instead of opposing the particular and the general, Dewey rather focuses on their necessary entwinement, thus opening a way to re-assessing the meaning of "ethical theory" instead of simply rejecting it.

I develop my argument in three principle steps. First, turning to Bernard Williams as an exemplary anti-theorist, I show how his position is bound to a wrong assumption, namely, that science is essentially a theoretical affair ("Anti-theory as a Critique of Generality" section). Then, I focus on Dewey's alternative understanding, according to which the logic of science follows the model of experimental practice. Rationality, therefore, should be understood as a constitutively practical response to an open situation ("Thinking as the Affirmation of Change" section). According to this understanding, theory is essentially a tool, which has the function of introducing new perspectives on action and understanding ("Theory as a Tool of Thought" section). Finally, I focus more on the specific problem of ethical rationality and argue that for Dewey, the very idea of action already presupposes a generalized conception of the acting self ("The Moral Self as a General Form" and "Choosing the Self" sections). Given Dewey's experimental understanding of generality the self is inevitably subject to change and influence, simply in virtue of being "general." In this way, Dewey manages to give weight to the particular individual and the specific situations it is acting in, without having to dismiss the value of systematic moral theorizing.

Anti-theory as a Critique of Generality

Following the outline presented above, I begin with the claim that Williams' criticism of ethical theory is actually targeting a certain conception of generality, and not just theory proper. His famous statement that "*reflection can destroy knowledge*" (Williams 2006, 148) will serve us as a starting point. It rests on the thesis that ethical knowledge is constitutively bound to the culture in which it is applied. This assumption is defended on roughly Wittgensteinian grounds. According to this understanding, issuing an ethical judgment—and thus articulating ethical knowledge—depends on the proper use of ethical concepts. Yet such conceptual knowledge, according to Williams, is dependent on a thorough practical immersion in the culture in which this concept is used. The members of this culture quite naturally master the fine distinctions and subtle complexities which govern their use; to them, these "thick" concepts, as Williams calls them, have a distinct and recognizable shape. In particular, they are able to rationally discuss their proper use, e.g., whether a certain judgment is appropriate. Yet according to Williams, this kind of reflection and rational scrutiny has to remain in touch with the practices that ground it. The attempt to find a *more general* justification of such a "thick" ethical conception, he claims, will eventually come to its limit. In "thinning" out these concepts, as it were, they become detached from the shared practical ground which governs their understanding.

The early Platonic dialogue *Laches* can serve as an illustration of Williams' point. One of Williams' examples of a "thick" concept is "cowardice." Now this dialogue, which is about courage, ends aporetically. Even though its participants all know very well how to use these ethical concepts, they are unable to find a satisfying general definition. In this sense, the search for a general description of ethical knowledge ultimately turns on the concept itself: In finding that we do not "know" anymore why we call some acts brave, reflection has actually destroyed moral knowledge, or so Williams claims.

Note that the problem for Williams is not the mere existence of "thin" concepts like "justice" in ethical reflection. The problem is created by the additional philosophical claim that in order to be rationally binding, *all* morally relevant concepts in such a reflection have to assume a generalized, context-transcending shape. In lifting the essentially "thick" ethical concepts to such heights, they risk losing their anchorage within the culture from which they are taken. As a result, these concepts also lose their evidential quality for those who had used it with a lesser degree of reflectivity. Their local application now appears to be unfounded, and the initial demand for rational justification remains unsatisfied.[3]

For Williams, it is in particular the modern scientific conception of rational justification which introduces that problematic demand to "thin" out all of our ethical concepts. Even though Socrates can already serve as an illustration of the problem, Williams argues that it was the success of the modern sciences which has eventually changed the shape of moral philosophical theorizing. For the modern scientific approach presupposes, Williams argues, what he calls an "'absolute conception' of the world," for which knowledge holds independently of any observer. According to this conception, knowledge ideally consists of "nonperspectival materials available to any adequate investigator, of whatever constitution" (Williams 2006, 140). Under these premisses, it seems natural to transfer this understanding of knowledge to ethical matters. Yet such a "nonperspectival" conception of knowledge, Williams argues, is doomed to fail when applied to morals. It implies a universal subject which can only be conceived of as a "featureless self," a subject which has neither character nor any particular wants or interests. Consequently, the resulting conception of morality ultimately loses its power to move individuals ethically. It presents an overly abstract conception of the self and deforms morality to being a rational system that has lost all points of contact with concrete moral problems. Under the pressure of a certain conception of theory, the ethical subject is thus forced to identify itself with a merely formal point of view—but such a position is the position of no one in particular. It perforce misses the specific contours of what it means to be confronted with ethical questions in a real social context.

As our reconstruction shows, Williams' careful skepticism towards modern ethical theory is far from a wholesale rejection of rationality. His motive, rather, is to *reattach* ethical thinking to practice, as it were. He is criticizing a certain theoretical understanding of ethical rationality, which he sees as grounded in the scientific "absolute conception" of the world. In doing so, however, Williams actually reaffirms a problematic modern idealization of scientific rationality. He fully identifies systematic theory with abstract scientific universalism, and thus claims that it creates contents which are necessarily *less* particular than the individual life with which it is concerned. Consequently, it looks as if systematic moral theory imposes its general judgment on a matter it cannot really understand. The result is an unhealthy and, as a matter of fact, artificial separation of general theory and less general practice.

Williams' dualistic separation of the "general" from the "particular" is actually typical for the anti-theoretical literature. It opposes scientific form and literary description, general rules and context-aware responsiveness, abstract concepts and particular intuitions, universal principles and culturally bound valuations.[4] Such an approach, however, in fact simply reverses the order of priorities. In turning their attention to the particular, the anti-theorists retain the modern scientific conception according to which systematic theory alone is responsible for the general and abstract. As a result, they do not touch the true problem of modern rationality. This comes to the fore if we look at Kant, who takes the *very same dualism* between the general and the particular as an argument for the former (cf. Kant 2005). This is made possible by a different ethical estimation. In contrast to the anti-theorists, Kant locates the problem of the ethical on the side of the particular, which he identifies with those inclinations and tendencies that stand in the way of ethical generality. For him, the particular is the problem which has to be overcome in the name of the general—or universal—power of reason. Thus, Kant claims that ethical practice has to accept moral theory as an uncompromising master—a claim which pivots on the very same categorical difference against which the anti-theorists turn.

We can therefore conclude that the anti-theorists are misled by a prejudice about the nature of theory. If there is something wrong with the modern way of theorizing ethics, it is necessary to attack the very dualistic understanding of theory and practice instead of just reversing the order of priorities. The problematic anti-theoretical understanding of generality, however, is not an isolated case. It mirrors the positivist image of science which was widely accepted in the 20th century, and according to which scientific rationality consists, in its core, in universal, or minimally law-like explanations of particular phenomena.[5] Yet as post-positivist science studies have shown, this image has no hold in reality. It turns out that the true use of "theory" in scientific practice is quite different from what positivism took it to be. Scientific discovery and justification operates on rich and dynamic social-historical grounds, of which "theory" proper is just one element. Put differently, positivism takes the final systematic presentation of scientific findings, such as it can be found in handbooks and articles, already for the whole of scientific practice.[6] Thus, it is blind to the possibility of understanding theory *itself* as a practical activity, in which both abstractions and particular attachments are jointly at work—a position which is naturally close to Dewey's pragmatism, to which we turn now.

Thinking as the Affirmation of Change

From the perspective of the anti-theoretical criticism of modern ethics, Dewey occupies an ambivalent position. In many respects, Dewey certainly shares the anti-theoretical impulse. He rejects the sterile type of theory which appeals to rational principles as if they were laws with unconditional authority. Theory "cannot take the place of personal decision" (LW 7, 166), he insists. He was also critical of the wide-spread scientism of his times. For him, thinking cannot be reduced to a universal method. Furthermore, throughout his mature work, we can find direct criticisms of the modern idolatry of truth, as in such passages as the following with a familiar Nietzschean ring:

> Meaning is wider in scope as well as more precious in value than is truth, and philosophy is occupied with meaning rather than with truth. ... truths are but one class of meanings.
>
> (LW 3, 4)

Yet in spite of all this distance from what is often taken to be the essence of modern rational thought, Dewey is also a fervent defender of both modernity and theory. Books such as *The Quest for Certainty* or *Experience and Nature*, among others, all tell the modern tale of progress through science. In the tradition of pragmatism, he calls problem-oriented thinking *inquiry* and declares scientific practice to be its most successful and paradigmatic realization. Consequently, his *Ethics* defines its topic as "the science that deals with conduct" (LW 7, 9), and I have already quoted Dewey's belief that moral thinking needs *more* rather than less theory.

We can begin to resolve that apparent conflict by pointing out how Dewey's understanding of science and rationality differs from the standard narrative shared by "theorists" and "anti-theorists" alike. Most importantly, Dewey does not identify the success of science with *theory*, but rather with *the practice of experimentation*. This change of perspective introduces a divergent understanding of the binding authority of rational thought. Instead of attributing it to some general level of theory or conceptual abstraction, thinking is identified with the experimental practice as a whole. Theory, in this view, thus loses its exclusive position and is integrated into a functional whole, to which it contributes.

For Dewey, experimentation is a practice of inquiry with a life of its own. It is an "adventure" (MW 14, 163), not just a confrontation with the facts.[7] It also cannot be reduced to an abstract mechanism which simply aims to affirm or falsify an assumption. Rather, it demands creatively working with the given material while heeding to suggestive details in the surrounding environment. The experimenter is therefore doing more than just issuing judgments. She has further to be sensitive to those vague signs and symptoms which are not yet fully articulated, nor understood, but somehow promise to be of help. A problem, Dewey remarks, "must be felt before it can be stated" (LW 12, 76), and thus demands a form of creativity which cannot be reduced to formal reasoning.

In locating theory within the wider context of experimental practice, cognitive attention thus moves away from the merely intellectual to its *interaction* with the ongoing practice as a whole. For Dewey, this shift is the product of a logical requirement. Following the pragmatist tradition, he takes all inquiry to be a response to a problem; as a consequence, some aspects of the problematic situation have to *change* in order to gain footing again. For that reason, a problem can only be solved by means of introducing something new; a change has to be made. The experiment is such a paradigmatic form of thinking, for Dewey, because it is organized around this requirement. It valorizes change as a methodological tool. There are many ways to introduce changes: it might be a new way of understanding something, an analogy, or a new concept; it could also be a new tool or research method, or a second try under newly refined conditions. Yet the common denominator is that these acts, for Dewey, all engage in the situation. For our purpose, however, the important point to note is that the actual course of experimental inquiry, in this view, is fundamentally dependent on what is contingently available. From this perspective, the experiment is not a machine for generating truths, but an open field of mindful practice.

Understood this way, scientific experimentation turns out to be the controlled version of what Dewey takes to be the human condition in general. As Dewey emphasizes in particular in the second chapter of *Experience and Nature*, life, for him, is fundamentally uncertain, full of immanent tensions, contradictions, and conflicts. Thus, to live means to embark on that open "adventure," whether one wishes to or not. The institutionalization of scientific experimentation, in this sense, marks such an important point in the history of thought, for Dewey, precisely because it *affirms* change, rather than working against it. It uses the fact of change itself in order to find knowledge, instead of denying it in the name of a preconceived rational order. Thus, paradoxically, the most stable knowledge has been found by accepting the inescapable fact of permanent change.

Furthermore, the ubiquity of change extends beyond the objects of inquiry. In experimentally responding to the problems, *the form of thought itself* changes. After all, the practice of experimentation acknowledges that our way of approaching the subject-matter might be wrong, and that alternatives have to be found. There are, of course, problems which are resolved in a routine way, by applying established rules, standards, and concepts. Yet the more intractable a problem turns out to be, the more does its resolution double back on our further ways of acting. Standards change, concepts are corrected, new principles emerge, and established principles lose their authority. New ways of thinking emerge.

As a matter of fact, this transformative feedback can already be discerned in these rather unproblematic cases where the solutions are ready to hand. Recall that for Dewey, any application of an instrument of thought is a response to an experienced conflict, and thus an expression of the *belief* that this instrument, in this particular case, will have this specific desirable consequence. Therefore, even the simple repeated use of such a means has the transformative consequence of confirming that belief, and thus stabilizing it. The repeated application of an intellectual schema will turn it into a habit. Eventually, it will even lose its distinct intellectual quality and become a routine response. That way, the distinctive ways in which problems are solved form the manner in which problems will be approached in the future.

In conclusion, change, as Dewey conceives it, cannot be restricted to the mere contingency of objective facts. Rather, the individual is itself permanently changing, simply due to the fact that it is always confronted with failure, conflicts, and other kind of problems. According to this point of view, change is not the exception, stability is, since it has to be won *against* the sheer contingency of being. From Dewey's perspective, stability and change are thus intertwined.

The question, therefore, is not *whether* we change, but *how* (cf. MW 14, 57f.). The real choice is whether we act blindly or with some foresight. For Dewey, it is the disposition to do the latter which characterizes human intelligence (cf. LW 1, 126), or what has been traditionally called "reason."[8] For Dewey, the disposition to intelligent acting can be realized in many different forms. There is not one single form of rationality. Problems can be approached in many different ways. And this means, of course, that for Dewey, there is no *ontologically* distinguished role of theory. Systematized thinking is just one aspect of our manifold attempts to "render choice more intelligent" (LW 7, 316). Keeping in mind that we want to better understand Dewey's take on ethics, let us now examine how exactly theory can play that role.

Theory as a Tool of Thought

For Dewey, theory is just a part of the functional whole of inquiry. Yet how can theory, thus conceived, contribute to individual choice without somehow imposing its generality on the particular situation? The anti-theoretical challenge is thus still open. To begin with an answer, note first that for Dewey, "theory" and "practice" are both modes of practice. Their difference is the degree in which problems become the explicit object of reflection. Ordinary practice, in this view, is marked by "a minimum of incidental reflection," whereas "theory" is a practice with "continued and regulated reflective inquiry" (LW 1, 15). First and foremost, a theory is thus a tool—a product of this latter kind of practice.

This conception still entails that theory is marked by a higher degree of generality and systematicity. Yet in contrast to the anti-theorists, Dewey does not think that these abstractive features somehow render theoretical thought "crude." Quite to the contrary, Dewey actually assigns "crudeness" to the *non-theoretical* practice, which he sees as reigned by routine, quick decisions, and a vague and shifting cognitive focus. Conversely, it is theoretical practice, for Dewey, which produces "refined objects" and a mode of inquiry where "isolated details" acquire fuller meaning and context (LW 1: 16).

From Dewey's perspective, abstraction cannot be understood as a deficit which, like Frege's unsaturated function, has somehow to be supplemented by particularity. The reason for this is simply that, given Dewey's understanding of rationality, it is not the function of theory to replace rational decision. Strictly speaking, a theory capable of directly replacing individual choice would not be a theory anymore. If a theory can be used blindly, like a calculus, it becomes a mere habit and ceases to be an instance of thought. Thus, there remains a constitutive gap between systematic thought and each actual inquiry. As Dewey puts it, with regard to ethical thinking: "the rule, to be applicable to all cases, must omit the conditions which differentiate one case from another" (LW 7, 276). Even if we simply subsume something under a given theory, this very act is a selective act, an implicit wager that *this* application of theory is actually adequate.

Given the overall experimental structure of inquiry, the task of theory is therefore not to replace the particularities at hand, but to offer a different perspective on them. A good theory discloses alternative possibilities of acting or points out important consequences. Dewey gives the example of the Golden Rule. It cannot be sensibly understood as a simple prescription which tells us what we should do: "Because I am fond of classical music it does not follow that I should thrust as much of it as possible upon my neighbors" (LW 7, 280). Its function, rather, is to provide "*a point of view from which to consider acts*" (LW 7, 280), in this case by "considering how our acts affects the interests of others" (LW 7, 280f.).

The main function of theory, on this account, is thus to offer new perspectives. This conception can be traced back to Dewey's experimentalist understanding of the practice of thought. In experimentally working *with* material, the experimenter has to be open to the suggestions of the material. What might happen if we alter this variable? Is it worth the trouble to try an instrument which is much more difficult to use and to maintain? Should we really pursue the present issue further instead of turning to other aspects of the problem?—these and other questions come to the experimenter's mind. The primary role of theory, then, as well as that of any other tool used within the context of inquiry, is not to provide an answer, but rather to open perspectives wherein potential answers can be found.

Applied to ethical thinking, Dewey thus finds no problem postulating a deep continuity between ordinary moral reasoning and moral theory. "Moral theory begins, in germ, when any one asks: 'Why should I act thus and not otherwise?'" (LW 7, 163). In theorizing, we simply pick these questions up and focus on them in a more systematic and rigorous manner. The resulting product is a tool, or better, it is *something*—a set of propositions, a body of insights, a complex account of some philosophical sort—which is, like all tools of thought, to be ultimately judged against its capacity to contribute to the moral problems at hand. Theory, on this account, neither replaces individual judgment nor does it imply a special power which irreconcilably distances it from particular thought and action.

The Moral Self as a General Form

We are now in a position to give a first reply to the anti-theorist's challenge. The use of theory is not *intrinsically* problematic, from Dewey's perspective, because it cannot replace individual judgment. Theory is useful insofar as it provides a more generalized and systematic point of view; yet its worth is limited—it depends on its capacity to effectively "render choice more intelligent" (LW 7, 316).

From the point of view of the anti-theorists, however, all of this is still begging the question. For what does it mean to apply a theory in the moral case? In non-ethical inquiries, it might well be the case that theory does open up new perspectives. In ethics, however, it seems that the problem of the "featureless self" (Williams) still persists. For in moral reflection, we are dealing with a particular individual, with particular wants and desires. Ethical theory is not a reflection about a distanced object, but rather addresses our very way of being. How does that focus square with Dewey's concession that ethical theory actually *is* in fact general and abstract?

The first thing to note here is the implicit premise of this anti-theoretical argumentation. It suggests that any abstract conception of the self is already cut off from the particular individual *due to its highly general nature*. We had already reconstructed this kind of thinking in the previous sections, in particular Williams' identification of systematic moral theory with a non-perspectival "absolute conception of the world." At bottom, this kind of thinking reproduces the positivist separation of the general and the particular it wants to escape from.

Dewey's alternative is to understand the "moral self" as a notion which is connected with the general *and* the particular, in the same way experimental theory is. For Dewey, the very idea of the self already is a general idea. This generality, however, is not at a distance from the individual self in the particular situation, but rather constitutes an essential part of it. More importantly, the general is present in the form of a *potentiality* to act, and thus is subject to change without thereby ceasing to be general. From Dewey's point of view, the notion of the self thus signifies a general understanding not of what a person ultimately is, but of how she potentially acts and responses. It points to a sum of tendencies and dispositions which Dewey often subsumes under the concept of "habit" (LW 7, 170–172; cf. MW 14). Recall that for pragmatism, habits are no blind routines. Rather, they embody pragmatic orientations with an intrinsic practical intelligence, giving form to the specific emotional and cognitive response of an individual. Being dispositions, however, these habits do not manifest themselves continuously in action, but only "under special conditions" (MW 14, 32). They are no innate rules, but general "*ways* or modes of response" (MW 14, 32).

The general self, thus conceived, is not somehow set over and against the particular acting individual. Rather, it is by itself an important, and morally speaking indispensable, factor in determining the moral character of an individual act. Its essential role comes to the fore in all conscious and voluntary action. Long before the advent of what is called "action-theory" today, Dewey, in his ethical writings, reflects about the constitutive role of the self in action. Any given act will remain under-determined, he argues, if it is taken solely as a mere occurrence. What does it signify if an arm moves, a word is uttered, or a course of action is undertaken? Or if these were *not* to happen? A single act or series of acts only *make sense*, according to Dewey, if they refer back to a habit or self as that which binds them or gives them coherence (MW 14, 29–30). In order to know what an act is, and to see if it succeeds and how it succeeds, we have to establish a meaningful connection between the acts and its consequences, or between one act and a series of acts.

Of course, such a connection need not necessarily have a moral character. It might simply be a description of what somebody does. Such a description is general, however, insofar as we explain the act with the help of a principle which integrates the act into a wider context, such as by finding a motive for the action. Now such a description acquires a moral dimension if this explanatory principle is *itself* placed in a wider context, and reflected back as a consequence of other, previously undertaken acts. Thus, the judgment becomes moral if the self is not simply identified as the cause of what happens, but also being hold *responsible* for being the cause. In any case, there is a logical correlation between self and act, or between conduct and character.[9]

It is important to see the logical nature of Dewey's argument. Dewey is not simply postulating that we judge others or ourselves in this or that way. The idea is rather that we *cannot understand* an act apart from its relation to a self, which therefore becomes a constitutive part of what it means to refer to action. A variant of this conception can be found in Dewey's definition of intelligence—rationality—as a skillful practice which converts "causal bonds, relations of successions, into a connections of means-consequences, into meanings" (LW 1, 277). Two events happen one after another, and we begin to understand them if we can say *how* they are related together. In the case of action, this "how," this *way* of acting, is to a large degree constituted by habits and the self. In this conception, simply to see an event as an action already implies the postulate that there is "something" more general which serves as a cause of the event observed.

There are, of course, other determinants of an event, such as the laws of physics or simply chance influences of any kind. Dewey therefore admits a "running scale of acts, some of which proceed from greater depths of the self, while others are more casual, more due to accidental and variable circumstances" (LW 7, 167). But even the failure to make sense of a given act confirms the underlying logical structure. We understand an act if we succeed at postulating a meaningful relation between the act and further acts, or between the act and its consequences. We say, for example, that a person *wants* to reach that thing, or that she walks to the train *in order to* get home. Thus, the reference to the self or to the habit plays an indispensable explanatory role. The self is identified as an "agency of accomplishing consequences" (LW 7, 287).[10] This identification allows to switch from the mere observation of two events to an explanation of their more general form, possibly even to a proper prediction of the outcome.

Unlike the anti-theorists, Dewey thus does not set the particular individual against the general notion of the self. Rather, both are intrinsically related with each other. In particular, understanding an act *already is* postulating a general relation, even though in Dewey's experimentalist ontology, such a conception is always "of the nature of a possibility" (LW 12, 262). The general is thus not somehow imposed on the acting subject, but rather constitutive for the very fact that it is an intentionally acting subject.

Choosing the Self

We are in a position now to finally summarize Dewey's alternative to the scientistic separation of the general from the particular, or theory from practice. For Dewey, systematic theory is valuable insofar as it offers a more rigid, more exhaustive, and more general perspective on moral issues (LW 7, 166). The general nature of theory, however, does not conflict with the needs of the particular individual. *Pace* anti-theory, Dewey assumes that the very form of action already relates the particular acts, wants, and desires to the self. We cannot understand an intentional act apart from this relation. Yet such a relation, for Dewey, is already general in nature. It postulates that something is done *for a reason*, and thus integrates the action in a wider net of descriptions.

From this view, the self emerges as a *moral fact* to which we already relate in ordinary moral practice, even if unwittingly. All intentional action, for Dewey, is implicitly governed by a conception of the acting agent. Morality proper, Dewey claims, thus consists in raising awareness of that fact. In agreement with his general understanding of human intelligence, moral reflection, for Dewey, thus consists in making explicit that "acts are connected with one another" (LW 7, 169). More specifically, what we do connects with our own conduct and has consequences for others. From the moral point of view, we are not acting *simpliciter*. Instead, our acts are reflected as expression of a certain tendency, a predisposition. The real object of ethical reflection, therefore, is the potential worth not of this act or the other, but the more general tendency it embodies.

On a more general level, we can thus conclude that for Dewey, the nature of moral theory is to systematically reflect on the *possibilities of being a moral agent*. It examines the possible consequences of action as well as the nature and worth of certain dispositions. Thus, Dewey claims that traditional moral theories, which have been the subject of detailed studies in his *Ethics*, are in sum controversies about the importance of certain "aspects of the good self" (LW 7, 285). In both moral theory as well as in ordinary discourse, we are therefore actually reflecting upon the moral value of certain *types* of conduct and of certain general ways of behavior.

At this point, we are now able to formulate a Deweyan reply to Nietzsche's challenge. Remember that Nietzsche most prominently raised doubts about the possible value of reason and rationality; he asks why there is any *moral value* in rationally reflecting about moral problems. In Dewey's pragmatist perspective, the value of these reflections is that they respond to a real need. For it is in moral conflicts, Dewey claims, that the moral problem of the "good self" comes explicitly to the fore. In such conflicts, the acting agent experiences herself caught in contrary tendencies to act, e.g., as "torn between duties" (LW 7, 165). In such cases, the general nature of the self becomes manifest. For in these genuine moral conflicts, the agent is not simply confronted with an opposing force or with some other external obstacle. Rather, the problem is that the agent's action is caught between at least two opposing descriptions, each pointing to a different understanding of the agent. Should one be loyal to a state at war, or rather be firm in one's conviction "that all war is a form of murder and hence wrong" (LW 7, 165)? Up to that moment of crisis, both convictions could coincide in the same subject. They were compatible explanatory principles of her actions. Yet now, the agent is confronted with the necessity to choose, or more generally, to find a way to deal with that conflict.

Moral conflicts, as Dewey sees them, therefore force the agent to a more explicit self-determination. In confrontation with the issue, she has to determine how to act. Yet in these cases, the significance of such a decision always reaches beyond the issue at hand. It doubles back on the acting agent herself, because what she does is also an affirmative determination of how she takes herself to be. She is making up her mind of what she *really* wants to do (LW 7, 286), and for Dewey, that implies that she is deciding about what *kind* of self she wants to be (LW 7, 295). It is here that moral theories, or systematic forms of moral theorizing, become productive. Being tools that open up new perspectives, they offer different visions of the self, as well as reasons why one general way of acting is preferable to another. Furthermore, they allow to better understand what implications a choice will have.

Note, however, that in the case of a real conflict, the agents involved will most likely not be fully aware of the far-reaching consequences of their choice. They will not see themselves as choosing between rival self-understandings. Dewey's position, therefore, is itself an instance of moral education. It points out that as a matter of fact, all moral choices do affect what kind of self we will be. Dewey emphasizes that this issue cannot be evaded. Whatever choice is made, and regardless of how it is made, the "resulting choice also shapes the self, making it, in some degree, a new self" (LW 7, 187).

The metaphysical foundation of that position is Dewey's experimentalist understanding of thought and its wholesale affirmation of change. It is a general trait of inquiry that the application of a means doubles back on its cognitive status as a tool. Likewise, in the case of a moral conflict, choosing one option rather than another inevitably also transforms the agent. Here, the agent is affected in its role as a further means of action. Her choice either stabilizes an existing predisposition to act, or changes its power or direction. In sum, these choices eventually reveal what kind of self one really wants to be, because they show on what kind of self-understanding we are actually willing, or capable, to act.

Conclusion

Our discussion began with the necessity of choice, and it ends with it. We were asking Nietzsche's question whether the tradition is right in holding a *rational* treatment of moral choices in high regard, and we have found an affirmative answer. It turned out that Nietzsche's question is actually based on a misunderstanding of the role of theory and of rationality in general. We have seen how Williams, who we take to be a more contemporary exemplary "anti-theorist," identifies rationality with a dimension of reflective generality which cannot do justice to the individual particular wants and desires. Yet in Dewey's alternative conception of rationality, such a stark opposition of the general and the particular is avoided.

Dewey offers several arguments against such a dualist approach. First, he denies that theory is the expression of a specific power of generalizing thought. Instead, he integrates theory in the overall practice of thinking, which he models on the impressively successful pattern of modern scientific experimentation. From that perspective, the general dimension of thought turns out to be constitutively dependent on the particular aspects of the situation to which it is applied to. Second, Dewey's philosophy agrees with the anti-theoretical skepticism against abstract rationality. For him, the functional role of abstract theory is not to solve problems, but rather to *assist* the individual in doing so. Thus, theory cannot replace individual choice, but is rightly estimated for its power to assist it. Being a tool, however, this power cannot be isolated from the concrete working context in which it is applied. As a third point, Dewey offers arguments against the anti-theorist's suggestion that the individual agent is *merely* a particular agent, and thus essentially different from any abstract conception theory could provide. For Dewey, the very idea of action already presupposes a generalized notion of oneself as an acting entity, as a self. Thus, the mere fact of intentional action already intermingles the general and the particular, and thus does not allow to oppose them in the way some anti-theorists want to.

As a last point, it is important to keep in mind the overall experimental dimension of Dewey's central concepts. The self and its acts are not simply identical. Rather, the acts form the self, as much as the self causes the acts. Consequently, any judgment about a stable relation between self and act is always a postulate. To put it differently, such a judgment expresses a *potential* classification of conduct which has to be confirmed in the further course of experience and reflection. The logical relation between self and act is inherently unstable. As a matter of fact, the self and the act are not identical, and yet, they have to be treated as a unity. Whatever general form our behavior thus assumes, it can never be said to be *simply* given. Our general ways of response are general, but precisely because of this generality, they are also essentially contested. With regards to the position held by representatives of both "theory" and "anti-theory," it is finally this experimentalist understanding of generality which distinguishes Dewey's approach.[11]

Notes

1 For a comparable assessment (see Louden 1992; Hämäläinen 2008; Fotion 2014).
2 With respect to the assessment of situated judgments, moral particularism (Dancy 2002) represents an interesting middle position. It also emphasizes the need of understanding ethical judgment more practically, likening it to the Aristotelian sense of "phronesis," yet it also attempts to *theoretically defend* that conception. From the point of view of an anti-theorist, such a philosophical foundation cannot be given.
3 A reconstruction of Williams' claim on reflection along the lines presented here can be found in Hall (2014).
4 A further prominent example of this dualistic opposition can be found in Nussbaum (1990). Even though she concedes that in ethics, there is a need for "general rules," this concession is based on the premise that these general rules, *taken by themselves*, are ethically suspect—simply due to their generality. For her, all "moralities based exclusively on general rules" perforce exhibit a certain "ethical crudeness" (Nussbaum 1990, 37) which has to be countered by individual ethical sensitivity. For another, more recent example of such a dualistic understanding of theory (see also Chappell 2009, 184–213).
5 As in illustration of this "rationalist understanding of rationality" and how it dominated academic thinking in the first half of the 20th century (see Toulmin 1992, 5–45, esp. 13–17).
6 For an oversight of the science-studies in the 20th century (see Rheinberger 2010).
7 In this reading, Dewey's approach is deeply different from Peirce's, which can be reconstructed as a pragmatized version of empiricism (Misak 2004). In its core, the difference is whether "experience" is assigned the task to merely inform the thinking subject, thus preserving its sovereignty, or if it is further granted the power to fundamentally *change* its relation to the world and to itself. For a fuller defense of that position (see also Volbers 2018).
8 Dewey uses the term "intelligence" instead of the more traditional "reason," not least because the latter is usually not associated with feelings, imagination, or qualities. I will, however, not adhere to this terminological decision. As long as we keep in mind that reason and rationality can assume many forms, there is no reason, to my mind, to deny that Dewey is, in fact, working on a very traditional theme. His philosophy, in the main, proposes a theory of rationality. See, for example, Dewey's definition of "rationality" as "an affair of the relation of means and consequences" (LW 12, 17).
9 Dewey talks interchangeably about the "correlation of conduct and character" or "the unity of self and action." This unity is, as Steven Levine (in this book) shows, "speculative" in the sense that it is a *postulate* which governs action, and not necessarily a statement of fact. See also the discussion of the role of the "habit" in Dewey's moral theory by Stéphane Madelrieux, also in this volume.
10 Not accidentally, this description bears great resemblance to Anscombe's analysis of intentional action. Both Dewey and Anscombe have been strongly influenced by Aristotelian thought (Sleeper 2001; Rogers 2007). For Anscombe, however, intentional action is marked by the genuine practical knowledge that "I do what happens," as opposed to knowledge gained by observation. Dewey would not draw such a sharp dividing line, because knowledge, for him, is rather a future-oriented term designating a solution to a problem, and not a given state of mind.
11 I want to express my gratitude to both Steven Levine and James Matthew Fielding for important advice when writing and editing this chapter.

References

Anscombe, Gertrude Elizabeth Margaret. 1958. "Modern Moral Philosophy." *Philosophy* 33, no. 124: 1–19.

Chappell, Sophie Grace. 2009. *Ethics and Experience: Life beyond Moral Theory*. Durham, NC: Taylor and Francis.

Chappell, Sophie Grace. 2015. *Intuition, Theory, and Anti-theory in Ethics*. Oxford: Oxford University Press.

Dancy, Jonathan. 2002. *Practical Reality*. Oxford: Oxford University Press.

Fotion, Nicholas. 2014. *Theory vs. Anti-Theory in Ethics: A Misconceived Conflict*. Oxford: Oxford University Press.

Hall, Edward. 2014. "Contingency, Confidence, and Liberalism in the Political Thought of Bernard Williams." *Social Theory and Practice* 40, no. 4: 545–569.

Hämäläinen, Nora. 2008. "Is Moral Theory Harmful in Practice?—Relocating Anti-theory in Contemporary Ethics." *Ethical Theory and Moral Practice* 12, no. 5: 539–553.

Kant, Immanuel. 2005. "Ideen zu einer allgemeinen Geschichte in weltbürgerlicher Absicht." In *Schriften zur Anthropologie, Geschichtsphilosophie, Politik und Pädagogik*, 6th Edition. Darmstadt: Wissenschaftliche Buchgesellschaft.

Louden, Robert B. 1992. *Morality and Moral Theory: A Reappraisal and Reaffirmation*. New York: Oxford University Press.

Misak, Cheryl. 2004. *Truth and the End of Inquiry: A Peircean Account of Truth*. 2nd Edition. Oxford: Oxford University Press.

Nussbaum, Martha C. 1990. *Love's Knowledge*. Oxford: Oxford University Press.

Rheinberger, Hans-Jörg. 2010. *On Historicizing Epistemology: An Essay*. Palo Alto, CA: Stanford University Press.

Rogers, Melvin L. 2007. "Action and Inquiry in Dewey's Philosophy." *Transactions of the Charles S. Peirce Society: A Quarterly Journal in American Philosophy* 43, no. 1: 90–115.

Schacht, Richard. 2008. *Nietzsche, Genealogy, Morality: Essays on Nietzsche's on the Genealogy of Morals*. Berkeley: University of California Press.

Sleeper, Ralph W. 2001. *The Necessity of Pragmatism: John Dewey's Conception of Philosophy*. Champaign: University of Illinois Press.

Taylor, Charles. 2007. "Modern Moral Rationalism." In *Weakening Philosophy: Essays in Honour of Gianni Vattimo*, edited by Santiago Zabala. Montreal: McGill-Queen's University Press, 57–76.

Volbers, Jörg. 2018. *Die Vernunft der Erfahrung: eine pragmatistische Kritik der Rationalität*. Hamburg: Meiner.

Williams, Bernard. 2006. *Ethics and the Limits of Philosophy*. Abington: Routledge.

Notes on Contributors

Roberta Dreon is Associate Professor of Aesthetics in the Department of Philosophy at the Ca' Foscari University, Venice.

Steven Fesmire is Professor of Philosophy at Radford University.

Roberto Frega is Permanent Researcher at the CNRS (French National Center for Scientific Research) in Paris.

Mathias Girel is Associate Professor in the Department of Philosophy, École Normale Supérieure, Paris.

Céline Henne is PhD Candidate in History and Philosophy of Science at the University of Cambridge.

Steven Levine is Professor of Philosophy at the University of Massachusetts Boston.

Federico Lijoi is Assistant Professor in the Department of Philosophy at Sapienza Università di Roma.

Stéphane Madelrieux is Associate Professor at the University of Lyon.

Sarin Marchetti is Associate Professor of Philosophy at Sapienza Università di Roma.

Conor Morris holds a PhD from University College Dublin.

Gregory Fernando Pappas is Professor of Philosophy at Texas A and M University.

Matteo Santarelli is Junior Fellow at the Max Weber Center for Advanced Cultural and Social Studies in Erfurt, Germany.

Jörg Volbers is Visiting Professor of Philosophy at the Free University of Berlin.

Justo Serrano Zamora is Postdoctoral Researcher in the DFG-ANR project "DemoFutures" at the University of Groningen.

Index